Living in Technical Legality

EDINBURGH CRITICAL STUDIES IN LAW, LITERATURE AND THE HUMANITIES

With a global reach, this innovative series critically reimagines the interdisciplinary relationship between legal and literary (or other aesthetic) texts through the most advanced conceptual frameworks and interpretive methods of contemporary theory available in the humanities and jurisprudence.

Available or forthcoming titles

Schreber's Law: Jurisprudence and Judgment in Transition
Peter Goodrich

Living in Technical Legality: Science Fiction and Law as Technology
Kieran Tranter

edinburghuniversitypress.com/series/ecsllh

Living in Technical Legality

Science Fiction and Law as Technology

Kieran Tranter

EDINBURGH
University Press

For Sophia and Alexander

Edinburgh University Press is one of the leading university presses in the UK. We publish academic books and journals in our selected subject areas across the humanities and social sciences, combining cutting-edge scholarship with high editorial and production values to produce academic works of lasting importance. For more information visit our website: edinburghuniversitypress.com

Edinburgh University Press Ltd
The Tun – Holyrood Road
12 (2f) Jackson's Entry
Edinburgh EH8 8PJ

First published in hardback by Edinburgh University Press 2018

Typeset in 11/13pt Adobe Garamond Pro by
Servis Filmsetting Ltd, Stockport, Cheshire

A CIP record for this book is available from the British Library

ISBN 978 1 4744 2089 1 (hardback)
ISBN 978 1 4744 7479 5 (paperback)
ISBN 978 1 4744 2091 4 (epub)
ISBN 978 1 4744 2090 7 (webready PDF)

Contents

Figures

Preface

This book has had a complicated, cosmopolitan gestation. Its genesis was at the 2000 Critical Legal Studies Conference in Helsinki in Finland, where, as a young junior academic from a small Catholic law school in Fremantle, Western Australia, I presented some half-conceived ideas about 1950s American science fiction and international space law on a panel titled 'Law and Popular Culture' alongside William P. MacNeil. A slightly better thought-out iteration of that paper was eventually published by *Law and Critique*,[1] and it gave impetus to two further papers on science fiction and the car, and the cloning narratives in *Star Trek*.[2] However, my thematic exploration of law, technology, and science fiction would almost certainly have remained a passing distraction from what may be seen as the more serious scholarly tasks if it had not been for the opportunity to present on another 'Law and Popular Culture' panel at the 2006 Law and Society Association Conference in Baltimore, Maryland, United States. By this stage, I was slightly less young and less junior, and due to serendipity found myself working alongside William MacNeil at Griffith Law School in Australia. For this panel, I wrote a paper that looked at the jurisprudential articulations of the technical in the fabulously reimagined *Battlestar Galactica*. The reception of this paper, the enthusiasm with which it was published by *Law and Literature*, the sheer personal joy at being able to be what Henry Jenkins has termed an 'aca-fan',[3] and the understanding that I had hit on a rich insight concerning the essential relations between law, technology, and science fiction were revelatory. My doctorate – which until then was plodding along as a study of Australian responses to emergent technology over the twentieth century – morphed, under the supervision of MacNeil, into an examination of the science fictionality of law and technology scholarship. It is from that work that this book has mutated.

1 Tranter, 'Terror in the Texts: Technology – Law – Future'.

2 Tranter, '*Mad Max*: The Car and Australian Governance'; Tranter and Statham, 'Echo and Mirror'.

3 Jenkins, 'Confessions of an Aca-Fan'.

Ultimately, this book is a celebration of monsters. It is a monster of a book and its final message is for the monsters that have inherited the West to live well – to live as responsible for becoming – in their technical existence. Monsters, too, have complicated origins. Intra-myth they often owe their existence to many progenitors, and as stories of profanity, horror, and hybridity they have relied on all those who have shared their stories around fires, in texts, and on screens for them to live in the world. Likewise, this book owes its monstrous being-in-the-world to many.

I wish to thank Lyndal Sleep, whose companionship, encouragement, love of speculative fiction, and own theoretical orientation have very much helped to make this book what it is. I also must mention our children, Sophia and Alexander Tranter-Sleep, who have grown into *Doctor Who* and *Star Trek* as this book has developed, and whose commentary and insights were very important for Chapter 5.

I also must thank William MacNeil, whose work, support, and encouragement have made this book. His pioneering work in law and popular culture is clearly the laboratory from which this book has escaped. However, it also would not have been possible without the long and dedicated support he has shown me as a colleague, a doctoral supervisor, and an editor. This is the moment to credit the institutional context of my creating. The idea of seriously pursuing the relationships between law, technology, and science fiction is novel and creative, and would not be possible in many law schools. I have been extremely fortunate to have been working at Griffith Law School during the formation and writing of this book, and to have had the opportunity to work with such creative, theoretically sophisticated, and serious scholars as Shaun McVeigh, Sandra Berns, Paula Baron, Rob McQueen, Allan Ardill, Charles Lawson, Edwin Bikundo, Jay Sanderson, Chris Butler, Roshan de Silva, Karen Crawley, Tim Peters, and Ed Mussawir, all of whom have had an impact on the ideas, tone, and orientation of the text that follows. I also need to thank my own PhD students, particularly Robbie Skyes, Samuli Haataja, Skye O'Dwyer, Jing-Yueh Hsu, and Mark Brady, whose energy, struggles, and triumphs directly and indirectly informed the book.

However, this book has benefited from the input of scholars beyond Griffith Law School. David Caudill (Villanova University in Pennsylvania, United States) and Sherryl Vint (University of California, Riverside in United States) deserve credit as the examiners of my doctoral thesis, whose comments critically informed the development of Chapters 3 and 4. Maria Aristodemou (Birkbeck University in London in the United Kingdom) and Vicky Saker Woeste (American Bar Association) deserve special mention as facilitators of my presentations at Helsinki and Baltimore respectively. Martha Merrill Umphrey (the University of Massachusetts Amherst in the

United States) and Peter Goodrich (Benjamin N. Cardozo School of Law at Yeshiva University, New York City, the United States) both helped my thinking on *Battlestar Galactica* to develop. Finally, I would like to acknowledge Lyria Bennett Moses (the University of New South Wales in Australia), Art Cockfield (Queen's Law, Queen's University, Kingston, Ontario), Thom Giddens (St Mary's University in London) and Mitch Travis (the University of Leeds in the United Kingdom), Cassandra Sharp (the University of Wollongong in Australia), Jason Bainbridge (the University of South Australia), Thalia Anthony (University of Technology Sydney in Australia), Georgine Clarsen (the University of Wollongong in Australia), and Kylie Doyle (Commonwealth Department of Public Prosecutions), whose collegiality around theorising law, technology, and speculative fiction has had a significant impact on arguments to follow.

I would also like to express my thanks to John Watson and Laura Williamson at Edinburgh University Press for their support and encouragement and Sue Jarvis for her excellent copy editing.

An early version of Chapter 2 was first published as '"Frakking Toasters" and Jurisprudences of Technology: The Exception, the Subject and *Techné* in *Battlestar Galactica*', *Law and Literature* 19:1 (2007), pp. 45–75 and parts of Chapter 6 have had a previous life as 'Mad Max: The Car and Australian Governance', *National Identities* 5:1 (2003), pp. 67–81.

Kieran Tranter
Gold Coast, Australia
October 2017

Introduction: Living in Technical Legality

This book is a monster. It has been stitched together from various disciplines: law and humanities, law and technology, science fiction studies and science technology and society. Beamed into science fiction, it would resemble something from a B-grade matinee – a rubber-suited mismatch of eyes, limbs, and antennae. However, as more sophisticated science fictions show, even BEMs (bug-eye monsters) (the derogatory term for such creatures) have purpose and humanity. Indeed, they can be – and often are – more human than the 'humans'.[1] This monster of a book has a purpose and humanity. Its purpose is to chart a way to live well within the total triumph of technology.

Law is often called upon to humanise technology. A current manifestation is the call for law in response to the 'disruption' of automated road vehicles.[2] Within this political truism that circulates endlessly within the politico-legal networks of the West, a specific set of concepts and relationships are projected. This technology that needs law is seen as primal, as something non-human and threatening. It is a monster. Humanity is located elsewhere. It is conceived as not technological, yet vulnerable to technology's monstrous pursuits. Mediating between technology and humanity is law. Law saves. It is an instrument through which technology is collared and made to serve human ends. Two observations suggest themselves. The first is that these characterisations of technology, humanity, and law have a pedigree. They belong to none other than Frankenstein, that quintessential modern myth in which an amoral, asocial techno-thing threatens and kills humans. It is a story that calls out for a saving supplement to intervene between creator and monster.[3] The second is a fundamental irony. The law that saves

1 Parrinder, 'The Alien Encounter'.

2 Brock, 'Where We're Going, We Don't Need Drivers'; Glancy, 'Autonomous and Automated and Connected Cars'.

3 Cranny-Francis, 'The "Science" of Science Fiction'; Caudill, 'Scientific Narratives in Law', p. 253.

humanity from technology is tool-like. It is a law that is instrumental, plastic, and capable of being called upon and fashioned towards any end. Following Carl Schmitt, this quintessential modern law – empty, yet all-powerful – can be seen clearly: it is law as technology.[4] From this ironic vantage point, the monster can be seen as a trickster, and the political truism of law called upon to humanise technology implodes. Humanity is not saved from technology by law; rather, the technical, tool-like nature of law reveals humanity as given over to technology. What is left after this is not 'technology', 'humanity', and 'law', but a monstrous hybrid figure, the revelation that modern humanity and modern law are thoroughly technological.

This is why this book is about technical legality. It is about the technical legality that conditions law's responses to technology, the multiple calls for regulation, rights, and code. However, it is also about law at its essence being technical legality – that is, law as technology – of regulation, rights, and code as manifestations of an epoch-defining 'technicity' – and the implications of this for both the theory and cultural life of law. The term 'technicity' is intended to capture a profound sense of *technē*. That technology – cloned sheep, motor vehicle, smart watch, or a hydroelectric plant on the Rhine – should not properly be considered as objects, but rather as part of a worldview associated with instrumentality, calculation, repetition, and procedure, which makes possible the networks of contemporary Western life.[5]

This book argues that this epoch-defining technicity revealed in the technical legality of modern law is not a cause for despair. This is why the book is about 'living in technical legality'. Within thinking about technology and society, there is a tragic strand that regards modern technological existence as the end of true human life, its vitality replaced by empty exchange.[6] The theoretical foundation for this literature is Martin Heidegger's account of technology.[7] For Heidegger, the course of Western metaphysics has been one of decline. The call to reveal the truth of the world has become subsumed by the technological imperative to order the world as ready and in reserve, capable of being deployed towards any ends.[8] This tragic strand, with its yearnings for past, simpler, and more meaningful technologies, does not see anything that resembles living in technical legality. However, it undersells Heidegger's legacy. Heidegger can be seen as clearing the way for thinking about technology and humanity as co-located, as conceiving humanity as

4 Schmitt, *Political Theology*, p. 28.
5 Stiegler, *Technics and Time, 1*, pp. 4–6.
6 Tabachnick, 'Techne, Technology and Tragedy'.
7 Feenberg, *Heidegger and Marcuse*, p. 25.
8 Heidegger, 'The Question Concerning Technology'.

a thoroughly and wholly technical entity, as 'technological Being-in-the-world'. In so doing, Heidegger provides a space for alternative theorising of the triumph of technology that escapes the closed binaries of human/technology, being/thing, and culture/nature.[9] It is in this space that Donna Haraway's focus on cyborgs, becoming, and the networks of the everyday has allowed the charting of politics and ethics, from within technological Being-in-the-world.[10] Haraway and others suggest that it is possible to 'live in' technical legality. They identify embodied locations where a possibility of 'responsibility for becoming' can emerge, which offers ways of living within the total triumph of technology.

The question of technical legality is how this living with, this active engagement with law and technology encapsulated by the phrase 'responsibility for becoming', can be substantiated. In Haraway's work, science fiction grounds theorising. Haraway's inspiration for both understanding the real of technological Being-in-the-world and sketching an empowering critique of technological existence is specific science fiction texts by Joanne Russ, Anne McCaffrey, Samuel R. Delany, Isaac Asimov, and Octavia E. Butler.[11] This rapprochement between the speculative and literary in Haraway can be seen as a hallmark in thinking about technology. As Istvan Csicsery-Ronay (2008) argues in *The Seven Beauties of Science Fiction*, it is from science fiction's 'thesaurus of images that we draw many of our metaphors and models for understanding our technologized world and it is as [science fiction] that many of our impressions of technology-aided desire and technology-riven anxiety are processed back into works of imagination'.[12] Firmly located within this cultural milieu of 'science fictionality',[13] the political truism of law humanising technology not only mirrors the Frankenstein myth in its basic structure – humanity vs technological monstrosity and the need for law to mediate between them – but draws its urgency from science fiction's potent imagining of technological possibilities: of brave new worlds, big brothers, space wars, clones, and killer robots.[14]

9 McNamee, 'An Egg Shaped Bowl'.

10 Wajcman, *TechnoFeminism*, pp. 108–30.

11 Haraway, 'A Manifesto for Cyborgs', pp. 97–9; Haraway, *Modest_Witness@Second_Millennium*, pp. 70, 74–8; Haraway, *Primate Visions*, pp. 368–82.

12 Csicsery-Ronay, *The Seven Beauties of Science Fiction*, p. 2.

13 Ibid., p. 5.

14 Tranter, 'The Speculative Jurisdiction'.

Science Fiction and Law

In recent years, law and the humanities have begun to engage with science fiction. Explorations of science fiction in law and the humanities that occurred prior to 2010 can be catalogued briefly. The most well-known is Paul R. Joseph and Sharon Carton's article that pieces together the 'domestic law' of the Federation from *Star Trek: The Next Generation* (1987–94) episodes.[15] This article inspired Michael P. Scharf and Lawrence D. Robert to map the Federation's 'international law'.[16] This mapping approach was repeated by Walter A. Effross, who catalogued the image of lawyers from cyberpunk texts.[17] A version of this mapping approach can be identified in a brief chapter by Joseph, where he sketched how a variety of science fictions, particularly the *Star Trek* franchise, could illuminate substantive issues facing North American lawyers.[18] It can also be seen in works by Christine A. Corcos, who catalogues science fictions that explore artificial intelligence (AI), cloning, imprisonment, and rights-talk,[19] and in Anna Lorien Nelson and John S. Nelson's examination of bureaucracies within Ursula Le Guin's *The Left Hand of Darkness* (1969).[20]

These photon bursts have become a slightly steadier beam in recent years, as a next generation of law and humanities scholars increasingly focus on science fiction. Tim Peters has investigated 'The Force' as law and theology in the first six *Star Wars* movies and the legal theology manifests within the film adaptions of *I, Robot*.[21] Peter J. Hutchings has explored the subjectivity of liminal legal spaces through *Blade Runner*[22] and Steven Kapica has approached similar themes within the *Battlestar Galactica* (2003–9) universe.[23] Juliet Rogers and Kirsty Duncanson have both pursued the fractious legalities screened in *The Matrix*,[24] while Duncanson has also thought

[15] Joseph and Carton, 'The Law of the Federation'.

[16] Scharf and Roberts, 'The Interstellar Relations of the Federation'.

[17] Effross, 'High-Tech Heroes, Virtual Villains, and Jacked-In Justice'.

[18] Joseph, 'Science Fiction', pp. 157–66; Joseph and Carton, 'Perry Mason in Space'; Joseph, 'A Course Whose Time Has Come'.

[19] Corcos, 'More Human Than Human'; Corcos, Corcos, and Stockhoff, 'Double-Take'; Corcos, 'I Am Not a Number I Am a Free Man!'; Corcos, 'Visits to a Small Planet'.

[20] Le Guin, *The Left Hand of Darkness*; Nelson and Nelson, 'Institutions in Feminist and Republican Science Fiction'.

[21] Peters, '"The Force" as Law'; Peters, 'Allusions to Theology'.

[22] Hutchings, 'From Offworld Colonies to Migration Zones'.

[23] Kapica, '"I Don't Feel Like a Copy"'; Kapica, '"What a Glorious Moment in Jurisprudence"'.

[24] Rogers, 'Free Flesh'; Duncanson, 'Tracing the Law through *The Matrix*'.

cultures of sovereignty through *Doctor Who*.[25] Jay Sanderson has utilised Margaret Atwood's *Oryx and Crake* (2003)[26] to frame thinking about legal responses to genetically modified animals,[27] while Chip Stewart has catalogued how various science fictions have projected intellectual property law's future.[28] Thomas Giddens has recently rethought the persona of justice in *Judge Dredd*.[29] Further Orna Ben-Naftail and Zvi Triger have a symposium forthcoming in *Law, Culture and the Humanities* creating a discourse around science fiction and international law.[30]

These emergent engagements with science fiction suggest that law and humanities is beginning to fulfil its potential, but yet to reach its destiny. The study of law's cultural existence within a thoroughly technological culture, and especially thinking through the technicity of law within this culture, mandates taking science fiction seriously.[31] In 1989, Lawrence Friedman encouraged the nascent field of law and humanities to embrace science fiction.[32] Notwithstanding, the small but increasing scholarship, Cass R. Sunstein's populist *The World According to Star Wars* (2016),[33] catalogues of when judges have cited from *Star Wars*[34] or drawn upon science fiction's trove of robot imagery[35] or the High Court of Australia paraphrasing *Star Trek*'s Captain Jean-Luc Picard,[36] law and humanities has yet to substantially answer his call. This is the lacunae that this book occupies. Its purpose is to deal directly with the totality of technology for law and living in the modern West by taking science fiction seriously.

To embark upon this journey, it is first necessary to understand why law and humanities has not engaged more with science fiction. There are two related inhibiting factors at work.

The first is that within science fiction law, especially as regulation, rights

25 Duncanson, 'Bodies, Cinema, Sovereignty'.
26 Atwood, *Oryx and Crake*.
27 Sanderson, 'Pigoons, Rakunks and Crakers'.
28 Stewart, 'Do Androids Dream of Electric Free Speech?'
29 Giddens, '*Anderson v Dredd* [2137] Mega-City LR 1'; Lloyd, 'Judge, Jury, Executioner'.
30 Ben-Naftali and Triger, 'The Human Conditioning'; Lavi, 'Cloning International Law'; Kerr and Szilagyi, 'Evitable Conflicts, Inevitable Technologies?'
31 Travis, 'Making Space'.
32 Friedman, 'Law, Lawyers and Popular Culture', pp. 1,590–1.
33 Sunstein, *The World According to Star Wars*.
34 Browning, 'A Long Time Ago, in a Courtroom Far, Far Away'.
35 Calo, 'Robots as Legal Metaphors'.
36 *Phonographic Performance Company of Australia v Federation of Commercial Television Stations* (1998) 195 CLR 158 McHugh and Kirby JJ, 181.

or code seems to play a minor part.[37] Lawyer protagonists are few, as Joseph has pointed out, 'Buck Zeal: Space Lawyer' has yet to grace television, the paperback shelves, or the multiplexes.[38] When lawyers are portrayed, for example, 'Jubal Harshaw LL.B, M.D., Sc.D.', from Robert A. Heinlein's *Stranger in a Strange Land* (1961)[39] or Charles Mundin from Frederik Pohl's and C. M. Kornbluth's *Gladiator-at-Law* (1955)[40] or the kleptomaniac Romo Lampkin (Mark Sheppard) from *Battlestar Galactica,* the baseline representation is not a diligent officer of the court doing law jobs, but politically savvy realists, organising, exploiting connections, and politicking behind the scenes.[41] This limited appearance of lawyers in science fiction continues into the few science fiction courtrooms. In *Star Trek: The Next Generation* (1987–94), when Data (Brent Spiner) is the subject of a Star Fleet JAG hearing to determine whether he could be disassembled, argument and submissions revolved around ethical conjuncture about souls and the person/property distinction rather than the citing of 'hard law'.[42] Similarly, the two occasions that the Doctor from BBC's *Doctor Who* (1963–) was brought to account for his actions by his species, the images were of crime and punishment rather than indictments, procedure, and alleged transgression of specific provisions.[43] The mostly lawless nature of science fiction was parodied by Frank Herbert in his little-known *ConSentiency* series,[44] which featured the 'Bureau of Sabotage' (BuSab), that had the constitutional function of inhibiting the workings of planetary and galactic government, thus saving 'sentiency' from the oppression of hyper-legality.[45]

This talk of law in science fiction leads to the two best-known of science

[37] Per Schelde suggests that the two dominate personas in science fiction film are the scientist and the 'everyman' – 'lawyers' does not make it to the list. See Schedle, *Androids, Humanoids, and Other Science Fiction Monsters*, pp. 27–37.

[38] Joseph, 'Science Fiction', pp. 156–7.

[39] Heinlein, *Stranger in a Strange Land*, p. 75.

[40] Pohl and Kornbluth, *Gladiator-at-Law.*

[41] Travis and Tranter, 'Interrogating Absence', p. 33.

[42] Scheerer, 'Measure of Man'; Joseph and Carton, 'The Law of the Federation', pp. 72–3; Short, '"The Measure of a Man"'; Nesteruk, 'A New Narrative for Corporate Law'; Carter and McCann, 'Measuring Humanity'.

[43] The finale of the 1969 season, culminating in the Doctor's regeneration (from Patrick Troughton to Jon Pertwee) and banishment to Earth. Maloney, 'The War Games'. The 1986 season comprised a single story arc; see Clough, Jones, and Mallett, 'The Trial of a Time Lord'.

[44] The ConSentiency series spanned the 1964 short story 'The Tactful Saboteur' and the novels *Whipping Star* and *The Dosadi Experiment.*

[45] Herbert, 'The ConSentiency and How it Got That Way'.

fiction's laws, Asimov's 'Three Laws of Robotics'[46] and the *Star Trek* franchise's 'Prime Directive'.[47] Both appear and disappear within their respective texts. Asimov's laws are static,[48] hardwired into the 'positronic brain'. His stories come from the ambiguity of application.[49] Consequently, the profession called forth by Asimov's '*roboticus lex*' is not the positronic lawyer, but the 'robopsychologist', suggesting that the laws are immutable and the only opportunity for professional – indeed clinical – intervention involves understanding the manifestations of pathology to avoid situational exposure. For Dr Asimov, one-time Assistant Professor in Chemistry at Columbia,[50] the laws of robotics seem more akin to 'laws of nature' than 'law properly called'.[51] *Star Trek*'s Prime Directive has a more substantial jurisprudential aura. The Directive – generally stated as Starfleet must not interfere in the domestic affairs of a pre-warp planetary social system – has been identified by the literature concerned with law in *Star Trek* as allowing a Captain's fiat, a way of rationalising chosen actions against what manifests as a fairly vague standard of non-interference, 'unless . . .'[52]

It has been this general lawlessness of science fiction that has inhibited law and humanities' engagement with science fiction. As a field of study, law and humanities has its origins with the law and literature movement and its preoccupation with the representation of 'law in literature'[53] of the courtroom drama. Notwithstanding the flowering and diversity of contemporary law and humanities beyond the written word and beyond mapping the appearance and meaning of law tropes within texts,[54] there is a residual

[46] The first 'Robot' short story, 'Robbie', was published in *Astonishing Stories* in 1940. Reprinted in Asimov, *I, Robot,* pp. 1–24.

[47] First mentioned in the second season episode Senensky, 'Bread and Circuses', *Star Trek.*

[48] Asimov, *The Rest of the Robots*, p. 1: 'A robot may not injure a human being or through in-action allow a human being to come to harm. A robot must obey the orders given it by human beings except when such orders would conflict with the First Law. A robot must protect its own existence as long as such protection does not conflict with the First and Second Law.'

[49] Leslie-McCarthy, 'Asimov's Posthuman Pharisees'.

[50] Asimov, *In Memory Yet Green*, p. 641.

[51] Austin, *The Province of Jurisprudence Determined*, p. 130.

[52] Peltz, 'On a Wagon Train to Afghanistan', pp. 639–52; Scharf and Roberts, 'The Interstellar Relations of the Federation', pp. 608–10; Wingfield, 'Lillich on Intersteller Law', p. 96.

[53] The phrase 'law in literature' is from Weisberg, 'The Law–Literature Enterprise'.

[54] For example, Young, *The Scene of Violence* (graffiti); Skyes and Tranter, '"You Gotta Roll/ Rule with It"' (popular music); Pearson and Tranter, 'Code, Nintendo's Super Mario and Digital Legality' (computer games); Giddens, 'Natural Law and Vengeance'; Sharp, '"Riddle Me This . . .?"' (comics); and Marusek, 'License Plates' (motor vehicle licence plates).

reluctance to boldly go beyond texts that do not immediately signify law. Hence, science fiction, with its minimal law content, has been a shadowy blip on law and humanities' scanner.

This connects with the second inhibition to a taking seriously of science fiction by law and humanities. Science fiction is popular, mass produced and mainstream. When in print it is often lacking in the hallmarks of literary skill, with clunky writing, predicable plots and unengaging characters – a fantastic made mundane.[55] When on the screen it has a tendency towards hyper-visuality epitomised by the dominance of special effects to the detriment of story and higher-brow engagement.[56] This tendency towards technicity is a manifestation of science fiction as the culture of technological culture.[57] Law and humanities has expressed insecurity about its place in the legal academy.[58] Its emphasis on culture, meaning, and language is at odds with the dominant law school tropes of 'reality', 'practice', and 'authority'.[59] By taking seriously science fiction, with its surrounding markers as populist, speculative, and non-literary, the law and humanities scholar could be seen as inviting a double dose of institutional marginalisation.

Yet this exercise in self-othering – in making monstrous – is exactly what this book does. It addresses both of these inhibitions by participating in the reconceptualising of law and humanities pioneered by William P. MacNeil.[60] MacNeil's concern is with the existence and circulation of wisdom about law within, and through, popular culture. In *Lex Populi* (2007) MacNeil reads popular cultural texts '*jurisprudentially*'.[61] His key observation is that popular culture is not divorced from the ambient legality of contemporary life, but is a participation in and an analysis of, living within the rule of law. What MacNeil established, and this book develops, is a way of considering seemingly lawless texts – MacNeil examines such non-law texts as *Harry Potter and the Goblet of Fire* (2000), *Buffy the Vampire Slayer* (1997–2003), *Fight Club* (1999), and the science fiction film *Minority Report* (2002)[62] – as encoding, dissecting, and critiquing core legal concepts. Following MacNeil, this book addresses the two inhibitions that have slowed law and humanities from engaging with science fiction. First, by reading popular texts to elicit the

[55] Broderick, *Reading by Starlight*, pp. 8–11.

[56] Csicsery-Ronay, *The Seven Beauties of Science Fiction*, p. 11.

[57] Sobchack, 'Science Fiction Film and the Technological Imagination', pp. 157–8.

[58] Sarat, Douglas, and Umphrey, 'On Film and Law: Broadening the Focus', p. 4.

[59] Thornton, 'Technocentrism in the Law School'.

[60] Reichman, 'The Production of Law (and Cinema)', pp. 495–6.

[61] MacNeil, *Lex Populi*, p. 2; italics in original.

[62] Ibid., pp. 11–96.

jurisprudential content within, this book allows key works of science fiction – all of which fly under a radar attuned only to the most obvious textual signifiers of law – to shine as exemplars of technical legality. Second, it locates this analysis not on the margins of legal institutions, but at the centre of law in its institutional guise, as the essence of law that lies behind the modern law-talk of regulation, rights, and code. This book is not necessarily concerned with the fleeting jurisdictional and temporal specificities of lawyers, controversies, and doctrines, but with law and life within this technological epoch. However, this book does depart and develop from MacNeil. Where MacNeil wants to 'recall jurisprudence to life'[63] by showing how popular culture presents richer, diverse, and more nuanced accounts of law than those found within the texts of jurisprudence, this book orbits the question of technical legality. This means that the following analyses of science fictions combine to pursue and comprehend technical legality and to chart a living, a lawyering, and a scholarship within this totality. This leads to a consideration of the chapters that follow.

The Chapters to Come

Reflecting the descriptive dimensions of 'technical legality' and the normative of 'living in technical legality' this book is divided into two parts. Part I (Chapters 1 to 3) describes technical legality and the forms of life that it shapes. Its narrative arc begins with law responding to technology, moves through to the revelation of law as technology and the jurisprudential implications of this revelation as a monstrous project located in death and time. It then considers this totality of the technical and the attended narratives of loss and decline, but glimpses an alternative in responsibility for becoming. Part II (Chapters 4 to 7) focuses on the potential for these forms of life to live well in technical legality. In particular, the 'ethical' possibilities for three forms of life are explored; the legal subject, the lawyer, and the legal scholar.

Chapter 1 opens Part I by beginning the process of describing technical legality through identifying law as technology. It is argued that law can be seen as technological when, ironically, law is called to respond to technological change. Through a focus on the legal responses to cloning, it is shown that the called-for laws were responding to visions of cloning futures directly sourced from science fiction. Having located these legal acts within science fiction, the essential elements of this future-oriented process – monstrous technology, vulnerable humanity, and saving law – can be seen. This will be identified as the 'Frankenstein myth'. What is revealed is that science fiction

[63] Ibid., p. 156.

holds the technical and legal together at the level of substantive dreaming and also at the level of basic commitments. The irony intrudes at this point. This saving law that can determine the future has a particular character. It is a species of pure power, manufactured through procedure in the present to determine the future. It has the same characteristics that have been ascribed to technology. With this the categories established by the Frankenstein myth of 'technology', 'humanity', and 'law' are imploded. What is glimpsed is the singularity of technical legality.

Chapter 2 continues the description of technical legality through looking in detail at how modernity allowed law as technology. This is undertaken through a jurisprudential reading of Frank Herbert's 'Dune cycle' (1965, 1969, 1976, 1981, 1984 and 1985). The Dune cycle has been read as involving an affirmation of chaos over rationality in public activities – religion, politics, and ecology – concluding with the message of self-care and Zen-like calm in coping with an uncertain universe. But these accounts sell Herbert's imagining short. This chapter re-examines *Dune* (1965) (the italic *Dune* reserved for the foundational 1965 text) and the Dune cycle as a story of tyrants and Leviathan sandworms. In this re-reading, Dune can be seen as an account of the metaphysics of law as technology. The themes identified in the established secondary literature on Dune can be rewoven into a critical elaboration of Hobbes' 'mortal God', which exposes the essential commitments of sovereignty and its technical law. These commitments are death and time. Located within the bloody alchemy of modernity, the monstrousness of the law as technology is revealed – the consumption of bare life in time. This brutal realisation seems to end with Schmitt's representative sovereign deciding to make the world.

Chapter 3 builds directly on the previous chapter by further exploring technical legality, and particularly the forms of life made by technical legality, through the re-imagined series *Battlestar Galactica.* It is argued that *Battlestar Galactica* deals directly with the triumph of technology and in so doing charts a way for living within technical legality. Like Chapter 2, which moved from the public to the personal and back to the public, this chapter opens with the sovereign and moves to the personal. *Battlestar Galactica*, however, does not invite a return to the public. Rather the personal is the technical and the distinction between essence and artefact becomes blurred. Here *Battlestar Galactica* seemingly performs Heidegger's foundational account of technology that sees technology as consuming humanity leaving a false, destructive, and empty shell. *Battlestar Galactica* does not quite follow this script. It affirms that living remains after the end. Humanity as it has been known has been changed, but agency and 'life' remains. This location, identified by Haraway, and developed by Rosi Braidotti, offers the possibility for living well in technical legality through knowing and feeling the 'networks of the present'. This possibility of an 'ethics of affect' closes Part I of the book and provides the basis for the argument in Part II.

Chapter 4 begins Part II by arguing that a detailed reading of Octavia E. Butler's *Xenogenesis* series (1987, 1988, and 1989) clarifies how, notwithstanding the challenges to its being and its agency by technical legality, the 'ethics of affect' identified in Chapter 3 can allow the technical legal subject to live well in the present. The technical legal subject is revealed as a node within the networks, a blob of natureculture, a nexus point for biopolitical operations. Through Butler's narrative of Lilith and her monstrous, hybrid human-alien children possibilities for the technical legal subject to be 'embodied' within a 'location' and 'navigate' the networks of the present emerge. Not only is agency empowered, notwithstanding the weight of the technical networks and the inclination to automation, but so is a form of ethics. Butler's afrofuturism present a powerful affirmation that knowing and acting well to nurture life remains ever present, even in technical legality.

Chapter 5 argues that the seemingly immortal British science fiction television show *Doctor Who* (1963–) provides guidance on how to live well as an entity designated 'lawyer' within the networks of technical legality. Technical legality challenges the received tradition of legal ethics. Lawyering is revealed not as a 'profession' with imagery of human respectability and sound judgement, nor as a technical exercise of going through the motions of the law of lawyering and client wishes, but as a demonic calling to be an alchemist of death and time. To be a lawyer is to be responsible for death and to master time. This calling to be a 'time lord' who brings 'death' immediately suggests *Doctor Who*. A consistent theme through the unfolding text that is *Doctor Who* has been the 'ethics' of the Doctor in his working of death and time. Alien, proudly not human, and supremely technically competent, the Doctor suggests how to live from the alchemist's location. The Doctor overcomes and endures because the weight of his responsibility for death and time is within his Time Lord being. There is neither sound judgement nor technical somnambulism in the Doctor's actions. Instead, his actions appear as a hybrid of both, unified by an acceptance that actions performed from this location break, change, and destroy the networks of the present. Ultimately, the Doctor shows that lawyering within technical legality demands an accepting of the powers of time and death to safeguard 'life'.

Chapter 6 examines living in technical legality from the location of the legal scholar. Technical legality means that thinking about law and especially law and technology has to escape the circularity of the Frankenstein myth. Technical discussions of law reform remain valid but need to be more deeply informed. This provides an opportunity for those located at the law scholar-node to aspire to know the complex networks of technical legality. In this chapter, George Miller's classic Australian post-apocalyptic film *Mad Max 2: The Road Warrior* (1981) is presented as providing a map of the functions of a very familiar manifestation of technological humanity, the human-automobile. Through foregrounding the depth and intimacy of the human–automobile relationship, *Mad Max 2* charts how this monster functions across identities, myths, and biopower. Refracted through Australian culture, these locations are shown to be critical for the knowing and ordering of self and others, essential to collective myths of possession and prosperity, significant in the distinguishing of 'place' from 'space' and to specific, Australian biopolitical projects such as the programmed removal of indigenous children over the twentieth century. What is shown through this cartography is a way of thinking law and technology that goes beyond the closed metaphysics of the Frankenstein myth. In mapping complexity, complicity, collusions, and surprises within the networks of the present, the law scholar-nodes functions at a privileged location whereby technical legality can be self-reflective – where the effects and affects of the continually changing world are seen. Further, in generating knowledge about the networks of the present, law scholar-nodes can empower others, other embodied nodes in the networks, the monsters that have come to inherit the Earth, to live well in technical legality.

The concluding chapter, Chapter 7, summarises the argument of the book through emphasis on the reoccurrence of deserts throughout the book. Like deserts, technical legality could appear empty and harsh, but such superficial glances mislead. With closer looking deserts are revealed as full of ingenious life – so to with technical legality. The ingenious forms of life are not the humans of an earlier epoch, but these monsters live and can live well within technical legality.

The central imagery in this book is that of the 'monster'. The monster is a rich trope. In its primary sense the monster is a figure of horror arising from its status as impure and as such defiling and tainting cultural norms and expectations.[64] The paradigm of the monster is the eponymous monster from *Frankenstein*. Shelley's Frankenstein describes his monster thus:

> How can I describe my emotions at this catastrophe, or how delineate the wretch whom with such infinite pains and care I had endeavoured to form? His limbs were in proportion and I had selected his features as beautiful. Beautiful! Great God! His yellow skin scarcely covered the work of muscles and arteries beneath; his hair was of a lustrous black and flowing; his teeth

[64] Carroll, *The Philosophy of Horror*, p. 32.

> of a pearly whiteness; but these luxuriances only formed a more horrid contrast with his watery eyes, that seemed almost of the same colour as the dun-white sockets in which they were set, his shrivelled complexion and straight black lips.[65]

Frankenstein's monster is a parody of a human, something rendered more obvious in the stock twentieth-century image of the monster – established by the actors Boris Karloff and Glen Strange – tall, flat-toped, neck electrodes, and cragged face.[66] The monster's physical appearance emphasises its manufactured-ness; it is a product of technicity and it is othered to the human and to the good. It is a figure that violates established boundaries between nature and culture, and object and being – a violation that is reinforced by its murderous rampage.

However, the monster has alternative imaginings. As Robin Wood has identified, the horror monster has a more sympathetic double – as the location for empathy and a progressive politics of difference.[67] Within technology studies, this alternative coding of the monster can be seen in the work of Donna Haraway and Bruno Latour, as not the demonic being of technology, but a celebratory figure of what N. Katherine Hayles has termed the 'posthuman'.[68] In this literature, to which this book owes a considerable debt, the monster becomes the symbol for hybrids that 'be' in the contemporary West: the cyborg and the trickster.[69] In this sense, the monster as trickster can be seen as an active creator of the world. For Joseph Campbell:

> This ambiguous, curiously fascinating figure of the trickster appears to have been the chief mythological character of the palaeolithic world of story. A fool and a cruel lecherous cheat, an epitome of the principle of disorder, he is nevertheless the cultural bringer also.[70]

As trickster, the monster as technology is not the danger to human society, as it is cast in the Frankenstein myth, but the creator and innovator of social relations.[71] However, this talk of the Frankenstein myth moves this book on. It is time to begin examining the technicity of law and with it the primacy of the Frankenstein myth.

65 Shelley, *Frankenstein*, p. 56.
66 Glut, *The Frankenstein Archive*, pp. 35–6.
67 Wood, *Hollywood from Vietnam to Reagan*, p. 80.
68 Hayles, *How We Become Posthuman*, pp. 2–3.
69 See Haraway, 'A Manifesto for Cyborgs'; Penley and Ross, 'Cyborgs at Large', p. 9; Latour, *We Have Never Been Modern*, p. 47.
70 Campbell, *The Masks of God*, p. 273.
71 Leeming and Page, *God*, p. 24.

Part I

Technical Legality

1

From Law and Technology to Law as Technology

One of the most influential accounts on law and technology has been Lawrence Lessig's *Code* (1999).[1] It is a remarkable text: conversational, passionate, and funny, yet communicating a forceful repudiation of 1990s Internet exceptionalism (the argument that the Internet was either technologically beyond state control, or ideologically should be beyond state interference) with a more sophisticated theoretical account of the law–technology interface.[2] It was a manifesto for the future, a technically competent constitutionalist's account of how to do things with systems and rules. The language in *Code* was urgent – it was written within a 'revolution'[3] – and its registry was the prophetic, full of hypotheticals and what-ifs.[4] In a single bound, Lessig makes it obvious that the horizon for law and technology is the 'future'.

About the same time that Lessig was combating excessive libertarian zeal in cyberspace, the politico-legal networks of the West were starting to react to the 1997 announcement of the existence of a physically unremarkable Scottish sheep.[5] 'Dolly' – named after the American country singer-songwriter (a chauvinist joke based on the fact that Dolly was derived from a mammary cell)[6] – has gone on to be a technological icon as the first mammal cloned from an adult cell. In the immediate aftermath of her announcement, Dolly circulated within Western politico-legal networks – old and Lessig's new media, legislators, health departments, law reform commissions, bioethics centres, and law schools – as a future that must be stopped. Over

1 Lessig, *Code and Other Laws of Cyberspace*. On the influence of Lessig see Brownsword, 'So What Does the World Need Now?'

2 Lessig, *Code and Other Laws of Cyberspace*, pp. 6–7.

3 Ibid., p. 234.

4 This anticipatory voice of *Code* is made more obvious by Lessig's revisiting of the text; in the preface, he discusses the vindication, or otherwise, of his prescience. Lessig, *Code 2.0*, p. x.

5 McKie 'Scientists Clone Adult Sheep'.

6 Kolata, *Clone*, p. 3.

the early years of the 2000s, Dolly came to represent a family of less woolly anxieties and hopes concerning reproductive cloning, therapeutic cloning, and embryonic stem cell research. These projections called forth law within Western jurisdictions to secure preferable versions of a Dolly-induced future.

This future focus, seen in Lessig, within the cultural legal event of Dolly and within all the other ceaseless calls echoing around the West for law to 'keep up' with technology,[7] is a fundamental realisation for the comprehension of technical legality. The exposure of 'law' to 'technology' is chronologically explosive. It hastens the temporal vector. Thinking and legislating lurches from the 'what is' to the speculative 'what could be'. It is this futurity that is pursued in this chapter. The argument substantiated is that this futurity reveals the essential technicity of modern law – that is, it is law as technology.

This revealing has three stages. The first begins with the Dolly event within the politico-legal networks of the West. Dolly birthed law. It will be shown how Dolly was conceptualised according to the negative images, tropes, and narratives associated with science fiction's 'clone canon'. In this, science fiction provided the content through which Dolly was transmuted into law. The second stage identifies the essential configuration within the West that drove this transmutation: monstrous technology, vulnerable humanity, and saving law – as located in the Frankenstein myth. In the third stage, having revealed the science fictionality behind conventional thinking about law and technology, a fundamental irony manifests. The called-for law – the law that is to save – is modern law. There is a confident claim that law-tools can make the future. This account of the reality of modern law is law as technology. In this, the monster of technology can be seen to be not so categorically bounded as in the Frankenstein myth. There is no saving law – just a monster-trickster, and a not so pure humanity. It is this constellation of the technicity of modern law – of the monster-trickster and a contested, compromised humanity – that orientates the next two chapters.

Cloning Law

Dolly the sheep could be described as legally promiscuous. Beyond giving birth to six healthy lambs, Dolly gestated much law in the West. In the United Kingdom, Dolly called forth the Human Reproductive Cloning Act 2001 (UK)[8] and cloning-related amendments to the Human Fertilisation and Embryology Act 1990 (UK).[9] For the rest of Europe, the announcement of

[7] Bennett Moses, 'Recurring Dilemmas'.

[8] Human Reproductive Cloning Act 2001, Chapter 23.

[9] Human Fertilisation and Embryology Act 1990, Chapter 37. These were later repealed and amended by the Human Fertilisation and Embryology Act 2008, Chapter 22.

Dolly led to the Council of Europe's Additional Protocol to the Convention for the Protection of Human Rights and Dignity of the Human Being with regard to the Application of Biology and Medicine, on the Prohibition of Cloning Human Beings in January 1998[10] and the inclusion of a prohibition on human reproductive cloning in Article 3 of the European Union's Charter of Fundamental Rights of the European Union 2000.[11] This was followed by national laws concerning cloning in Belgium, Demark, Finland, France, Italy, Portugal, and Spain,[12] but not Germany, which maintained that human cloning was already regulated under its Embryo Protection Law of 1990.[13] In Australia, Dolly gave impetus to the Prohibition of Human Cloning for Reproduction Act 2002 (Cth) and the Research Involving Human Embryos Act 2002 (Cth).[14] Canada passed the Assisted Human Reproduction Act 2004 (Canada),[15] New Zealand the Human Assisted Reproductive Technology Act 2004 (NZ),[16] and South Africa the National Health Act 2004 (South Africa),[17] which all prohibited human reproductive cloning. In the United States, while regular attempts to introduce federal laws have not been successful,[18] Arizona, Arkansas, California, Connecticut, Iowa, Indiana, Louisiana, Maryland, Massachusetts, Michigan, Missouri, New Jersey, North Dakota, Rhode Island, South Dakota, and Virginia all have legislation concerning cloning.[19] At the international level, Dolly's influence can be seen in the November 1997 General Conference of United Nations

[10] Additional Protocol to the Convention for the Protection of Human Rights and Dignity of the Human Being with Regard to the Application of Biology and Medicine, on the Prohibition of Cloning Human Beings, 12 January 1998, Europ. T.S. No. 168, <http://conventions.coe.int/Treaty/en/Treaties/html/168.htm>, last accessed 9 February 2017.

[11] Available at <http://www.europarl.europa.eu/charter/pdf/text_en.pdf>, last accessed 9 February 2017.

[12] Isasi and Knoppers, 'Mind the Gap'.

[13] Gesetz zum Scvhutz von Embryonen [Embryo Protection Law], v. 13.12.1990 (BGB1. I S. 2746); see Hoeren and Rodenhausen, 'Constitutional Rights and New Technologies in Germany', p. 150.

[14] Nemes, 'Therapeutic Cloning in Australia'.

[15] Assisted Human Reproduction Act, S. C., c.2; Downie, Llewellyn, and Baylis, 'A Constitutional Defence of the Federal Ban on Human Cloning for Research Purposes'.

[16] Human Assisted Reproductive Technology Act 2004 (NZ) no 92, s.8, schedule 1.

[17] National Health Act, 2003 (no. 61 of 2003), s 57.

[18] Human Cloning Prohibition Act of 2009, H.R. 110, 111th Cong. (2009); Human Cloning Prohibition Act of 2007, H.R. 2560, 110th Cong. (2007); Human Cloning Research Prohibition Act, H.R. 222, 109th Cong. (2005); Human Cloning Prohibition Act of 2005, H.R. 1357, 109th Cong. (2005); Human Cloning Prohibition Act of 2003, H.R. 534, 108th Cong. (2003).

[19] Payne, 'Stem Cell Research and Cloning for Human Reproduction'.

Educational, Scientific and Cultural Organization's (UNESCO's) adoption of the Universal Declaration on the Human Genome and Human Rights, which declared that the cloning of humans 'shall not be permitted'[20] and the slow to emerge[21] 2005 United Nations Declaration on Human Cloning.[22]

Each of these ewe-induced legislative moments represented the end-point of a process that transmuted, through highly formalised, lengthy, and complex politico-legal processes, the possibility of mammalian cloning as represented by Dolly into law. In Australia, for example, the legislative scheme emerged after five Commonwealth-level institutional inquiries, two Coalition of Australian Governments (COAG) agreements, two 'conscience votes' in the Commonwealth Parliament (where the members of Parliament were free to vote outside party discipline), and a substantial library of jurisdictional specific academic comment.[23] These post-Dolly laws in the West dealt with three issues. Although there is a minor debate on nomenclature, these have generally been organised by the terms 'human reproductive cloning', 'human therapeutic cloning', and 'stem cell research'. Human reproductive cloning captures the possibility of applying the Dolly techniques, in conjunction with assisted human reproduction, to bring to full term babies who have an identical nuclear deoxyribonucleic acid (DNA) to another human.[24] Human therapeutic cloning anticipated the possibility of using clone embryos, or material derived from clone embryos, in medical treatment.[25] 'Stem cell research' covers techniques enabling the propagation and manipulation of human stem cells, both embryonic and adult. When twinned with therapeutic cloning, stem cell research is often accompanied by attendant claims of cures for cancer, Parkinson's, and Alzheimer's disease, rejection-free organ transplants and healed spinal cords.[26]

The laws covering therapeutic cloning and stem cell research are diverse.

[20] *Universal Declaration on the Human Genome and Human Rights*, UNESCO, 29th General Conference, 11 November 1997, Art. 11, <http://unesdoc.unesco.org/images/0010/001096/109687eb.pdf>, last accessed 9 February 2017.

[21] Cameron and Henderson, 'Brave New World at the General Assesmbly'.

[22] *United Nations Declaration on Human Cloning*, G. A. Res. 59/280, U.N. Doc A/RES/59/260 (23 March 2005), <http://www.un.org/en/ga/search/view_doc.asp?symbol=A/RES/59/280>, last accessed 9 February 2017.

[23] For the history and scope of the controversy in Australia and the academic literature, see Tranter, 'Biotechnology, Media and Law-making'.

[24] Australian Health Ethics Committee, *Scientific, Ethical and Regulatory Considerations Relevant to Cloning of Human Beings*, p. 51.

[25] Ibid., pp. 17–19.

[26] Brownsword, *Rights, Regulation and the Technological Revolution*, pp. 48–50.

In some jurisdictions – the United Kingdom being the most notable – a pro-research stance of facilitation can be seen.[27] Others – like Italy, Germany, and New Zealand – have been less facilitative.[28] Some jurisdictions regulate therapeutic cloning through the denial of public-research monies,[29] others through centralised command and control bureaucracies.[30] However, notwithstanding the diversity in how the politico-legal networks of various jurisdictions responded to therapeutic cloning and stem cell research, there can be seen a uniform constant: the prohibiting of human reproductive cloning.[31]

Indeed, in the law of the West, human reproductive cloning is a serious offence. In most jurisdictions, the 'cloner' should be added to the heinous parade of murderer, terrorist, and paedophile. In the United Kingdom, a reproductive cloner can face ten years' imprisonment,[32] a period that could outlast the duration of many murderers' mandatory life custodial sentences.[33] In Australia, a reproductive cloner could be liable for fifteen years,[34] while in France reproductive cloners could be sentenced to thirty years' imprisonment and a €7.5 million fine.[35] In California, a reproductive cloner escapes imprisonment, but risks a $250,000 fine and institutions that harbour such felons face a $10 million fine.[36]

But why have the clone and cloner attracted this opprobrium? Textbooks define a clone as an entity with an identical genetic sequence to another individual.[37] However, this definition fails to explain the onerous nature of the penalties. There are natural 'clones'. Normal cellular reproduction by mitosis involves the splitting of a single cell into two identical daughter cells. Plant propagation by cutting produces siblings with the same genes as the parent, and identical twins also satisfy the definition.[38] Various animals can undergo unisexual reproduction, whereby females produce clone offspring independent and unmolested by males.[39] Clearly, there is something about

27 Luk, 'The United Kingdom and Germany'.
28 Isasi and Knoppers, 'Mind the Gap', p. 20.
29 Ibid., p. 21. Most notably the United States.
30 Ibid., p. 17. Most notably the United Kingdom, Australia, and Canada.
31 Ibid., p. 18.
32 Human Fertilisation and Embryology Act 1990, Chapter 37, ss 3(2), s 41.
33 Cotton, 'Mandatory Life Sentence for Murder'.
34 Prohibition of Human Cloning Act 2002 (Cth), ss 9.
35 Act No. 2004-900 of 6 August 2004 relative to bio-ethics [*relative à la bioéthique*] *JO* 7 August 2004, art 28.
36 Cal. Health & Safety Code §§ 24185, 24187, 24189 (2001).
37 Lodish, Berk, Zipursky, Matsudaira, Baltimore and Darnell, *Molecular Cell Biology*, p. G-4.
38 David and Kirkhope, 'Cloning/Stem Cells and the Meaning of Life', p. 368.
39 Loxdale and Lushai, 'Maintenance of Aphid Clonal Lineages'.

clones that is to be feared beyond the widespread, natural occurrence of entities with genetic sameness.

The answer to this question should be obvious to anyone with a well-tuned law and humanities antenna. The legal reception of Dolly, and the subsequent prohibition of human reproductive cloning, were framed by, and responded to, Western myths of clones and cloning that have been nurtured by the 'clone canon' in science fiction.[40] Clones were already terrifying, repulsive, evil creatures within Western culture decades before the Roslin Institute began experimenting with *Ovis Aries* embryos.[41] There had been earlier media controversies concerning human cloning, most notably the public debate that surrounded David Rorvik's hoax cloning novel *In His Image* (1978).[42] Before Rorvik, there was a proto-bioethics discourse concerned with the possibility of human cloning and the ethical dilemmas that it posed.[43] Indeed, human cloning as terrifying, repulsive, and evil was used by pioneering bioethicists during the recombinant DNA and in vitro fertilisation (IVF) controversies of the 1970s as the extreme case of an out-of-control, amoral science.[44] By the late 1970s, there existed enough serious consideration of cloning to inspire legal scholars to write about possible legal responses to human cloning,[45] and by the time of the birth in 1978 of Louise Brown – the first in vitro fertilisation (IVF) child – the possibility of cloning was a regular feature in legal scholarship concerned with artificial human reproduction.[46] In the mid-1980s, the prospect of cloning was regularly anticipated in law reviews[47] and books,[48] to the point where some Western jurisdiction possessed legislative prohibitions on human cloning prior to 1997.[49]

The beginning of this negative cultural role for the clone is with the images of mechanised human reproduction in the opening chapter of Aldous Huxley's *Brave New World* (1932).[50] Huxley's text is rich in imagery: there

40 Corcos, Corcos, and Stockhoff, 'Double-Take', pp. 1,045–6; Hamilton, 'Traces of the Future', p. 267.

41 Turney, *Frankenstein's Footsteps*, p. 214.

42 Rorvik, *In his Image*. On this book and its media impact, see Kolata, *Clone*, pp. 93–119.

43 Lederberg, 'Experimental Genetics and Human Evolution'; Ramsey, *Fabricated Man*, pp. 78–100.

44 Zaner, 'Surprise! You're Just Like Me!', p. 116; Klugman and Murray, 'Cloning, Historical Ethics, and the NBAC', pp. 16–18.

45 Pizzulli, 'Asexual Reproduction and Genetic Engineering'.

46 Steeves, 'Artificial Human Reproduction'; Humphreys, 'Lawmaking and Science', p. 429.

47 For example, Smith II, 'Intimations of Immortality'.

48 For example, Carmen, *Cloning and the Constitution*.

49 Nicol, Chalmers, and Gogarty, 'Regulating Biomedical Advances', p. 46.

50 Huxley, *Brave New World*, pp. 15–26.

is 'decanting', 'sow's peritoneum', 'Alphas', 'Gammas', and 'Ninety-six identical twins working ninety-six identical machines!'[51] From this shocking, dystopian origin, the clone has featured across a variety of science fiction genres and mediums: from *The Boys from Brazil* (1976)[52] and (1978)[53] to celebrated texts in feminist science fiction, such as Fay Weldon's *The Cloning of Joanna May* (1989)[54] and James Triptree Jr's novella *Houston, Houston, Do You Read?* (1976)[55] to space opera,[56] cyberpunk,[57] monster action films such as *Jurassic Park* (1990, 1993),[58] and comedies.[59] Indeed, prior to Dolly, John Clute and Peter Nicholls' *Encyclopaedia of Science Fiction* (1993) suggested a non-conclusive list of the cloning canon running to more than forty entries.[60] The clone joins the robot, spaceship, alien, and cyborg as one of the core motifs of science fiction. Christine Corcos, Isabel Corcos, and Brian Stockhoff suggest that, while the narratives and themes within the cloning oeuvre are diverse, 'most of them are negative'.[61] Outside of feminist science fiction, where critiques of heterosexuality allowed more positive stories about clones (like in *Houston, Houston, Do You Read?*),[62] the clone has generally been a figure associated with corruption, power, death, and destruction. In particular, the clone is tied to authoritarianism and mad scientists, as in *The Boys from Brazil*,[63] and the clone invokes the manufactured, the unnatural, and the end of human dignity, as in *Brave New World*.[64]

These two specific texts, and the narratives and tropes popularly attributed to them, circulated within the politico-legal networks that moved from Dolly to law. With its haunting imagery of young Hitlers and a harrowed

51 Ibid., p. 18.
52 Levin, *The Boys from Brazil.*
53 Schaffner, *The Boys from Brazil.*
54 Weldon, *The Cloning of Joanna May.*
55 Tiptree Jr, 'Houston, Houston, Do You Read?'
56 Clarke, *Imperial Earth*; Lucas, *Star Wars: Attack of the Clones*; Baird, *Star Trek Nemesis.* In Chapter 4, the Cylons from *Battlestar Galactica* are clones, and the early episodes clearly reference all the negative tropes from the clone canon.
57 In the *Neuromancer,* the Tessier-Ashpool family turn out to be a hive of clones, cryogenically frozen in their villa Straylight atop the Freeside orbital platform. Gibson, *Neuromancer,* pp. 95–6.
58 Crichton, *Jurassic Park.* Spielberg, *Jurassic Park.* Other action fantasy science fictions featuring clones are Spottiswoode, *The 6th Day*; Bay, *The Island.*
59 For example, Ramis, *Multiplicity*; Allen, *The Sleeper.*
60 Clute and Nicholls, *Encyclopedia of Science Fiction,* pp. 236–7.
61 Corcos, Corcos, and Stockhoff, 'Double-Take', p. 1,052.
62 Wasson, 'Love in the Time of Cloning', p. 141.
63 Rose, 'How to Teach Biology', p. 293.
64 Hartouni, '*Brave New World*', p. 96; Back, '*Frankenstein* and Brave New World', p. 330.

Gregory Peck, *Boys from Brazil* surfaced repeatedly during the immediate post-Dolly announcement as signifying the institutional evils of cloning – that is, that cloning would only be pursued by corrupt and morally bankrupt entities. Graeme Leech, writing in the *Australian* on 1 March 1997, set out the elements of this coding:

> [A] mad dictator or an unscrupulous government wanting to conduct a secret experiment, or even a deranged billionaire, could, within a few years, have the capacity to gather the necessary personnel and equipment to clone a human. The frequently cited scenario contained in the movie *The Boys from Brazil,* in which Nazi fanatics plot to clone copies of Hitler, is no more than an entertaining piece of science fiction . . . But the fictional idea might still hold sufficient fascination for someone to undertake the work in secrecy . . . So who would deny with any confidence that someone such as Saddam Hussein might not be tempted to clone himself?[65]

These connections between *Boys from Brazil* and depraved scientists and despots were repeated in other Western media.[66] They can be seen in the California Advisory Committee on Human Cloning, which noted that 'discussions of human reproductive cloning have often focused on evil or frivolous uses of cloning such as to create clones of Adolph Hitler, of superior warriors, of excellent athletes, or of rich egomaniacs'.[67] They can also be seen in the citing of *Boys from Brazil* and its referents by legislators[68] and legal scholars.[69] The commonality of association of *Boys from Brazil* with the institutional evil of cloning can also be seen in its circulation in commentary by pro-research advocates. In these representations, *Boys from Brazil* and its connotations are something from which the therapeutic cloning or stem cell research needs to be distanced.[70]

65 Leech 'The Genetic Gene', p. 22.

66 For example, see Crane, 'Don't Rush to Ban Cloning Research', p. 2; Hawkes, 'Legal Barriers will Prevent Apocalypse Now, if Not Later', p. 3; Devine 'Crackpot Reasoning Behind Ungodly Cloning Rush', p. 13.

67 California Advisory Committee on Human Cloning, *Cloning Californians*, p. 20 [II.2.A].

68 For example, see *Commonwealth Parliamentary Debates*, House of Representatives, 21 August 2002, p. 6,068 (Alexander Downer, Minister for Foreign Affairs), *Commonwealth Parliamentary Debates*, Senate, 12 November 2002, p. 6,105 (Nick Sherry); Hansard (House of Lords) 28 April 1999 Col 329 (Lord Rea).

69 See, for example, Korobkin, 'Stem Cell Research and the Cloning Wars', p. 116; Cohen, 'Cloning and the Constitution', p. 519; Chester, 'Cloning for Human Reproduction', p. 321; Eibert, 'Human Cloning', p. 1,097.

70 See, for example, Birkett, 'Cloning is Good', p. 20; Sutherland, 'The Ideas Interview', p. 24.

Often in the same statement, *Boys from Brazil* was complemented by *Brave New World*. For example, in the House of Lords, Lord Alton of Liverpool considered that 'there was a time when human cloning was regarded as being in the realms of science fiction. It made good reading in books like *Boys from Brazil* or *Brave New World*.'[71] Whereas *Boys from Brazil* signified the corruption of cloners, *Brave New World* referenced the corruption to the clone: that the clone would be unnatural, mass produced, and not possess human dignity. Lord Brennan in the House of Lords articulated these connotations of *Brave New World*:

> Within the field covering the use of stem and adult cells for various purposes, it is natural that a primeval fear has taken hold among many people; namely, that at the hands of science they face the risk of copies being made of human beings . . . In Huxley's *Brave New World*, written 70 years ago, genetic engineering was a commonplace in his fictional world. Human beings were created by cloning and were mass produced. Mothers and fathers became 'controllers' and 'predestinators'.[72]

As such, *Brave New World*, with its connotations of '"photocopying" a human being'[73] and 'human mass production, slave factories and carbon-copied armies',[74] circulated in newspaper reports,[75] governmental reports,[76] and law reviews.[77] Like *Boys from Brazil*, *Brave New World* was identified as a source of misinformation and hysteria by pro-research advocates.[78]

This discussion of an obvious moment of law and technology shows that one of the primary discourses that mediated the reception of Dolly within the politico-legal networks of the West was science fiction. Specific texts, and popular imagery and tropes, were referenced as the primary location

71 Hansard (House of Lords) 28 April 1999 Col 317 (Lord Alton of Liverpool). See also Trafford, 'Fear of Cloning And the Ewe To-Do', p. Z.06; Kaveny, 'Cloning and Positive Liberty', p. 15.

72 Hansard (House of Lords) 26 November 2000 Col 20 (Lord Brennan).

73 House of Representatives, *Human Cloning*, p. x.

74 Editorial, 'To Clone a Sheep', p. 18.

75 See, for example, Ragg, 'Right or Wrong? Cloning Ourselves', *The Australian*, p. 10; Ahuja, 'Could the Cure for all Diseases be Banned?', p. 8; Colman, 'Why Cloning Would Be Inhuman', p. 17; Brown 'Cloning: Where's the Outrage?', p. 1.

76 See, for example, Human Fertilisation and Embryology Authority and Human Genetics Advisory Commission, *Cloning Issues in Reproduction, Sience and Medicine*, p. 19 [5.1].

77 See, for example, Robertson, 'Liberty, Identity, and Human Cloning', p. 1,387; Annas, 'Human Cloning'; Greene, 'The Regulation of Human Cloning', p. 342; Bell, 'Human Cloning and International Human Rights Law', p. 217; Lavi, 'Cloning International Law'.

78 See, for example, Postrel 'Should Human Cloning Be Allowed?', A.20; Blackford, 'Who's Afraid of the Brave New World?'

for 'public' or 'immediate' reactions to a technological event such as Dolly. Indeed, it was often just 'science fiction' that was cited as the location for alarm and the justification for the law that was to come, in the media,[79] in the governmental reports,[80] by politicians,[81] and in law reviews.[82]

This event of 'cloning law' in the West reveals three characteristics that distinguish the usual way in which technical legality has been conceived and practised. The first is the future. There was little concern with the cloning of sheep per se – particularly in the Antipodean lands of Australia and New Zealand, where sheep are rather plentiful. Rather, the hyperbole was anticipatory. Dolly was a concern because she heralded the possibility of human reproductive cloning. This speculative reception of Dolly locates the significance of science fiction for technical legality. Dolly represented an anxious future of human reproductive cloning precisely because of the monstrous images, tropes, and narrative associated with clones, cloning, and cloners made popular through science fiction's clone canon. This science fictionality behind the legal engagement with cloning technology has a final revelation. It is trite – it almost goes without saying – but through science fiction, the scientific announcement of a new technique in mammalian embryology gave impetus to the making of law. While more complicated and ambiguous possibilities of therapeutic cloning and stem cell research came to occupy the politico-legal networks and the texts of law over the 2000s, the founding moment was the science fictional reception of Dolly that triggered the law-making processes. In this, the public union of Dolly and the clone canon was not platonic. It was – like Dolly – fertile, and it gave rise to an offspring: law.

This suggestion of science fiction mixed with talk of future, law, and technology moves this chapter along. Having shown the connections between science fiction and technical legality in the context of the politico-

79 Friend, 'Hello Dolly! Breakthrough with Sheep Could Herald Human Cloning', p. 1; Coyne, 'Think Twice before Fearing the Advent of Cloning',, p. 29; Kolata, 'Gene Genie', p. 14.

80 National Bioethics Advisory Committee, *Cloning Human Beings*, p. 3; Australian Government, *Legislation Review*, p. 153.

81 'The stuff of nightmares and horror movies has come of age . . . a confirmation of our prejudices that mad scientists lurk in the shadows in their white coats with anti-social habits.' Despoja, 'To Clone or Not to Clone', p. 12. Hansard (House of Commons) 19 December 2000 Col 221 (Yvette Cooper, Pontefract and Castleford); Hansard (House of Lords) 28 April 1999 Col 317 (Lord Alton of Liverpool).

82 For example, see Annas and Robertson, 'Human Cloning', pp. 80–1; Scheckel, 'The Prospect of Cloning Human Beings', p. 609; Lawton, 'The *Frankenstein* Controversy', pp. 298–9, 301; Sevanthinathan, 'Heavy Regulation of Human Cloning as an Alternative to a Complete Ban', p. 227.

legal responses to cloning, the scope can be expanded. The claim is that the Dolly event was not unique – indeed, its basic structure has been replicated whenever law is faced with technology. From this, science fiction can be seen as occupying two positions within technical legality. The first, as was seen with the operation of the clone canon in the Dolly event, is as the source of images, tropes, and narratives through which the implications of a technology can be projected into the future. It forms a primary place of reckoning in the West for anxieties over its technological disruptions and becomings. The second is that it informs the very structure of this process – a structure that has a primal name: Frankenstein!

Frankenstein Myth

The identification of science fiction as the nexus between technology and law in the Dolly event is not an isolated incident. The history of law and technology reveals a fundamental science fictionality.[83] Responses to Sputnik in the late 1950s and early 1960s were motivated by images of space-faring humanity – of planetary colonies, alien contact, and space war, made popular by space opera.[84] Julies Verne and H. G. Wells were mentioned[85] as 'prophetic'[86] of humanity's space-faring future[87] and as the embodiment of speculating on technological futures.[88] Indeed, popular space opera texts – the 1920 and 1930s *Buck Rogers* franchise was the most common[89] – were cited and space opera images of planetary travel, alien encounters, exploitation of celestial resources, and space war circulated in the legal literature from the period.[90] The eventual international laws of space – which provide for humankind space sovereignty, registration of space vehicles, liability for space accidents, and royalty distribution from lunar mining – can be seen as directly leg-

83 Tranter, 'The Speculative Jurisdiction'.

84 Westfahl, 'Space Opera', pp. 197–8.

85 Verne, *From Earth to the Moon*; Jenks, 'International Law and Activities in Space', p. 99; Lee, 'The Legal Implications of McGill's High Altitude Research Project', p. 158.

86 Simeone Jr, 'Space – a Legal Vacuum', p. 43.

87 Jenks, 'International Law and Activities in Space', p. 99; Lee, 'The Legal Implications of McGill's High Altitude Research Project', p. 158; Simeone Jr, 'Space – a Legal Vacuum', p. 43.

88 Dembling, 'National Coordination for Space Exploration'; Smirnoff, 'The Legal Status of Celestial Bodies', p. 385; Menter, 'Formulation of Space Law', p. 3.

89 See, for example, Wurfel, 'Space Law – Is There Any?', p. 269; Teller, 'Peace and National Security in the New Space Age', pp. 283–4; Keating, 'Reaching for the Stars', p. 56.

90 See, for example, Haley, 'Space Law and Metala', pp. 438, 448–9; Menter, 'Formulation of Space Law', p. 3; McDougal and Lipson, 'Perspectives for a Law of Outer Space', pp. 408–9; Jessup and Taubenfeld, *Controls for Outer Space*, p. 200; Pépin, 'Space Penetration', p. 233.

islating for a future imagined by E. E. 'Doc' Smith and the *Buck Rogers* serial matinees.[91] The reception of Louise Brown prefigures the dystopian texts and images that accompanied Dolly, with *Brave New World*, *Nineteen Eighty-Four*, and the anticipated spectre of centralised, authoritarian state control over reproduction circulating in the politico-legal discourses.[92] In more contemporary moments, the reception of the Internet in the 1990s was shadowed by William Gibson's term-defining cyberpunk classic *Neuromancer* (1984),[93] with its sprawling future of freedom, illicitness, and corporate excess.[94] Even Lessig felt the pull to cite Gibson in the opening pages of *Code*.[95] Further, during the 2000s, conceptualising the possibilities of virtual worlds was projected against the more comic cyberpunk tomorrow of Neal Stephenson's *Snow Crash* (1992).[96] The public debate about the regulation of nanotechnology remains haunted by Greg Bear's animation in *Blood Music* (1985)[97] of the 'grey goo' scenario, where self-replicating nanobots consume the biosphere, leaving a uniform nothing.[98]

In these events, science fiction is the myth-source for technological futures. It stores up, examines, and projects anxieties and also hopes for technological-driven change. In this, science fiction is the airbag for future shock. It provides the interpretative schema – the images, lexicon, and narratives – to cushion the alleged jarring disruption of the endless technological (r) evolution. Furthermore, this cushioning does not just occur in the realm of

91 Pop, 'The Men who Sold the Moon'.

92 Mulkay, *The Embryo Research Debate*, pp. 120–7; Annas and Elias, '*In Vitro* Fertilization and Embryo Transfer', pp. 200–1; Porte, 'Government Regulation of In Vitro Fertilization', p. 103; Lorio, '*In Vitro* Fertilization and Embryo Transfer', p. 983; Clapshaw, 'Legal Aspects of Artificial Human Reproduction', p. 254; Lane, Cross Bolton, and Alexander, '*In Vitro* Fertilization', p. 320.

93 Gibson, *Neuromancer*.

94 McCaffery, 'The Desert of the Real', p. 9. On the appearance of Gibson's cyberpunk in early cyber law discourse, see, for example, Katsh, 'Rights, Camera, Action', p. 1,684; Horning, 'The Enforceability of Contracts Negotiated in Cyberspace', p. 109; Burke, 'Cybersmut and the First Amendment', p. 89; Cockfield, 'Designing Tax Policy for the Digital Biosphere', p. 348; Hunter, 'Cyberspace as Place and the Tragedy of the Digital Anticommons', p. 472.

95 Lessig, *Code and Other Laws of Cyberspace*, p. 5.

96 Stephenson, *Snow Crash*. See, for example, Lastowka and Hunter, 'The Laws of the Virtual Worlds', p. 6; Balkin and Noveck, 'Introduction', p. 3; Chin, 'Regulating Your Second Life', p. 1,306; Sheldon, 'Claiming Ownership, but Getting Owned', p. 786; Dougherty and Lastowka, 'Virtual Trademarks', p. 758.

97 Bear, *Blood Music*.

98 See, for example, Reynolds, 'Nanotechnology and Regulatory Policy', p. 181; Drexler and Wejnert, 'Nanotechnology and Policy', pp. 14–15; Fiedler and Reynolds, 'Legal Problems of Nanotechnology', p. 605; Lin, 'Size Matters', pp. 355–6.

the personal. Science fiction is present in discourses around water coolers and shopping malls and in social media feeds; however, more significant is its breaching of the public–private divide. As shown in the Dolly event and within other moments of public reckoning with technology, science fiction is there feeding content into the formal networks of public power in the West. These serious, practical, and important institutions engage in a speculative jurisdiction or 'legal futurism'[99] through an inherent taking seriously of science fiction as the storehouse for technical futures. Through these networks, science fiction's technological futures become transmuted into law. What this means for technical legality is the immediate and intimate association of science fiction with law and technology. Science fiction presents technology as a glimpse of a future that calls for law.

This suggests a cultural logic that bounds up technology, future, and law, a set of structural relationships that configure the politico-legal networks of the West to transmute science fiction into law. This configuration has a name and pedigree. It was first given form by Mary Shelley in *Frankenstein: Or the Modern Prometheus* (1818).[100]

Within science fiction studies, there is dispute about whether science fiction as an identifiable genre begins with Shelley. Such prominent authors-turned-critics as Brian Aldiss and Isaac Asimov both specify *Frankenstein* as science fiction's ur-text.[101] Don Idhe and Robert Adams separately argue that the substantive origins of science fiction lie with the interstellar journey texts of the seventeenth century, of which Cyrano de Bergerac's are the best known,[102] while Darko Suvin regards Thomas More's *Utopia* (1516)[103] as a key text.[104] However, these claims are not denials of the significance of *Frankenstein* for the genre. Both within the scholarly community and within popular culture, *Frankenstein* is synonymous with science fiction, and only a controversial critic would want to argue that *Frankenstein* belongs outside of the genre.[105]

The formal elements of *Frankenstein* are well known: scientist creates monster and immediately rejects monster,[106] monster learns about humanity

[99] Beebe, 'Fair Use and Legal Futurism'.

[100] Shelley, *Frankenstein.*

[101] Aldiss, *Trillion Year Spree*, p. 25; Asimov, 'Introduction: The First Century of Science Fiction', pp. 11–12.

[102] Ihde, *Bodies in Technology*, pp. xiii–ix, 48–9.

[103] More, *Utopia.*

[104] Suvin, *Metamorphoses of Science Fiction*, p. 92.

[105] Pierce, *Foundations of Science Fiction*, p. 20.

[106] Shelley, *Frankenstein*, pp. 56–8.

and its own monstrousness,[107] monster becomes pathological,[108] and monster destroys scientist.[109] This familiarity has allowed critics to argue that *Frankenstein* is mythic rather than textual, that it has been freed from its text to circulate as a myth within the supposed modern – and therefore myth-less – West.[110] A consequence of the mythic essence to *Frankenstein* has been the emergence of the '*Frankenstein* archive'.[111] The 1818 text has become the fountainhead for an immense catalogue of popular cultural material that has invoked, recycled, parodied and extrapolated from Shelley's text.[112] It is this archive that has allowed *Frankenstein* to be regarded as a myth, manifesting differently in different articulations yet still possessing a stable symbolic content.[113]

However, *Frankenstein* is not just a problematic modern myth; it has been regarded as 'the' myth of modernity.[114] It is common ground among literary, cultural, and technology studies that the 'Frankenstein myth' enacts the quintessential modern relationship between humans and technology.[115] In this common reading, *Frankenstein* provides what amounts to a series of interlinked characterisations and associations concerning scientists, technology, and society. Victor Frankenstein, the protagonist, becomes the epitome of the rational scientist too preoccupied with his techniques to consider the wider context of his creating.[116] As a metaphor for technology, the monster is ambiguous. It has the potential for good:[117] rescuing a child;[118] not stealing from the De Lacey's meagre stores;[119] and appreciating classical literature and history such as Goethe, Plutarch, and Milton.[120] It also has the potential for

[107] Ibid. pp. 98–129.
[108] Ibid. pp. 136–90.
[109] Ibid. pp. 205–11.
[110] Baldick, *In Frankenstein's Shadow*, pp. 1–9; Turney, *Frankenstein's Footsteps*, pp. 26–8; Back, '*Frankenstein* and Brave New World'.
[111] Glut, *The Frankenstein Archive*.
[112] Ibid.; Forry, *Hideous Progenies*.
[113] Ong, *Orality and Literacy*, p. 12.
[114] Baldick, *In Frankenstein's Shadow*, p. 5.
[115] Gaylin, 'The *Frankenstein* Factor'; Levine, 'The Ambiguous Heritage of *Frankenstein*', pp. 16–17; Botting, *Making Monstrous*, pp. 164–84; Cranny-Francis, 'The "Science" of Science Fiction', pp. 64–6; Caudill, 'Scientific Narratives in Law', p. 253.
[116] Winner, *Autonomous Technology*, p. 313.
[117] Olorenshaw, 'Narrating the Monster', p. 165.
[118] Shelley, *Frankenstein*, p. 134.
[119] Ibid., p. 106.
[120] Ibid., pp. 122–4.

evil:[121] murdering Frankenstein's young brother, William;[122] framing Justine for that murder;[123] and murdering Henry Clerval[124] and Frankenstein's bride Elizabeth.[125] The monster is a thing to be both pitied and feared, and in most commentaries it is Victor, with his acontextual rationalism, bourgeois irresponsibility, and petty revulsion, who is the true monster.[126] The monster's 'thing-ness' – its status as external to humanity – is repeatedly emphasised through its exclusion from human society[127] and its desire for a mate of its own kind.[128] In this, the monster animates an amoral and non-human conceptualisation of technology. *Frankenstein* also shows the vulnerability of human society to the revolutionary, and often bloody, product of science. The scientist concocts in his private rooms while society remains passive and impotent against the depravity of his monstrous creation.

Frankenstein is therefore a modern myth, not just because of its archive's blurring of authoritative text and communal orality, but for its articulation of anxieties about technology. However, to return to technical legality, *Frankenstein* can clearly be seen as inhabiting the 'technical', but not the 'legal'. Absent from Shelley's text is any institutional counterforce; there is no Inquisition, Royal Society, or ethics committee to control scientist and creation. As William P. MacNeil has acknowledged, there is law work occurring throughout the text. There is excessive talk of crime, murders, and guilt.[129] There are also some obvious institutional legal moments: the trial of Justine for the murder of the child William,[130] Frankenstein's subjection to the Irish legal process,[131] and Frankenstein's 'confession' to the Genevan magistrate.[132] However, Shelley presents an impotent law: Justine's trial is a farce, Ireland frees Frankenstein without asking hard questions, and the Genevan magistrate reluctantly agrees to hunt the monster with the caveat that it will be 'impracticable'.[133] Faced with the monster's campaign of terror,

[121] Turney, *Frankenstein's Footsteps*, pp. 38–9.
[122] Shelley, *Frankenstein*, p. 136.
[123] Ibid., p. 137.
[124] Ibid., p. 169.
[125] Ibid., p. 186.
[126] Milner, *Literature, Culture, Society*, p. 155.
[127] Shelley, *Frankenstein*, pp. 128–31 (rejected by the De Laceys), p. 135 (shot by the father of the child the monster rescued).
[128] Ibid., p. 137.
[129] MacNeil, 'The Monstrous Body of the Law', pp. 23–4.
[130] Shelley, *Frankenstein*, pp. 78–85.
[131] Ibid., pp. 168–74.
[132] Ibid., pp. 189–90.
[133] Ibid., p. 190.

law does not respond and the monster and creator are left to chase on the northern ice, alone.[134] However, through negation law becomes included. Shelley's cast – irresponsible scientist, ambiguous monster, and vulnerable society – calls out for a hero to thwart Frankenstein and control the monster in society's name. A continuing feature of the *Frankenstein* archive has been the provision of this heroic supplement through policeman, 'good' scientists, monster hunters, superheroes, and/or enraged townsfolk.[135] In this, the Frankenstein myth can be seen as the basic articulation of the configuration in the West that bundles technology, humanity, and law. Its monstrous, non-human technology threatens a passive, pure, and vulnerable humanity, calling forth law in the present to control, regulate, and render human the technology monster in the future.[136]

In essence, the Frankenstein myth posits a humanity whose fate is determined by a primal battle between two forces. On the one side – the dark side – is the monster of technology: 'more machine than man: twisted and evil'[137] – indeed, all machine and not human, perpetually challenging and disrupting the human present with anxieties and hopes of inevitable technological futures. On the other side – the light side – is law, the instrument through which present humanity can combat or entrench specific technological futures. The Frankenstein myth says that technology will change human futures, but that through law the human present can influence this changing. This is what the politico-legal networks of the West did when they transmuted Sputnik, Louise Brown, cyberspace, nanotechnology, and Dolly into law: the dark of technology was made human and light.

So, science fiction intersperses technical legality at two points. The first is as the storehouse of technological futures, the keeper of images, motifs, and narratives concerning the impact of technological change and especially the anxieties and hopes for the future of human life. The second, through the Frankenstein myth, involves having a programming function within the politico-legal networks. Stated, animated, and anticipated in Shelley's tale of naïve, immature scientist, and other, death-bringing monster lies the basic configuration – monstrous technology, vulnerable humanity, and saving law – that transmutes the cultural imaginings of technological change into law. This is why technical legality must deal seriously with science fiction. It is an exercise in science fiction, and to talk of law and technology without science fiction would be to completely compress the cultural life from the enterprise

134 Huet, *Monstrous Imagination*, pp. 143–4.

135 Winner, *Autonomous Technology*, p. 307; Glut, *The Frankenstein Archive*.

136 Tranter, 'Nomology, Ontology and Phenomenology of Law and Technology', p. 458.

137 Marquand, *Star Wars: The Return of the Jedi*, Obi-Wan Kenobi (Alec Guinness).

– the colour, characters, and narratives that give meaning to technologies and laws. More importantly, engagement with technical legality without science fiction would disconnect its essential futurity.

In this, the future keeps coming back. Science fiction is the West's storehouse of technological futures, and the saving law of the Frankenstein myth is the law of the present to influence those futures. As Andy Miah observes, the prohibitions on human reproductive cloning were not because there had been reproductive cloning – not withstanding five sensationalist media announcements of to-be human clones from 1997 to 2005.[138] The laws were anticipatory; they responded to the possibility that there *could* be clones and cloners in the future if there was not legal intervention in the present. In this, Dolly – through the Frankenstein myth – manifested an inverse temporal polarity from that other Western crisis event of the 2000s: 9/11. In 9/11, the politico-legal networks processed the images of the fall of the two towers – themselves anticipated by science fiction's alien invasion genre from *Independence Day* (1996)[139] back to H. G. Wells' *War of the Worlds* (1898)[140] – into laws to prevent this past from recurring, from ever happening again. However, the Frankenstein myth means that technical legality can be seen as operating according to a different schema. It makes laws, as in the prohibitions on human reproductive cloning, to prevent a dark speculative imagining from ever being – or, in the case of the distribution mechanisms of lunar resources in the Moon Agreement, to facilitate the dream of a humanity enriched by celestial wealth through calling it into being. This legislating for the future presupposes an account of law – or, more precisely, an instrumentality to law.

Law as Technology

It is commonplace in contemporary legal discourses to talk of law instrumentally. Law is conceived as a tool, an instrument to achieve social goals in the future. Thinking like a lawyer means being able to manufacture arguments about law involving terms such as 'mischief', 'policy', and 'intent of the legislators'.[141] Legal research and legal scholarship mean identifying the effectiveness of various law tools – regulations, rights, and codes – to secure specific futures. As James Boyd White stated in 1985, this means:

[138] Miah, 'Genetics, Cyberspace and Bioethics'.

[139] Emmerich, *Independence Day*; Bell-Metereau, 'The How-To Manual, the Prequel, and the Sequel in Post-9/11 Cinema', p. 147.

[140] Wells, *The War of the Worlds*.

[141] Schauer, *Thinking Like a Lawyer*, pp. 148–70.

> Law then becomes reducible to two features: policy choices and techniques of implementation. Our questions are 'What do we want?' and 'How do we get it?' In this way, the conception of law as a set of rules merges with the conception of law as a set of institutions and processes.[142]

This can be seen in some of the key scholarship on law and technology. Lessig's fundamental contribution was to emphasise to legal scholars the significance of code in the normative toolbox. His *Code* presents the thesis that the technology itself can be considered a law tool. Roger Brownsword has argued for a reformulated rights discourse to anchor responses to technology in the twenty-first century.[143] Earlier, Laurence H. Tribe, in his 1973 opus *Channelling Technology through Law*, advocated for risk assessment to comprehend technology's problematic futures,[144] which then was to feed into law-based regulatory schemes.[145] Tribe's talk of institutionalised mechanisms for law-making was mirrored in Australia over the 1980s by Justice Michael Kirby, foundational chairman of the Australian Law Reform Commission, who championed the Commission as an institutional 'technique of law development',[146]

> with its procedures for interdisciplinary consultation, public hearings, discussion on the media and widespread community involvement, [the law reform commission] provides legislators with a well fashioned instrument by which to tackle the 'too hard basket' of legal change.[147]

In each of these accounts, technological futures become the subject of law-mechanisms in the present. However, what is significant in these moments of thinking technical legality is that there is a change in emphasis between White's two questions of 'What do we want?' and 'How do we get it?' The dominant question is the getting it, not the policy choices of what is wanted. Here the future appears to retreat. Lawyers can be seen as vacating the policy position, leaving it to legislatures or community, or a more abstract 'us', to make choices about what values should manifest in technological futures. The prevailing modus is captured by Kirby's lexicon of 'technique', 'procedures', and 'instrument' – in White's terms, 'The overriding metaphor is that of the machine.'[148]

142 Boyd White, 'Law as Rhetoric, Rhetoric as Law', p. 686.

143 Brownsword, *Rights, Regulation and the Technological Revolution*; Brownsword, 'So What Does the World Need Now?'

144 Tribe, *Channeling Technology through Law*, pp. 6–9.

145 Ibid., pp. 634–40.

146 Kirby, 'IVF – the Scope and Limitation of the Law', p. 10.

147 Kirby, *The Law and Modern Technology*, p. 14.

148 Boyd White, 'Law as Rhetoric, Rhetoric as Law', p. 686.

For modern lawyers, this is exactly how it should be. Jurisprudence has a well-established name for this mechanistic, value-free account of law: positivism.[149] Modern law, in the Weberian definition, was stripped of custom, values, and transcendent authority, reduced to a species of institutionalised power within the nation state.[150] Law in modernity became a question of authority, its validity a question of institutional competence – not, as in pre-modern legal orders, its continuity with past custom, or its organic association with community.[151] In this, the paradigm of positive law is legislation – and, as most forcefully shown in the debates concerning the injustice of retrospective legislation,[152] the addressee of legislation is properly the future. Legislation is law made now to affect the future. Within jurisprudence, this definition is entirely uncontroversial. Jeremy Bentham's wax eyes at University College London could be seen twinkling in agreement.[153] However, in the context of technical legality, with its founding narrative within the Frankenstein myth, such a conception of law becomes problematic.

Carl Schmitt has, until recent years, been a marginal influence on post-World War II jurisprudence.[154] At one time 'Crown Jurist' of the Third Reich,[155] Schmitt's refusal to undergo de-Nazification meant that he became a shadow figure within jurisprudence and also progressive and conservative political theory. However, his Weimar writings represent one of the first theoretical accounts of technical legality, of connecting modern law and technology.

For Schmitt, and for many conservatively inclined German intellectuals, Weimar Germany faced obliteration by the Soviet machine.[156] It was the identification of the machine nature of Russian communism that was specifically the danger. In Sovietism, Schmitt saw the full manifestation of the technological epoch: a hollowing out of substance and meaning, leaving only mechanisms for the efficient pursuit of goals.[157] Technology for Schmitt was agnostic between a 'silk blouse and poison gas'.[158] From within the system, both were outputs to be put to ends. Values and meaning – human life – came from outside. This is the Frankenstein myth of amoral non-human

149 Drahos, 'Law, Science and Reproductive Technology'.
150 Weber, *Economy and Society*, p. 848.
151 Postema, *Bentham and the Common Law Tradition*, pp. 1–33.
152 Fuller, *The Morality of Law*, p. 53.
153 Bentham, *Of Laws in General*, pp. 74–5.
154 Manderson, *Kangaroo Courts and the Rule of Law*.
155 Müller, *A Dangerous Mind*, p. 40.
156 Bourdieu, *The Political Ontology of Martin Heidegger*, pp. 26–7.
157 Schmitt, 'The Age of Neutralizations and Depolitcizations'.
158 Schmitt, *The Idea of Representation*, p. 39.

technology. Indeed, Schmitt's speculative engagements runs early and deep. One of his first publications, the 1918 short essay 'Die Buribunken',[159] was a satirical account of what jurisprudence would later call the 'internal point of view' of bureaucratic cyborgs (the Buribunken) to come, whose bodies had merged with office machinery[160] and whose compulsive continuous self-diarising seems to anticipate an obsessed social media user, who is compelled to

> write myself. Who writes me? I write myself. What is the content of my writing? I write that I am writing myself. What is the great motor that lifts me out of this self-satisfying circle of 'I'-ness? History! I am a key on the typewriter of history.[161]

What Schmitt saw in the future echoes of the Red Army's tanks and the self-important prattle of the Buribunken was the implications within Weber's characterisation of modern law as 'rational'. It was neutral and procedural. In this, Schmitt was commenting on the arrival of modern law, heralded by Weber with his analogy of the mechanised factory:

> The fully developed bureaucratic apparatus compares with other organizations exactly as does the machine with the non-mechanical modes of production. Precision, speed, unambiguity, knowledge of the files, continuity, discretion, unity, strict subordination, reduction of friction and of material and personal costs – these are raised to the optimum point.[162]

While, for Weber, the arrival of 'mechanised' law was the ultimate step in the long process of rationalisation ending with the procedural framework for efficient bureaucracy, for Schmitt the emergence of modern law as a framework that experts could wield to specific ends represented fundamental danger; it indicated that the law had become, in his own terms, 'technology'.[163] As Philippe Nonet comments, 'positive law is the metaphysics of modern technology'.[164]

This characterisation of modern law as technological allows for a telling re-reading of the laws that the politico-legal networks of the West produced in response to the Dolly event. Notwithstanding the diversity of responses and regimes dealing with therapeutic cloning and stem cell research, there is a

159 Schmitt, 'Die Buribunken'.

160 Kittler, *Gramophone, Film, Typewriter*, p. 231.

161 Schmitt, 'Die Buribunken', quoted in Kennedy, *Constitutional Failure*, p. 45.

162 Weber, *Economy and Society*, p. 973.

163 Schmitt, *Political Theology*, p. 28.

164 Nonet, 'What is Positive Law?', p. 683.

fundamental technicity to the post-Dolly cloning laws in the West. The prohibition on reproductive cloning that arrived in most Western jurisdictions over the 2000s was manufactured and applied to the future. For example, in Canada reproductive cloning was permissible on 28 March 2004, but not after 29 March 2004.[165] The politico-legal networks' processing of the controversy climaxed on a specific date with the coming into force of law. The future was rendered accountable by a specific action in space and time – in Canada, by assent on that date. This ability to make law has its origins in modernity's freeing of legality into a raw power that can be moulded into any shape or form, provided the procedures and manufacturing protocols are adhered to. It is this combination of substance-less plasticity with determinative procedure, the turning of law into a framework for executive power, that is central to Schmitt's declaration of it as technical.

Furthermore, in the jurisdictions whose laws went further and regulated therapeutic cloning or stem cell research, the technicity that was evident in the prohibitions on reproductive cloning can be seen more strongly. For example, in Australia the technicity of the Prohibition of Human Cloning for Reproduction Act 2002 (Cth), in both substance and in its gestation, is obvious. First, it is procedural law. While much of the Act directly prohibits various monsters and activities from the cloning canon (human reproductive cloning, chimeras, hybrids stitched together from the genetic materials of more than two humans, bio-traders in human reproductive bits), the new (in 2006) Division 2 provides the basic machinery for a licensing regime for therapeutic cloning. What is mentioned is 'licence',[166] which is defined in section 8 as a licence granted under the Research Involving Human Embryos Act 2002 (Cth).[167] In turn, Division 4 of that Act sets out the procedure through which an application for a licence by a 'person'[168] is decided by the 'NHMRC [National Health and Medical Research Council] Licensing Committee'.[169] In making the decision, the NHMRC Licensing Committee must ensure that appropriate 'protocols' are in place concerning consent[170] and verifying the origins of embryos,[171] and must consider the 'likelihood of significant advance in knowledge'.[172] Further, the committee

165 Assisted Human Reproduction Act, S. C., c.2.
166 Prohibition of Human Cloning for Reproduction Act 2002 (Cth), ss 22, 23, 23A, 23B.
167 Ibid., s 8.
168 Research Involving Human Embryos Act 2002 (Cth), s 20.
169 Established by section 13 of the Research Involving Human Embryos Act 2002 (Cth).
170 Ibid., s 21(3)(a).
171 Ibid., s 21(3)(b).
172 Ibid., s 21(4)(b).

needs to consider the report on the application by the Human Research Ethics Committee,[173] any relevant guidelines issued under the National Health and Medical Research Council Act 1992 (Cth),[174] and any matters specified by regulations.[175] Here, the critical decision-making has been turned over to an expert body; the legislation just provides for the mechanics for the decision. Further, the substance of the decision – the details of what content and considerations these experts should use to decide the application – is predominately left to other experts, the Human Research Ethics Committee, guidelines, and regulations. The law itself has been, in Schmitt's 1929 term, 'neutralised'[176] – stripped of values – leaving only an apparatus through which technicians can exercise power. This neutralised structure, where technical experts within the executive are empowered as decision-makers on morally contested cloning-related activities, has been mirrored in other Western post-Dolly laws.[177]

The Prohibition of Human Cloning for Reproduction Act 2002 (Cth) as modern law appears to substantiate Schmitt's suggestion in *Political Theology* (1922) that the modern state had not only become a 'great machine', but one in which the 'machine runs itself'.[178] However, there can be seen another marker of technicity to the Act. In *The Crisis of Parliamentary Democracy* (1923), Schmitt writes that the alleged 'intellectual foundations'[179] for parliament in openness and debate have been contradicted in its modern manifestation, where, '[s]mall and exclusive committees of parties or of party coalitions

173 Ibid., s 21(3)(c).

174 Ibid., s 21(4)(c).

175 Ibid., s 21(4)(e). The Prohibition of Human Cloning for Reproduction Act 2002 (Cth), s 26 allows for executive regulations, as does section 48 of the Research Involving Human Embryos Act 2002 (Cth). There is a Research Involving Human Embryos Regulation 2003 (Cth), which regulation 2.3 specifies that the committee under section 21 must also consider the 'ART guidelines' and the *National Statement on Ethical Conduct in Human Research*, issued by the CEO of the National Health and Medical Research Council.

176 Schmitt, 'The Age of Neutralizations and Depoliticizations'.

177 For example, Canada's Assisted Human Reproduction Act, S. C., c.2 mirrors the Australian scheme of layers of procedure and expert, technical decision-making. Section 10(2) allows for a licence to be granted to 'alter, manipulate, treat or make any use of an *in vitro* embryo.' Sections 21–39 establish the Assisted Human Reproduction Agency of Canada as the responsible decision-maker, and section 40 specifically empowers the Agency to issue licences. Further, for stem cell research, section 40(3.1) specifies that the Agency follow the procedure in *Human Pluripotent Stem Cell Research Guidelines* issued by the Canadian Institute of Health Research, and regulations.

178 Schmitt, *Political Theology*, p. 48.

179 Schmitt, *The Crisis of Parliamentary Democracy*, p. 49.

make their decisions behind closed doors.'[180] The Australian response to cloning can be seen to take Schmitt a step further.

The 2002 Act and its 2006 amendments essentially enacted the recommendations of the major reports: the Andrews report of 2001 and the Lockhart report of 2005. Notwithstanding the media debates, subsequent Senate reports, and conscience votes, the laws corresponded with the expert reports. A common comment by Australian parliamentarians was that responding to cloning was 'difficult'.[181] It can therefore be seen that many parliamentarians deferred to the reports, as evidenced by the numerous parliamentary comments commending and approving of the reports.[182] As texts, the Andrews and Lockhart reports exude authority. Both present their recommendations as the outcome of a detailed inquiry that has considered the science, the ethics, and community standards.[183] Both acknowledge the complexity – indeed, the intransigent character – of the ethical debate.[184] In the Lockhart report, an attempt is made to apply a neutral technical approach to the gathering and synthesising community attitudes.[185] Finally, both reports share the framing of their respective recommendations as 'balance'.[186]

The way that Australian law responded to cloning is a further demonstration of the technicity of modern law. If the 'machine runs itself' in terms of positive law providing a neutral framework for the modern executive, within

[180] Ibid., pp. 49–50.

[181] *Commonwealth Parliamentary Debates*, House of Representatives, 20 August 2002, p. 5,255 (Nicola Roxon); *Commonwealth Parliamentary Debates*, House of Representatives, 20 August 2002, p. 5,884 (Daryl Melham); *Commonwealth Parliamentary Debates*, House of Representatives, 28 August 2002, p. 6,087 (Bruce Scott).

[182] See, for example, concerning the Andrews Report, *Commonwealth Parliamentary Debates*, House of Representatives, 20 August 2002, p. 5,242 (Simon Crean); *Commonwealth Parliamentary Debates*, House of Representatives, 28 August 2002, p. 6,055 (Petro Georgiou); *Commonwealth Parliamentary Debates*, House of Representatives, 28 August 2002, p. 6,066 (Barry Wakelin). See, for example, the Lockhart Report, *Commonwealth Parliamentary Debates*, Senate, 6 November 2006, p. 5 (Natasha Stott Despoja); *Commonwealth Parliamentary Debates*, House of Representatives, 30 November 2006, pp. 13–16 (Julia Gillard); *Commonwealth Parliamentary Debates*, House of Representatives, 30 November 2006, p. 25 (Julia Irwin); *Commonwealth Parliamentary Debates*, House of Representatives, 30 November 2006, p. 63 (Dick Adams).

[183] House of Representatives, *Human Cloning*, pp. ix–x; Australian Government, *Legislation Review*, p. v.

[184] House of Representatives, *Human Cloning*, p. 94; Australian Government, *Legislation Review*, p. 161.

[185] This was emphasised by the authors of the report in a separate journal article: Skene, Kerridge, Marshall, McCombe, and Schofield, 'The Lockhart Committee'.

[186] House of Representatives, *Human Cloning*, p. 166; Australian Government, *Legislation Review*, p. xiii.

the Australian law-making in response to cloning, it can be seen that the very making of this law has become technical. The machine runs itself, not just at the level of the everyday decision, but at the macro level of institutional change. This pattern of technical law-making through the mechanism of inquiries and expert reports can also be seen in other jurisdictions' cloning laws.[187] This is particularly so when considering the Lockhart report in Australia. The Lockhart Committee was anticipated in the Andrews report in the recommendation for a three-year review,[188] and this was legislated for in section 25 of the Prohibition of Human Cloning Act 2002 (Cth). In this context, the 2006 amendments, which followed Lockhart's 2005 reporting, can be seen as autonomous – as the cyclic operation of a self-maintaining machine.

So, in the specific instance of the Dolly event, the laws that emerged can be seen as technological. They were technological in their calling, produced by the politico-legal networks to secure certain technological futures from the science fictional repercussions of a specific sheep. They were technological in their substance: beyond the prohibitions on human reproductive cloning, many jurisdictions established neutralised mechanisms for technical, expert decision-making on therapeutic cloning and stem cell research. Further, they were often technical in their making. The 'balanced' reports of commissioned experts tended to provide the blueprint for the manufactured law.[189]

This is an ironic moment for technical legality. The law called forth by technology is law as technology. While a few law and technology scholars have noted the irony,[190] the full implications for technical legality and the Frankenstein myth have not been thought through. The closest that has come has been Tribe's remarkable self-rebuff of *Channelling Technology*

[187] For example, the United Kingdom's response to stem cell research followed the recommendations of the joint Human Fertilisation and Embryology Authority and Human Genetics Advisory Commission and the Chief Medical Officer. See Human Fertilisation and Embryology Authority and Human Genetics Advisory Commission, *Cloning Issues in Reproduction, Sience and Medicine*; Department of Health Chief Medical Officer's Office Expert Group Reviewing the Potential of Developments in Stem Cell Research and Cell Nuclear Replacement to Benefit Human Health, *Stem Cell Research: Medical Progress with Responsibility*; House of Lords Select Committee on Stem Cell Research, *Stem Cell Research*; Brownsword, 'Stem Cells, Supermen and the Report of the Select Committee'.

[188] House of Representatives, *Human Cloning*, p. 235 recommendation 15.

[189] California Advisory Committee on Human Cloning, *Cloning Californiams?* Evaluation of the various scientific and ethical arguments, with the Committee justifying the ban on reproductive cloning on safety grounds and the regulation of 'non-reproductive cloning' as a balance. See Quintero, 'Cloning Californians'.

[190] Cockfield, 'Towards a Law and Technology Theory', p. 402; Murphy, 'Technology, Tools and Toxic Expectations', p. 183.

through Law, before he left the field for constitutional pastures, where he presented a critique of instrumentality through affirming a groovy 1970s claim of intellectual transcendence of the material.[191] Tribe's grokking and going has meant that technical legality has only glimpsed its monstrous self-reflection.

Let us clinically make clear what is at stake. It is the stake. Ever since Joss Whedon freed through subversion the received popular mythology of vampires and the supernatural with *Buffy the Vampire Slayer*, many a monster in popular culture has been put to the stake only to come back to live and love again.[192] The Frankenstein myth – the West's dominant narrative of technical legality – is pre-Whedon. Its three protagonists play traditional roles. The monster threatens human futures and law slays these monstrous possibilities. The monster and humanity are mutually exclusive, and law is the stake. However, a stake is a tool. If the law to humanise technology is technological, then the Frankenstein myth's 'monstrous technology', 'vulnerable humanity', and 'saving law' are illusionary. The monster, it seems, is more complex than it may appear to be. Its monstrousness extends to possessing a dimorphic being.[193] It is a trickster, for the law cannot be seen as 'channelling' technology; rather, in being called to face technology in the battle for the future, the law itself has become technology. The monster of technology and the saving law are one. The Frankenstein myth is just that – a myth, an illusion supposedly preventing knowledge of the real.[194]

This revelation represents the liberation of technical legality from the accretions of half-thought connections between law and technology in the West. It is also the liberation of science fiction for thinking technical legality. In the Frankenstein myth, science fiction was the storehouse for the monstrous. It was the repository for images, tropes, and narrative on technological futures, and in Shelley's *Frankenstein* the origin of the Frankenstein myth itself. In this chapter, the registry of future has moved law and technology to the revelation of law as technology. In revealing the technicity of modern law, science fiction can now be opened up as the site for the manifestation and critical engagement with technical legality. In pursuing this through Dune and through *Battlestar Galactica*, the implications of technical legality for humanity become clearer. Instead, of the

[191] Tribe, 'Technology Assessment and the Fourth Discontinuity', p. 652; Tribe, 'Ways Not to Think about Plastic Trees', pp. 1,338–46.

[192] Tyree, 'Warm-Blooded'.

[193] Jay, 'Must Justice be Blind?'

[194] Malinowski, 'Magic, Science and Religion', pp. 83–4.

pure, innocent, and vulnerable being of the Frankenstein myth, the human emerges as contested, compromised, and ultimately monstrous. And, as will be presented in the following chapters, this is good.

2

Dune, Modern Law, and the Alchemy of Death and Time

The previous chapter presented a troublesome conclusion for law and technology. It suggested that the 'saving law' transgressed the boundaries of the Frankenstein myth. Instead of securing a future for humanity against the monstrous of technology, it was revealed, in itself, as technological. This glimpse of technical legality suggests two lines of enquiry. First, is technical legality an adequate account of contemporary law? Second, if it is, what does this mean for the remaining element of the Frankenstein myth – the human? It was further suggested that science fiction is a privileged location for exploring technical legality.

This chapter takes up these strands. It argues that Frank Herbert's Dune cycle exposes the essential commitments of law as technology. Dune is a coriolis storm from the title planet that 'cut[s] metal like butter, etch[es] flesh to bones and eat[s] away the bones'.[1] The bones of law as technology that are exposed are sovereignty and positivism. However, the abrasiveness of Dune goes beyond exposing skeletal matter; it dissolves the very notion of sovereignty, leaving its essential commitments – death and time.

Structuring this argument is the law and humanities' method of reading a popular text jurisprudentially. Dune is not read as an analogy of legal theoretical concepts – namely sovereignty and positive law – but as a contribution to thinking sovereignty and positivism. Dune's dusty vistas, superhuman galactic emperors, and sandworm hybrids reveal the commitments behind law as technology in ways that have been forgotten or missed by jurisprudence's formal texts. To do this, Dune is engaged with 'thickly'. It is through a detailed shifting of the sands of Herbert's imagined universe and the decades of secondary literature that it has spawned that allows this jurisprudential reading.

The argument of this chapter is in three stages. The first stage reviews

[1] Herbert, *Dune*, p. 219.

the cycle.[2] The second stage re-examines the secondary literature on Dune. Critics have identified that *Dune* reflects on messiahs, politics, and ecology. The commonality identified between these is a meta-theme concerning the illusion of control. This meta-theme has led critics to summarise Herbert's opus as a rejection of the public and as encoding a message of self-care and disengagement with the world. However, the 'public' nature of Herbert's protagonists suggests another accounting of Dune.

The third stage takes up this alternative accounting of Dune. It is shown that the themes identified in the critical literature can be rewoven, taking as a starting point the desire for control in Dune. Dune emerges as an articulation of the essential elements of sovereignty. In its bloody pages, it embraces the consumption of bare life that modern Western jurisprudence has mystified. In its primacy of sovereignty, it also highlights one constant within a universe of change: time. In conclusion, in animating the necessary death inherent in sovereign attempts to lock in a desirable future, Dune is revelatory of the monstrous being of law as technology, its alchemist origins with death and time.

Sand, Spice, and Empire

Dune is often regarded as a seminal work of twentieth-century science fiction. Winner of both the Hugo and Nebula Awards in 1966,[3] for some critics Dune is considered a creative tour de force comparable with J. R. R. Tolkien's *Lord of the Rings* (1954–5).[4] Similar to Tolkien, the bare structure of *Dune* and its immediate sequels can be summarised as variations on the mono-myth.[5]

Dune, the 1965 novel, is divided into three 'books'. Book I introduces Paul Atreides, a boy of unique parentage (born of the union of a planetary ruler, Duke Leto Atreides, and his concubine, the Lady Jessica, who herself possessed uncanny powers), whose life is changed when his family's mortal enemy, the Baron Vladimir Harkonnen, invades the planet Arrakis/Dune and kills his father.[6] The boy and his mother escape into the deep desert of Arrakis and are presumed dead.[7] In Book II, Paul and Jessica meet up with the indigenous inhabitants of Arrakis, the Freman.[8] Paul, through the train-

[2] In this chapter, *Dune* (in italics) refers to the first novel of the series, originally published in 1965. Dune (no italics) refers to the cycle as a whole.

[3] Scholes and Rabkin, *Science Fiction*, p. 243.

[4] Touponce, *Frank Herbert*, p. 8; Riggs, 'Future and "Progress" in *Foundation* and *Dune*', p. 113.

[5] Palumbo, *Chaos Theory*, pp. 139–82.

[6] Herbert, *Dune*, pp. 1–192.

[7] Ibid.; Campbell, *The Hero with a Thousand Faces*, p. 78.

[8] Herbert, *Dune*, pp. 257, 264.

ing given to him by Jessica, his genetic inheritance, and using concentrated drugs as a catalyst, discovers that he is prescient and able to access his ancestors' memories.[9] In Book III, set two years later, Paul has taken a Freman name, Muad'Dib,[10] a Freman woman, Chani, as his mate,[11] has exploited Freman mythology concerning an outsider saviour, and has become their military leader, waging a guerrilla war against the Harkonnens.[12] The climax has Paul returning as a man, leading his Freman hordes riding on the backs of the gigantic sandworms of the desert, conquering the Harkonnens, and not only claiming his rightful Ducal title, but also becoming Emperor of the Known Universe.[13]

The immediate sequel, *Dune Messiah* (1969), set twelve years after *Dune*, tells a story of decline. The establishment of the Atreides' empire had precipitated a bloody jihad across the universe. Paul is a broken character in *Dune Messiah*, riddled with grief at the galaxy-wide slaughter in his name, distressed that his empire and religion have 'fallen into old patterns'[14] and surrounded by plotting Freman and the disgruntled institutions of the Imperium (the Spacing Guild, the Bene Gesserit, and the Bene Tleilaxu). Unable to foresee any better alternative, Paul allows himself to succumb to the plotting, becomes blinded, and exiles himself in the desert, leaving the Empire to his newborn twin children with his sister, Alia, as regent.

The action in the third novel, *Children of Dune* (1976), occurs nine years after *Dune Messiah*. In many respects, it is a replaying of *Dune*, complete with the Baron Vladimir Harkonnen returning to possess Alia,[15] an escape into the desert for the male son, Leto II, his testing and discovering even more special powers than his father, and his merging with the nymph stage of the sandworms to become physically invulnerable.[16] The novel concludes with Leto II, now superhuman in mind and body, taking the throne to reign for thousands of years.[17]

The fourth novel, *God Emperor of Dune* (1981), deals with Leto II's 'death' some 3,500 years after the third book. Now a small sandworm with a bloated, vaguely human face, Leto II rules a stagnate empire as a living

9 Ibid. p. 281; Campbell, *The Hero with a Thousand Faces*, pp. 90–1.
10 Herbert, *Dune*, p. 292.
11 Ibid., p. 344.
12 Ibid.; Campbell, *The Hero with a Thousand Faces*, p. 126.
13 Herbert, *Dune*, pp. 425–64; Campbell, *The Hero with a Thousand Faces*, pp. 193–237.
14 Herbert, *Dune Messiah*, p. 109.
15 Herbert, *Children of Dune*, p. 58.
16 Ibid., pp. 307–13.
17 Ibid., p. 373.

god.[18] This novel is predominately a palace drama of feints, plans, and plots, culminating in Leto II's death by submersion, birthing a new generation of sandworms.[19] The final two novels, *Heretics of Dune* (1984) and *Chapter House Dune* (1985), set 2,000 years further on, deal with the aftermath of Leto II's reign, the return of descendants of refugees who escaped from the Atreides Empire and the final destruction of some of the lingering institutions and entities from that earlier period.[20]

On the surface, this 'swords and sandals' science fiction does not seem to offer much as a critical site for the reflection on technical legality. Indeed, contemporary readers could be forgiven for dismissing *Dune* as a fifty-year-old book that became popular through counter-culture iconography of shamanic orgies and psychedelic excess. Critics have rightly identified misogyny behind Herbert's central female characters – the Lady Jessica, Chani and Alia Atreides[21] – made obvious by the Bene Gesserit order of superwomen who seem content with playing a behind-the-scenes manipulative role within imperial politics, while breeding the 'Kwisatz Haderach', a male capable of their skills.[22] Herbert's portrayal of the homosexual Baron Harkonnen is particularly repugnant to contemporary sensibilities.[23] It is tempting to suggest that science fiction has moved on and by the 1980s the last three novels[24] – not to mention David Lynch's 'disastrous' 1984 film,[25] the low-budget mini-series of 2000[26] and 2004,[27] and the endless Brian Herbert and Kevin J. Anderson prequels and sequels – give the impression that the franchise has outlived its cultural moment.[28]

Further, both technology and law seem to be very much in the background of the Dune universe. Technology lies literally in the background. The cycle is set millennia after the 'Butlerian Jihad', where humanity revolted

18 Herbert, *God Emperor of Dune*, p. 107.

19 Ibid., p. 444.

20 Herbert, *Heretics of Dune*; Herbert, *Chapter House Dune*.

21 Roberts, *Science Fiction*, p. 46; Silliman, *Conserving the Balance*, p. 120.

22 Hand, 'The Traditionalism of Women's Roles in Frank Herbert's Dune'; Youngerman Miller, 'Women of *Dune*: Frank Herbert as a Social Reactionary?', p. 191; Knězková, *Frank Herbert's Heroines: Female Characters in Dune and its Film Adaptations*, pp. 37–51, 62–3.

23 Roberts, *Science Fiction*, p. 43; Silliman, 'Conserving the Balance', p. 131.

24 Spinrad, *Science Fiction in the Real World*, p. 156.

25 Lynch, *Dune*. 'Disastrous' was Brian Aldiss's judgement on the film: Aldiss, *Trillion Year Spree*, p. 343.

26 Harrison, *Dune*.

27 Yaitanes, *Children of Dune*. See Booker, *Science Fiction Television*.

28 Gough, 'Speculative Fictions for Understanding Global Change Environments', pp. 6–10.

and destroyed 'thinking machines'.[29] This plot device facilitated two structural elements of the Dune universe.

The first element is that it explains the technological primitiveness of Dune. The Butlerian Jihad allowed a science fiction that could be sustained without gee-wiz high technology. This does not mean that technology is absent from Dune. There is hard technology – the Spacing Guild's interstellar Heighliners; the ornithopter, carry-alls and harvester factors associated with spice gathering on Arrakis; the adapted technology of the Freman, the windtraps, stillsuit, fremkit, and thumper; and the more exotic technology of royal households, poison snoopers, distrans, and hunter-seeker – but it never occupies centre stage. Instead, the Butlerian Jihad allowed Herbert to manifest an alternative technology in the training of human capacity.[30]

This alternative technology is the second structural element that Herbert's imagined history of the Butlerian Jihad allowed. The Jihad, with its central dogma that 'Thou shalt not make a machine in the likeness of a man's mind . . . forced human minds to develop. Schools were started to train human talents.'[31] The resulting specialisation, of mentats (human computers), Guild Navigators (beings capable of limited prescience, allowing the piloting of a spacecraft at trans-light speed) and the Reverend Mothers of the Bene Gesserit (formidable beings adept at controlling others using voice alone, discerning 'truth', and accessing the memories of female ancestors) reveals Herbert's focus on technical skills. There are fantasy elements to this. The elixir that stimulates and sustains these extraordinary mental powers is melange, the spice incapable of synthetic manufacture and only found on Arrakis, registering the significance of the title planet.

So, while there is technology in Dune, there seems to be little law.[32] Technology and law intersect in Herbert's backstory with the conclusion of the chaos of the Butlerian Jihad in the enacting of the 'Great Convention', with the central provision being the prohibiting of the use of atomic weapons against humans.[33] Beyond this, though, mentions of law in Dune are perfunctory and cynical. Early in Dune, Duke Leto comments on the poster declaring him ruler of Arrakis: 'Who was fooled by that fatuous legalism?'[34]

29 Herbert, *Dune*, pp. 495–6.
30 O'Reilly, *Frank Herbert*, p. 58.
31 Herbert, *Dune*, p. 17.
32 Erman and Möller, 'What's Wrong with Politics in the Duniverse?', p. 65.
33 Herbert, *Dune*, pp. 494–5.
34 Ibid., p. 78.

Paul – rightly, it turns out[35] – justifies his use of nuclear weapons on a technical distinction:

> It's fear, not the injunction that keeps the houses from hurling atomics against each other. The language of the Great Convention is clear enough: 'Use of atomics against humans shall be cause for planetary obliteration.' We're going to blast the Shield Wall, not humans.[36]

Beyond this interpretive moment, there is no real sense in Dune of law-making. Imperial law is mentioned by members of the Great Houses as code for the ritual of politics that surrounds clandestine manoeuvrings.[37] The Baron plots a quasi-legal move that could place Feyd-Rautha on the throne, while Paul tries to buy the allegiance of Liet-Kynes with a 'legal' plan to discredit the Emperor.[38] There are no courtrooms and legal trials; the closest we come is the inconclusive cross-examination of the traitor Korba before the assembled Freman Naibs in *Dune Messiah*.[39] Judgement – made readily and often by the characters – is a product of trained intuition in identifying the non-verbal signs betraying 'guilt'. Here a law job appears to have been subsumed by technicity.

This final suggestion of devolution of the legal to the technical is revelatory. The Dune cycle does not make its legal and technological reflections obvious. There are many more obvious themes that Dune's critical literature has explored. Its jurisprudential content – glimpsed in its portrayal of the technicity of judgement – is another matter. This jurisprudential reading begins with the critical literature on Dune and the identification of the identified meta-theme of the illusion of control.

The Illusion of Control

The size of the Dune cycles, and the textual and character inconsistencies between instalments, have challenged critics.[40] In response, critics have tended to emphasise the themes threaded through Herbert's work. Three themes have been identified: messianism, politics, and ecology. However, as will be seen, all three are not independent but rather manifest a meta-theme on the failure of control.[41]

35 Ibid., p. 451.

36 Ibid., p. 428.

37 Ibid., p. 312.

38 Ibid., p. 214.

39 Herbert, *Dune Messiah*, pp. 173–8.

40 Levack, *Dune Master*, p. xvi; O'Reilly, *Frank Herbert*, p. 187.

41 Siegel, *Hugo Gernsback, Father of Modern Science Fiction*, pp. 66–7; Elgin, *The Comedy of the Fantastic*, p. 136.

Writing in 1980, Herbert suggested that *Dune* and its sequels were a reflection on the danger of messiahs.[42] This is not as clear from the novels as it may initially appear. In *Dune*, Paul plays a messiah character. He is referred to as such by the Freman[43] and he delivers on his messianic promises in ridding Arrakis of the Harkonnens. It is a poor story concerning the dangers of messiahs. Paul is bothered by his prescient visions of the jihad to come,[44] and there is the oft-quoted passage from a hallucinating and dying Liet-Kynes that, 'No more terrible disaster could befall your people than for them to fall into the hands of a Hero.'[45] However, *Dune* does not end with images of bloody jihad. Instead, it ends with images of bloody justice. The Harkonnens are dead, the Emperor and his Sardaukar defeated, and the Bene Gesserit humiliated. Indeed, 'at *Dune's* end we cheer . . . reading it has been an emotionally satisfying experience',[46] for the wrongs of the novel have been righted.

Herbert seemingly prioritises the evils of messiahs in the appropriately named *Dune Messiah*; however, in this text the message is also less clear. Herbert tells of the atrocities of the Atreides-Freman jihad.[47] Nevertheless, the jihad is not in the foreground; its horrors are seen mostly through Paul's blue-in-blue eyes coloured by his feelings of responsibility.[48] However, Paul's feelings of responsibility are contradicted. Herbert repeatedly emphasises the predestination of the jihad. In the climax of *Dune,* with the powers of the Imperium at his feet, Paul senses his jihad-to-come as fate.[49] This also appears in *Dune Messiah,* where Paul experiences the sweep of history 'like a gigantic tidal bore. He sensed the vast migrations at work in human affairs: eddies, currents, gene flows. No dams of abstinence, no seizures of impotence nor malediction could stop it. Muad'Dib's Jihad was less than an eye-blink in this larger movement.'[50] By *Children of Dune* and *God Emperor of Dune*, messianism is further in the background. Leto II is no messiah. He does not seize the throne with promises of a better future;[51] rather, he declares himself a tyrant.[52]

42 Herbert, 'Dune Genesis', p. 72.
43 Herbert, *Dune*, p. 497.
44 Ibid., pp. 294, 304, 306, and 369.
45 Ibid., pp. 263, 500. See Siegel, *Hugo Gernsback, Father of Modern Science Fiction*, p. 70.
46 Fjellman, 'Prescience and Power', p. 51.
47 Herbert, *Dune Messiah*, pp. 50, 92.
48 Ibid., pp. 43–4.
49 Herbert, *Dune*, p. 457.
50 Herbert, *Dune Messiah*, p. 110.
51 Herbert, *Dune*, p. 406.
52 Herbert, *Children of Dune*, p. 378. 'I have the cruelty of the husbandman and this human universe is my farm.'

Dune does not tell a cautionary tale of the dangers of messiahs; it tells a conflicted story that opens with a hero, shows that hero's mid-life crisis, and ends with an over-over-man dominating time and space. Timothy O'Reilly claims that Herbert's basic insight concerns the limits of human consciousness within an infinite universe.[53] In the partial messiah message, Herbert is being performative. Paul's loyalty in *Dune,* his tears when he first kills, and his remorse in *Dune Messiah* are not the characteristics popularly associated with evil, and the Harkonnens – with their oppression, amorality, and scheming – are seemingly foils for the 'noble Atreides' in this regard.[54] Yet Paul is Harkonnen, his mother the unacknowledged daughter of Baron Harkonnen.[55] For Herbert, such absolutes – who is good and who is bad – and the confidence of knowing are impossible. Herbert presents a universe that resists control: 'You do not take from this universe, he thought. It grants what it will.'[56]

An example of this illusion of control is Paul's prescient powers. John W. Campbell worried after reading the manuscript of *Dune* that in Paul Herbert had created a superman, with all the authorial difficulties for credibility of character and plot.[57] Herbert's response was to emphasise the limited nature of Paul's 'gift'.[58] The recurring image is the dance of an object caught in a jet-stream.[59] Paul can see the future, but this does not mean that he looks on fate as an absolutely known. Paul's vision, and with it his ability to control, is limited. He can see some of the tensions and forces at play in alternatives futures, but he is also blind to the working of other oracles.[60] Displaying the classic behaviour of addiction, Paul keeps taking greater quantities of spice, but the hit is never enough.[61] However, Herbert confounds this simple explanation. Once Paul succumbs to the vision that leads to his blindness and Chani's death, he is shown as able to function as if sighted, relying on his memory of that future to live in it.[62] By giving in and not fighting the vision, it becomes true. Except it is not entirely the case: the birth of the twins was unforeseen.[63]

[53] O'Reilly, *Frank Herbert*, p. 3.

[54] Mulcahy, '*The Prince* on Arrakis', p. 27; DiTommaso, 'History and Historical Effect in Frank Herbert's *Dune*', p. 321.

[55] Herbert, *Dune*, p. 191.

[56] Herbert, *Dune Messiah*, p. 108.

[57] Herbert, Herbert, and Anderson, *The Road to Dune*, p. 275.

[58] An edited extract of Herbert's response can be found at O'Reilly, *Frank Herbert*, p. 153.

[59] Herbert, *Dune*, p. 187; Herbert, *Dune Messiah*, p. 51.

[60] Ibid., p. 19.

[61] Ibid., pp. 107–8.

[62] Ibid., pp. 162–9, 201–8.

[63] Ibid., p. 208.

Paul's prescience is a working of Herbert's meta-theme of the illusion of control. The complexities of *Dune* arise because this message is coded in the very presentation of the messiah theme. The book and sequels elude determinative judgement: at times they are sophisticated texts warning of the peril of messiahs[64] and at other times 'masturbatory power fantas[ies]'.[65] It is this meta-theme of the desire for control in an uncontrollable universe that is reiterated through Herbert's other themes of politics and ecology.

With its machinations in the corridors of power, critics have considered *Dune* a popular window into the writing of Niccolò Machiavelli.[66] Kevin Mulcahy has observed that the Baron's strategy of subduing the reconquered Arrakis is a straight take from *The Prince*, where Machiavelli praises Cesare Borgia's use and then disposal of a known cruel lieutenant to win over a conquered people.[67] However, notwithstanding this *Prince*-like plan, the Harkonnens are not Machiavellians. They are not only prepared to kill and deceive to gain power and wealth; they are also sadists.[68] This is not Machiavelli's ideal tyrant.[69] Machiavelli's prince should be restrained in the ways of violence. He must have the character and confidence to do all that is necessary to secure order and peace, including unpleasant and dirty work.[70] But violence is a tool with known strengths and weaknesses, and the torture chamber should not be used when there are more peaceful means available. In this, the Harkonnens are more properly characterised as 'Machiavels' from Elizabethan and Jacobethan theatre.[71] The Machiavel is a figure of evil, cruelly calculating, and a lover of over-complicated plots.[72] The Baron is more Richard III or Iago than Borgia. His plot to destroy the Atreides meanders around cumulating with the betrayal by the Atreides' physician, Dr Wellington Yueh. Yet with Yueh, the Baron could efficiently have had the Atreides killed off at any time. Instead, in fine Machiavel style, the Baron spends Book I of *Dune* floating and gloating about his genius in pulling off the 'biggest mantrap in history'.[73]

This leaves the Atreides to take up the mantle of Machiavelli. The Atreides

64 Roberts, *The History of Science Fiction*, p. 236.

65 Spinrad, *Science Fiction in the Real World*, p. 155.

66 Mulcahy, '*The Prince* on Arrakis'; Minowitz, 'Prince Versus Prophet'.

67 Machiavelli, *The Prince and the Discourses*, p. 27. See Mulcahy, '*The Prince* on Arrakis', p. 24.

68 Minowitz, 'Prince Versus Prophet', pp. 126–31.

69 Berlin, *Against the Current*, p. 51.

70 Machiavelli, *The Prince and the Discourses*, pp. 56–7.

71 Meyer, *Machiavelli and the Elizabethan Drama*, pp. 41–8.

72 Raab, *The English Face of Machiavelli*, p. 56.

73 Herbert, *Dune*, p. 19.

do what is necessary. In *The Prince*, Machiavelli emphasises that the statesman should display what Isaiah Berlin has identified as the Roman Republic ideals of *virtu*: 'courage, vigour, fortitude in adversity, public achievement, order, discipline, happiness, strength, justice and above all assertion of one's proper claims and knowledge and power needed to secure their satisfaction'.[74] This reads as a character description of both Duke Leto and Paul. Herbert portrays both as courageous, projecting a manly bravura, big on public achievement, order, discipline, and strength, coupled with confidence in their claim to rule. While a bit short in the happiness registry, Herbert paints the Atreides as leaders of *virtu*, whose strength of character has been rewarded with loyal subjects.

It is this cultivation of followers that reveals the Machiavellian style of the Atreides. The Atreides' followers are there to be used for the Atreides' power.[75] Duke Leto does not flinch in risking his family, his army, and his people to gamble on the occupation of Arrakis. Paul's rise to leader of the Freman reveals his skills as a master opportunist, seizing strategic alliances through Chani as Liet-Kynes' daughter and Stilgar's niece, and manipulating Freman mythology to locate himself at the power apex.

The Atreides therefore appear to be a fairly successful rendering of Machiavelli's prince. All the political players in *Dune* – the Baron, the Emperor, and the Bene Gesserit – fail to control the situation on Arrakis. The Baron kills off Duke Leto and re-establishes Harkonnen rule only to trigger the cycle that ends with his own death. The Emperor succeeds in destroying Duke Leto, a dangerous rival to the throne, only to create Paul, who takes the throne. The Bene Gesserit spend centuries on their breeding program only to have the dreamed-of Kwisatz Haderach arrive one generation early and outside of their control. Mark Siegel suggests that these players fail because their over-confidence prevents a cool assessment of the consequences of their actions.[76] In Machiavellian terms, these princes lose through poor judgement based on a failure to assess consequences. The symmetry to this analysis is that Paul wins because he considers consequences, helped in this regard by his uniqueness.

Except Paul does not win: the ends of Paul in *Dune Messiah* and *Children of Dune* cannot be taken as wins except by the most committed stoic. Even in the victorious climax of *Dune*, the nascent jihad is poised to inflame the universe. Mulcahy argues that the message is the corruption for both leader

[74] Berlin, *Against the Current*, p. 45.
[75] O'Reilly, *Frank Herbert*, p. 45.
[76] Siegel, *Hugo Gernsback, Father of Modern Science Fiction*, p. 71.

and the lead that arises from cynical manipulation.[77] Paul goes from appealing youth in Book I to God-like leader in Book III. In Book II, he sheds water for the dead when killing Jamis, but by Book III he cannot grieve for his dead son. The Freman devolve from a fierce and independent people in *Dune* to divided sycophants in *Dune Messiah*. For Mulcahy, this is Herbert's critique of Machiavelli.[78] The drive for charismatic leaders to give certainty in an uncertain universe gives rise to power-hungry monsters. In placing responsibility for the leadership with the people who follow, Mulcahy suggests that Herbert's prince-like novel affirms democracy. However, nowhere in the *Dune* universe do the people go, to adopt the Bene Gesserit terms, from 'animals' to 'humans'.[79] Again, the meta-theme of uncertainty is disclosed: if *Dune* is a democratic critique of Machiavelli, it is a very problematic one that borders on rather undemocratic celebrations of the *überman*.

For Peter Minowitz, Herbert's biological metaphor for the people is instructive. Not only does it remind of Machiavelli's description of a leaderless people as an escaped beast,[80] but it links Herbert's politics with his ecology. Herbert's biographers have suggested that the origins of *Dune* lay in his 1957 newspaper assignment looking at the use of grasses to stabilise desert in Oregon.[81] *Dune* has been hailed as an ecological novel,[82] as evidenced by the 'Ecology of Dune' appendix,[83] the narrative of ecological destruction and rejuvenation through the cycle, and Herbert's well-documented paraphrasing from ecologist Paul B. Spears.[84]

At this point, Herbert's illusion of control meta-theme intervenes: notwithstanding the ecological veneer, questions can be put regarding the depth of Herbert's engagement with ecological thought. An emphasis on ecology is not particularly evident in the bare narrative of *Dune*.[85] Paul is the focus, not Liet-Kynes, and the Atreides' adoption of the planetologist's plan appears to be just another policy strategically adopted to secure the allegiance of the

[77] Mulcahy, '*The Prince* on Arrakis', p. 33.

[78] Ibid., p. 34.

[79] Herbert, *Dune*, pp. 12–17; Siegel, *Hugo Gernsback, Father of Modern Science Fiction*, p. 70.

[80] Minowitz, 'Prince Versus Prophet', p. 143 referring to Machiavelli, *The Prince and the Discourses* 'The Discourses Book 1:XXIV', p. 161.

[81] Touponce, *Frank Herbert*, p. 16.

[82] Schmitt-v Mühlenfels, 'The Theme of Ecology in Frank Herbert's Dune Novels'; Elgin, *The Comedy of the Fantastic*, pp. 125–52; Parkerson, 'Semantics, General Semantics, and Ecology in Frank Herbert's Dune'.

[83] Herbert, *Dune*, pp. 467–74.

[84] Herbert's adoption of Spears phrase 'law of the minimum' and other terms has been documented by Scigaj, '*Prana* and the Presbyterian Fixation', p. 348.

[85] Ellis, 'Frank Herbert's *Dune*', p. 104.

Freman. Further, Joseph Meeker has argued that eco-literacy should be in the comic rather than tragic genre.[86] Dune's seriousness – along with characters like the Atreides, whose name was poached from Greek mythology (King Atreus, whose children were called Atrides) – suggests that it should be seen as lying towards the tragic end of the continuum.[87]

In addition, the prevailing ecological motif is that of predator and prey. This primal image harks back to an earlier era of biological thinking and not the systemic interconnectedness that characterises ecology.[88] The Baron styles himself like a predator, feeding off lesser prey in his gloating over the Atreides solders trapped in the caves of the Shield Wall,[89] while the Duke Leto worryingly paces: 'I must rule with eye and claw – as the hawk among lesser birds.'[90] It is possible to argue that Herbert's use of the predator–prey image with the Baron and Duke Leto is to suggest their shared thinking in the ways of domination and ignorance of connection, distinguishing Paul as more ecological in orientation. Yet Paul does not seem to escape the fascinating pull of the 'red in tooth and claw'.[91] His arrival at Sietch Tabr exactly in the middle of *Dune* is heralded by predation.[92] In becoming Freman, Paul – ironically – renounces the Atreides Hawk for Muad'Dib, the Freman name for the Kangaroo Mouse, yet the image of predator and prey remains, just the identification of Paul's father and grandfather with the predator shifts to prey. Seeing the future does not necessarily mean that Paul appreciates consequences, as evidenced by his twin failures of jihad and climate change.

There has been observed elements of a stance against global capitalism and its exploitation of environments and indigenous communities in *Dune*.[93] The monopolistic trading company Combine Honnete Ober Advancer Mercantiles (CHOAM), the Guild and Bene Gesserit can be read as trans-galactic corporations maintaining a spice-dependent universe grounded on oppression of the Freman and exploitation of the Arrakian ecosystem. However, Paul's jihad is not against the Imperium's economic structures and its environmental degradations; it is a more primal revenge. Paul is prepared

86 Meeker, *The Comedy of Survival*, pp. 15–16.
87 Elgin, *The Comedy of the Fantastic*, p. 126.
88 'The term *ecology* is therefore intended to refer to the study of the conditions of existence that make up our larger, cosmic household.' Fox, *Towards a Transpersonal Ecology*, p. 32; italics in original.
89 Herbert, *Dune*, p. 176.
90 Ibid., p. 100.
91 Tennyson, *Tennyson: Poems and Plays*, 'in memoriam a. H. H.' IVI (p. 243).
92 Herbert, *Dune*, p. 257.
93 Morton, 'Imperial Measures'; Stratton, 'The Messiah and the Greens', p. 309; Ellis, 'Frank Herbert's *Dune*', p. 119.

Figure 2.1 John Schoenherr, 'Defeat of the Sardaukar', for *Analog Magazine*, 1966. Permission to reproduce from Ian Schoenherr

to destroy the entire ecosystem with his spice bomb,[94] he is prepared to use nuclear weapons, and, as Emperor, he allows the Fremans to change the basic ecology. Safely ensconced on the 'Lion Throne' (another celebration of the predator), he does not dismantle the economic system that has oppressed 'his' people, but rather takes it over, continuing the spice system as an Atreides monopoly.

The ultimate ecological image in *Dune* is the sandworms. Immortalised by John Schoenherr's terrifying artwork, the worms have entered popular culture as definitional alien monsters.[95] The effectiveness of the worms lies in the repetition of the predator–prey dualism. The worms devour anything moving on the sand. It is in the act of predation that they rise from the text:

> A wide hole emerged from the sand. Sunlight flashed from the glistening white spokes within it. The hole's diameter was at least twice the length of the crawler, Paul estimated. He watched as the machine slid into that opening in billow of dust and sand. The hole pulled back.[96]

[94] Herbert, *Dune*, p. 424.
[95] Schmitt-v Mühlenfels, *The Theme of Ecology in Frank Herbert's Dune Novels*, p. 29.
[96] Herbert, *Dune*, p. 121.

In casting the worm as predator, the worms become the ultimate sign of human dominance and exploitation of nature. The worms dominate nature – yet the Freman control the worms.[97]

In this, Herbert's meta-theme is performed. *Dune* has much ecological content, yet the ecological message is mixed. This incompleteness of Herbert's ecological imagining is challenged by O'Reilly, who regards the ecology theme and the illusion of control theme as one: 'Paul's vision is to take ecological concepts to a much deeper level. Paul comes to see opposition between the aims of civilisation and those of nature, as represented by the human unconscious.'[98] O'Reilly turns this into an inner struggle between consciousness and unconsciousness that locates the meta-theme of *Dune* as personal – how to thrive in a changing world. It has been suggested that Paul is Zen; he engages in life and takes risks.[99] However, Paul is not a very successful demonstrator of Zen calm, notwithstanding the Zen-like statements that he makes to his followers.[100] Paul is not at rest.[101] Like other tragic characters, Paul is always questing.[102] It is perhaps only as the Preacher in *Children of Dune* that Paul appears to be at rest in the world he has had a hand in creating.[103]

It is Leto II who has been seen as embodying the heightened subjectivity of the Zen-aware. Leonard M. Scigaj argues that Leto II emerges from *God Emperor of Dune* as a being who flows with the universe.[104] Leto II mocks the attempts by the Bene Tleilaxu and the Ixians to plot and control.[105] He celebrates surprises and he claims to be teaching humanity a lesson: not to desire the stagnate future promised by messiahs, but instead to be responsible for self in adapting to change.[106] Leto II's victory is not political (he won on that field in the climax of *Children of Dune*); it is personal. He has mastered himself – a uniquely difficult task for the son of a superman, born with both the memories of all his ancestors and the faculty of prescience.

Slavoj Žižek has described what he calls the 'Western Buddhism' of New Age, spiritualist and Eastern mysticism that has become popular in the West. He contends that these movements are not an innocuous flowering

[97] Ibid., p. 441.
[98] O'Reilly, *Frank Herbert*, p. 50.
[99] Ibid., pp. 68–9.
[100] Ibid., p. 77.
[101] Siegel, *Hugo Gernsback, Father of Modern Science Fiction*, p. 73.
[102] Elgin, *The Comedy of the Fantastic*, p. 152.
[103] Herbert, *Children of Dune*, pp. 320–6.
[104] Scigaj, '*Prana* and the Presbyterian Fixation', p. 343.
[105] Herbert, *God Emperor of Dune*, pp. 164–5.
[106] Ibid., pp. 21–31.

of empowered subjectivity, but encode at a fundamental level the very ideological commitments of globalised capitalism.[107] Faced with rapid change, information overload, and the isolation of Western urban existence, Western Buddhism allows a gap between complicit engagement with the realities of competitive social existence and the self. [108] This seems to be very close to the ultimate message of Dune. The universe denies control. A mere human – even a superhuman like Paul – fails to control it. Public enterprises, like religion, politics, and ecology, are seen as incomplete. Human doing in the world is failure; all that exists is a coming to peace with oneself within the chaos.

This personal message of *Dune* can be read the other way. The beginnings of this reading can be glimpsed in one of the more successful multimedia offshoots of Dune. In Westwood Studios' 1992 computer game *Dune II: The Building of a Dynasty*, the game players take command of rival houses, build bases, control units, harvest spice, and try to destroy opposing artificial intelligence (AI)-controlled enemies.[109] *Dune II* is celebrated as defining the genre that has become known as 'god games',[110] or real-time strategy (RTS).[111] RTS allows players to fulfil total control fantasies within a virtual-world: building empires, conquering opponents, and also controlling individual units.[112] For Steven Poole, the message of RTS games is:

> The gameplayer doesn't count as an individual: he or she is, after all God. What matters is the inexorable march of the corporate machine. There seems to be a pernicious subterranean motive here: such games offer you a position of infinite power in order to whisper the argument that, as an individual in the world, you have none at all.[113]

RTS games exploit the tension between control and the lack of control as symptom and therapy for the 'lost souls' of the West. With this at their core, it seems entirely fitting that the founding game of the genre should have been inspired by Herbert.

However, the game *Dune II* offers a different narrative from that of Herbert. Within the game, the gamer rules supreme. The game climaxes with total victory. There are no future echoes of jihad or *Dune Messiah*-like sequels of entropy. This exposes something absolutely fundamental in Dune.

107 Žižek, *On Belief*, p. 12.
108 Ibid., p. 13.
109 Westwood Studio, *Dune II: The Building of a Dynasty*.
110 Herz, *Joystick Nation*, pp. 30–1.
111 Egenfeldt-Nielsen, Smith, and Pajares Tosca, *Understanding Video Games*, p. 86.
112 Postigo, 'From *Pong* to *Planet Quake*', p. 595.
113 Poole, *Trigger Happy*, p. 49.

Even with the Western Buddhism messages of disengagement and self-care, the public, 'the plans within plans',[114] and the questing for order continually reappear throughout the novels – whether it is Paul's failed attempt at grabbing power to prevent jihad or Leto II's multi-faceted Golden Plan. While the universe remains outside of willed control, the humans and superhumans of Herbert's far-future keep trying.

This desire for order is something that resonates with law. The ultimate jurisprudential being that keeps the chaos at bay is the sovereign. The suggestion is that Dune can be seen as a sophisticated examination of the essential commitments of sovereignty.

Sovereignty as the Alchemy of Death and Time

Law as technology, as seen in Chapter 1, is about control. It is about making law so as to render the disruptions and anxieties of an uncertain future more known and managed. As such, law as technology makes the world-to-come. It conjures out of the ether new criminal offences, institutions, and new rights. In Dune, the makers of the world are the sandworms. Freman culture acknowledges this in the terms 'little maker' for the worm's nymph stage and Shai-Hulud – the destroyer – for the adult form. Within a jurisprudential frame, Dune conjures the being that can make law: the sovereign. This reading of Dune should be obvious from the sandworms on the covers: Dune is about Leviathan.

What does it mean to make law? Law's response is a tale of transformation. The common law did not make law. Located in time immemorial, it claimed that it emanated from the very soil of the 'Sceptred Isle'.[115] The judicial function was to declare the law, not make it, and legal training amounted to memorising speeches and decisions of the past.[116] Written records, where they existed, were mnemonic aids for those initiated in Sir Edward Coke's 'artificial reason'[117] of the law.[118] Established legal history notes that, with the wider Reformation, England experienced legal reformation with the expansion of the influence of the Crown and Parliament.[119] Politically, the common law negotiated this period by aligning with the Crown and nationalising its jurisdiction as the King's Court.[120] It also developed the doctrine of parlia-

[114] Herbert, *Dune*, p. 217.
[115] Goodrich, *Languages of Law*, pp. 210–13.
[116] Goodrich, *Law in the Courts of Love*, pp. 86–90.
[117] *Prohibitions del Roy* [1607] EWHC KB J23; 77 ER 1342.
[118] Goodrich, *Law in the Courts of Love*, p. 108.
[119] Murphy, *The Oldest Social Science?*, pp. 72–4.
[120] Goodrich and Grey Carlson, *Law and the Postmodern Mind.*

mentary supremacy, reinventing itself as a body of inferior rules.[121] Such a story is familiar. The narrative of the Reformation birthing a spirit of rational activity that refashions the pre-modern into the modern has its origins in Max Weber's rationalisation thesis.[122] Weber, however, underplayed a critical creature that emerged during this development: the sovereign.

Familiarity dims awareness of how radical Thomas Hobbes' account of sovereignty was within Western political and legal thought.[123] While it is trite to say that Hobbes' sovereign emerged from the social contract, what is missed is the form of being that arises. The sovereign is human, but is not. The sovereign retains – and I use Hobbes' gendered possessive pronoun – his 'natural' freedom:[124]

> There is only one way to erect such a common power that will be able to defend men from the invasions of foreigners and from the injuries of one another . . . This way is to confer all of their power and strength upon one man, or assembly of men, that will reduce all of their wills . . . Everyone thereby submits their wills to his will and their judgments to his judgements. This is more than consent or concord; it is a real unity of them all into one and the same person, made by covenant of every man with every man . . . This is the generation of that great Leviathan, or rather, to speak more reverently, of that mortal god, to which we owe our peace and defense under the immortal God.[125]

In this celebrated passage from *Leviathan* (1651), a key differentiation of Hobbes' sovereign from the latter liberals can be seen. The sovereign is not party to the social contract; the contract is only between would-be subjects. Hobbes makes this clear:

> The right of bearing the person of all the multitude is given to the one made sovereign by the people making the covenant with each other and not to the one who is the sovereign. Therefore, there can be no breach or covenant on the part of the sovereign.[126]

This sovereign freedom has been well recognised by public international lawyers.[127] However, what this freedom means domestically has been overlooked.

[121] Postema, *Bentham and the Common Law Tradition*, pp. 102–3.
[122] Weber, *The Protestant Ethic and the Spirit of Capitalism*, pp. 180–2.
[123] Saunders, *Anti-Lawyers*, pp. 4–6.
[124] Sorell, 'The Burdensome Freedom of Sovereigns'.
[125] Hobbes, *Leviathan*, p. 116.
[126] Ibid., p. 119.
[127] Douzinas, *Human Rights and Empire*, p. 35.

As suggested in Chapter 1, Hobbes' modern sovereign meant that questions of authority became temporal.[128] Law was because of a valid law-making act of the sovereign in a specific space and time. This is a point about which Hobbes was consistent throughout his long career:

> The civil laws are the rules that the commonwealth has commanded to every subject either by word, writing or other sufficient sign of his will. These laws distinguish right from wrong in terms of what is contrary or in agreement with the rules . . . The laws are the rules of what is just and unjust, as nothing can be considered unjust that is not contrary to some law.[129]

Having rendered all law positive law of the commonwealth, Hobbes reveals who is behind the commonwealth:

> The sovereign is the only legislator in a commonwealth . . . Only the commonwealth prescribes and commands the observation of those rules that are called laws. Therefore the commonwealth is the legislator. But the commonwealth is not a person and does not have capacity to do anything. The person is the representative, which is the sovereign and therefore the sovereign is the sole legislator.[130]

Hobbes articulates the defining feature of modern law: its origin and authority depend entirely on positive action by the sovereign and this posited law is the sole arbitrator of just and unjust within a commonwealth. Banished from the legal system are any claims to independent legal authority in Bible, conscience, or judiciary.[131] As Norberto Bobbio observes, the key to understanding Hobbes is 'unity over anarchy. Hobbes is obsessed by the idea of dissolution of authority.'[132] In pursuit of this unity, the sovereign must be free to make law on any topic, unconstrained by nature, custom, or any other power.[133] The law becomes another tool at the sovereign's disposal to maintain peace and unity.[134]

It is at this point of unity that Dune can be read as Hobbesian. There are many parallels between Hobbes' and Herbert's texts. Immediate similarities

[128] Postema, *Bentham and the Common Law Tradition*, p. 48.

[129] Hobbes, *Leviathan*, pp. 183–5. See also Hobbes, *A Dialogue between a Philosopher and a Student*, p. 29.

[130] Hobbes, *Leviathan*, p. 184. See also Hobbes, *The Elements of Law*, p. 112.

[131] Hobbes, *Leviathan*, pp. 186–8; Hobbes, *Behemoth*, p. 51.

[132] Bobbio, *Thomas Hobbes and the Natural Law Tradition*, p. 29.

[133] Although Hobbes, anticipating John Austin, seems to indicate that law must have a general character, something he emphasises in working through the example in *Behemoth* commanding a subject to kill his father. See Hobbes, *Behemoth*, p. 51.

[134] Gauthier, *The Logic of Leviathan*, p. 108.

are that both seem to affirm monarchy as the most stable form of government and that Dune animates Hobbes' desire for unity in showing the faction-ridden Corrino Empire giving way to the unitary Atreides regime. Some of Herbert's text could have been penned by Hobbes:

> 'Mankind has ah only one mm-m-m science,' the Count said.
>
> . . .
>
> 'And what science is that?' the Baron asked.
>
> 'It's the um-m-m-ah-h science of ah-h-h discontent.'[135]

This cynicism would fit well within Hobbes' reflections on the civil war, *Behemoth, or the Long Parliament* (1681).[136] There are deeper relations. Hobbes, for all his postulating of rationality leading to social contract, was not blind to the ingredients behind human fanaticism.[137] A theme within the 'Hobbes industry'[138] concerns what weight should be given to Hobbes' detailed engagement with theology and religion.[139] Hobbes understood that for humans the fear of death paled in comparison with the fear of eternal damnation.[140] Furthermore, Hobbes observes that this weakness intensifies in a group setting and can be manipulated by rhetoric-savvy leaders[141] In this, Paul's self-coronation in the Cave of Birds[142] takes on particular meaning – not as a demonstration that the Freman are fools, but as a view of humanity that seems remarkably coherent within a Hobbesian frame. Further, not only are Herbert's humans 'irrational' in their passions – so too are his sovereigns.

While the secondary literature that reads Dune through Machiavelli considers it to be a drama of 'princes', it is more properly a drama of sovereigns. Herbert animates a succession of sovereigns. The Atreides are not just Machiavellian leaders of *virtu,* but Hobbesian sovereigns. The maintenance and unity of power are Paul's and Leto II's fundamental motivations.[143] Here, Herbert's animation of Hobbes is particularly insightful. Paul falls. Victorious in the battle of Arrakeen, he sits as undisputed sovereign over the political, economic, and religious institutions of the Imperium. Yet Paul's religious state fractures within itself – paralleling his own divisions between guilt and

135 Herbert, *Dune*, p. 313.

136 Holmes, *Passions and Constraint*, p. 73.

137 Ibid., pp. 75–7.

138 Goldsmith, 'The Hobbes Industry', p. 145.

139 See Martinich, *The Two Gods of Leviathan*; Pasquino, 'Hobbes, Religion and Rational Choice'; Kateb, 'Hobbes and the Irrationality of Politics'.

140 Hobbes, *Behemoth*, pp. 14–15.

141 Ibid., p. 38.

142 Herbert, *Dune*, pp. 403–7.

143 Zeender, 'The "Moi-peau" of Leto II in Herbert's Atreides Saga', p. 230.

irresponsibility. Paul's residual humanity – that he loves and expresses grief – is the fault that leads to his fall. The conspirators' complicated plotting in *Dune Messiah* aims to polish Paul's love for Chani and Duncan Idaho into a cruel mirror in which he will see and despise the monster he has become.[144]

This monstrous self is exactly who Paul's son Leto II becomes with his catch-cry that 'his skin was not his own!'[145] In the succession from Paul to Leto II, Herbert brings to the fore an aspect of sovereignty implicit in Hobbes: Leto II merges with Leviathan.[146] This physical act is symbolic of the unitary state that he commands as God Emperor for 3,500 years.[147] Leto II becomes the 'mortal god' and achieves galaxy-wide peace. He criticises his father for failing to take this essential step,[148] and Herbert confirms this choice with Leto II's defeating the weathered Paul as Preacher in a duel of prophecy.[149] The message seems to be that sovereignty demands the losing of Paul's vestiges of humanity. It involves a full and conscious union with the worm, resulting in something other than human – indeed, something more animal. This is exactly what Hobbes proposes. Hobbes can be observed as caught in the paradox of the social contract. In the state of nature:

> there is no industry because its fruits would be uncertain. There is no culture of the earth, no navigation . . . there is no knowledge of the face of the earth, no account of time, no arts, no letters and no society. Worst of all there is continual fear and danger of violent death and the life of man is solitary, poor, nasty, brutish and short.[150]

In other words, the hallmarks of humanity are absent, yet it is human reason in the state of nature that rescues humanity from this animal existence.[151] The paradox is an assumption of rationality prior to the alleged rationality-securing event. Herbert does not provide a solution to this 'puzzle'.[152] But what Herbert does in Leto II is show what it means to say, as Hobbes does, that the sovereign remains in the state of nature. It means that the sovereign is not human – at least not human as they may be known after the social contract. Just like Leto II, the sovereign contains the animal. This makes sense of the predator–prey imagery that interrupted Dune's ecological message. The biblical Leviathan is

144 Herbert, *Dune Messiah*, p. 19.
145 Herbert, *Children of Dune*, p. 243.
146 Ibid., pp. 308–12.
147 Herbert, *God Emperor of Dune*, p. 155.
148 Herbert, *Children of Dune*, p. 204.
149 Ibid., p. 321.
150 Hobbes, *Leviathan*, p. 81.
151 Hampton, *Hobbes and the Social Contract Tradition*, pp. 68–9.
152 Fitzpatrick, *Modernism and the Grounds of Law*, p. 26.

described as the ultimate predator,[153] and Leto II declares that 'my purpose is to be the greatest predator ever known'.[154] As God Emperor, he is represented as possessing two natures: the Zen-like Atreides Emperor who, even encased in his seven metres-long 'pre-worm' body,[155] is capable of play, love, and regrets,[156] and the worm that kills.[157] This seems a perfect representing of Hobbes' sovereign, terrifying in thought and action.

For Hobbes, it is the sovereign's terrifying nature that facilitates sovereign peace. As Leo Strauss and Schmitt both note, Hobbes is foremost a theorist of fear,[158] and Herbert is quite clear that Leto II's empire is maintained through fear: fear of his female Fish Speaker army[159] and fear based on his monopoly over the last of the spice.[160] Hobbes' humans, just like Herbert's, are motivated by fear – especially fear of violence.[161] It is fear that drives the social contract[162] and it is fear of that common power that keeps, most of the time, irrational and seditious human passions in check.[163] Law works in Hobbes' schema not because it is just, or custom, but because it is coded sovereign violence. Its register is the irrational.

Law as a species-sovereign violence has been overlooked by much twentieth-century legal thought.[164] Hans Kelsen proposed a legal order rationally unfolding from a shared grundnorm: that the legal order is legitimised by a fundamental 'political' acceptance of its legitimacy.[165] In this, he was condemned by Schmitt for 'negating' the actuality of sovereignty.[166] Liberal political thought has tried to deny the violence of positive law; having inherited Leviathan, liberals have put it in the chains of constitutions, rights, separation of powers, and due process.[167] This was Schmitt's argument. Schmitt saw that

[153] Job 41: 33–4, The Bible Society in Australia, *Good News Bible*, p. 536. On Hobbes' iconography, see Farneti, 'The "Mythical Foundation" of the State'.

[154] Herbert, *God Emperor of Dune*, pp. 16, 69.

[155] Ibid., pp. 7, 94.

[156] Ibid., pp. 192–5.

[157] Ibid., pp. 29–30.

[158] Strauss, *The Political Philosophy of Hobbes*, p. 128; Schmitt, *The Leviathan in State Theory of Thomas Hobbes*, p. 19. On Strauss and Schmitt on Hobbes, see McCormick, *Carl Schmitt's Critique of Liberalism*, pp. 258–65.

[159] Herbert, *God Emperor of Dune*, pp. 125, 313.

[160] Ibid., pp. 76–82.

[161] Blits, 'Hobbesian Fear', p. 424.

[162] Hobbes, *Leviathan*, pp. 84, 116.

[163] Ibid., p. 113.

[164] Nonet, 'What is Positive Law?', p. 669.

[165] Kelsen, *Introduction to the Problems of Legal Theory*, p. l.

[166] Schmitt, *Political Theology*, p. 21.

[167] Holmes, *Passions and Constraint*, pp. 69–70.

Hobbes opened the way for law 'to become decision and command in the sense of a psychologically calculable compulsory motivation'.[168] Schmitt's imagery was specific and telling. Hobbes opened the way for Leviathan to be not only the awe-inspiring mythic monster, but the mega-machine:[169]

> For technically represented neutrality to function, the laws of the state must become independent of subjective content, including religious tenets or legal justifications and propriety and should be accorded validity only as the result of the positive determinations of the state's decision-making apparatus in the form of command norms.[170]

Schmitt was prepared to declare the modern state producing positive law as 'a huge industrial plant'.[171] He saw in Hobbes' Leviathan wielding plastic law, the fear of law becoming formalised – that is, turned into a form to be deployed for whatever end,[172] including, as discussed in Chapter 1, the end of securing certain technological futures.

However, Dune does more than expose the sovereignty behind law as technology: it shows the essential commitments on which sovereignty and, with it, law as technology, arises. Dune not only shows the Leviathanic monster behind law as technology, but shows just how monstrous law as technology is. In one of Paul's rants against his Empire in *Dune Messiah*, Herbert provides a glimpse of a more essential contribution, explicitly linking law and death:

> 'Ahh. Laws,' he said. He crossed to the window, pulled back the draperies as through he could look out. 'What's law? Control? Law filters chaos and what drips through? Serenity? Law – our highest idea and our basest nature. Don't look too closely at the law. Do and you'll find the rationalised interpretations, the legal casuistry, the precedents of convenience. You'll find serenity which is just another word for death.'[173]

There is ample death in Dune.[174] Paul achieves sovereignty over the deaths of (in order) Shadout Mapes,[175] most of the Atreides' army,[176] Wellington

168 Schmitt, *The Leviathan in State Theory of Thomas Hobbes*, p. 70.
169 McCormick, *Carl Schmitt's Critique of Liberalism*, p. 271.
170 Schmitt, *The Leviathan in State Theory of Thomas Hobbes*, p. 44.
171 Schmitt, *Political Theology*, p. 65.
172 Ibid., p. 28.
173 Herbert, *Dune Messiah*, p. 168.
174 McLean, 'A Question of Balance'.
175 Herbert, *Dune*, p. 155.
176 Ibid., p. 169.

Yueh,[177] his father,[178] Duncan Idaho,[179] Liet-Kynes,[180] Jamis,[181] numerous unnamed Freman who challenge his leadership,[182] Gurney Halleck's smuggler crew,[183] his first-born son, Sardaukar,[184] and Freman during the Battle of Arrakeen,[185] Baron Harkonnen,[186] Thufir Hawat,[187] and Feyd-Rautha Harkonnen.[188] Leto II's sovereignty follows the death of his mother, Chani, in childbirth,[189] the Preacher's guide Assan Tariq,[190] Paul as Preacher,[191] and Ali Atreides.[192] Accompanying these actual deaths are Paul's and Leto II's faked deaths: Paul's in flying the ornithopter into the sandstorm in *Dune*[193] and then again marching into the desert in *Dune Messiah*;[194] and Leto II in faking the success of the Corrino assassination attempt in *Children of Dune*.[195] Finally, these deaths are just a prelude to the deaths that flow once Paul and Leto II install themselves as Emperor. Billions die in Paul's jihad,[196] and billions of billions are slaughtered ensuring the eons of Leto's Peace.[197] Herbert seems to be sending a clear message that death is entwined with sovereignty.

This relationship is something that Hobbes underplayed. For Hobbes, the sovereign is a source of fear and awe emanating from its potential to do violence.[198] However, Hobbes was caught in a bind. While he was not prepared to claim an independent source of authority in the individual as a bulwark against the sovereign, Hobbes nevertheless conceived the sovereign as necessary for the protection of the individual from the chaos of

177 Ibid., p. 171.
178 Ibid., p. 176.
179 Ibid., p. 215.
180 Ibid., p. 264.
181 Ibid., p. 290.
182 Ibid., pp 362–3.
183 Ibid., p. 391.
184 Ibid., p. 432.
185 Ibid., p. 443.
186 Ibid., p. 440.
187 Ibid., p 450.
188 Ibid., p 461.
189 Herbert, *Dune Messiah*, p. 205.
190 Herbert, *Children of Dune*, p. 322.
191 Ibid., p. 363.
192 Ibid., p. 368.
193 Herbert, *Dune*, p. 220.
194 Herbert, *Dune Messiah*, p. 216.
195 Herbert, *Children of Dune*, pp. 163, 175–81.
196 Herbert, *Dune Messiah*, p. 92.
197 Herbert, *God Emperor of Dune*, pp. 73, 14–125, 134.
198 Hobbes, *Leviathan*, p. 113.

the state of nature.[199] In his major works, Hobbes turns to natural law to attempt to weave sovereign and individual into a mutually reinforcing system.[200] However, as Schmitt identifies, in building his theory of sovereignty 'geometrically' off the individual to natural law, Hobbes sowed the seeds that were to grow into liberal claims of rights against the state.[201] Hobbes seems to suggest in *Leviathan* that individuals have a right to resist when the sovereign sends for the executioner.[202] Yet he is particular in emphasising that 'the sovereign never lacks the right to do anything . . . It may and often does happen in commonwealths that a subject may be put to death by the commands of the sovereign and yet neither does a wrong to the other.'[203] It seems that, in Hobbes' own schema, the decision by the sovereign to kill allows a micro-state of nature to engulf sovereign and doomed subject. This means that neither is 'wrong' – the sovereign in bringing death and the subject in resisting. The outcome of this staged 'original' clash of wills is inevitable. Herbert's celebrated image of sandworms obliterating humans seems apt.[204]

Schmitt's concern with the transformation of Leviathan into a 'technically neutral state'[205] that followed from Hobbes was exactly the capacity of this state to consume its subjects. Postulating alternative Judaic imagery for the state, Schmitt suggests that 'the very mention of the name "leviathan" could evoke the recollection of dreadful Asiatic myths of an all-demanding Moloch or an all-trampling Golem'.[206] Schmitt does not hold with this reading, preferring in *Political Theology* (1922) the mythic and representative manifestation of Leviathan as the solution to the mechanistic state.[207] Here, Schmitt's preference for myth sends warnings. Schmitt's (and Strauss's) criticisms of Hobbes' proto-liberalism reveal their preferred vision of humanity as 'needed to be ruled'.[208] While concerned with the state as Moloch, par-

199 Ibid., p. 146.

200 Ibid., pp. 86–107; see also Hobbes, *The Elements of Law*, pp. 81–95; Hobbes, *De Cive*, pp. 51–76.

201 Schmitt, *The Leviathan in State Theory of Thomas Hobbes*, pp. 84–97.

202 Hobbes proposes that a natural law is that: 'A covenant not to defend myself from force by force is always void.' Hobbes, *Leviathan*, p. 93. This is taken up in Chapter 21 to be a liberty to defend their own bodies even against those who lawfully invade them, p. 149; see Dyzenhaus, '"Now the Machine Runs Itself"', p. 16.

203 Hobbes, *Leviathan*, p. 146.

204 Ibid., pp. 124–5; McCormick, *Carl Schmitt's Critique of Liberalism*, p. 275.

205 Schmitt, *The Leviathan in State Theory of Thomas Hobbes*, p. 45.

206 Ibid., p. 95. See Agamben's concerns with Schmitt's engagement with the Jewish-Kabbalistic tradition in Agamben, *Statis*, p. 45.

207 Schmitt, *Political Theology*, pp. 33–5.

208 McCormick, *Carl Schmitt's Critique of Liberalism*, p. 275.

ticularly if it was seized by the communists,[209] Schmitt was more concerned with the liberal undermining of the state's capacity for collective protective violence 'when the organizations of individual freedom were used like knives by anti-individualistic forces to cut up leviathan and divide his flesh among themselves'.[210] Schmitt tried to articulate another Leviathan and found it – at least from 1933 to 1938 – in the National Socialist state.[211]

Remembering Schmitt's problematic involvement with the Nazi regime reminds of its horrors, wars, and deaths. Nevertheless, the liberal aversion to speaking about sovereignty has prevented an appreciation of death within legal theory. John Austin spoke of commands backed by threats, but did not dwell on the necessary consequences of disobedience, beyond a fairly unspecific 'evil'.[212] H. L. A. Hart could only speak of this through agricultural metaphors when he suggested that a society composed solely of subjects whose obedience to law was secured by external force would be 'deplorably sheep-like; the sheep might end up in the slaughter house'.[213] Lon L. Fuller tried to get around the necessity for death in sovereignty through excluding such elemental violence from the study of law,[214] an approach that was continued with the interpretative turn in jurisprudence and Ronald Dworkin's account of law as a rational Herculean activity of best fit.[215] It took the reception of another Weimar intellectual, a correspondent with Schmitt[216] but from a radically different political and religious tradition – Walter Benjamin – for a more thoughtful engagement with death. Through what has become an iconic text of 'postmodern or deconstructive' jurisprudence,[217] Jacques Derrida introduced Benjamin's 'Critique of Violence' (1921) to Anglo-American jurisprudence.[218] Via Derrida, Benjamin reminded jurisprudence that legal order was founded on two violences: the violence that founds and the violence that preserves the law.[219] Both become indistinguishable in the modern apparatus of the police state. The shared commonality of

[209] Schmitt, *The Leviathan in State Theory of Thomas Hobbes*, p. 95.

[210] Ibid., p. 74.

[211] McCormick, *Carl Schmitt's Critique of Liberalism*, pp. 282–6. On Schmitt's career under the Nazis, see Müller, *A Dangerous Mind*, pp. 37–41.

[212] Austin, *The Province of Jurisprudence Determined*, pp. 12–14.

[213] Hart, *The Concept of Law*, p. 114.

[214] Fuller, *The Morality of Law*, p. 110

[215] Dworkin, *Taking Rights Seriously*, pp. 105–23. The absence of death in Dworkin is clearly brought out by Cover, 'Violence and the Word'.

[216] Weber, 'Taking Exception to Decision'; Agamben, *State of Exception*, pp. 52–64.

[217] Douzinas and Gearey, *Critical Jurisprudence*, p. 70.

[218] Benjamin, 'Critique of Violence'; Agamben, *State of Exception*, p. 37.

[219] Derrida, 'Force of Law', pp. 35–40; Douzinas, *Human Rights and Empire*, p. 252.

both founding and preserving violence is as species of 'mythic violence', as opposed to 'divine violence', and the defining characteristic is the need for blood.[220] In Benjamin's words:

> Mythical violence is bloody power over mere life for its own sake, divine violence pure power over all life for the sake of the living. The first demands sacrifice, the second accepts it.[221]

It is tempting to locate Benjamin's essay within his life and to consider, in his suicide in 1940 while fleeing occupied France, that the text was a response to the Nazi state. However, 'Critique of Violence' anticipated rather than 'witnessed' Nazism.[222] Giorgio Agamben, drawing upon Schmitt and Benjamin, does attempt to construct a juridical account of Nazism's signature excess: the concentration camp. For Agamben, the camp is not to be understood as just an evil – the tragic production of madmen – but rather is a manifestation of the perfection of modern sovereignty in the West.[223] In Benjamin's terms, sovereignty demands 'bloody power over mere life for its own sake'. The camp makes explicit that the ultimate fact of sovereignty is violent power over bare life, the very physical bodies of subjects.[224] Agamben shows that, in the brute existence of sovereignty, the human becomes an animal: a material substance to be used and consumed.[225] The fear of death that was the basic commitment on to which Hobbes erected his mythic Leviathan is revealed in the camp as dependent on something more basic. In order to fear Leviathan, the sovereign must have capacity to deliver on its promise: it must bring death. In essence, it is not Leviathan the sea serpent that all but God fear; nor is it Behemoth, Hobbes' code for the state of nature; nor is it a Golem, an animation of lifeless matter; nor is it a Moloch, with the connotation of complicated, ritual sacrifice. It is something more primal. To raid, like Herbert and Schmitt did, kabbalah mythology, the more appropriate deification of modern sovereignty would be the Angel of Death: Samael.[226]

220 Derrida, 'Force of Law', pp. 42–5, 52.

221 Douzinas, *Human Rights and Empire*, p. 297.

222 Derrida, 'Force of Law', p. 57.

223 Agamben, *Homo Sacer*, pp. 166–74.

224 Ibid., p. 175.

225 Ibid.; Agamben, *The Open*, p. 76.

226 While the sources are many, most accounts have Samael in two related, yet different, manifestations, as the faithful servant of God who brings death and also a demon closer to Satan of the New Testament who was the serpent in Genesis. Unifying the representations is Samael as bringer of death. See Jung, 'Fallen Angels in Jewish, Christian and Mohammedan Literature'; Dan, 'Samael, Lilith, and the Concept of Evil in Early Kabbalah'.

Herbert, unlike contemporary legal theory, does not need the continental philosophic supplement to reveal that death is the sovereign's being. This is what he shows in *Dune*. Paul becomes sovereign through learning how to kill.[227] This is the importance of the Jamis. In taking Jamis's life, Paul is confirmed on the path to sovereignty. Paul is innocent of all the deaths that surround him up to that moment; however, after Jamis he is responsible for the deaths. The play on 'Janis' is possibly deliberate: Jamis looks back to Paul the human boy, subject to the vagrancies of the world and forward to Paul the sovereign, maker of worlds and killer of humans. Looking forward further, Leto II is represented as Samael, particularly in the Gnostic image of Samael as a lion-headed serpent.[228] Leto II brings death. Beyond claims to predator status, Herbert has Leto killing or threatening to kill throughout the text. He crushes the aged Duncan Idaho;[229] he orders the execution of the Corrino heir;[230] he runs over Face Dancer assassins with his cart;[231] he discloses that he had killed one of Hwi Noree's ancestors;[232] he threatens to crush the Ixian civilisation;[233] he threatens to kill Reverend Mother Luyseyal; he enters the fray outside the Ixian embassy as a 'terrible death-machine';[234] and he 'orders' the killing of the ex-ambassador from Ix, Malky.[235] Leto II emerges from the text as a death-bound figure, from descriptions of his underground lair as a mausoleum,[236] to the awed Fish Speaker description of his involvement in the embassy skirmish.[237] Leto II does 'not play hide-and-seek with death'.[238]

In Leto II, Herbert shows what sovereignty must do: it must kill. This is a truth that Hobbes and also Schmitt obscured. This means that the plastic law of modernity is grounded on death. Herbert has Paul anticipating this realisation:

[227] O'Reilly, *Frank Herbert*, p. 70.

[228] Davies, 'The Lion-Headed Yaldabaoth'. See Samael's status as guardian angel of Rome and Leto's curse on the Romans to have infected humanity with the curse of government. Herbert, *God Emperor of Dune*, p. 42.

[229] Herbert, *God Emperor of Dune*, p. 30.

[230] Ibid. This execution is remembered by the replacement Duncan Idaho as a 'fat little man lying in a pool of his own blood': p. 209.

[231] Ibid., p. 141.

[232] Ibid., p. 158.

[233] Ibid., p. 165.

[234] Ibid., p 270. The fight is described at pp. 264–5.

[235] Ibid., p. 408.

[236] Ibid., p 37.

[237] Ibid., p 289.

[238] Ibid., p 234.

> The convoluted wording of legalisms grew up around the necessity to hide from ourselves the violence we intend toward each other. Between depriving a man of one hour of his life and depriving him of his life there exists only a difference of degree. You have done violence to him, consumed his energy. Elaborate euphemisms may conceal your intent to kill, but behind any use of power over another the ultimate assumption remains: 'I feed on your energy.'[239]

However, this is not the end of Dune as jurisprudence. Dune not only shows the commitment of death on which modern sovereignty is erected, but it shows the other essential commitment: time.

It is surprising that the received literature on Dune does not make more of Herbert's preoccupation with time throughout the series.[240] First, Herbert plays with what could be called 'epoch time', the meta-timescale of civilisations. The events in Dune occur 10,000 years after the formation of the Empire in the aftermath of the Butlerian Jihad, which in turn was the culmination of thousands of years of machine age that stretched back to the twentieth century. Book I and II of *Dune* unfold chronologically, yet Book III leaps several years into the future, while *Dune Messiah* occurs twelve years later. *Children of Dune* jumps another seven, leading to the 3,500-year fast-forward to the end of Leto II's reign in *God Emperor of Dune* and 2,000 years of famine, scattering, and revival until the events of the final two books. Second, there is the phenomenon shared by the Atreides and the Bene Gesserit Reverend Mothers of 'remembering' past lives. Here the past is animated in the present. Finally, there is Paul's and Leto II's faculty of prescience, shared in a lesser way with the Guild Navigators, which has portents of the future revealed in the present. This emphasis on time is reaffirmed in Herbert's many asides, pontificating and gesturing about time. Paul's first forays into his exceptional being are described as follows:

> Awareness flowed into that timeless stratum where he could view time, sensing the available paths, the winds of future . . . the winds of the past: the one-eye vision of the past, the one-eye vision of the present and the one-eye vision of the future – all combined in a tri-ocular vision that permitted him to see time-become-space.[241]

In Dune, Herbert can be seen playing with time, both timescales and the personal experience of time.

239 Herbert, *Dune Messiah*, p. 160.

240 DiTommaso, 'History and Historical Effect in Frank Herbert's *Dune*'.

241 Herbert, *Dune*, p. 281.

Louis E. Wolcher has written about the essence of time for law. Drawing on established resources within the philosophy of time,[242] he suggests that the West imagines time in two ways. The first is the timescale, which is the formal progression of time as a linear series of events ('Past→Present→Future'), each a known space through which objects move.[243] The plotting of events of Herbert's future universe represents this image of time. The second is existential time, the experience of beings living in the present. Here, past and future do not occupy known space, but 'the future as the wellspring of an unseen force that ceaselessly renews and surrounds the present, continually pushing the past into oblivion over the horizon of the now'.[244] Wolcher represents this as ('Future→PRESENT→Past').[245] In Dune, this is the Freman's life before the Atreides, with the immediate concerns of weather, spice, Harkonnen patrols, and dreams of a green Arrakis that fade into distant recollections of past injustices and planetary migrations. Wolcher attempts to synthesise, through Martin Heidegger and Kafka's *Er(He)* (1920), a Western truth about time: 'that time is not an objective property or determination of things in themselves, but rather a medium or mode of ordering which finds its true home only in the context of *human* experience'.[246]

There are moments in Dune when time is experienced in a human context. Leto II comments, 'Time runs out for a finite observer. There are no closed systems. Even I only stretch the finite matrix.'[247] He later says, 'Sometimes, time rushes by me; sometimes, it creeps.'[248] However, Leto II is not human; Herbert even has him declaring himself 'the ultimate alien'.[249] He is sovereign and, as with the identification of death for sovereignty, Dune tells something about the relationship of sovereignty to time.

Hobbes' sovereign was to maintain peace, and killing was the basic tool within the sovereign's peace-keeping arsenal. The sovereign, remaining in the state of nature, possessed the baseline rationality that is the natural inheritance of humanity.[250] Inherent in this rationality is an assigning of temporal mastery. It involves thinking about the future and taking active steps in the present to achieve future goals. This 'prudence'[251] is a function of a thinking

242 McTaggart, *The Nature of Existence*.
243 Wolcher, *Law's Task*, p. 213.
244 Ibid.
245 Ibid. The faded past and the future is in the original.
246 Ibid., p. 216; emphasis in the original.
247 Herbert, *God Emperor of Dune*, p. 70.
248 Ibid., p. 309.
249 Ibid., p. 172.
250 Hobbes, *Leviathan*, p. 23.
251 Ibid., pp. 12, 44.

being in time: 'prudence is a *presumption* of the *future* contracted from the *experience* of *past* time'.[252] In this, Hobbes maps the constituents of reason – projection of future events based on reflection of past events. A clearer awareness that modern reason emanates from time is one of Heidegger's gifts to the West.[253] However, it is a gift that has yet to be appreciated by legal theory. That law is grounded on time appears a truism. Legal practice is dominated by time: limitations, sentences, court dates, appointments, billable hours.[254] Jurisprudence talks excessively about time, but not about Being-in-time. The common law speaks to history, custom, and notions of continuity with the past.[255] Positivism – as critics like Dworkin identify – involves a succession of law-making events located in an institutionalised history.[256] In response, the interpretative jurisprudence of Dworkin focuses on legal decision-making in the present, while deconstructive replies orientate on future.[257] Yet, beyond recognition of the temporality of law,[258] how law and time interpose has yet to be theorised adequately.[259]

Dune opens the ground for theorisation of time and sovereignty. In particular, Dune shows that sovereignty involves a different relationship with time then either the linear or experiential times summarised by Wolcher or his Heidegger/Kafka-informed claim that time is human experience. The sovereign has to be prudent in a way that the human subject does not. Humans fear for their own in the state of nature – a fear based on the immediacy of violence of the war of all against all. However, the sovereign is responsible for all the subjects of the commonwealth. It must sort 'friends' from 'enemies'. It must, in Dune-speak, deal with '[f]eints within feints within feints' of a civilised War of Assassins,[260] the double and triple-speak of ambitious power groups at banquet,[261] and ensure that the spice flows. In short, the sovereign's prudence involves making decisions within a much more complicated tangle of activities and projects than either the human in the state of nature or

252 Ibid., p. 44. Italics in original.

253 Cornell, 'The Relevance of Time to the Relationship between the Philosophy of the Limit and Systems Theory', p. 1,590.

254 French, 'Time in Law', pp. 664–5.

255 Postema, *Bentham and the Common Law Tradition*, pp. 3–38.

256 Dworkin, *Taking Rights Seriously*, p. 17.

257 Cornell, 'Time, Deconstruction, and the Challenge to Legal Positivism', p. 279; Cornell, 'The Relevance of Time to the Relationship between the Philosophy of the Limit and Systems Theory', p. 1,579.

258 Tontii, *Right and Prejudice*, p. 180.

259 Nonet, 'Time and Law'.

260 Herbert, *Dune*, p. 353.

261 Ibid., pp. 123–42.

the human who has been freed by the social contract to get on with 'peace and profit'.[262] The sovereign requires, to use Herbert's phrase, 'a tri-ocular vision'[263] of past, present, and future. It must imagine futures based on a reasoned appreciation of how activities of the present can be understood as unfolding. Its vision must be beyond that of a mere human. Here Herbert's Atreides animate this time-mastery of sovereignty. They directly embody the 'experience' of the past, the memory of countless ancestors and they 'sampled the time-winds'[264] of the future. As the political and ecology reading of the Atreides emphasised, they have the capacity to appreciate consequences, at least better than their rivals, within the complex systems that they master.

This suggests that the sovereign is outside time, looking down as God, or at least Samael, at the unfolding of the world. This is why Hobbes described Leviathan as a god. However, Hobbes' deification of the sovereign is partial: his famous phrase is 'mortal god' and the adjective 'mortal' makes a profound difference. While being sovereign – killing in the name of peace or, more mundanely, making law for technological futures – involves a striving towards timelessness, Hobbes specifies that sovereignty lives within time. It is mortal and can die. It was the death of the sovereign that rallied Hobbes to raise his pen in sovereignty's defence. Hobbes' sovereign was birthed in the social contract and remains vulnerable to political pathogens. Leviathan can be consumed by a bigger Leviathan or torn apart by behemoth.[265] Ultimately, Paul dies – ironically stabbed by one of his own priests – and Leto II disintegrates after his plunge into the Idaho river; his animal selves 'slough away' leaving a pathetic remnant of bone and flesh.[266] Here sovereignty is in history. The sovereign's acts are not timeless. The sovereign is not located in a mythic time of creation, but merges with lived time to be an ever-present possibility.

Further, the sovereign is not just in history, but becomes the author of history.[267] The past as experience needs to be known and ordered, made useful to the present. Here, Herbert is insightful. The past, represented as the cellular ancestral memory, is perceived as a dangerous thing. It is feared that the 'pre-born' would be an 'abomination' because an ancestor's memory would dominate, demonstrated by the Baron's possession of Alia. The first task that Paul and Leto II undertake on their road to sovereignty is to master their memorial inheritance: they archive the past into something useful, into

262 Hobbes, *Behemoth*, p. 113.
263 Herbert, *Dune*, p. 281.
264 Ibid., p. 457.
265 Holmes, *Passions and Constraint*, p. 71.
266 Herbert, *God Emperor of Dune*, p. 451.
267 Douzinas, 'Theses on Law, History and Time', p. 17.

history. Derrida regarded this ability to create history in present time as a critical element of modernity, giving it the name 'white mythology'.[268] The phrase plays on ambiguities.[269] 'White' is used in two ways: it is a white mythology because it belongs to the West; and it is white because it is colourless. In merging mythic and lived time, the colour and poetry of the creation stories of pre-modernity are lost. Creation becomes a bland task of the sovereign's officers writing dates and decrees on white paper.

Thus, sovereignty possesses, to use Costas Douzinas' phrase, 'a dual time'. [270] In being sovereign, it must be timeless, outside time looking at past, present, and future with a tri-ocular vision. Yet sovereignty remains time bound, experiencing linear time, and with that birth and death and an immediate present that becomes more than past; it becomes history. In animating sovereignty in the Atreides, Herbert reveals this complicated relationship of sovereignty to time. However, there is a shared character to the sovereign's dual time. Herbert's sovereigns do not know the future: they can see more than mere humans, but total prediction eludes them.[271] In this, they remain future-focused, facing a universe that they cannot ultimately control. Similarly, their linear temporal existence opens to an unknown future; both Paul and Leto II fail to foresee the moment of their death. This discloses something about sovereignty and time. To be sovereign is to be future orientated. The sovereign does not write timescale; they make timescales. Nor does the sovereign experience the present as a 'human experience'; they decide the limits on what subjects experience. The sovereign forever sifts the 'time-winds', predicting, anticipating, responding, deciding, and ultimately killing for the future. To rework Wolcher's syntax images of time, sovereign time as revealed through Dune is FUTURE←past+present.

In summary, Dune reveals sovereignty emerging from the alchemy of death and time. Herbert's texts are not entirely about religion, politics, or ecology. Drawing upon the meta-theme of failure to control, Dune has been read as a detailed rumination on the existence of sovereignty and, beyond that, how sovereignty is constituted in the alchemy of death and time. Leviathan, or more correctly Samael, kills for the future. Dune reveals the essential commitments of law as technology, a desire for decisions that transform a potential, formless legality into structures that facilitate a preferred technological future. In this, there is a parallel figure. Cowering before the

268 Derrida, *Margins of Philosophy*, p. 213.

269 Fitzpatrick, *The Mythology of Modern Law*, p. 32.

270 Douzinas, 'Theses on Law, History and Time', p. 17.

271 Herbert, *God Emperor of Dune*, p. 21. Leto II: 'Absolute prediction which equals death to me.'

sovereign is a naked animal – what has been known as the human, impotent and vulnerable, fearful and shadowed by death.

Dune therefore achieves two things. First, in its allusions to Hobbes, it thinks law as technology stripped of its mundane technicity and seen as the monster that it is – a creature of death and time. Second, its monstrousness is seen in what it leaves as the 'human' – bare life that can be consumed. It also possibly suggests a resolution.

In Dune, it is possible to see Schmitt's 'solution' to law as technology in the 'representative' sovereign – the sovereign who represents the people as an organic whole, as the People, in the making of decisions. Instead of hiding the sovereign decision within procedures and technicalities, Schmitt celebrated the deciding sovereign, famously in the catchphrase that the 'sovereign decides the exception'.[272] Schmitt's sovereign decides when emergencies require the negation of the normal legal system. As an exposé of sovereignty, there is much in Dune that speaks to Schmitt's representative and deciding sovereign. The Atreides are very keen to embody their people, whether it is Paul and the Freman, or Leto II and the multitude of his empire. They, notwithstanding Paul's cynicism or Leto II's hubris, style themselves as the representatives of the multitude as a political unity. Further, Herbert's Atreides are full of decisions that negate law. Paul's career in *Dune* amounts to a sustained exercise in law-breaking,[273] and Leto II, discussing his favourite topic – himself – observes, 'I can play at being callous and I can make the necessary decisions, even decisions which kill, but I cannot escape the suffering.'[274]

Leto II's linking of decision, killing, and suffering points to the limit of Dune in progressing understanding of technical legality. Herbert's exposé of the essential commitments of sovereignty means that once Paul, and also Jessica, are off-stage, what is left is desert – a fairly dry palace drama of tyrants and superhumans. The engaging connection with humanity embodied by both of them – youth coming of age, a mother coping with life's vagrancies – is lost. This is performative of sovereignty, that it comes from humanity to be something animal and alien. What is left undone in Dune is how bare life is lived in the shadow of Samael. In this demonic age, is Being still worth being? This is the other essential question left by the implosion of Frankenstein myth. If law is technology, then what is the proper relationship of the 'human' to the technical? The next chapter crafts a response to this question through looking at a text whose core revolves around 'just' living in the midst of decision, killing, and suffering: *Battlestar Galactica.*

272 Schmitt, *Political Theology*, p. 5.

273 Barton-Kriese, 'Exploring Divergent Realities', pp. 211–12.

274 Herbert, *Children of Dune*, p. 313.

3

Battlestar Galactica, Technology, and Life

This chapter continues the examination of technical legality through a detailed analysis of *Battlestar Galactica*. Whereas, in the previous chapter, Dune emerged as a jurisprudential text that explored the base elements of sovereignty, revealing that law as technology is founded on the alchemy of death and time, this chapter shifts the focus directly to technicity. It argues that *Battlestar Galactica* shows that technology collapses the received Western metaphysics, yet it affirms that Being continues as 'technological Being-in-the-world'. *Battlestar Galactica* is a journey through the darkness of law as technology to a possibility that is 'responsibility for becoming'.

This argument is in three stages. The first stage reviews the series, noting a significant shift in emphasis from the politics of Season 1 and 2 to the metaphysics of Seasons 3 and 4. The second stage begins by taking seriously the suggestion of Schmitt that closed the previous chapter, but shows that *Battlestar Galactica* does not re-enact science fiction's tendency to fascist fantasies.[1] In *Battlestar Galactica*'s identification of sovereign and subject, the public becomes personal. This movement away from the public to identity is not complete. Behind the show's animation of identity lies a now familiar monster, but in an unfamiliar environment. Closing this stage is a fundamental realisation that the personal, threatened by essence, discloses the technical.

The third stage draws upon these strands. *Battlestar Galactica* challenges the metaphysics of technology. In *Battlestar Galactica*, the distinction between human and technology has been completely blurred. Here *Battlestar Galactica* seemingly performs Heidegger's 'end' of Western metaphysics in the occupation of Being by Enframing. This climax appears to be the total triumph of the monster, seen in the implosion of the Frankenstein myth in Chapter 1. However, *Battlestar Galactica* – notwithstanding its apocalyptic sensibilities – suggests that living remains after the end. The occupation of

[1] Roberts, 'Adama and Fascism'.

Being by Enframing can lead to technological Being-in-the world, which opens to 'responsibility for becoming'.

Battlestar Galactica Redux

Any analysis of *Battlestar Galactica* must begin with the original television series of the same name.[2] The original series had a short run during 1978–9,[3] with a dismal spin-off, *Galactic 1980* (1980),[4] and was essentially a *Star Wars* rip-off.[5] In contrast, the reimagined series ran for four seasons and was a ratings and critical success,[6] even ranked as the top television series by *Time* magazine for 2005.[7]

The basic framework of *Battlestar Galactica* remains faithful to Glen A. Larson's original, with images and narratives from post-apocalyptic science fiction mixed with space opera. The post-apocalyptic elements form the backbone of the story. Human society lived in a federation of 'colonies' on twelve planets. All the colonies are destroyed in a sudden attack, leaving the refugees to form a 'rag-tag fleet' of spaceships led by the sole surviving battleship/aircraft carrier, the *Galactica*.[8] The surrounding imagery is space operatic. The destructive enemy are malignant robots, the Cylons. The backdrops are planets, stars, and mile-long spaceships, providing for *Star Wars*-style space combat action. Further, the initial myth that these refugee humans are in search of the thirteenth tribe of humanity on the lost planet of Earth conjures Erich von Däniken's 'God is an Astronaut' pop archaeology.[9]

However, the reimagined *Battlestar Galactica* modifies these basics. First and foremost, the Cylons are not the dim, oscillating red-eye robots of the original. While there are some Cylons – denigrated as 'toasters' by the humans – that resemble the chrome originals, the reimagined series adds two twists. The first is the Frankenstein twist that the Cylons are humankind's

2 Marshall and Potter, '"I See the Patterns"', p. 3.

3 Colla, 'Saga of a Star World'; Bellisario, 'The Hand of God'.

4 Hayers, 'Galactica Discovers Earth Part I', *Galactica 1980* – Satlof, 'The Return of Starbuck', *Galactica 1980*.

5 Muir, *An Analytical Guide to Television's* Battlestar Galactica, pp. 37–40. The similarity did not escape George Lucas, who commenced proceedings, *Twentieth Century-Fox Film Corp v MCA, Inc* (1983) 715 F.2d 1327 (9th Circ).

6 Dempsey, 'Sci Fi's "Battlestar" Shines Brightly'; on critical fronts, there are four edited volumes devoted to the reimagined *Battlestar Galactica*: see Kiersey and Neumann, Battlestar Galactica *and International Relations*; Eberl, *Battlestar Galactica and Philosophy*; Potter and Marshall, *Cylons in America*; Hatch, *So Say We All*.

7 Poniewozik, 'Best of 2005: Television'.

8 Sontag, 'The Imagination of Disaster', pp. 40–7.

9 Muir, *An Analytical Guide to Television's* Battlestar Galactica, p. 5.

own rebelled creations. The second is that the Cylons have 'evolved' organic humanoid models, termed 'skin jobs' in an obvious borrow from *Blade Runner* (1982).[10] The two series are very different stylistically. The original presented Loren Greene's Commander William Adama leading, to the rallying sounds of an orchestral score, a futuristic humanity from the brightly lit bridge of his spaceship.[11] In contrast, the reimagined *Galactica* is a brooding ribbed beast, an old warship constructed fifty years earlier. Its poxed exterior mirrors the new Adama's (portrayed by *Blade Runner* alumni Edward James Olmos) marked face. Its interior lacks the techno-lavish aesthetics usually associated with television spaceships.[12] Designed to fight an enemy that infected computer networks, its grey interior resembles a World War II military vessel with manual airlocks, paper correspondence, and a scurrying crew.[13] In this universe, there are no lasers or advanced medical cures: spaceships shoot bullets; cancer kills after a long, painful decline; old equipment breaks down; and the weapons of mass destruction are nuclear bombs.[14] Bear McCreary's musical score is low key, featuring Celtic chants, ethnic drumming, and Bob Dylan's cryptic 'All Along the Watchtower'.[15] The space battles are a quiet chaos of movement and explosions overlaid by the garbled communication of pilots swearing (the oft-heard 'Frak/Fraking'), chimed with ethereal laments. Finally, the production values between the old and new diverge. The new series has a documentary style: hand-held cameras, rapid oscillations between characters and space battles where the camera itself is caught and flung about unable to track and zoom in on the action – all very unlike the sound stage scenes and static spaceship models of the original.

All this follows creator Ronald D. Moore's desire that the new series take the 'opera out of space opera'.[16] This is manifested in the inclusion of strong female characters, a challenge to the traditional sexism of the genre.[17] Complicating Adama's leadership of humanity is Laura Roslin (Mary McDonnell), the Education Secretary who is elevated to 'President of the Twelve Colonies' when the rest of the executive die in the Cylon attack.[18]

10 Scott, *Blade Runner*.

11 Muir, *An Analytical Guide to Television's* Battlestar Galactica, p. 5.

12 The aesthetics of *Battlestar Galactica* was conceived as a contrast to *Star Trek*: see Casey, '"All this has Happened Before"', p. 242.

13 Rymer, 'Battlestar Galactica Mini-series'.

14 Rose, 'Cyborg Selves in *Battlestar Galactica* and *Star Trek*', p. 1,205. On the nuclear bomb in *Battlestar Galactica*, see Fey, Poppe, and Rauch, 'The Nuclear Taboo'.

15 Papanikolaou, 'Of Duduks and Dylan'.

16 McNamara, 'The Hit that Zaps Sc-Fi Cliches'.

17 Russ, *To Write Like a* Woman, pp. 41–59.

18 Rose, 'Cyborg Selves in *Battlestar Galactica* and *Star Trek*'.

Also, much to the consternation of fans of the original,[19] the charismatic swashbuckling hero character of Lieutenant Kara 'Starbuck' Thrace is a woman (Katee Sackhoff). This gender reassignment in the new series also happens to the pilot, Lieutenant Sharon 'Boomer' Valerii (Grace Park), who is further revealed as a Cylon (Number Eight). While the other major characters retain their gender from the original, they are presented in significantly more complex ways. Captain Lee 'Apollo' Adama (Jamie Bamber), Adama's surviving son and *Galactica*'s chief pilot, is not the all-American hero of Richard Hatch's original. Richard Hatch returns as the political prisoner and sometime vice-president, Tom Zarek. Nor is Dr Gaius Baltar (James Callis) the traitor commanding the Cylons in their genocide that he was in the original;[20] instead, he begins the series as a lascivious, self-serving civilian scientist whose intimate cavorting with a Number Six Cylon (the blonde and leggy 'Caprica Six', played by Tricia Helfer) allowed the Cylons to infiltrate the human defences.

One element developed by Moore (and co-creator David Eick) was the religious themes of the original series.[21] The original series borrowed from classical, Old Testament, and Mormon mythology.[22] Unlike the original, where the humans were a militant theocracy,[23] in the new series the 'Twelve Colonies' appear as a pluralistic, democratic, secular, contemporary Western society, with liberal constitutionalism and civilian control of the military. The cityscape of the planet Caprica possesses the familiar high-rise office blocks and river promenades of a Western metropolis.[24] Religion is not a dominant feature and, when it is involved, it is the pluralism of the Hellenistic pantheon that calls the humans' devotion. In contrast, the Cylon occupation of Caprica shows a hive of identical-looking duplicates going through the motions of being human, referencing the uncanny horrors of the clone canon.[25] This sameness is reflected in the Cylons' monotheism, justifying their destruction of humanity as 'God's will'.[26]

As with Dune, a summary of *Battlestar Galactica*'s four seasons is difficult, although a touch of the monomyth can be discerned. Core to the series is the destabilising of certainties, and a clear distinction can be made

19 Kungl, 'Long Live Stardoe'.

20 Muir, *An Analytical Guide to Television's* Battlestar Galactica, p. 167.

21 Basson, *Battlestar Galactica: The Official Companion*, p. 18.

22 Ford, '*Battlestar Gallactica* and Mormon Theology'.

23 Muir, *An Analytical Guide to Television's* Battlestar Galactica, p. 153.

24 This was later explored through the unsuccessful spin-off sequel *Caprica* (2010). Reiner 'Pilot' *Caprica*. On that show see Kapica, '"I Don't Feel Like a Copy"'; Tranter, 'I, Archive'.

25 Woolnough, 'Downloaded', *Battlestar Galactica*.

26 Kukkonen, 'God against the Gods'.

between the mini-series and Seasons 1 and 2, and Seasons 3 and 4.[27] The first half of the series emphasised the politics of survival. The occupation of the human settlement of New Caprica for the opening episodes of Season 3 marked a changed set of identifications, with a movement to the metaphysical as the Fleet jumped through various astrophysical events chasing the legend of Earth. This metaphysical turn was cemented in the finale of Season 3, with Starbuck returning from the dead and the revelation that four characters, seen so obviously as human, were the 'final Cylons'.[28] Season 4 continued this destabilising of certainties with the Cylons' civil war,[29] the discovery that the 'thirteenth colony' of Earth was settled by Cylons[30] and the realisation that the Colonial and Cylon survivors become the ancestors of the beings-that-are-us.[31]

While the emphasis moved in Seasons 3 and 4 to the metaphysical, this was not at the expense of the political, which continued throughout the series. The seemingly obvious coding of a religious-based 'clash of civilizations'[32] established the series as an allegory of contemporary global politics,[33] and with that terrorism, counter-terrorism, suicide bombers, torture of enemy combatants, religious fanaticism, *coups d'état*, occupation, and resistance.[34] This political emphasis, explored in the secondary literature,[35] suggests that this is the place to begin with *Battlestar Galactica* – particularly Schmitt's politics of the exception.

Sovereigns and Subjects in *Battlestar Galactica*

Like Dune, there seems to be little law in *Battlestar Galactica*. In Season 1, Adama responds to a series of terrorist attacks aboard the *Galactica* by allowing an 'independent tribunal' to investigate.[36] When the direction of that investigation leads back to Adama, he shuts it down. In another episode, viewers are never shown the working of the colonial military justice system that led to the death sentence being imposed on two of *Galactica*'s

27 Charles, 'War Without End?, p. 451.

28 Rymer, 'Crossroads Part II', *Battlestar Galactica*.

29 Hemingway, 'Six of One', *Battlestar Galactica*.

30 Nankin, 'Sometimes a Great Notion', *Battlestar Galactica*.

31 Rymer, 'Daybreak Part II', *Battlestar Galactica*.

32 Huntington, *The Clash of Civilizations and the Remaking of World Order*.

33 Ott, '(Re)Framing Fear: Equipment for Living in a Post-9/11 World'.

34 Howie, 'They Were Created by Man'.

35 See, for example, Johnston-Lewis, 'Torture, Terrorism and Other Aspects of Human Nature'; King and Hutnyk, 'The Eighteenth Brumaire of Gaius Baltar'; Ip, 'Two Narratives of Torture'.

36 Hardy, 'Litmus', *Battlestar Galactica*.

crew.[37] Both of these episodes show scenes of individuals claiming the protection of rights and those claims being brushed aside. Starbuck justifies her torture of the Cylon Leoben Conoy/Number Two (Callum Keith Rennie) because, 'It's a machine, Sir, there are no limits to the tactics I can use.'[38] Talk of establishing a tribunal system in the Fleet through 'Executive Order 112' becomes clouded in politicking.[39] There are occasional references to legal documents, the constitutional 'Articles of Colonisation',[40] or the colonial military regulations,[41] but the precise wordings and concepts are left unspoken.

The two representations of courts in the series – Baltar's trial at the end of Season 3 and Adama's trial by the mutineers in Season 4 – are both farce. Baltar's trial for his actions as president when collaborating with the Cylons on New Caprica becomes a stage for airing of the recriminations from occupation and Baltar's 'innocence' is won not so much by the weight of evidence as through his lawyer, Romo Lampkin (Mark Sheppard), bringing the compromises of occupation out into the open.[42] Adama's trial by the mutineers, with the chief mutineer Lieutenant Felix Gaeta (Alessandro Juliani) as prosecutor and with his co-conspirator Tom Zarek as judge, is not a trial but a 'conclusion' – even with Lampkin as defence attorney.[43] In providing a lawyer as a character – admittedly a minor one – *Battlestar Galactica* does go further than most science fictions in providing some substance for a mainstream law in literature analysis.[44] However, Lampkin is less a lawyer and more a knower of characters. Hiding his eyes behind sunglasses, Lampkin is deeply flawed. He is a kleptomaniac, egotistical, and cynical ('Lampkin's First Rule of Legal Dynamics: When an irresistible force meets a moveable object, stand aside and wait for the class action')[45] yet, against his better judgement, he is also empathetic and caring.[46]

37 Rymer, 'Pegasus', *Battlestar Galactica.*

38 Turner ,'Flesh and Bone', *Battlestar Galactica.*

39 Nankin, 'The Ties that Bind', *Battlestar Galactica.*

40 Mentioned in the swearing-in ceremonies for Roslin and Baltar as President and Apollo as Acting President. Rymer, '*Battlestar Galactica* Mini-series', *Battlestar Galactica* (Roslin); Rymer, 'Lay Down Your Burdens Part II', *Battlestar Galactica*, (Baltar); Hardy, 'Sine Qua Non', *Battlestar Galactica* (Apollo).

41 Rymer, 'The Road Less Traveled', *Battlestar Galactica.*

42 Rymer, 'Crossroads Part II', *Battlestar Galactica.* Kapica, '"What a Glorious Moment in Jurisprudence"'.

43 Rose, 'Blood on the Scales', *Battlestar Galactica.*

44 Travis and Tranter, 'Interrogating Absence', p. 33.

45 Hardy, 'Sine Qua Non', *Battlestar Galactica.*

46 Notwithstanding whinging, he cares for and about his deceased wife's cat (Young, 'The Son

Notwithstanding talk of 'writs of forfeiture' and Lampkin making cynical comments that 'one of the less ennobling features of a legal culture, [is that] no one wants to take responsibility',[47] *Battlestar Galactica* does not show this legal culture 'boarding a wagon train to the stars'.[48] Nor does it present, as will be discussed in relation to *Mad Max 2* in Chapter 6, a post-apocalyptic context for a retelling the social contract. Life is nasty and brutish for the refugees in the Fleet, particularly for the civilians crammed into 'Dogsville' on *Galactica*'s lower decks,[49] but there are forms of order, self-generated by factions and cults, augmented and imposed by the military. Also, there are not the techniques of surveillance and control to manage populations, as featured in dystopian science fiction.[50] Indeed, the few attempts by the *Galactica* to control civilians end not with governing, but rather with death.[51]

However, death is what there is in *Battlestar Galactica*. The series is set after the death of the human home worlds in the Cylons' nuclear holocaust. In the opening sequence of each episode, a figure is flashed on to the screen showing the total number of human survivors – they are fewer as the series goes on.[52] This death is not abstracted. Bodies are thrown into space from exploding spaceships and humans kill one another with monotonous regularity. This killing goes beyond war casualties or unfortunate policing to official ex-judicial killings; Apollo's ad hoc murder investigation climaxes with him summarily executing a crime boss;[53] and the New Caprica resistance leaders start executing those they see as collaborators.[54] President Roslin disposes of Starbuck's tortured Cylon by flushing him out an airlock,[55] and Gaeta's and Zarek's mutiny ends with their execution by firing squad.[56] Seemingly,

also Rises', *Battlestar Galactica*; Hardy, 'Sine Qua Non', *Battlestar Galactica*) and he helps Starbuck with a wounded Sam Anders (Michael Trucco) in Rose, 'Blood on the Scales', *Battlestar Galactica*.

47 Hardy, 'Sine Qua Non', *Battlestar Galactica*.

48 Peltz, 'On a Wagon Train to Afghanistan'.

49 Rymer, 'The Woman King', *Battlestar Galactica*.

50 Sisk, *Transformations of Language in Modern Dystopias*, p. 2.

51 Kroeker, 'Resistance', *Battlestar Galactica*.

52 Season 1 begins with a survivor count of 47,973. The count at the end of Season 2 was 49,550. The increase comes from the fleet finding the *Pegasus*. Aside from this one-off increase, the numbers decrease each week. By the finale it is down to 38,516.

53 Head, 'Black Market', *Battlestar Galactica*.

54 Rymer, 'Collaborators', *Battlestar Galactica*.

55 Turner, 'Flesh and Bone', *Battlestar Galactica*. This execution was threatened to be used against Boomer in Mimica-Gezzan, *Home Part I: Battlestar Galactica* and carried out against the two Cavil/Number One Cylons (Dean Stockwell) in Rymer, 'Lay Down Your Burdens Part II', *Battlestar Galactica*.

56 Rose, 'Blood on the Scales', *Battlestar Galactica*.

the rule of law – the bedrock for liberal accounts of legality, the interlinking of roles and offices with the judicial utterance of 'the law' at its apex – is problematically manifested in *Battlestar Galactica*.

However, this order of death is still an order. It is an order of uniforms and salutes, of titles (Sirs, Commander, Lieutenant, Madam President), of pilot call signs (Starbuck, Apollo, Boomer, Helo, Hot Dog, Race Track and so on), of abbreviations (CAG – Captain of Air Group; CIC – Command, Intelligence, Control), of briefings, and a life of booze and card games interrupted by the adrenal rush of action. It is, in short, military order. The series only occasionally depicts the civilian society aboard the fleet – the crowds in Dogsville, the wealthy living it up on the luxury liner *Cloud Nine*, the grubby proletariat on the refinery ship *Hitei Kan*.[57] The focus is on the military and the relationships between the military and the civilian order.[58] This is visualised whenever the *Galactica* is shown. It is rarely pictured in its entirety; usually just its alligator-shaped snout fills the screen, dwarfing any of the civilian ships, including the Presidential *Colonial One*. The image is of an apex predator scattering lesser beasts. The message seems to be that, at the point of the annihilation of a society, the brute violence of the military is called to the fore.

This usurpation of the rule of law to military order in a time of enemies and annihilation seems particularly Schmittian. *Battlestar Galactica* presents a people on the brink of extinction facing an indefatigable and mechanical foe – similar sentiments to Schmitt's fear of the Soviet Union as mentioned in Chapter 1. The civilian population is represented as impulsive and fractious – suggesting Schmitt's feared demise of the state in street-level anarchy.[59] The episodes dealing with the political workings of the civilian government reflect Schmitt's attacks on parliament as involving much talk but little action.[60] The final episode of Season 1, 'Kobol's Last Gleaming Part II', manifests these themes.[61] The Fleet has found the origin of humanity, the planet Kobol. Adama disagrees with Roslin on how it should be explored; he believes that Roslin is being reckless. Roslin's position creates divisions within *Galactica*, leading to Starbuck mutinying. This triggers Adama to send in the marines

57 Rose, 'Dirty Hands', *Battlestar Galactica*.

58 Dellamonica, 'Stripping the Bones', p. 166.

59 Schmitt, *The Concept of the Political*, p. 32.

60 Pate, 'Colonial Day', *Battlestar Galactica*; Nankin, 'The Ties that Bind', *Battlestar Galactica*. 'The essence of parliament is therefore public deliberation of argument and counterargument, public debate and public discussion, parley and all this without taking democracy into account.' Schmitt, *The Crisis of Parliamentary Democracy*, pp. 34–5.

61 Rymer, 'Kobol's Last Gleaming Part II', *Battlestar Galactica*.

to take Roslin into custody. Adama, faced with division at home, an implacable external enemy, and poor political leadership, declares an exceptional circumstance and ousts the civilian government.

It is tempting to read Adama as Schmitt's preferred Hindenburg, although it glosses much of Schmitt's discussion of the legitimacy of dictatorship called forth by the exception. However, there is some support within Schmitt for a military coup d'état as a legitimate basis for dictatorship.[62] In the rapid progression of work during Weimar, Schmitt appears to move from an affirmation of a 'classical' dictator appointed by the ordinary political process in times of crisis,[63] to a more radical account of the 'sovereign' who represents the people. In this representing, the sovereign can decide between the ordinary and the exceptional[64] and through that decision recast the political machinery of the nation.[65] In announcing to Roslin that her 'Presidency is terminated',[66] Adama appears to be motivated by the belief that he possesses 'reserve' sovereign powers to preserve the nation. However, any affirmation that in this decision he 'represents' the nation is uncertain. Minutes after he is shot and for the following episodes of Season 2, he is unconscious and critically wounded in the sick bay. His leadership is left to his drunken executive officer (XO), Colonel Saul Tigh (Michael Hogan), who 'Fraks things up good' to the point where the crew and the Fleet revolt.[67]

However, *Battlestar Galactica*'s animation of Schmittian concepts reveals a problem. Schmitt's fundamental orientation – the basis for his distinction between normal and exception and his account of sovereignty[68] – lies in his infamous notion that 'the specific political distinction to which political actions and motives can be reduced is that between the friend and enemy'.[69] For Schmitt, the ability to distinguish between friend and enemy is a public act:

> The friend and enemy concepts are to be understood in their concrete and existential sense, not as metaphors or symbols, not mixed by economic,

62 Böckenförde, 'The Concept of the Political', p. 44. Piccone and Ulmen suggest that in the halcyon days of 1933, Schmitt was encouraging the army to seize power as an alternative to Hitler; Piccone and Ulmen, 'Uses and Abuses of Carl Schmitt', p. 16. However, one of Schmitt's biographers seems to suggest otherwise: Bendersky, *Carl Schmitt*, p. 28.

63 McCormick, *Carl Schmitt's Critique of Liberalism*, pp. 122–33.

64 Schmitt, *Political Theology*. See generally Schwab, *The Challenge of the Exception*, pp. 29–43.

65 McCormick, *Carl Schmitt's Critique of Liberalism*, p. 147.

66 Rymer, 'Kobol's Last Gleaming Part II', *Battlestar Galactica* (Adama).

67 Hardy, 'The Farm', *Battlestar Galactica*.

68 Schmitt, *Political* Theology, p. 5; Kalyvas, 'Carl Schmitt and the Three Moments of Democracy', p. 1,535.

69 Schmitt, *The Concept of the Political*, p. 26.

> moral and other conceptions, least of all in a private-individualistic sense as a psychological expression of private emotions and tendencies . . . An enemy exists only when, at least potentially, one fighting collectivity of people confront a similar collectivity. The enemy is solely the public enemy.[70]

He continues: 'In its entirety the state as an organized political entity decides for itself the friend/enemy distinction.'[71] Schmitt, like Hobbes, regarded the political as emerging from the possibility of war.[72] Unlike Hobbes, where the individual – vulnerable and alone – contracts to form the sovereign,[73] Schmitt presents an a priori nation declaring which other nations are friends or enemies. The key elements are summarised by Chantal Mouffe: 'this involves the creation of a "we" which stands in opposition to a "them" and this is located, from the outset, in the realm of collective identifications'.[74] This seems quite acceptable within *Battlestar Galactica*. In science fiction, what can be more 'collective enemy' than swarms of evil robots?[75] However, in its paralleling of Schmitt, the series identifies the limits of the friend/enemy distinction.

The Cylons do not all present as killer toasters. The skin jobs not only look human, but as the series progresses they manifest all the vagaries, emotions, and individuality displayed by the humans. Individual Cylons are portrayed sympathetically – the tortured Gina/Number Six, the Number Eight, who becomes known as Athena, when her child 'dies',[76] Caprica Six when she miscarries.[77] By Season 4, the deaths of rebel Cylons allied with the humans – whether in Doctor Cottle's (Donnelly Rhodes) sick bay[78] or shot in battle[79] or vented into space in explosions from *Galactica*'s increasingly dilapidated hull[80] – are poignant moments. The Cylons are shown as growing ambivalent about the direction of their extermination of humanity,[81] a tension that contributes to their civil war.[82] What this means is that the obvious imaging of

70 Ibid., p. 28.
71 Ibid., pp. 29–30.
72 Howse, 'From Legitimacy to Dictatorship'.
73 Robin, *Fear*, p. 42.
74 Mouffe, *The Return of the Political*, p. 132.
75 Ryan and Kellner, 'Technophobia', pp. 58–65.
76 Woolnough, 'Downloaded', *Battlestar Galactica*.
77 Young, 'Deadlock', *Battlestar Galactica*.
78 Nankin, 'Someone to Watch Over Me', *Battlestar Galactica*.
79 Rymer, 'Daybreak Part II', *Battlestar Galactica*.
80 Nankin, 'Someone to Watch over Me', *Battlestar Galactica*.
81 Woolnoughm, 'Downloaded' *Battlestar Galactica*; Rymer, 'Lay Down Your Burdens Part II', *Battlestar Galactica*.
82 Nankin, 'The Ties that Bind', *Battlestar Galactica*.

friend and enemy breaks down. For all his polemic about the public national character of the friend/enemy distinction, what Schmitt is actually suggesting is that it is the sovereign leader who holds the deciding power of friend and enemy. The friend/enemy distinction, like the exception, is another manifestation of Schmitt's decisionism.[83] While not necessarily a subjective decision for the public – indeed, according to Schmitt individuals can 'love your enemy',[84] something that Baltar represents a bit too literally – the distinction is rendered personal and an ongoing responsibility of leadership. Repeatedly in *Battlestar Galactica*, Adama and Roslin are seen to be making this call, ordering the destruction of the *Olympic Carrier* due to a suspicion that it has been overtaken by Cylons[85] and deciding that Admiral Helena Cain (Michelle Forbes), the commander of the found Battlestar *Pegasus*, must be executed as an 'enemy' of the fleet.[86] This decision of who is friend and who is enemy also goes the other way. Roslin and Adama decide, against the popular mood of the people, that the rebel Cylons should become 'friends'.[87] *Battlestar Galactica* suggests that 'friend' and 'enemy', in 'their concrete and existential sense',[88] do not originate in the nation, but rather reside within the person of the leader.[89]

Battlestar Galactica manifests the way that the friend/enemy distinction discloses a focus on the person of the leader in its emphasis on Adama. Adama's relationships with his sons and with the Colonial military tradition are shown to influence his decisions, particularly the decisions to reunite the Fleet, to 'reinstate' Roslin as president,[90] and to prevent Roslin and Tigh from rigging the presidential election.[91] In this, Admiral Cain of the *Pegasus* is Adama's foil.[92] Like *Galactica*, the *Pegasus* attracts a fleet of civilian ships in the aftermath of the Cylon attack.[93] While Adama makes the reluctant choice to flee the conquered homeworlds to protect the civilian fleet,[94] Cain feeds her civilian fleet – both ships and people – to her war machine to maintain

83 Hurst, 'Carl Schmitt's Decisionism'.
84 Schmitt, *The Concept of the Political*, p. 29.
85 Rymer, '33' *Battlestar Galactica.*
86 Rymer, 'Resurrection Ship Part II', *Battlestar Galactica.*
87 Olmos, 'Islanded in a Stream of Stars' *Battlestar Galactica.*
88 Schmitt, *The Concept of the Political*, p. 28.
89 Howse, 'From Legitimacy to Dictatorship'.
90 Woolnough, 'Home Part II', *Battlestar Galactica.*
91 Rymer, 'Lay Down Your Burdens Part II', *Battlestar Galactica.*
92 Mulligan, 'The Cain Mutiny', p. 54.
93 Alcalá, 'Razor', *Battlestar Galactica.*
94 Rymer, '*Battlestar Galactica* Mini-series', *Battlestar Galactica.*

her offensive.[95] Cain, the younger and more senior officer, makes a very different decision from that made by the older war veteran commander.

Furthermore, *Battlestar Galactica* exposes another tension within Schmitt's account of the friend/enemy distinction. Schmitt's critique of liberalism was that it transformed the life-and-death of politics into mere subjectivity: questions of economics or debating.[96] Schmitt responded to this privatisation of politics through a valorisation of the public, as revealed in his idealisation of the German people as a unified *volk*.[97] However, he distanced this ideal from the actual manifestation of the Weimar population, whose individuality had been dangerously freed by liberalism.[98] Schmitt presents an ambiguous account of the public as the collective entity manifesting in the state and also a fractious rabble threatening the state.[99] Agamben has observed that this dualism is significant in the Western political tradition through his account of people/People – people being the population governed by a sovereign, while People accounts for the sovereign-forming collective.[100] For Agamben, the people/People distinction grounds a sovereignty that transmutes people into People; however, this is a perverse transmutation, as it is founded on human existence as bare life.[101] *Battlestar Galactica* shows a population not playing its role according to this logic. In this, the series could be *Polis Galactica* for, in response to the exception, the people manifest a flowering of politics, elections, interest groups, rival leaders, and resistance to marshal law. Even while continually being killed, the people refuse to be *homo sacer*,[102] and they also refuse to play Schmitt's allocated representative public role of mass politics.

A Schmittian response would be to emphasise that this 'failure', like the failure of the German people during Weimar, manifests the terminal stages of liberalism: rapid individualism eroding clear collective thinking about who is a friend and who is an enemy. Alternatively, this steadfast representation of a politicised civil society could be explained as Moore's and Eick's residual liberal arts college education,[103] projecting Frances Fukuyama not just to the end of history, but to the end of worlds.[104] However, these alternatives

95 Rymer, 'Resurrection Ship Part I', *Battlestar Galactica*; Alcalá, 'Razor', *Battlestar Galactica.*
96 Schmitt, *The Concept of the Political*, p. 28.
97 Schmitt, *Political Theology*; McCormick, *Carl Schmitt's Critique of Liberalism*, p. 194.
98 Schmitt, 'State Ethics and the Pluralist State', p. 309.
99 Kennedy, '*Hostis* Not Inimicus', p. 103.
100 Agamben, *Homo Sacer*, pp. 176–9.
101 Ibid., p. 123.
102 Ibid. p. 83.
103 Edwards, 'Intergalactic Terror'.
104 Fukuyama, *Our Posthuman Future.*

– an adherence to metaphysical totalities or a triumphant affirmation of liberal individuality – do not capture the complexity presented by *Battlestar Galactica*. In the series, collectives organised according to the friend/enemy distinction are powerfully represented. However, these collectives are occupied by subjects. The category 'leader' is occupied by an embodied person whose personality and role mingle when called to decision. Similarly, the category 'people' comprises a collective unified through fleeing an annihilating enemy, yet is also a multitude of subjects clamouring for a say over their destiny. Addressing Schmitt, *Battlestar Galactica* highlights the problems within his metaphysics of leader and people in the 'concrete'.[105] Questions of embodied existence, agency, or subjectivity are theorised out by Schmitt.

This means that *Battlestar Galactica* offers enticing parallelisms for thinking about Schmitt, and in animating the friend/enemy distinction it also shows some of Schmitt's limits. Projected into a fleet of spaceships, Schmitt's abstractions of friend and enemy give way to 'the leader' and 'the people', which are not abstractions but embodied subjects. It shows the tension between category and existence – between metaphysics and embodiment – and this leads to the way that *Battlestar Galactica* opens the subject to essence.

Battlestar Galactica offers a reflection on the tensions within Schmitt posed by subjectivity because at another level the series allegorises concerns with identity. It successfully presents a world that, at least initially, appears to enact substantive gender equality. The starting point is simply that Starbuck appears as a post-feminist pin-up.[106]

The society presented in *Battlestar Galactica* seems to be post-feminist in its substantive gender equality. Women can be president and priests, admirals and front-line fighter pilots. Starbuck begins the series respected as *Galactica*'s 'top gun'. She does not pilot her Viper in a 'different voice'.[107] In the mini-series and Season 1, she is arrogant, disrespectful of senior officers, a spectacular risk-taker, cigar smoking, hard drinking/fighting/gambling, and bed hopping – in summary the archetype top-gun pilot.[108] In this, Starbuck's foil is Apollo. Apollo begins the series more concerned with others:

> *Starbuck:* You're the CAG, act like one.
> *Apollo:* What the hell does that mean?
> *Starbuck:* It means that you're still acting like you're everyone's best friend.[109]

105 Schwab, *The Challenge of the Exception*, p. 115.

106 Kungl, 'Long Live Stardoe'; Raney and Meagher, 'Gender in the Aftermath'.

107 Conly, 'Is Starbuck a Woman?', p. 234.

108 Sharp, 'Starbuck as "American Amazon"', p. 62; Wolfe, *The Right Stuff*; Konas, 'Traveling "Further" with Tom Wolfe's Heroes'.

109 Rymer, '33', *Battlestar Galactica*.

It is tempting to read Starbuck's 'masculinity' and Apollo's 'femininity' as a visioning of radical feminism's desire of the negation of the biological.[110] In *Battlestar Galactica*, it seems that gender does not relate to identity or social roles. There are some female characters who occupy more traditional female roles. Lieutenant Anastasia 'Dee' Dualla (Kandyse McClure), *Galactica*'s communications officer, supports and encourages dialogue and is also the focus of a love contest between Apollo and Roslin's first personal assistant, while Ellen Tigh (Kate Vernon), Saul Tigh's wife, is – at least until Season 4 – a behind-the-scenes jezebel, manipulative and self-promoting.[111] Nevertheless, the impression – especially from the four main characters – is that gender has a marginal place when it comes to identity. These characters are shown to be driven by conflicts, past traumas, and their relationships; there is no simplistic gender determinism. Adama's serious engagement with the military tradition and its dictates of leadership and loyalty gives him conflicting responsibilities to his 'family' – both his son and his crew. Roslin's mortality and disarming countenance contrast with her skill in political manipulation and her confidence in decision-making.[112] Starbuck's macho-nihilism is explained as a combination of her guilt in contributing to the death of Adama's other son, Zak,[113] and her upbringing as the daughter of a military-obsessed mother.[114] Apollo lives in the shadow of his father; he is initially hostile and distant, but as the series progresses he evolves more in his father's image, which he breaks out of by resigning and taking to civilian politics.[115] These characters are highly fallible: Adama stages a coup after insisting on the primacy of civilian government; Roslin starts believing that the hallucinations associated with her cancer treatment are divine messages; Starbuck, in common with her 'enemy' Tigh, turns too much to the bottle; and Apollo, who supported the established legal order in resisting his father's coup, executes a civilian in cold blood. It is these characters as believable humans that allow *Battlestar Galactica* to show the absence of the subject in Schmittian jurisprudence.

If *Battlestar Galactica* seems to represent progressiveness concerning gender, it is not as progressive concerning race.[116] Following *Star Trek*'s

110 Firestone, *The Dialectic of Sex*, p. 270.

111 Olmos, 'Tigh Me Up, Tigh Me Down', *Battlestar Galactica*; Rymer, 'Scattered', *Battlestar Galactica*; Alcalá, 'Exodus Part II', *Battlestar Galactica.*

112 Hardy, 'Epiphanies', *Battlestar Galactica.* 'The interesting thing about being President is you don't have to explain oneself to anybody' (Roslin).

113 Hardy, 'Act of Contrition', *Battlestar Galactica.*

114 Nankin, 'Maelstrom', *Battlestar Galactica.*

115 Hemingway, 'Six of One', *Battlestar Galactica.*

116 Greene, 'The Mirror Frakked', p. 21.

template, *Battlestar Galactica* attempts to 'white' out race.[117] In doing so, it animates criticisms of positive discrimination made by critical race theorists.[118] There are different races aboard *Galactica* – Boomer/Athena/Number Eight (Asian), Dee (African), and Gaeta (Hispanic) – but they are token representatives within a sea of Caucasians.[119] Race, it seems, does matter in this galaxy.[120] This is particularly so regarding Africans. Aside from Dee, the only other Africans are the marine who guards Roslin during her arrest and the representative from the planet Picon. These two are shown as the most religious of all the humans within a secular and rational society, channelling old prejudices of Africans as superstitious.[121]

When it comes to racial diversity, the skin job Cylons seem to be more progressive. The African Cylon, Simon/Number Four (Rick Worthy), was allowed to play a doctor (Galactica's chief medical officer, Doctor Cottle, is Caucasian). The sour note is that the Cylons have other types. The chrome toaster variety, the Centurions, are initially treated as disposable by the skin jobs.[122] The Cylon space fighter, the Raider – revealed as a sentient biomechanical being[123] – is explained by Boomer as she lovingly strokes it:

> It's not really a thing, you know. It's probably a Cylon itself. [Pause] More of an animal maybe than the human models. Maybe they genetically design it to perform a task. To be a fighter. Can't treat it like a thing and expect it to respond. You have to treat it like a pet.[124]

The Cylon Basestar, again a sentient biomechanical being personalised by a controlling hybrid – a human head and upper body in a fluid-filled bath – is not given the franchise by the skin jobs when it comes to political and military decisions. The Cylons, like the humans, seem to account for physical diversity through the imposition of hierarchy, with this tendency a cause of their civil war.[125]

This hierarchical ordering of difference within *Battlestar Galactica* returns, rendering problematic its treatment of gender.[126] Among the

117 Alessandria Hurd, 'The Monster Inside'; Huh, 'Race in Progress, No Passing Zone'.

118 Bell, 'Racial Realism'.

119 Although Edward James Olmos is well regarded as a Hispanic actor, his Adama presents as 'white' in *Battlestar Galactica*.

120 Nishime, 'Post-9/11 Global Migration in *Battlestar Galactica*'.

121 Deis, 'Erasing Difference', pp. 164–6.

122 Rymer, '*Battlestar Galactica* Mini-series', *Battlestar Galactica* (Number Six).

123 Mimica-Gezzan, 'You Can't Go Home Again', *Battlestar Galactica*.

124 Hardy, 'Act of Contrition', *Battlestar Galactica*.

125 Nankin, 'The Ties that Bind', *Battlestar Galactica*.

126 Wimmler, *Religious Science Fiction in* Battlestar Galactica *and* Caprica, p. 97.

skin job Cylons, there are three females: Boomer/Athena/Number Eight; Caprica Six/Shelly/Gina/Natalie/Number Six; and D'anna Biers/Number Three (Lucy Lawless). The problem originates in how the Number Eights and Number Sixes are consistently represented as sexual beings.[127] In the scenes depicting consensual sex, there is a misogynist undercurrent that the Cylon women are using intercourse as an instrument of manipulation.[128] This misogyny is rendered explicit in the episode 'Pegasus',[129] where Baltar, as *Galactica*'s Cylon expert, is sent to investigate *Pegasus*'s captured Cylon. He finds Gina/Number Six comatose, chained to the floor, having been interrogated by gang rape. Further, the chief perpetrator is interrupted while attempting to rape *Galactica*'s interned Boomer. The gender equality initially projected is negated by these scenes: women are reduced to biological beings located within a sexualised regime of violence, powerlessness, and vulnerability.[130]

This sexual violence of human towards Cylon is reciprocated. When Starbuck returns to Caprica, she is shot in a Cylon ambush. When she awakes, the Cylon Simon convinces her that she is in a resistance-run hospital.[131] She is then subjected to numerous undisclosed operations on her lower abdomen. In the episode 'The Farm', during her escape from the hospital, Starbuck finds in the other wards the familiar science fiction/horror image of the 'robot rape': rows of drugged women obscenely connected to various machines. The Cylons seem not to be content with their mass production of skin job Cylons, but need to 'fulfil God's command to multiply'[132] through mastering sexual reproduction. This has two effects. The first is that Starbuck is forcefully reallocated as female, as possessing a body intimately connected with reproduction.[133] The second is it redefines the series' survival theme. Adama, during *Galactica*'s decommission ceremony early in the mini-series, questions the worthiness of a people to survive:

> You know, when we fought the Cylons we did it to save ourselves from extinction. But we never answered the question, 'Why?' Why were we as a people worth saving? We still commit murder because of greed, spite, jealousy. And we still visit all of our sins upon our children. We refuse to accept

127 Pegues, 'Miss Cylon', p. 205; George, 'Fraking Machines', pp. 166–7.

128 See, for example, Nankin, 'Someone to Watch over Me', *Battlestar Galactica*; Kamir, *Every Breath You Take*, p. 41.

129 Rymer, 'Pegasus', *Battlestar Galactica*.

130 Sharp, 'Darwin's Soldiers', p. 218.

131 Hardy, 'The Farm', *Battlestar Galactica*.

132 Ibid. (Boomer/Number Eight).

133 Sharp, 'Starbuck as "American Amazon"', pp. 64–7.

> the responsibility for anything that we've done . . . Sooner or later, the day comes when you can't hide from the things that you've done any more.[134]

'The Farm' recasts Adama's introspection that, prior to any evaluation concerning survival, there is the more basic question of reproduction. What is presented is the claim that before culture and, with it, memory and justice, there is biology.

Reproduction becomes a recurring theme from Season 2 onwards.[135] Season 2 not only has the return of the biological in its depictions of sexual violence towards women, but has Roslin – contrary to her past as an advocate for women's rights – banning abortion on the grounds that all pregnancies must be carried to term to boost population numbers.[136] In Season 3, on New Caprica, Leoben keeps a captured Starbuck in an apartment, playing out a grotesque charade of happy family, complete with a young child named 'Kacey' – allegedly Starbuck's daughter, the product of violations of 'The Farms'.[137] For the Cylons, reproduction becomes increasingly more significant, with mortality coming mid-way through Season 4 with the destruction of their ability to 'resurrect'.[138] This leads to a false hope that Caprica Six's pregnancy may open the way for Cylon sexual reproduction.[139] When that does not eventuate, the promised return of resurrection technology from the 'Final Five' Cylons to the Cylon leader John Cavil/Number One (Dean Stockwell) halts the bloodshed during the *Galactica*'s assault on the Cylons' colony in the ultimate finale.[140] All this emphasis on reproduction prioritises the biological and in doing so sketches a world comprising of essence.

The capstone of this emphasis on essence is the birth of Athena's and Lieutenant Karl C. 'Helo' Agathon's (Tahmoh Penikett) child, the Human–Cylon hybrid, Hera.[141] However, the birth of a human-toaster destabilises the focus on reproduction. Hera points towards something more radical. In Seasons 3 and 4, Hera becomes an embodied symbol of reproductive security for both Cylons and humans, as she is alternatively kidnapped and rescued.[142] Rosi Braidotti has attempted to think through the dilemmas

134 Rymer, '*Battlestar Galactica* Mini-series', *Battlestar Galactica* (Adama).

135 Hellstrand, 'The Shape of Things to Come?'

136 Mimica-Gezzan, 'The Captain's Hand', *Battlestar Galactica.*

137 Mimica-Gezzan, 'Precipice', *Battlestar Galactica.*

138 Edwards, 'The Hub', *Battlestar Galactica.* See Leaver, '"Humanity's Children"', p. 137.

139 Moore, 'Disquiet Follows My Soul', *Battlestar Galactica*; Horder-Payton, 'No Exit', *Battlestar Galactica*; Young, 'Deadlock', *Battlestar Galactica.*

140 Rymer, 'Daybreak Part II', *Battlestar Galactica.*

141 Woolnough, 'Downloaded', *Battlestar Galactica.*

142 Alcalá, 'Exodus Part II', *Battlestar Galactica*; Rymer, 'Rapture', *Battlestar Galactica* (res-

in feminist theory offered by the binary alternatives of essence and anti-essences.[143] For her, feminism has remained at core anti-essential, believing in culture over nature, yet in doing so it has remained problematically engaged with essences.[144] This seems to be animated in *Battlestar Galactica*'s projected failure of post-feminism: images of equality and the freeing of the subject from gender and race are undermined by hard nature. In response, Braidotti draws inspiration from the recent discovery of transposition in the biological sciences, which has diminished DNA's status as the location for essentialism in revealing how organisms can influence DNA sequences.[145] Her motivation lies within the challenge of the technical for critical theory. She accepts that contemporary technology should properly be understood in the conflating of nature and culture, and she follows Bruno Latour's founding observation that the West's technologically mediated life is marked by the proliferation of 'hybrids', which are not capable of being consigned to either 'nature' or 'culture'.[146]

Within *Battlestar Galactica*, Hera – the combination of nature (biology) and culture (technology) – imagines this wider thematic. With her birth, the prioritising of essential biological nature by the emphasis on reproduction is undone. 'Tranpositing' the essence is the Cylon, the technological object. In *Battlestar Galactica,* essence – as well as also non-essence – appears to lose essentiality. This presents *Battlestar Galactica* as a text that focuses on the metaphysics of technology as opening an alternative between essence and anti-essence.

The Metaphysics of Technology

Battlestar Galactica rethinks the metaphysics of technology. Its blurring of what is natural and what is cultural can be read as the story of technology in the West. The place to begin is with the representations of technological relationships within the series.

Battlestar Galactica provides many images of the relationships between humans and machines. At a primary level, the series presents images of mundane technological objects. The visible technologies in *Battlestar Galactica* are recognisable as familiar, dated domestic instruments: Adama's and Roslin's 'cut

cued by Athena using resurrection technology); Nankin, 'Someone to Watch over Me', *Battlestar Galactica* (kidnapped by Boomer posing as Athena); Rymer, 'Daybreak Part II', *Battlestar Galactica* (rescued in the assault on the Cylon colony).

143 Braidotti, *Nomadic Subjects*, p. 177.

144 Ibid.

145 Braidotti, p. 6.

146 Ibid., pp. 37–8.

corners' paperwork and the corded telephones. This continues to the humans' spaceships as objects that are used, lived in, and junked. The *Galactica* and her ageing Vipers are analogous to old motor vehicles: simple, long-lasting designs, endearing in their mechanical quirks. These images of humans using domestic technology are complemented by more industrial iconography. The interior of the *Galactica*, with humans pushing Vipers, manhandling airlocks, and working on ships with manual tools, suggests a heavy industrial workplace. These multiple images combine to present the human society of *Battlestar Galactica* as a thoroughly technological one; technology is not external – the monster to be banished, the Cylon to be fought – but integral. Even at the level of keeping technology as things and humans as beings, *Battlestar Galactica* presents a technological society composed of human–machine interactions. The message seems to be that there is no nature aboard spaceships, just human life fundamentally involved with machines.

These images of technological society are interrupted, for *Battlestar Galactica* does not keep technology as things and humans as beings. The supposed external robotic enemy turns out to be very natural. Not only are the skin job Cylons flesh and blood, but the Cylon spaceships are sentient, organic beings. While the representations of technological society in *Battlestar Galactica* notice human–machine interaction, the Cylons present the intimacy of humanity and technology. This seems to be manifested in the relationship between Baltar and 'Inner Six'. Baltar begins the series haunted by Caprica Six, who sacrificed herself to save him in the nuclear destruction of Caprica.[147] Throughout the series, this Inner Six is often shown accompanying him, making cynical comments, telling him what to say and distracting him.[148] Up until the epiphany as to Inner Six's nature, the series is ambiguous about whether she is actually there, the personification of a link between Baltar and the Cylons, or whether she is a symptom of psychosis. The suggestion is that Baltar is infected by technology; his love of a 'machine' has internalised the machine. But the series also goes the other way. Resurrected in Season 2, Caprica Six is shown as possessing an 'Inner Baltar', who acts similar to Inner Six.[149] In this, the love of a human haunts the machine. However, it gets even more complicated when, by Season 4, Inner Baltar joins Inner Six in Baltar's increasingly crowded delirium.[150]

[147] Rymer, '*Battlestar Galactica* Mini-series', *Battlestar Galactica.*

[148] For example, Woolnough, 'The Hand of God', *Battlestar Galactica.* On speculation as to Inner Six and what her interactions with Baltar may mean for relations with technology, see George, 'Fraking Machines', p. 166.

[149] Beginning with Woolnough, 'Downloaded', *Battlestar Galactica.*

[150] Hemingway, 'Six of One', *Battlestar Galactica.* Causing the Baltar, played by Briton James

In other words, what is 'human' and what is 'technology' – already under pressure with the existence of Hera, and the skin job Cylons – becomes, like Baltar's delirium, increasingly confused as the series progresses.[151] Indeed, by Season 4, identification of human from Cylon or Cylon from human becomes near impossible. The rebel Cylons are incorporated into the human fleet. They are referred to as 'people'.[152] This blurring is epitomised in the very structure of the *Galactica*. By Season 4, the battered *Galactica* is falling apart. To save his terminal ship, Adama agrees that Cylon resin (a smelly biological gloop) be applied.[153] The outcome is that the ship changes from an industrial human-made robot destroyer to begin to show some of the sentience of the Cylon Basestars.[154]

Further, not only does the simple-ish human tool that is the *Galactica* take on a more complex technological hybridity, but discovery of the Final Five Cylons and their revelations about Earth complete the confusion. In 'Crossroads, Part II', after some build-up, four of the Final Five Cylons – XO Saul Tigh, Chief Galen Tyrol (Aaron Douglas), Sam Anders (Michael Trucco), and Tory Foster (Rekha Sharma) – are 'switched on' by a ghostly version of Bob Dylan's 'All Along the Watchtower'.[155] This is a confounding revelation. Tigh's alcoholism,[156] his fractious relationship with Ellen,[157] his relationship with Adama, and his blunt personae had all suggested that he was flawed, but very human. Similarly, Senior Petty Officer Tyrol, *Galactica*'s deck 'Chief' responsible for maintenance and repairs, had come across as paradigmatically human. The genuineness of Tyrol's life – from his caring leadership style[158] to his lack of emotional control, his marriage to Cally (Nicki Clyne) and the mundane pressures of their life together with a young child[159] – strongly contrasted with the calculated duplicity that characterised

Callis to exclaim 'oh my giddy aunt' – paraphrasing another science fiction character who sometimes appeared to himself, the Second Doctor (Patrick Troughton) from *Doctor Who*.

151 Rose, 'Cyborg Selves in Battlestar Galactica and Star Trek', p. 1,208.

152 Rose, 'Guess What's Coming to Dinner?', *Battlestar Galactica* (Adama).

153 Horder-Payton, 'No Exit', *Battlestar Galactica*.

154 Olmos, 'Islanded in a Stream of Stars', *Battlestar Galactica*; Rose, 'Cyborg Selves in *Battlestar Galactica* and *Star Trek*', p. 1,206.

155 Rymer, 'Crossroads Part II', *Battlestar Galactica*.

156 Tigh is introduced as drunk in the mini-series. Rymer, '*Battlestar Galactica* Mini-series', *Battlestar Galactica*.

157 Olmos, 'Tigh Me Up, Tigh Me Down', *Battlestar Galactica*; Kroeker, 'Resistance', *Battlestar Galactica*. Tigh poisons Ellen on New Caprica to silence her leaking of resistance intelligence to the Cylons: Alcalá, 'Exodus Part II', *Battlestar Galactica*.

158 As seen in Hardy, 'Litmus', *Battlestar Galactica*; Rymer 'Scattered', *Battlestar Galactica*; Rose, 'Dirty Hands', *Battlestar Galactica*.

159 Hardy, 'A Day in the Life', *Battlestar Galactica*.

the 'human' lives of Caprica Six and Boomer. A further irony was that Tigh, Tyrol, and Anders formed the leadership of the resistance on New Caprica, while Foster was shown as an active member.[160] Anders was also introduced as leader of the resistance movement on Caprica.[161] To have these characters – especially Tigh and Tyrol – revealed as Cylons means that demarcation between human and machine, between being and thing, becomes impossible.[162]

This conflating of human and technology can ultimately be discerned in the backstory of the Final Five and Earth. The finding of Earth in the mid-season finale of Season 4 was a profound disappointment.[163] A nuked wasteland, Earth turned out to be a settlement of Cylons. The mythology of a lost thirteenth tribe of humanity was not quite accurate. The destruction of the human origin world Kobol occurred because of a familiar robotic uprising, which also involved a familiar evolution of machines to organic humanoid models. It was these humanoid models that settled on Earth, eventually losing the knowledge to resurrect and – continuing the reproduction theme – acquiring natural procreation. After a thousand years, these natural Cylons are destroyed by their own 'lesser' machines. The survivors Tigh, Tyrol, Anders, Foster, and the last of the Final Five, Ellen Tigh, having re-engineered resurrection, are reborn on an orbiting ship, in which they rush to warn the humans.[164] Arriving at the Twelve Colonies, they halt the Cylon War through offering to help the first-generation Centurions with the development of humanoid Cylons.[165] In turn, they are 'boxed' by their first-born, John Cavil/Number One and then released over a thirty-year period into the Colonies with false memories in a Machiavel-like plot by Cavil to show the creators of the skin jobs the mistake of making machines in the image of humans.[166]

This clunky backstory of science fiction clichés allows explanations for many of the anomalies that accompanied *Battlestar Galactica*'s metaphysical turn in its later seasons.[167] Further, this myth of successive creation and usurpation, and of the indistinctiveness of humans and technology, in itself

[160] Alcalá, 'Exodus Part I', *Battlestar Galactica*.

[161] Kroeker, 'Resistance', *Battlestar Galactica*.

[162] Gumpert, 'Hybridity's End', pp. 144–6.

[163] Rymer, 'Revelations', *Battlestar Galactica*.

[164] Nankin, 'Sometimes a Great Notion'.

[165] Horder-Payton, 'No Exit', *Battlestar Galactica*; Wimmler, *Religious Science Fiction in* Battlestar Galactica *and* Caprica, p. 85.

[166] Horder-Payton, 'No Exit', *Battlestar Galactica*; Olmos, 'The Plan', *Battlestar Galactica*.

[167] For example, Tyrol's discovery of the 'Temple of the Five' on the algae planet – Rymer, 'The Eye of Jupiter', *Battlestar Galactica* – and Tigh's age and memories of fighting the First Cylon war: Horder-Payton, 'No Exit', *Battlestar Galactica*.

holds significance.[168] It suggests that the 'human' from the Frankenstein myth is not so pure. In *Battlestar Galactica,* the representations of technology move from the human (beings) using machines (things) to a disorientating conflating of being and thing. What can be seen in this movement is the animation of Martin Heidegger's influential account of technology as the end of Western metaphysics.

For Heidegger, technology did not just amount to machines, but was a fundamental way of revealing the world as is:

> The revealing that rules throughout modern technology has the character of a setting-upon, in the sense of a challenging-forth. That challenging happens in that the energy concealed in nature is unlocked, what is unlocked is transformed, what is transformed is stored up, what is stored up is, in turn, distributed and what is distributed is switched about ever anew.[169]

This led Heidegger to name the essence of technology 'Enframing':[170]

> Enframing means the gathering together of that setting-upon which sets upon man, i.e., challenges him forth, to revel the real, in the mode of ordering, as standing-reserve. Enframing means that way of revealing which holds sway in the essence of modern technology and which is nothing technological.[171]

This quote suggests three elements concerning the essence of technology. The first is that technology 'revel[s] the real' – that is, it occupies the very essence of humanity. For Heidegger, to be human means to be 'thrown' into the world, and human fate is to come to a dwelling in this finite totality.[172] Second, in their 'thrown-ness', humans are gifted with the responsibility towards truth: 'man is given to belong to the coming-to-pass of truth'.[173] Heidegger's use of truth was not to invoke correspondence,[174] but rather a pre-Socratic notion of 'truth' (*alētheia*) concerned with how the world is revealed. The destiny of humanity is in bringing forth what is undisclosed.[175] Third, Heidegger understood technology as a way of revealing, allowing him to situate technology within Being: 'Technology is a mode of revealing. Technology comes to

168 Malley, '"Does All This Have to Happen Again?"'
169 Heidegger, 'The Question Concerning Technology', p. 16.
170 Ibid., p. 19.
171 Ibid., p. 20.
172 Heidegger, *Being and Time,* pp. 127–9.
173 Heidegger, 'The Question Concerning Technology', p. 32.
174 Heidegger, 'The Age of World Picture', p. 127.
175 Heidegger, 'The Question Concerning Technology', p. 32.

presence in the realm where revealing and un-concealment take place, where *alētheia*, truth, happens.'[176]

Having located technology within Being, Heidegger sets out the ontological commitments of such a Being. Enframing involves 'setting upon'. Rather than letting beings reveal themselves to humanity, humanity imposes a technological 'truth' on to entities.[177] This truth is as a 'standing-reserve' in a stockpile, kept at hand ready to be deployed.[178] The fate of the world is it becomes atomised, abstracted, and commensurable.[179] There is a danger in this:

> As soon as the unconcealed no longer concerns man even as object, but does so, rather, exclusively as standing-reserve and man in the midst of the objectlessness is nothing but the orderer of the standing-reserve, then he comes to the very brink of a precipitous fall; that is, he comes to the point where he himself will have to be taken as standing-reserve.[180]

Heidegger seems to be capturing the conflating of human and technology in *Battlestar Galactica*. Heidegger does not place the essence of technology in a material thing – the hydroelectric plant on the Rhine,[181] a decrepit spaceship, or a shiny robot; rather, it occupies Being: 'Machine technology remains up to now the most visible out-growth of the essence of modern technology, which is identical with the essence of modern metaphysics.'[182] Technology *is* the way in which the 'unfolding' of Western metaphysics has led the West to conceive the world. While this extends to the way that humans see themselves, the ultimate concern is that technology in occupying this place within modern existence deprives Being from seeing the 'truth' of the world.[183] The universe becomes a realm of 'ends', of resources to be accumulated and used. This is what being human has become in the West. In *Battlestar Galactica*, the human leaders who resisted the integration of the Cylon rebels are executed.[184] Similarly with the Cylons, Cavil/Number One – with his continual desires to be more like a machine: 'I don't want to be human. I want to see gamma rays, I want to hear X-rays and I want to smell dark matter . . . but I'm

[176] Ibid., p. 13.
[177] Ibid., pp. 15–18.
[178] Ibid., p. 14.
[179] Ibid., p. 19.
[180] Ibid., pp. 26–7.
[181] Ibid., p. 16.
[182] Ibid.
[183] Ibid., p. 28.
[184] Rose, 'Blood on the Scales', *Battlestar Galactica.*

trapped in this absurd body'[185] – commits suicide as the remaining 'loyal' Cylons are sucked into a black hole.[186] The message seems to be that attempts to maintain the distinction between human and technology have no future. This appears to be the essential message of *Battlestar Galactica*: Being has been occupied by technology.

In technology studies, the claim of the occupation of Being by technology has had a decisive influence. Herbert Marcuse,[187] Jacques Ellul,[188] and, more recently, Albert Borgmann[189] and Francis Fukuyama,[190] can be seen as grounding their critiques of modern technology on metaphysical foundations. There is a tragic aura surrounding this tradition.[191] The absolute of technology and Heidegger's charting of the decline of a more authentic Being mean that it is difficult to theorise strategies for overcoming technology.[192] Indeed, there is a tendency to pastoral romance, as seen in the yearning for simpler 'human-scaled' technologies in Borgmann.[193] *Battlestar Galactica* appeared to also have purchased this way out of its confounding of human and technology. Having found 'New Earth', the inhabitants of the Fleet decide to abandon technology and begin life on the new planet in a state of primitive agrarianism.[194] The *Galactica* and the rest of the ships of the Fleet are sacrificed to this new start – sent to burn into the heart of the sun. However, the images of African plains that accompany Roslin's death give way to two other images. The first is the child Hera playing in the light; the second is a lurch of 150,000 years to the present day. In this scene, Inner Six and Inner Baltar – now to be understood as celestial beings – stroll the streets of broadcast present New York City. In their banter, it is confirmed that the busy humans of this technological metropolis, whose screens flash images of contemporary real-world robots, are the descendants of the human and Cylon settlers. This penultimate scene suggests that the pastoral solution to technology would only delay the inevitable cold flowering of Enframing.

This seems to explain both the persistence and implosion of the Frankenstein myth. It endures because of a tragic yearning for a time before

185 Horder-Payton, 'No Exit', *Battlestar Galactica.*

186 Rymer, 'Daybreak Part II', *Battlestar Galactica.*

187 Marcuse, *One Dimensional Man.* See Feenberg, *Heidegger and Marcuse,* p. 25.

188 Ellul, *The Technological Society.* See Feenberg, *Questioning Technology*, p. 3.

189 Borgmann, *Holding on to Reality.* See Verbeek, 'Devices of Engagement'.

190 Fukuyama, *Our Posthuman Future.* See Tabachnick, 'The Politics and Philosophy of Anti-Science'.

191 Hill, *The Tragedy of Technology.* See Tabachnick, 'Techne, Technology and Tragedy'.

192 Norris, 'Heideggerian Law beyond Law?', p. 344.

193 Borgmann, *Holding on to Reality*, pp. 223–4.

194 Rymer, 'Daybreak Part II', *Battlestar Galactica.*

humanity was menaced and compromised by the monster of modern technology. However, it also explains the implosion of the Frankenstein myth that was charted in Chapter 1. Within Heidegger's legacy of thinking about technology, the modern human has become totally technological in their engagement with the world. This is the occupation of Being by Enframing that Heidegger charts. It explains the implosion of the Frankenstein myth. There is no 'human', or 'law', separate from the totality that is technicity. The monster just does not rule supreme – Leto II from Dune; it is all there is.

Having arrived at this totality of technology, there does not seem, to quote the Cylons' favourite Dylan track, 'some kind of way out of here'.[195] The images of New York City resemble the images of doomed Caprica City from *Battlestar Galactica*'s opening montage.[196] Inner Caprica suggests that history may not repeat, offering simple epistemological ('When a complex system repeats itself something new is bound to happen') and theological ('It is also part of God's plan') justifications. A more satisfying 'way out' can be gleamed in Heidegger.

Heidegger's way out begins with the paradoxical step that the 'saving power' is to be found in thinking of the essence of technology itself.[197] For Heidegger, meditation on the essence of technology leads to remembering technology's ancient sibling. Referring to pre-Socratic Greece, he observes that once 'there was a time when the bringing-forth of the true into the beautiful was called *technē*. And the *poēisis* of the fine arts also was called *technē*.'[198] He suggests that 'revealing lays claim to the arts most primally, so that they for their part may expressly foster the growth of the saving power'.[199] Art, the uncorrupted twin to the monster, remains the glimmer of that more primal revealing to which Being is called.

Heidegger's affirmation of art is contested. Walter Benjamin suggests that in art technique rules and as such the technicality of art demarks 'humanity's entire mode of existence'.[200] Benjamin can be seen as pointing towards another direction from Heidegger: a turning away from metaphysics and also a turning away from attachment to an idealised past of authentic Being. This is what is suggested by Inner Six's and Inner Baltar's street-side revelation that the humans-that-are-us are Hera's descendants.[201] There are toasters on

195 Dylan, 'All Along the Watchtower'.
196 Rymer, 'Daybreak Part II', *Battlestar Galactica*.
197 Heidegger, 'The Question Concerning Technology', p. 28.
198 Ibid., p. 34.
199 Ibid., p. 35.
200 Benjamin, 'The Work of Art in the Age of Mechanical Reproduction', p. 222.
201 Rymer, 'Daybreak Part II', *Battlestar Galactica*.

our maternal line, which suggests that authentic Being is already technological. In this revelation, the art that Heidegger regarded as 'fine'[202] and his exemplar, a hand-wrought silver chalice,[203] along with the technologies that have called for law in Chapter 1 and the sovereign's plastic law from Chapter 2 exist in continuity. They, *Battlestar Galactica* suggests, are all *technē*, different manifestations of the same Being-in-the-world. It means an acceptance of technicity and the monster that humans in the West have become. It means love thy toaster; love thyself.

In *Battlestar Galactica*, Starbuck ends with being the Angel of Death;[204] having 'returned from the dead' in the Ionian Nebula,[205] she finds her rotting corpse in a crash site on old Earth.[206] Rather than Samael, the prophesied doom to which she leads the Fleet is the end of their journey with New Earth.[207] In Starbuck, the end marked a beginning – a possibility for Hera's children to escape the destructive cycle of human and technology that doomed Kobol, old Earth, and Caprica. What can be gleaned from reading Heidegger in *Battlestar Galactica*'s wake is 'technological Being-in-the world', the concern not with metaphysics and essences, but with life – and that means life with technology – in the here and now. This was why sustained talk of essences and essential nature was not possible within *Battlestar Galactica*. In animating the occupation of Being by technology, *Battlestar Galactica* shows many falls, but not Heidegger's fear of a primal 'precipitous fall'.[208] Instead, it is an invitation to move from the watchtower guarding essence and to join company with 'the joker and the thief'.[209] In technology studies, this post-Heideggerian strand can be identified in the work of Donna Haraway.[210]

Haraway expressly rejects metaphysical approaches to thinking about technology, with their tragic aura.[211] For Haraway, such sentimentalism distracts from clear appreciation of the technological present. Her account is distinctly materialist. She is concerned with what it means to live at the particular moment when technology has undermined the past certainties of existence.[212] Her project is orientated towards the search for political

[202] Heidegger, 'The Question Concerning Technology', p. 35.

[203] Ibid., pp. 6–8.

[204] As heralded by the hybrid in Alcalá, 'Razor', *Battlestar Galactica.*

[205] Rymer, 'Crossroads Part II', *Battlestar Galactica.*

[206] Nankin, 'Sometimes a Great Notion', *Battlestar Galactica.*

[207] Rymer, 'Daybreak Part II', *Battlestar Galactica.*

[208] Heidegger, 'The Question Concerning Technology', p. 27.

[209] Dylan, 'All Along the Watchtower'.

[210] Braidotti, *Transpositions,* p. 57.

[211] Haraway, 'A Manifesto for Cyborgs', p. 71.

[212] Haraway, *Modest_Witness@Second_Millennium,* p. 51.

engagement in a world where it must be accepted that technology has destabilised old binaries – male/female, nature/culture – that orientated past political action.[213] In short, '[t]he cyborg is our ontology'.[214] In this, Haraway can be seen to reiterate Heidegger's declaration of the occupation of Being by technology. Haraway's polemics of cyborgs can be distracting, conjuring 1980s imagery of obvious prosthetic augmentation rather than the intimate and invisible location of technology that was her focus.[215] Unlike Heidegger, Haraway does not talk of the saving power of art, but affirms active engagement with the contemporary 'informatics of domination'.[216]

Braidotti, in recognising the influences of Michel Foucault and Gilles Deleuze in Haraway's cyborg, has argued for the 'embodied, materialist foundations of the subject in a non-essentialist yet accountable manner'.[217] In doing so, Braidotti affirms that this approach takes as its orientation Heidegger's recognition that the horizon of humanity rests in being thrown into the world, yet it avoids his metaphysics.[218]

Haraway's call for 'taking responsibility for social relations of science and technology . . . means embracing the skilful task of reconstructing the boundaries of daily life'[219] is the lasting message of *Battlestar Galactica*. In moving from a 'demonology of technology',[220] to use Haraway's phrase, to the revelation of the occupation of Being by technology, *Battlestar Galactica* returns both to life and responsibility. The redemption of Gaius Baltar is instructive. Baltar, the very human scientist and opportunist – the personification of *technē*, the user of techniques to organise the world around him to his will – has a charmed existence through the series. He is often threatened with exposure as a traitor, or death, but luck – or, as Inner Six regularly intones, 'God's plan' – intervenes to save him. However, in Season 4, while taking on the mantle of monotheistic prophet,[221] Baltar begins to feel responsible, culminating in his 'one selfless act' of choosing to stay on *Galactica* and participate in the assault on the Cylon Colony to rescue Hera.[222] In this, the other major characters reflect this responsibility to life in the wake of the technological collapse of metaphysics. Roslin, Adama, Apollo, and Starbuck,

213 Haraway, 'A Manifesto for Cyborgs', p. 100; Braidotti, *Nomadic Subjects*, pp. 104–5.
214 Haraway, 'A Manifesto for Cyborgs', p. 65.
215 Ibid., p. 70.
216 Ibid., p. 79.
217 Braidotti, *Transpositions*, p. 137.
218 Ibid., p. 142.
219 Haraway, 'A Manifesto for Cyborgs', p. 100.
220 Ibid.
221 Rymer, 'He that Believeth in Me', *Battlestar Galactica.*
222 Rymer, 'Daybreak Part II', *Battlestar Galactica.*

flawed humans with different orientations, share with the redeemed Baltar high technical skills – Roslin, Adama, Apollo, and Starbuck are all skilled leaders and tacticians – but this *technē* is accompanied by a responsibility to life, a life precariously represented by the declining survivor count. Their worlds have ended, the divisions between friend and enemy, nature and culture, human and machine are evaporating, yet for Roslin, Adama, Apollo, Starbuck, and the people of the Fleet, life continues. Politics remains, hardship remains, personal failings remain, guilt from the past remains, and grief over loss remains. But also love happens, faith is found, loyalty is affirmed, and heroism, bravery, and sacrifice occur. In *Battlestar Galactica* life endures after the end. It may be a difficult life where there can be 'great human satisfaction, as well as a matrix of complex dominations',[223] but it is a life that possesses the possibility to be responsible for becoming.

This is what technological Being-in-the-world means. It discloses a world in flux, a world that is always 'becoming'. Technicity is continually making the world anew. Old patterns and networks are reorganised and reprogrammed. New connections, institutions, and relationships form, while others change, decay, or implode. Life in its material generative sense – Braidotti uses the term *zoe* to capture this[224] – unfolds. This is not a return to some naturalistic fantasy of a primal and possibly, sovereign nature; rather, it acknowledges the freedom of our monstrous selves, selves that are non-unitary, changing, and decentred, in the world that our unavoidable doing-in, our inherent technical engagement, makes. Creation is always in play.[225]

This ever-present agency of creation that is technological Being-in-the-world can clearly be seen in *Battlestar Galactica.* Haraway would 'rather be a cyborg than a goddess';[226] however, she has no such qualms with the trickster.[227] The trickster, the destroyer, and the creator is Baltar in *Battlestar Galactica.* His comic role, the surrounding Christological iconography and also his hyper heterosexuality all suggest the trickster, but more significantly, Baltar spends the series creating. While Roslin and Adama preserve, Apollo communicates and Starbuck guides, Baltar makes. He was the 'traitor' who facilitated the Cylon destruction of the Twelve Colonies, unwittingly making the Fleet.[228] He builds the Cylon detector; he attempts to raise a civilisation on New Caprica; he ferments tensions within the Cylons that eventually lead

223 Haraway, 'A Manifesto for Cyborgs', p. 100.
224 Braidotti, *Transpositions*, p. 37.
225 Ibid., p. 178.
226 Haraway, 'A Manifesto for Cyborgs', p. 101.
227 Haraway, *Modest_Witness@Second_Millennium*, p. 127.
228 Rymer, '*Battlestar Galactica* Mini-series', *Battlestar Galactica.*

to the civil war; and, with his cult, he builds hope and a civil society in the Fleet.[229] In every situation and role – as scientific adviser to the president, stranded on Kobol, as president of the colonies in occupation, prisoner of the Cylons, and cult leader – Baltar as the trickster causes change. It is Baltar who, on New Earth, confirms that the observed higher bipedal mammals are genetically human and who promises to bring farming to the planet; his *technē* fathers both the future race that 'inherits the Earth' and the Neolithic jump to agriculture.[230] In this, Baltar is shown to be not just a minor trickster character, but to occupy a fundamental role in the escape from metaphysics to *zoe* and becoming. This reading becomes affirmed in the penultimate scene when Inner Baltar suggests that the God of the *Battlestar Galactica* universe 'doesn't like that name' and a stare from Inner Six provokes him to utter the final lines of the series, the cryptic, and seemingly self-referral, 'Silly me. Silly, silly me.'[231]

This screens Braidotti's calls for 'new cosmologies . . . that are appropriate to our own high level of technological development'.[232] It explains the place of myth in *Battlestar Galactica*. Unlike *Dune*, *Battlestar Galactica* is not cynical about myth; Roslin believes her prophecies, just as the skin job Cylons, with the exception of Cavil/Number One, earnestly believe in God, while Inner Six, Inner Baltar, and Season 4 Starbuck are ultimately revealed as mythic beings. While demonstrating how technology collapses Western metaphysics, *Battlestar Galactica* valorises myth. The myth of Earth – initially a cynical ploy by Adama to galvanise a distraught humanity[233] – becomes real. While old Earth disappointed, the Fleet does find a future on New Earth. In this, *Battlestar Galactica* suggests that to be responsible for becoming requires myth. It requires stories to make sense of the becoming of the world and to give meaning, quests, and purpose to technological Being-in-the-world. Creators, it seems, need a plan.

This need for myth to inform responsibility for becoming is reflected in Braidotti's call for a 'nomadic post-secular spirituality . . . beyond metaphysical life-insurance policies [that] enjoys gratuitous acts of kindness in the mode of a becoming-world of the subject'.[234] A similar anti-metaphysical grounding of the inescapability of technology leading to the possibility of being respon-

229 Young, 'Deadlock', *Battlestar Galactica.*

230 Rymer, 'Daybreak Part II', *Battlestar Galactica.*

231 Ibid.

232 Braidotti, *Transpositions,* p. 272.

233 Rymer, '*Battlestar Galactica* Mini-series', *Battlestar Galactica.* See Silverman, 'Adama's True Lie', p. 200.

234 Braidotti, *Transpositions*, pp. 258–9.

sible to becoming can be seen in Agamben's *State of the Exception* (2005). Agamben exposes the fundamental function of the exception within the Western 'juridico-political machine' as 'instituting a threshold of undecidability between anomie and *nomos*, between life and law, between *auctoritas* and *potestas*'.[235] Agamben suggests that once the exception is properly located, it can be realised:

> There are not first life as a natural biological given and anomie as the state of nature and then their implication in law through the state of exception. On the contrary, the very possibility of distinguishing life and law, anomie and *nomos,* coincides with their articulation in the biopolitical machine.[236]

Agamben presents an anti-metaphysical realm where the biopolitical machine determines becoming. His conclusion is similar to that of Braidotti: comprehending the material basis of exception opens the hopeful possibility of 'deactivation of the device that, in the state of exception, tied [law] to life'[237] and would 'open a space for human activity'.[238]

Notwithstanding their differences,[239] Braidotti and Agamben share Haraway's orientation that technological Being-in-the world is an opportunity for responsible becoming. Further, in its paralleling of this movement, *Battlestar Galactica* highlights something that was also clear in Braidotti's spiritualism and Agamben's hope: the necessity for myths, in order to give meaning to living. But where does this leave technical legality? It leaves it in search of earths that it can call home.

What *Battlestar Galactica* shows is that the Frankenstein myth's ignorance of technological Being-in-the-world means that its ontological grounding on being and thing leads to the irreducibility of being and thing. Instead of an essential humanity facing a non-essential technology, it seems that all that remains is technology. In *Battlestar Galactica*, decision gives way to the subject and the subject gives way to the technical – and this seems to be Heidegger's doom for the West: the occupation of Being by Enframing. However, *Battlestar Galactica* goes beyond Heidegger, showing that technological Being-in-the-world actually provides for responsibility for becoming.

235 Agamben, *State of Exception*, p. 86.

236 Ibid., p. 87. Italics in original.

237 Ibid., p. 88.

238 Ibid.

239 For Braidotti, Agamben's translation of *zoe* as bare life that can only be killed limits his contribution. Braidotti identifies that Agamben defers to the 'Heideggerian legacy that places mortality at the centre of philosophic investigation', and this closes his analysis to a vitalistic account of *zoe* that could ground a nomadic ethics. Braidotti, *Transpositions*, pp. 247, 39.

Haraway's cyborg lives precisely because of concerns regarding the end of humanity, just as the colonial society continues to live notwithstanding the nuclear destruction of the colonies. Further, this responsibility for becoming needs myth. Braidotti's and Agamben's stories end with spirit and hope, just as *Battlestar Galactica* ends with two 'angels' in lounge lizard attire on the streets of New York City.

That myth made real – albeit a tacky myth that doesn't like the name 'God' – is the final image of *Battlestar Galactica* also suggests the end, or doom, of law and technology. In Chapter 1, it was shown that law's engagement with technology was grounded on science fiction, both in its imagining of technological futures and also in its fundamental articulation of the Frankenstein myth. Law and technology, it turned out, was fundamentally a myth-soaked discourse. This can be seen as expected. If Being in the West has been given over to technology – or, indeed, was always technological – and this is not a disclosure to death, but responsibility for becoming, then the dwelling place of this saving is myth. Heidegger's saving power of art turns out to be perceptive. It is from poet Friedrich Hölderlin that Heidegger draws the inspirational quote concerning danger and the saving power.[240] And it is the poetry of art that is, for Heidegger, 'the setting-itself-into-work of truth'.[241] For Heidegger, earth 'is that which comes forth and shelters';[242] it can, then, be said that *alētheia* and *technē* find their earth in myth.

For technical legality, this means an acknowledgement of its essential mythic task. It needs to tell more stories about law and technology to reach for *alētheia* in comprehending technological Being-in-the-world and responsibility for becoming. It is a task that it already does. However, the ready-at-hand for these journeys needs to come out into the open. Science fiction is already present and has been presenting within this serious task. The task-to-come is a celebratory working through of what responsibility for becoming may mean for embodied locations within the networks of the West. This is what this book now journeys towards in examining responsibility for becoming of the technical legal subject, the lawyer, and the legal scholar. In this, science fiction moves from critique of law as technology to the raw mythic material through which responsibility for becoming can be narrated.

240 Heidegger, 'The Question Concerning Technology', p. 34.
241 Heidegger, 'The Origins of the Work of Art', p. 197.
242 Ibid., p. 171.

Part II

Living in Technical Legality

4

Xenogenesis and the Technical Legal Subject

The last chapter left some disturbing traces, and not just Baltar as trickster walking New York City. Humanity was left seeking a new, non-technological life on Earth with the great Battlestar *Galactica* condemned to a solar execution, yet the humans-that-are-us descend not from the Adama's and Roslin's pure humans, but rather from union with the Cylons. This replayed the message of *Battlestar Galactica*, the disintegration of the categories 'human' and 'technology' in seemingly an animation of Heidegger's account of the demise of Being into technicity. In this, the Frankenstein myth – so central to law's engagement with technology – is imploded. In Chapter 2, through Dune, modern law was shown as technological in its orientation on death and time, and Chapter 3 showed that the category 'human' was also compromised – indeed, riddled with technicity. This could reveal the feared grey goo scenario that informs thinking about nanotechnologies. As all categories are compromised by technology, technicity could be seen as absolute – a total technological world, undifferentiated, valueless, and devoid of meaning, hope, and what used to be known and cherished as human life.

But possibly the most profound disturbing trace was the emerging argument that this is not an end, nor is it a situation without hope. Following Haraway, what was suggested, and what *Battlestar Galactica* showed, was that life remains. It may be a non-essentialist form of life, a life without metaphysical guarantees, but it is still a life that remains within a world that is not grey, but rather a kaleidoscope of networks – relationships, discourses, structures, and bodies – that continually become. It was also argued that this ever-present agency of creation that is technological Being-in-the-world seeks myths to inspire, inform, and guide the making of the world. This leads to another disturbing trace. In *Battlestar Galactica*, the Cylons had a plan – at least in the first two seasons – and that plan was the extermination of humanity. Responsibility for becoming is an affirmation of activity and the need for mythic input amounts to a precondition. Schmitt found certain myths that he thought could liberate the polity from liberalism's failure to identify enemies, which became embodied by Nazism, but like the Cylons' plan, the making of world that accompanied this myth is abhorrent. This trace leads to an absolute concern, and a well-rehearsed one, in the context of recognising the totality of technicity. To argue that the reality of technology in the West has moved beyond the received metaphysics is a move beyond good and evil. In the undifferentiated, pure technicity of the world, there are no rules or measures for 'good' myths against 'bad' myths. The fear is that while there is agency, there are no limits to how the world can be made through this agency. The Cylon and Nazi terrors could be seen as indistinguishable to the work of humanitarians, saints, and kind and loving parents.

This chapter addresses the charge of nihilism directed to technological Being-in-the-world. It does so through looking at responsibility for becoming from the location of the entity known as the legal subject. The legal subject is revealed as a node within networks that constrain and empower. The primary text through which this revealing occurs is Octavia E. Butler's celebrated *Xenogenesis* trilogy, also known as *Lilith's Brood*.[1] These novels, *Dawn* (1987)[2], *Adulthood Rites* (1988),[3] and *Imago* (1989)[4] present a thoroughly technologised world of natureculture where both the individual and their doing in the world are curtailed, yet liberated, by multiple networks. Butler's protagonists emphasise 'embodiment' and 'location' in the 'navigation' of the networks of the present. In this, an ethics can be discerned. To be responsible for becoming involves a commitment to affect. In this, Butler can be seen as giving monstrous human-alien flesh to Braidotti's nomadic account of posthumanism.[5] Butler shows not nihilism, but rather the possibility of being responsible for becoming.

This argument is pursued in three stages. The first stage overviews Butler's *Xenogenesis* trilogy, noting the absence of orthodox law signifiers throughout, and emphasises a 'post-juridical' world of natureculture where biopower reigns. The second stage draws upon this reality to manufacture an account of the legal subject of technical legality, a non-essential subject that is a node in flux within multiple networks. This subject occupies an embodied location that is at once predetermined but also navigable. This opens to the third stage, which charts how the possible creating of the world and the identified need for myths of creation disclose an ethics of affect, a responsibility to nurture *zoe* as the becoming of the world.

1 Canavan, 'The Octavia E. Butler Papers', p. 43.

2 Butler, *Dawn*.

3 Butler, *Adulthood Rites*.

4 Butler, *Imago*.

5 Braidotti, *Transpositions*, pp. 32–3.

Biopower and Natureculture on an Alien Rehabilitated Earth

The *Xenogenesis* trilogy's meta-text meshes, to a degree, with that of *Battlestar Galactica*. Both are set in the aftermath of a nuclear holocaust and have a reoccurring theme of hybridity. There are also mile-long spaceships, although Butler's operating genre is neither space opera nor the dystopian tradition.[6] These tropes play in the background. Yet her story of the terrors and compromises, of 'alien invasion', and of a demise of free will within structures of total control, are more confronting than H. G. Wells' *The War of the Worlds* (1897)[7] or George Orwell's *Nineteen Eighty-Four* (1949).[8] Butler's narrative is the story of a woman of colour and that of her hybrid offspring. It is not a story of the disembodied, unnamed male observer from *The War of the Worlds*, or of Winston Smith's mid-life gestures to youthful rebellion in *Nineteen Eighty-Four*. *Xenogenesis* is a myth of living with, enduring, and negotiating the becoming-of-the-world.

Butler's work has generated a considerable dedicated scholarly opus.[9] Butler's twining together of themes from the African diaspora with strong, complex lead female characters,[10] along with clever twists on established science fiction tropes and narratives, places her in leading positions within Afrofuturism and also feminist science fiction.[11] Furthermore, Donna Haraway specifically anointed Butler as the preeminent storyteller of 'cyborg' origins[12] and returned to Butler and *Xenogenesis* specifically, across several of her iconic works. Following Haraway's approval, a central theme within the secondary literature has been whether Butler's work is actually progressive, 'postmodern', and/or feminist.[13] The dividing line has been whether Butler reinforces and enacts, or critiques and transcends, essentialist, sociobiological accounts of humanity.[14] The foundation for this debate, especially in relation

6 While many commentators see dystopian elements in Butler's work, there is a substantial literature suggesting that these are put to utopian ends. See Stillman, 'Dystopian Critiques'; Miller, 'Post-Apocalyptic Hoping'; Belk, 'The Certainty of the Flesh'.

7 Wells, *The War of the Worlds.*

8 Orwell, *Nineteen Eighty-Four.*

9 See Vint, *Bodies of Tomorrow*, p. 58; Mehaffy and Keating, '"Radio Imagination"', p. 45.

10 Salvaggio, 'Octavia Butler and the Black Science Fiction Heroine'.

11 Raffel, 'Genre to the Rear, Race and Gender to the Fore', p. 455; Scott, 'Octavia Butler and the Base for American Socialism', p. 107.

12 Haraway, 'A Manifesto for Cyborgs', pp. 92–7.

13 Tucker, '"The Human Contradiction"', pp. 165–8.

14 See Zaki, 'Utopia, Dystopia and Ideology in the Science Fiction of Octavia Butler'; Peppers, 'Dialogic Origins and Alien Identites in Butler's *Xenogenesis*'; Jesser, 'Blood, Genes and Gender'; Miller, 'Post-Apocalyptic Hoping'.

to *Xenogenesis*, is the dominant trope of the gene that runs through the trilogy. This trope grounds the overarching narrative that connects the three books: viral reproduction. What Xenogenesis tells is a story of reproduction by incursion and change.

The first book in the trilogy, *Dawn*, opens with Lilith Iyapo awakening, again, in a grey-white cubicle, one of a limited number of human survivors from a nuclear war and winter more than 250 years earlier. She has been in suspended animation, awoken for questions or experiments, and has now been given the gift of clothes to dress herself to meet her captors.[15] So attired, she meets Jdahya, a male Oankali, vaguely humanoid but covered in medusa-like sensory tentacles.[16] The first half of the book has Lilith discovering more about the alien Oankali: From their massive, living-organic ship *Chkahichdahk* to the tripartite sexes (female, male, and ooloi) and their purpose in saving humanity and restoring a nuclear ravaged Earth for 'trade'.[17] The Oankali are 'gene traders': they trade genetic information.[18] Their social structure is dedicated to trade, with three classes of Oankali destined to split through the trade with humanity and Earth: the 'Akjai' to remain apart from the trade and to continue in their pre-trade form; the 'Toaht' to genetically intermingle with humanity but continue aboard *Chkahichdahk*; and 'Dinso', who are to settle with humans and Earth and merge more fully with the terrestrial biosphere.[19] This narrative occurs mostly through Lilith becoming partnered (in more ways than she realised) with Jdahya's juvenile ooloi child Nikanj. Throughout this, the Oankali remain domestically alien. Lilith is accepted into Jdahya's Dinso family and the kin relationships that tie it to other Oankali groups, but also remains the outsider; her role is to return to Earth – indeed, to lead the terrestrial repatriation and participate in the birthing of the Oankali–human hybrid species.[20] The second half of the book sees Lilith strategically cooperating with the Oankali in the awakening of the first batch of humans to be trained how to survive on the newly 'naturalised', purged of pre-war human civilisation, Earth.[21] Yet, even while holding visions that once on Earth she and her human charges could escape, over the second half of the book Lilith becomes further bonded, emotionally and sexually, into the now mature Nikanj's family group. *Dawn* ends

[15] Butler, *Dawn*, pp. 3–9.
[16] Ibid., pp. 9–18.
[17] Ibid., pp. 18–111.
[18] Ibid., pp. 39–41.
[19] Ibid., pp. 33–4.
[20] Ibid., pp. 33–42.
[21] Ibid., pp. 115–248.

with the trainee humans, and especially the alpha males, violently rebelling against the Oankali in a confrontation that sees Lilith's human lover (Joseph) killed, Lilith choosing to 'nurse' a wounded Nikanj, and Nikanj – without permission – implanting in Lilith the first human–Oankali hybrid 'construct' foetus.[22]

A fundamental feature of the trilogy, introduced in *Dawn* and reiterated through the other novels, is a dark assessment of humanity. The Oankali discern in humanity what they call the 'Human Contradiction'; at the most fundamental genetic level, humans have evolved through 'hierarchy' – that is, through competition, inequity, and violence.[23] The destructive behaviour of the humans – both the pre-contact nuclear war and the post-contact violence – is explained by the Oankali as genetically inevitable. However, also deep in the human genome is intelligence. Indeed, humans are considered the most intelligent species that the Oankali have colonised. This combination of hierarchy and intelligence makes humans 'dangerous', yet also highly complex and 'seductive' to the Oankali.[24]

The following two books shift the focus to two of Lilith's hybrid children. The second book, *Adulthood Rites*, concerns Lilith's first male child, Akin. Like all of Lilith's children, Akin has been engineered by Nikanj from genetic material from Lilith, its two Oankali mates (Dichaan and Ahajas), and Joseph, who has been dead for thirty years. In his juvenile stage, which lasts for most of the narrative, Akin looks human although he shares with Herbert's Atreides children adult sensibilities within an infant body. Akin is a bridge, allowing Butler to explore the social differences within resettled Earth, between the fertile blooming of Lilith's Human–Oankali 'trader' settlement of Lo, the sterile, Hobbesian context of the human-only resister villages and the alien collective of *Chkahichdahk*. Mirroring *Dawn*, the first half of the book has a kidnapped Akin learning about the resister's barely civilised society in the optimistically named settlement of Phoenix, while being care for by some of the humans from Lilith's first training group.[25] The second half has a nearly mature Akin venturing to *Chkahichdahk* to make the case to the Oankali that the human resisters should be made fertile and allowed to permanently settle on a terra-formed Mars. This mission accompanies a growing recognition of what was a trace in the first book, that the Earth-as-is would be utterly destroyed in the coming century when settlements like Lo mature into new *Chkahichdahks*, enclosing their

[22] Ibid., pp. 223–46.

[23] Butler, *Adulthood Rites*, p. 16.

[24] Butler, *Imago*, p. 10.

[25] Butler, *Adulthood Rites*, p. 98.

Oankali–human hybrids, and spirit them always to the stars to find other life with which to trade.[26]

The third book, *Imago*, concerns Lilith's child Jodahs. Like *God Emperor of Dune*, this book is the most challenging, in that Jodahs' story of metamorphosis into the first-construct ooloi, like Leto II's tale, is quite alien, although mitigated through being the only book narrated in the first person. Jodahs' preoccupations, loves, drives, and supernatural mastery of life-materials seems one step removed from Lilith's compromises or Akin's empathy. Yet his human desire for independence, his running from the Oankali consensus that he was dangerous and needed to be exiled to *Chkahichdahk* and his essential need for mates invoke sympathy. This book finishes the saga through a heightening of tensions present in the earlier novels. Set some seventy years after Akin and *Adulthood Rite*, the central premise of *Imago* is the discovery of a resister village in which a crippled and degenerative form of human reproduction endures. Like Paul Atreides, who short-circuited the Bene Gesserits' plans, Jodahs represents the sooner-than-planned arrival of the sexually mature new hybrid species.[27] The pure hunger of Jodahs and his sibling Aaor to taste, record, change, and mate with humans animates the primal motivation of the Oankali to trade that was explained more abstractly in Lilith's and Akin's narratives.

Whereas the bloody battles over Hera in *Battlestar Galactica* affirmed heterosexual reproduction against mechanistic copying, *Xenogenesis* suggests viral reproduction. Sex with an ooloi, with its two profanely suggestive engorged trunk-like sensory organs,[28] mimics the virus. Bits of genes are spliced together in the ooloi's 'yashi', the defining Oankali organ that can store, process, and manipulate genetic material. The Oankali appear viral. At the individual level of ooloi manipulating and at the macro-level of Oankali civilisation, what can be seen is reproduction though colonisation. The Oankali need a vital living entity (Lilith, humanity, Earth) into which their code is injected, taking over that entity's autonomous reproduction, to produce more Oankali. The new species that emerges fully with Jodahs' metamorphosis takes its essential characteristics from the Oankali. It is Oankali-next, not human-next. This new species has three sexes, which possess the Oankali organelle and yashi and the concluding image of *Xenogenesis* is Jodahs' drawing into his yashi to nurture a *Chkahichdahk* seed that will feed upon Earth, grow, and eventually envelope these new Oankali for a future trade quest.

Therefore, like Butler's wider oeuvre, the viral places at the forefront

[26] Ibid., p. 229.
[27] Butler, *Imago*, p. 217.
[28] Butler, *Dawn*, p. 47.

of *Xenogenesis* themes of colonialism and miscegenation.[29] The figure that returns repeatedly in her texts is the Other. Indeed, with these themes and her surname, it is highly tempting to place Octavia E. Butler's work in relation to Judith Butler's. In *Xenogenesis,* the Oankali and humans, within a field entirely to the Oankali's advantage, circulate as Others. They remain to one another as Others to be feared, desired, resisted – markers of an ethical gulf that should, but cannot, be traversed.[30] Oankali remain beyond human knowing. Demanding to share Nikanj's reactions to Joseph's death, to do a true trade rather than the usual ooloi one-way sharing of human emotions, Nikanj grants to Lilith:

> a new color. A totally alien, unique, nameless thing, half seen, half felt or . . .
> tasted. A blaze of something frightening, yet overwhelmingly, compelling.
> Extinguished.
> A half known mystery beautiful and complex. A deep impossibly sensuous
> promise.[31]

While Oankali remain beyond human comprehension, humans remain dangerously unpredictable to the Oankali. Nikanj observes that Joseph's death was 'totally unplanned',[32] and so was Paul Titus' attempted rape of Lilith.[33] In this context of confronting the Other, the 'solution' of interbreeding – the recourse of colonisers all over the universe[34] – is, as it always has been, a perversion of the ethical imperative. The Oankali take to aid in their evolution. The complex diversity and vitality of Earth will be consumed, while the resister humans are relocated to the reserve of Mars where the Oankali 'know in their bones' that the Human Contradiction will eventually succeed in species-cide.[35]

This Otherness and the negation of the ethical by pure biopower – a power over life[36] rendered explicit in the text by the ooloi – positions *Xenogenesis* as seemingly a non-legal text. Its stories of self and other within a total colonialist context are, in the first instance, beyond the orthodox law

[29] Holden, 'The High Costs of Cyborg Survival', p. 51; Morris, 'Octavia Butler's (R)evolutionary Movement for the Twenty-First Century'.

[30] Butler, *Gender Trouble*, p. 144.

[31] Butler, *Dawn*, p. 225.

[32] Ibid., p. 224.

[33] Ibid., pp. 95–6.

[34] Wolfe, 'Nation and MiscegeNation'.

[35] Butler, *Imago*, p. 11.

[36] Foucault, *The History of Sexuality*, p. 143. I accept that biopolitics is an enigmatic phrase in contemporary theorising; nevertheless, this simple definition is relatively uncontroversial. Esposito, *Bios*, pp. 13–44.

signifiers of law and literature. Even further removed than Dune or *Battlestar Galactica* – which both had some accounts of law, legal interpretation, courts, judgment, and, in *Battlestar Galactica*'s case, a lawyer – there are no representations of Oankali or human law or legal institutions in these familiar senses. 'Not law. Consensus' is how Lilith describes Oankali normative practices.[37]

There is, across the three books, conflict and resolution that could travel under the name of justice. The Oankali respond to uncooperative or violent human behaviour with techniques of life. Disrupters are gassed, their moods biochemically modified, their bodies warehoused in suspended animation, their brains and genes reprogrammed.[38] This is done without consent; it is seen as necessary.[39] Even preferred humans, like Lilith, are interfered with – cancers are removed, immunity enhanced, lifespan extended, foetuses implanted – as beings that have no autonomy of self:[40] 'She did not own herself any longer. Even her flesh could be cut and stitched without her consent or knowledge.'[41] The colonial power manages its livestock.[42] Its justice ensures resources for Oankali manifest destiny.

The resister humans, in their quasi-state of nature, manifest a justice of a different kind. Theirs is the justice of retribution. Violence begets violence. Akin's kidnappers are butchered, conflict within Phoenix is met with aggression and the burning down of houses and the mountain village of degenerative humans is armed and trigger happy. Within this village, lorded over by a cohort of sterile, long-life Oankali tamped with humans from *Chkahichdahk*, a deformed version of the Oankali's biopower reigns. The malformed, fertile, short-lived humans are compelled to breed and breed in a frantic attempt to re-establish the human species.

However, the absence of orthodox law signifiers is precisely what makes *Xenogenesis* a text of technical legality par excellence. Law in the formal guises has been subsumed by biopower. This was the narrative of modern law as explained in Dune where the legal, emerging from the alchemy of death and time, establishes the absolute authority of law, not in metaphysical, ethical or transcendent realms, but in the base world of power over bodies in time. Modern law emerged from the potential to extinguish human life. *Xenogenesis* is a text about the post-juridical management of populations, to adopt Michel

37 Butler, *Imago*, p. 19.
38 Butler, *Dawn*, pp. 182, 192–4.
39 Riley, '"Your Body Has Made a Different Choice"'.
40 Butler, *Dawn*, p. 245.
41 Ibid., p. 5.
42 Stone, 'Biopower and Modern Genocide', p. 167.

Foucault's sense from his 'Governmentality' lecture.[43] As such, it enacts the experience of modern law, of law as a species within the biopower arsenal. While Dune highlighted this reality of modern law at a conceptual level and *Battlestar Galactica* located it within the totality of technology, *Xenogenesis*'s register is specifically the everyday, the living within a world that is completely constructed by techniques of – or, more precisely, over – life.

Biopower operates within a world of natureculture. There is no nature in *Xenogenesis* as conceived in a traditional Western sense, as an external site that originates beyond and before human culture and techniques.[44] *Chkahichdahk* and the rehabilitated Earth are living entities, but they are also manufactured, managed, and made by the Oankali.[45] The Oankali own this manufactured world. They talk openly about how their bodies were. The bipedal, vocal form that Lilith meets in *Dawn* was engineered as a more appropriate phenotype through which to instigate trade with humans.[46] The Akjai Oankali that are to remain aboard the *Chkahichdahk* and not engage in trade have kept their dumb centipede form. Oankali reproduction is not left to chance. Ooloi select traits deemed desirable in the next generation. The rainforest of resettled Earth appears thriving because of Oankali restoration; many of the plants and animals are modified or reconstructions taken from genetic 'prints'.[47] The resettled humans are not natural. Sterile, lifespans increased and with various other genetic tweaks, they are also the product of technical intervention. Yet this technical intervention is not the big-science, mechanic fantasies of earlier science fiction: it is organic and micro-scale. Akin's grey, elongated tongue is his technical instrument through which he codes the life that he tastes. The ooloi's sensory arms and yashi are a complete biolife laboratory, repository, and incubator. The Oankali are light-years beyond *Battlestar Galactica*'s Cylons, with their perverse, horror-inducing mixing of chromic mechanisation and bloody flesh. The Oankali moulding of life comes across not as transgressive, but as 'natural'. Butler has produced in *Xenogenesis* a world that renders explicit Haraway's claim of natureculture,[48] an account of the technologised world where identification of prior 'natural' entities and constructed 'cultural' practices is meaningless.

43 Foucault, 'Governmentality', p. 241.

44 Pepper, *The Roots of Modern Environmentalism*, p. 54; Frank, 'Science, Nature, and the Globalization of the Environment, 1870–1990', pp. 412–13.

45 Belk, 'The Certainty of the Flesh', p. 377.

46 Butler, *Adulthood Rites*, p. 209.

47 Butler, *Dawn*, p. 30; Butler, *Adulthood Rites*, p. 56.

48 Haraway, *Modest_Witness@Second_Millennium*, p. 149.

Indeed, there is little culture evident in *Xenogenesis*. The juvenile Nikanj tells Lilith stories of past trades,[49] but there is no singing, laughter, or play aboard *Chkahichdahk*. What passes for Oankali culture seems to be a preoccupation with trade, with finding and splicing with life and the technical discussions of its fulfilment.[50] The construct Akin objects to fairy tales as lies.[51] Similarly, the settlements on Earth – both trader and resister – seem occupied with industry. Trader communities focus on growing food and constructing children; what passes for cultural activity are humans recording their life history. Mated Oankali withdraw to save their hearing when humans begin a shindig,[52] while within and between resister communities there is violent competition for scarce resources. It does not seem that surplus value is directed to creativity in Oankali, human or the emerging construct societies. Instead, there are the manifestations of 'natural' tendencies: Oankali for trade, humans to conflict and constructs growing to maturity. In this blending of nature to culture and culture to nature, what is affirmed is that the world made by biopower is a world of natureculture.

Identifying this tension explains the 'Is Xenogenesis progressive or reactionary?' debate within the secondary literature. For critics like Hoda M. Zaki and Nancy Jesser, Haraway's championing of Butler, and *Xenogenesis* specifically, is misplaced. For Zaki, Butler links biology directly to behaviour.[53] The Oankali drive to trade is explained directly as a consequence of the cellular-level symbioses with the Oankali organelle,[54] while self-destructive human behaviour is a manifestation of the deep coding of the Human Contradiction.[55] This reveals not a progressive cyborg story, but a story of an essentialist nature determining being. Jesser develops this argument within a stronger feminist frame to see that Butler's essentialism appears particularly strong in the context of sexual difference. Indeed, for Jesser there is a sociobiological message in *Xenogenesis*. Males are shown again and again as violent, competitive, and sexually aggressive, while women – Lilith being the most obvious – are self-sacrificial in their care for children and community.[56] In this, 'Butler does manage to embrace the cyborg impurities that Haraway anoints her with. But

[49] Butler, *Dawn*, p. 61.

[50] White, 'The Erotics of Becoming: Xenogenesis and *The Thing*', p. 405.

[51] Butler, *Adulthood Rites*, p. 120.

[52] Ibid., p. 195.

[53] Zaki, 'Utopia, Dystopia and Ideology in the Science Fiction of Octavia Butler', p. 242.

[54] Butler, *Dawn*, p. 39.

[55] Ibid., p. 37.

[56] Jesser, 'Blood, Genes and Gender', pp. 46–50. See also Allison, 'The Future of Female'.

it is through a fairly conservative view based on common tenets of evolutionary and medical biology.'[57]

In the alternative to seeing a sovereign nature in *Xenogenesis* – that is, genes that make the world – numerous critics have emphasised that these essentialist elements are mediated by anti-essentialism.[58] The Oankali, master manipulators of natural material, represent the ultimate subjection of nature to technique. Their taking from trade biospheres is not total; it is selective. There is choice involved in considering what is 'useful'. While the Oankali seem to have an impoverished cultural life from a human perspective, what they do have is a joyous seeking of diversity, difference, and pleasure, so as to change.[59] Genes may determine life, but the Oankali technique determines the genetic sequence. There may not be teleology to the Oankali's meandering-viral evolution, but there is thought and reflection in their assimilating. In this reading, resister humans, replaying the 'cave man' narratives of 'Man the Hunter', manifest a genetic tendency that has not been corrected by Oankali surgery or by the 'intelligence' side of the Human Contradiction overcoming the tendency to hierarchy.[60] What can be seen is that the debate in the secondary literature amounts to differing readings of the strength of the gene theme – whether it tells an authoritative story of essential natures that determine being, or a malleable story of life materials that can be moulded by cultural practices, whether those practices be techniques of genetic manipulation and therapy, or technologies of education and care of the self, or governing institutions of social control.

For Cathy Peppers, *Xenogenesis* is not essence verse non-essence, nature verse culture, but:

> offers a third choice between: reveal[ing] science as yet one more meaningless master narrative . . . [and] as essentialist desire to claim some gender/race identity based in 'biology' outside of history or cultural construction . . . We can, as cyborgs, choose among alternative stories of our biological inheritance (themselves technologies of meanings) with which to interface.[61]

The constructs Akin and Jodahs – ooloi made hybrid beings – follow neither Oankali nor human ways. They both choose elements of each in the forging

[57] Jesser, 'Blood, Genes and Gender', p. 49. On the textual reflection of sociobiological texts within *Xenogenesis*, see Johns, 'Octavia Butler and the Art of Pseudoscience'.

[58] Peppers, 'Dialogic Origins and Alien Identites in Butler's *Xenogenesis*'; Holden, 'The High Costs of Cyborg Survival'; Vint, *Bodies of Tomorrow*, pp. 56–78.

[59] Ibid. p. 58.

[60] Peppers, 'Dialogic Origins and Alien Identites in Butler's *Xenogenesis*', pp. 56–8.

[61] Ibid., p. 59.

of their identity and their life's work. Akin's humanity makes him a grand story-teller and wanderer; Jodahs' gives him a desire for independence. In this, Peppers captures and elaborates on what Haraway found enticing about *Xenogenesis*: not that it was about the triumph of either nature or culture, but that it intertwined these foundational discourses of the modern West as a totalised space of natureculture through which activity and agency (choice) may be operationalised. It is this understanding of *Xenogenesis* that allows it to be a text about the technical legal subject.

The Technical Legal Subject of *Xenogenesis*

The modern West tells two stories of the legal subject. Most of one of these stories, the authoritative story, has been told in the previous chapters. In Dune, through Hobbes, the legal subject eked out a pathetic existence alongside the dominating sovereign-worm. As Agamben made plain, sovereignty was seen as emerging over and through the bare biological life of humanity. Positive law, for all its potential to make the world – especially to make the world so as to adapt to, manage and encourage technological change – does this precisely because of its alchemical basis in death and time. In this story, the legal subject is a nothing: mere matter whose agency, desires, relationships, subjectivity, future, and body can be changed by sovereign will, with law a potent manifestation of that will. This is what passes for the legal subject within the totality of technology. It is a product of the machine of law, a blob of natureculture crafted by political processes.

However, this is not jurisprudence's preferred myth of the legal subject. Indeed, it has been a counter-myth – a dangerous, subversive myth – associated with dangerous and subversive theorists, like Bentham, Foucault, and Deleuze.[62] For jurisprudence, the subject of law was a something, an entity in itself, existing before the law. Here is Hobbes' other legacy, which made him seem to Schmitt a problematic father to modern authoritarianism.[63] Hobbes was the theorist of fear and natural disorder that gave birth to the sovereign, but integrated within his origin story was an essential, natural humanity from which emanated rights.[64] Hobbes' humans were biological matter that could be – must be – moulded towards the common good, but as detailed in Chapter 2, they also had desires, tendencies, passions, needs, and intelligence that gifted them with agency in the world. This was a dangerous agency, all too easily given to the excess of asocial violence – murder, rape, kidnapping, theft, racism, misogyny, homophobia – that Butler attributes

[62] Mussawir, *Jurisdiction in Deleuze*, p. 24.

[63] See Chapter 2 text associated with notes 198–211.

[64] Hobbes, *Leviathan*, pp. 81–107.

to the resister males of *Xenogenesis*.[65] However, in Hobbes' story, strongly reiterated by Butler, dangerous, competitive, petty humanity preceded the sovereign.[66] In *Xenogenesis*, without the corrective institutions of the state, the resister humans are a failing civilisation. Guns are reinvented. Villages fight between themselves over goods and women.[67] Entire villages self-destruct, in violence or mass suicide,[68] while roving bands of males attack and loot.[69]

Yet for latter liberals it was the structure of Hobbes' story and not his misanthropy that was important. For John Locke, it was that the polity emerged after and through the pre-existing natural entity called human – a human not as wolfish as Hobbes believed.[70] This natural human proved to be a seductive location as the holder of rights. It came to be seen as the vessel for the remnants of an inherited primal freedom that could be safeguarded against the state and its technical apparatuses of control.

This tension runs through modern Western jurisprudence. On the one side there is the authoritarian story of sovereign, positive law, and a malleable humanity whose being could be modified, deleted, and reprogrammed by law.[71] This can properly be seen as a manifestation of the techno-utopian fantasy of non-essentialism, of mere matter needing culture (read science in its hard, biological, social, and juridical manifestations) to give it form and meaning – indeed, to make it live. On the other side is the liberal story of a recurring essential humanity. In this story, the human is the location for rights[72] and these rights mean something more than Bentham's limiting of the term to permissions under positive law.[73] In this story, the sovereign – with its power over death and time – allows for a plastic, biopower-facilitating law that has a tendency to the unnatural. Its *nomos* of control can go too far, illicitly impinging on essential freedoms safeguarded by rights. Rights are a time-portal connecting the free, natural human to its modern technologically mediated descendant, independent of the sovereign's mastery of matter and time. Rights ensure that something resembling the human endures in the midst of the mega-machinic totality of technology.

At play in jurisprudence's two stories of the subject is the same tension of non-essentialism and essentialism that circulates in the *Xenogenesis* secondary

65 Curtis, 'Theorizing Fear', p. 413.
66 Hobbes, *Leviathan*, pp. 82–3.
67 Butler, *Adulthood Rites*, p. 241–2.
68 Ibid., p. 31.
69 Ibid., pp. 257–8.
70 Locke, 'The Second Treatise', p. 108; Douzinas, *The End of Human Rights*, pp. 81–4.
71 Ibid., p. 236.
72 Douzinas, *Human Rights and Empire*, p. 53.
73 Bentham, 'Anarchical Fallacies', p. 69.

literature. Hard positivists commit to a species of non-essentialism. There are limits to what law can do, but those limits are cultural and, as such, changeable. A. V. Dicey's fictitious parliament, whose law authorised the killing of blue-eyed children,[74] was an example of the political, as opposed to natural, constraints on law-making. It was not a question of capacity but one of constraint based on cultural consequences. Lon L. Fuller disguised the essentiality of a preconfigured nature within his accounts of the legal subject. Fuller's inner morality of law has a content-neutral, technological-sounding, procedural gloss, but at its core it grows from the necessity for 'selfish, quarrelsome and disputatious'[75] yet is 'capable of understanding and following [the] rules'[76] of humanity to have clear structure and expectations regarding how humans will be treated into the future. H. L. A. Hart, in his chapter on 'Laws and Morality', identifies a biological reality-check for legal systems. For Hart, a system of law that tends to respect and accommodate his five truisms of Earth-bound humanity – human vulnerability, approximate equality, limited altruism, limited resources, and limited understanding and strength of will[77] – would more likely be 'accepted' by its human subjects.[78] While the superstructure of Hart's concept of law – primary and secondary rules, rule of recognition and officials – suggests law as a purely cultural practice, his five truisms explained in rather Hobbesian terms establish a naturalistic basis for a legal system in which is located essentialist humanity at the core of his theorising.

What Butler has achieved in the biopower-saturated natureculture of *Xenogenesis* are critiques of the West's two stories of the legal subject. Foremost, she dispels an essentialist location for rights. Without deciding in the secondary literature between the claims that *Xenogenesis* is utopian or dystopia, it is clearly illiberal.

Much of the narrative across the three books is dialogue. Lilith talks with her captors, with Jdahya, Nikanj, and the other humans. Akin, a mature mind in an infant's body, listens and then talks to the various resister humans with whom he comes into contact. Akin also 'talks' to Kohj, the Akjai centipedal ooloi aboard *Chkahichdahk*, who becomes his ally in advocating for the Mars reserve. Jodahs does less talking: as a metamorphosing construct ooloi, his dialogue is a continual stream of biolife data from the beings with which he engages. The main topic that circulates within all these discussions is that of freedom and constraint. Lilith identifies that her movement on

[74] Dicey, *Introduction to the Study of the Law of the Constitution*, p. 81.
[75] Fuller, *The Morality of Law*, p. 55.
[76] Ibid., p. 162.
[77] Hart, *The Concept of Law*, pp. 190–3.
[78] Ibid., p. 194.

Chkahichdahk is curtailed – and, indeed, what happens to her body is outside of her control, while the Oankali return with the alterative that without their discovery of post-war Earth and of a fatally injured Lilith (radiation after the war and a malignant cancer), she would be dead.[79] Akin implores both the resisters and the Oankali to be more free and flexible in how they face their constraints. For the humans, he urges engagement with the Oankali;[80] for the Oankali, he advocates restraint from the drive to totally consume a trade-species.[81] For Jodahs, it is the need to demark freedom for construct society away from both human and Oankali 'parents'.[82]

On occasion, this freedom-constraint tension discloses rights-talk. However, what becomes clear is the inability of rights to adequately articulate within natureculture. In *Xenogenesis*, they are neither trumps nor meaningful. Human claims to primary rights, rights of movement, and bodily autonomy occur against the absolute rights of the Oankali. As Lilith observes early in her bonding with Nikanj, 'They owned the Earth and all that was left of the human species.'[83] Rights become further irredeemable in the texts as they are claimed by male aggressors during attempted sexual assaults:

> 'We pair off!' Curt bellowed, drowning her out. 'One man, one woman. Nobody has the right to hold out. It just causes trouble.'
> 'Trouble for who!' someone demanded.
> 'Who the shit are you to tell us our rights!' called someone else.[84]

This interplay shows the emptiness of rights within a biopolitical world. There is no essence or juridical authority to decide competing rights claims. To have rights in the liberal sense as remembered by Butler's North American humans is alien and impossible in Oankali spaces. Even in human spaces, the resister villages, the invocation of rights is at best inconclusive, and at worst a symptom of escalating violence. As he lay metamorphosing in Phoenix during the climax of *Adulthood Rites*, Akin:

> heard and automatically remembered argument after argument over his mission, his right to be in Phoenix, the Human right to Earth. There was no resolution. There was cursing, shouting, threats, fighting, but no resolution.[85]

[79] Butler, *Dawn*, p. 31.
[80] Butler, *Adulthood* Rites, p. 245.
[81] Ibid., pp. 228-9.
[82] Butler, *Imago*, pp. 216–18.
[83] Butler, *Dawn*, p. 57.
[84] Ibid., p. 177.
[85] Butler, *Adulthood Rites*, p. 256.

To the Oankali, the very value at play in these claims of rights – hierarchical access to resources – manifests the deadly Human Contradiction.[86] To talk of rights to the Oankali as embodied beings of biopower is to just blow hot air at their tentacles. One human in Lo explains to a newly converted resister, 'You can do as you please here. As long as you don't hurt anyone, you can stay or go as you like . . . No one has the right to demand anything from you that you don't want to give.'[87]

So, unsurprisingly, the natureculture world of *Xenogenesis* presents an alien landscape for the liberal accounts of the legal subject. There is no nature from which essences and rights can be located. As such, no one in *Xenogenesis* is free to do their own thing, to accumulate resources and be master of their destiny. The Oankali's trade quest combined with the Human Contradiction has determined the fate of Earth and humanity. Both will cease. Liberty, that form of radical agency as freedom from all external constraints, is absent in the future but also in the immediate of the Oankali, human and construct lives. They are all programmed by biocultural networks to have certain tendencies and make certain choices.

This also discloses a critique of the other account of the legal subject. In the authoritarian account of freedom, it is supposedly with the sovereign in how they make their subjects. The sovereign has agency and choice in how they keep the peace. A simple symmetry between the two accounts of the legal subject can be discerned. In the liberal account, the subject is free while the sovereign is constrained; in the authoritarian account, the subject is constrained while the sovereign is free. Yet in *Xenogenesis* this simplicity is not manifest. Even if the Oankali are considered sovereign, they seem to have little choice in their assimilation. Jodahs' self-narrative in *Imago* provides insight into the Oankali's inability *not* to collect, record, manipulate, and mate with life-materials.[88] However, unlike the Emperors of Dune, or the President and Admiral of *Battlestar Galactica*, the Oankali are not easily coded as sovereign. *Xenogenesis* does not manifest a public realm of politics and power. Its scenes are always domestic: families, meal-taking, sleeping, and ooloi three-/five-way sex. Power, however, is never absent: the continual discussion of freedom and constraint; all those bodies, moods, and genes that are interfered with and the totality of the Oankali's colonialism mean that power – specifically biopower – is ever present. However, the focus is not on the macro-level politics of the Oankali assimilation of Earth. Lilith, Akin, and Jodahs are never invited into *Chkahichdahk*'s equivalent of the *Galactica*'s

[86] Butler, *Dawn*, p. 37.
[87] Butler, *Adulthood Rites*, p. 39.
[88] Butler, *Imago*, pp. 30–1.

Combat Information Centre (CIC) where big decisions are debated and made. Indeed, Butler's emphasis on the non-hierarchal nature of the Oankali seems to suggest that there is no such place, just a collective meeting of 'the people's' minds within *Chkahichdahk*'s neural-network.[89] However, Lilith, Akin, and Jodahs all play critical roles in the big-story of the renewal of the Oankali through trade with humans, although they do so not through decisions from a place of public authority, but rather through circumstance, choice, and inclination.

What emerges from this is a schizoid vision of the legal subject. The first is a global vision of the subject of modern law – that is, the technical legal subject. This is a node in fluxing networks. Multiple networks – of knowledge, of biology, of cultural practices – determine its present manifestation and its possibilities. Its extent, powers, property, relationships, and body are defined by positive law, and as such are ever-changing. There is no freedom in the liberal sense for the technical legal subject. There are authorities, licences, grants, discretions – all manifestations of the epochal technicity of law. Further, these do not last. As seen in Chapter 1, the legal machine is programmed to change: past authorities are reformed, widened, and revoked; conditions on licences change; grants are withheld; discretions are narrowed, abolished and liberalised. New laws are made and old ones repealed, while the ever-changing soft-law of regulations, directions, advices, forms, apps and algorithms greases the workings.[90] What is the legal subject, what does it do in the world, what is its body, what does it do with its biological bits (if it has such an embodiment), what relationships can it form, what powers does it have over other portions of the world? All of this continually becomes. This is the extreme anti-essentialism glimpsed by some commentators in *Xenogenesis*, and it is the extreme version of the traditional authoritarian story of the legal subject. However, this is a background vibration in *Xenogenesis.* Butler's focus is on the living-with inside this totality.

Lilith, Akin and Jodahs exhibit what it means to live within this moment. Foremost, each is embodied. Each is centred on a biological site. Their bodies – Akin's and Jodahs' as constructs especially, but also Lilith's Nikanj-modified flesh – dictate. Each has the need to eat, sleep, feel secure and desire sex. However, the body is not sovereign. Cancers can be removed and both genotype and phenotype can be technically mediated. Instead, their bodies – as blobs of natureculture – are nodes where biological and cultural networks intersect. There is both fluidity and rigidity in how their bodies

[89] Butler, *Adulthood Rites*, p. 227; Butler, *Imago*, p. 218.

[90] Sleep and Tranter, 'The Visiocracy of the Social Security Mobile App in Australia'.

are perceived and manipulated. As such, their bodies change. Lilith's body becomes integrated into Nikanj's Oankali family and becomes the primal progenitor of human-born construct offspring. Akin and Jodahs dramatically undergo metamorphosis. Their bodies matter to who they are and what they can do. They do not 'own' their bodies, yet they are not powerless in how their bodies are represented, or in the choices of their life missions.

This captures the second account of the technical legal subject. Instead of a global vision of endless change and plasticity, the vision is one of embodiment, of biological and cultural constraints but at the same time opportunities. Lilith takes the opportunity to train humans to resettle Earth so as to teach resistance to Oankali plans. Akin accepts his legacies – his status as the first human-born male construct and his kidnapping – to determine a life mission to represent and secure the Mars reserve for resister humans – while Jodahs weaves together human (independence, freedom) and Oankali tendencies (pleasure, life seeking) in his demarking of the sexually mature construct species. From their embodied locations, each works the biopower networks. From their locations, some networks seem rigid. Lilith cannot escape the Oankali, or Nikanj's quasi-insidious bonding. Akin aches with the longing to mate. Jodahs cannot but follow the Oankali prime directive of tinkering with genes. Yet others are malleable, open to use. Lilith uses her relationship with the Oankali to allow for the resettled humans to reject mating with Oankali and form resister communities. Akin blends human traits of storytelling and Oankali skills at direct neural communication to show the Oankali the resister humans' pain from the meaninglessness of their forced sterility. Jodahs, the construct ooloi, masters its raw biopower to strategically heal/reprogram/bond with members of the fertile resister village, cementing mates for itself and also an independent future for the construct species.

The vision of the technical legal subject that emerges from *Xenogenesis* is therefore that 'third way' of natureculture as identified in the secondary literature. In the narratives of self that occupy the texts, Xenogenesis is a story of individuals moving through – becoming – within natureculture. From the location of the legal subject, its being in the world is made by networks of power that determine and locate, but also facilitate, activity within this node. It is transitory. It changes what it becomes over time – its biological self, its identity, its doing in the world are in flux. These changes are both caused by networks beyond the subject's technical intervention and by exercises of technical intervention by the subject in the networks that constitute it. The technical legal subject is determined by the positive laws that appear, from the subject's location, to be immutable. Knowledge of the law is, after all, no defence, and legal change – while an ever-present possibility – involves an extremely high level of technical manipulation of the political, advocacy, and legal change networks that invariably is beyond a single embodied node in the network. Yet, even from this mundane, powerless position, the technical legal subjects make themselves – contracts, relationships, representations, exercise of rights, declarations of obligation by word or deed – through manipulation of the legal network. In doing so, their being-in-the world changes. Resources are accumulated and expended, desires fulfilled or transmuted, bodies become changed. This is what Butler has constructed in *Xenogenesis* as technical legality. She realises a fully technologised world of natureculture where being is made, and made again, through the exercise of biopower. Existing within a malleable, yet also rigid, naturecultural realm, Butler's protagonists are neither free nor constrained. In the alternative, they are nodes in flux within multiple networks that determine and locate, yet also allow choice and autonomy. It is this location of the every-present-becoming that is the identified technological Being-in-the-world that emerged from consideration of *Battlestar Galactica*. However, there is something more in Butler's storytelling. In her emphasis on that nodal location, responsibility for becoming – identified as a potential in *Battlestar Galactica* – can be elaborated on. In the everyday, embodied lived-ness of *Xenogenesis* can be glimpsed an 'ethics', a protocol for the navigating the networks of the present. In *Xenogenesis*, what is shown is a way to live well as a technical legal subject.

Living Well as a Technical Legal Subject

To live well in the present involves responsibility for becoming. This is a possibility created by the totality of technology in the modern West. As was seen in the narrative that unfolded in *Battlestar Galactica*, responsibility for becoming can happen because of the demise of essentialism, of hard nature, and also of metaphysical guarantees through the unfolding of technology. In Heidegger's questioning of technology, but also in Butler's projection of natureculture, technicity discloses a world without limit – a freedom to make the world that for Heidegger is a doom, but for Haraway is a statement of possibilities.

However, *Xenogenesis* shows that with regard to the embodied location of the little monster that was formally known as the human, the technical legal subject who is a node within the networks that are making and remaking the world, talk of freedom is partial. A world of Enframing may ultimately be a plastic, limitless world, but at specific embodied locations there is rigid fluidity. Some of the networks that intersect at a node are open to technical manipulation, while others constrain and dictate.[91]

[91] I note a parallel image of the technical legal subject emerging from Andreas Philippopoulos-Mihalopoulos's recent book, where the posthuman emerges and withdraws from the

So, having established *Xenogenesis* as a biopower, naturecultural text elaborating the technical legal subject, the critical question remains: How is this partial agency within the networks of the present to be exercised? In a world of total technicity, where the embodied agent is an ever-changing node, can there be an ethics? The possibility seems immediately paradoxical. The whole narrative of the totality of technology is the demise of the transcendent or natural that could have measured, evaluated, or judged being-in-the-world. The best that is sometimes suggested is the techno-economic standard of efficiency. However, Xenogenesis suggests something else.

Efficiency is not at play in *Xenogenesis*. The Oankali are patient, the humans irrational, and the constructs precocious. An over-arching motif may be trade, but the market is absent; the Oankali monopoly over power and resources, coupled with the resisters' inability to be rational enough to form a cross-village social contract, means that Akin cannot grasp the concept of money.[92] Even the social Darwinist argument of the efficiency of the survival of the fitness[93] has been blown away in the humans' nuclear war. Life on Earth is changing in a big way, but that change is due to the exercise of biopower by the Oankali. Competition and hierarchical behaviour are clearly coded by Butler as a one-way street to oblivion. There are no invisible hands of the market or natural selection in *Xenogenesis*; there are the much more visible sunflower-like 'sensory hands' of the ooloi mixing and manipulating individuals, gene-pools, and biospheres.[94] The everydayness of the narratives, unlike the sometimes heavy-handed concept-as-storyline in *Battlestar Galactica*, means that *Xenogenesis* does not animate such abstractions. But what it does show is life.

For all the representation of natureculture in *Xenogenesis*, there is a recurring image of life.[95] Butler suggests that there is always an excess, a something more, happening with this life. The biometrics and biomechanics of lived things may be the Oankali's domain, but they are never shown to possess complete technical mastery. Life surprises. Ultimately, what is hinted at is a vitalistic *zoe* that confounds even the perfect control of the ooloi. The human capacity for violence is always under-estimated. A critical rhetoric used by Akin in his argument for the Mars colony is that time and the challenging environment may allow a random mutation to dissipate the Human

'lawscape' and other material assemblages. Andreas Philippopoulos-Mihalopoulos, *Spatial Justice*.

92 Butler, *Adulthood Rites*, p. 122.

93 Huxley, *Evolution and Ethics*; Fitting, 'Eating Your Way to the Top'.

94 Walker, 'Destabilizing Order, Challenging History', p. 113.

95 Raffel, 'Genre to the Rear, Race and Gender to the Fore', p. 456.

Contradiction.[96] This nature as *zoe*, as 'the endless vitality of life as continuous becoming',[97] is taken a step further by Jodahs' unexpected transition to ooloi.[98] Butler's *zoe* is not a return to classical dualism of 'nature' and 'culture'; there is no harsh mistress of unruly nature needing order, control, and discipline, and it is not the death orientation of bare life and sovereign power of Agamben.[99] It is a generative force of absolute change, that can be technically learnt and manipulated, that can be known but can also surprise.

This explains the repeated becomings in *Xenogenesis*: the becoming of the new construct species, the becoming of a new *Chkahichdahks*, even the becoming of a possibly post-hierarchical humanity on Mars. The texts strain towards this future. Lilith in *Dawn* anticipates her repatriation to Earth. Akin anticipates a solution to the injustice done to the resister humans. Jodahs desires – as manifested by his chameleon body – to mate with humans and to experience sexual maturity. There is hope that the universe will become more diverse, more complex, and more life-filled through the Oankali–human interaction. From this meeting, we have the promise not only of the continuation of pre-contact Oankali with the Akjai, and pre-contact humanity on Mars, but many more diverse combinations from the Toaht groups and from the many Dinso communities. The precise biosphere of Earth will pass, but its contribution to galactic life will endure, diversify, and become anew.

It is at this very point, of life, becoming, endurance, and diversity, that *Xenogenesis* is a myth for the technical legal subject. Having shown the alienness of both the authoritarian and the liberal accounts of the legal subject in the technologised world of natureculture, Butler ultimately tells a story not only about becoming a node navigating the ever-changing techno-networks of the West; but how to live as an embodied, material entity at this location. Each of her protagonists chose to navigate natureculture so as to allow *zoe*. To misappropriate a slogan, they chose life – that is, they navigate the networks – utilise their circumstances and skills – to effect positive change in the world. They are not passive, empty vessels awaiting sovereign fulfilment as in the authoritative story, the warehoused humans in suspended animation aboard *Chkahichdahk* who could not cope with their new circumstances. Nor are they the aggressive human males whose violent affirming of rights ends, too often, with death. Rather Lilith, Akin, and Jodahs overcome the negativity of their circumstances to heal and to make. 'Of course, repugnant and unbearable

[96] Butler, *Adulthood Rites*, p. 228.

[97] Braidotti, *Transpositions*, p. 41.

[98] Vint, *Bodies of Tomorrow*, p. 69.

[99] Braidotti, *Transpositions*, pp. 39–40.

events do happen,' writes Braidotti.[100] Lilith suffers imprisonment, attempted rape, social rejection, the murder of her human lover, a pregnancy without consent, the kidnapping of her child and exile from her community because of another child's difference. Akin is kidnapped from kin and forced to witness violence, endures hardships, and undergoes metamorphose in hostile surrounds, while Jodahs experiences rejection and terrible isolation as the come-too-soon construct ooloi. Yet, as Braidotti continues, 'Ethics consists, however, in reworking these events in the direction of positive relations.'[101] At the critical moment at the end of the fight scene in *Dawn*, Lilith personally chooses Nikanj and a future life of construct children, but also has facilitated the Oankali to permit resister humans to be returned to Earth. Akin offers hope to the resisters through the Mars settlement and Jodahs liberates the malformed, fertile human breeding stock of the mountain village to make active choices about their bodies, reproduction, and future.

What emerges is affect.[102] This positivity to life is substantiated through the inherent relational nature of the node-network materiality of becoming.[103] Butler's characters are ethical in their striving to maintain and enhance relationships.[104] Lilith does not turn from her human kin; she struggles to maintain and develop relations with others. It is because of this disposition that the Oankali selected her as their 'trustee'.[105] As a node in a network that continually becomes, it is the relational – the points of interface and the energy for change – that matters. It is the recognition that 'these multi-layered levels of affectivity are the building blocks for creative transpositions, which compose a plane of actualization of relations'.[106] Ethics becomes an active force, working with this reality. The resister males, whose aggressive right-claims foster desire for a past-Earth that they ruled and nuked, sever relations.[107] They reject Oankali mating, they kidnap construct children, and they destroy communities through taking and killing women. It is also the opposite of the turning inwards of Western Buddhism that Dune seemed to preach. Instead of locking the self impossibly away from the contradictions, fluxes, and becomings of the world, there is a joyous invitation to engage. The flowering of social media – hyped, trivial, and superficial – reveals the

100 Braidotti, *Transpositions*, p. 208.
101 Ibid.
102 Olson, 'The Turn to Passion'.
103 Braidotti, *Transpositions*, p. 163.
104 Walker, 'Destabilizing Order, Challenging History', p. 109.
105 Butler, *Dawn*, p. 110.
106 Braidotti, *Transpositions*, p.173.
107 Pryor Ackerman, 'Becoming and Belonging', p. 28.

inherent propensity for embodied nodes in the network, the monsters of the West, to revel in connectivity.[108] What Butler, through Braidotti, shows is that affect both grounds and guides an ethical orientation of doing well within our technologised world. It provides a life-affirming myth through which the technical legal subject can exercise their responsibility for becoming, which will be partial and open to mistakes, but can provide for action that enacts the creative, positive potential of technological Being-in-the world.

In conclusion, Butler's *Xenogenesis* is a story of hybridisation and change. In portraying a biopower-saturated world of natureculture that is continually and obviously becoming, Butler emphasises what it means to be a technical legal subject circulating within the modern West. At one level, a being that has no essence – an entity that is made, stabilised, and changed by multiple and many networks – it is also an embodied node navigating these fluxes. It is not quite the 'human' of jurisprudence's authoritarian or liberal story. Instead, with her story of human-alien constructs, Butler shows a hybrid 'third way' of living well within this changing world. She acknowledges the node-network, relational basis of technological Being-in-the world and shows the positive potential that comes from fostering relationships and connections. Through embracing life as a primordial *zoe* of ever-change, Butler narrates an ethics of affect that can inspire living well as a component node in the modern West. By hybridising and manipulating the cabalist story of Lilith and her monstrous offspring,[109] Butler empowers a new myth of creation for our technological epoch.

Butler's concluding imagery is apt. The mountain resister community has been 'liberated' by Jodahs and a shuttle has landed, bringing Oankali from *Chkahichdahk*. Jodahs observes Francisco, one of the elder male resisters, talking with a female Oankali, 'She did not look in the slightest Human. He was laughing at something she had said.'[110] This simple relating, across radical difference, across the complicated history of Butler's imagined colonial legacy, as a cause of joy, captures Butler's central message. Within the three texts, genuine laughter – and not just the Oankali's flattening of tentacles in amusement or the cynical snorts by humans – is rare. This moment of affect – transient, yet full of future potential – encapsulates an aspiring myth for the

108 Hogan, 'The Presentation of Self in the Age of Social Media'; Bararova and Choi, 'Self-Disclosure in Social Media'; Hawi and Samaha, 'The Relations among Social Media Addiction'.

109 Haraway, 'The Biopolitics of Postmodern Bodies', p. 227; Osherow, 'The Dawn of a New Lilith'.

110 Butler, *Imago*, p. 215.

monsters of the West to embrace their monstrousness, their nodal location in the networks of change, as opportunities to nurture *zoe* as the becoming of the world – in other words, to share laughter.

5

The Doctor and Technical Lawyering

The previous chapter, drawing upon *Xenogenesis*, charted a myth for living positively within the totality of technology. The focused location was that of the monster formally known as the legal subject. No longer human, but not bare life, this transient entity was seen as a node within the networks of becoming – an embodied location of connections where, through affect, there is the potential to nurture life. Technicity is the defining feature of our world, ourselves, and our law and, rather than Heidegger's precipitous fall, this provides the possibility to be responsible for becoming.

Often this embodied node in the networks is a location for something more. Revealing the technical legal subject as a non-unitary self – changing yet enduring – allows for absolute and radical difference. The monstrous cyborgs of the West can have different attachments, be plugged into different networks, and have different identities, selves, relations, meanings, powers, and responsibilities. It would be a fundamental miscoding of the analysis over the past two chapters if what emerged was a vision of the inhabitants of the West as the same, the image rendered nicely by the 'battery' scene in *The Matrix* (1999)[1] or the clones from Lucas's *Attack of the Clones* (2002),[2] identical units within the mega-machine. The actual image is not so mechanical; we are not the same cogs in the machine or, looking back to earlier biological metaphors, we are not organs of the body politic. Rather, the scanner registers a primordial soup, eddies within a strange fluid of varying colours, movement, and density; it is a changing, swirling, fluxing complex, dynamic and full of potential. The totality of technicity means that difference cannot be accounted for by the binaries of the old West – nature/culture, male/female, sovereign/subject, black/white, bourgeoisie/proletariat; rather, fields of comparison, graduation, and uniqueness allow for representing difference. Ironically, the digitalisation of information has replaced the binary

[1] Wachowski and Wachowski, *The Matrix*.

[2] Lucas, *Star Wars: Attack of the Clones*.

mode with a much more graded and complex analogue process. The monsters of the West, even more than the monad of their ancestor, the liberal human, demark nodes that are radically unique.

This means that different embodied nodes in the network have different potentials, possibilities, and powers. Some are nexus points for legal networks and manifest the designation and duties known as 'lawyer'. In the same way that recognition of the totality of technology, technological Being-in-the-world, and responsibility for becoming, allowed, through *Xenogenesis*, an alternative myth for the technical legal subject's doing-in-the-world, recognising these recasts how to think about lawyering. If an ethics of affect can sustain the everyday of the technical legal subject, is there a myth for legal ethics that can accommodate and guide activity within the technicity of law? Reconnecting with the dusty quest from Chapter 2, if the base character of law as technology is its alchemical properties of death and time, what sort of monstrous – indeed demonic – being is the node in the network that has as its currency death and time?

This chapter finds the answer to this and a myth to live for as a lawyer of technical legality within the seemingly immortal BBC television phenomenon, *Doctor Who* (1963–present). To be a lawyer within technical legality is to be responsible for death and to master time. It is to be the eponymous Time Lord, face-changing, two-hearted, presiding over death and time. Alien, proudly not human and technically competent, the Doctor suggests how to be responsible for becoming from the alchemist's location. The Doctor overcomes and endures because his responsibility for death and time is within his Time Lord being. There is neither sound judgement nor technical somnambulism in the Doctor's actions; instead, they appear as a hybrid of both, unified by an acceptance that actions performed from this location break, change, and destroy the networks of the present. Ultimately, the Doctor shows that lawyering within law as technology demands an accepting of the powers of time and death to safeguard becoming.

This argument materialises in three stages. The first stage overviews the 'unfolding text' that is *Doctor Who*, emphasising that across its more than fifty years of broadcast history, time has been a consistent theme. In its 'timelessness' and 'timefulness', *Doctor Who* can be seen as manifesting the complex dual time of law as technology that was identified in Chapter 2. The second stage considers the nexus of these times in the 'event' to reveal the defining event in *Doctor Who* as death. At this point, *Doctor Who* can be seen – like Dune – as a text projecting the base elements from which law as technology is conjured. However, unlike Herbert's Atreides, who grasp the will to power from the mastery of death and time with cataclysmic consequences, the Doctor runs and dances through his texts as a much more endearing character. Indeed, the Doctor emerges as the preferred alchemist of time and death. The third stage interweaves the secondary literature's concern with the Doctor's ethics with legal ethics, to present the Doctor as a desirable myth-ideal for lawyer-nodes in their grappling with responsibility for becoming from their alien location. The Doctor shows how to live as a being who safeguards becoming through responsibility for time and death.

Time and a Blue Box

Doctor Who is bigger on the inside than just an extremely long-running science fiction created by the BBC. It is a cultural institution in the United Kingdom[3] and also in Australia, where the national broadcaster has beamed it into living rooms for more than fifty years.[4] First broadcast in 1963, the show was put in a production halt (not cancelled) in 1989.[5] A 1996 telemovie/pilot[6] was unsuccessful at returning the show to regular production.[7] It took until 2005, after intense lobbying by fans, that BBC Wales recommissioned new seasons (known as 'New Who' in the secondary scholarship, as distinguishable from the 1962–89 'Classic Who') under the stewardship of Russell T. Davies. New Who has had considerable ratings and award success in its traditional markets, and has also brought the Doctor (after decades of sporadic Public Broadcasting Service (PBS) broadcasting)[8] to much greater North American awareness.[9] New Who is not a 'reimagined' series like *Battlestar Galactica*, nor a sequel/pre-sequel set within a familiar universe, such as the various *Star Trek* generations. Instead, New Who continues to narrate the ongoing adventures of the Doctor with a fan-driven respect for the cultural heritage of the series.[10]

This continuity across more than fifty-five years of broadcasting – a continuity maintained and enriched by licensed, but generally considered non-canonical, novels, radio plays,[11] magazines, generations of fan-lit,[12] and, more recently, spin-off shows, the adult *Torchwood* (2006–11) and the child/teen orientated *Sarah Jane Adventures* (2007–11) and *Class* (2016) – presents significant hurdles for the cultural scholar. Even focusing on the

[3] Bould, 'Science Fiction in the United Kingdom', p. 213.
[4] McKee, 'Is *Doctor Who* Australian?'
[5] Chapman, *Inside the TARDIS*, p. 172.
[6] Sax, *Doctor Who.*
[7] Chapman, *Inside the TARDIS*, pp. 182–3.
[8] Sullivan, 'Transporting Television in Space and Time'.
[9] Porter, *The* Doctor Who *Franchise.*
[10] Hills, *Triumph of a Time Lord*, pp. 26–33.
[11] Hills, 'Televisuality without Television?'
[12] Perryman, '*Doctor Who* and the Convergence of Media'.

core canonical television broadcasts, as at October 2017 there had been 839 individual 'instalments' encompassing 275 distinct stories.[13] In *Doctor Who: The Unfolding Text* (1983), John Tulloch and Manuel Alvarado argue that '*Doctor Who* . . . [is] an "unfolding text" subtly shifting its ground in response to social and professional pressures, yet vindicating television's recipe for success: something different but something the same'.[14]

This openness of the *Doctor Who* text, its transposition during the 1960s from a family-history-quasi-educational show to a pure fantasy/science fiction[15] and then to regularly reinvent itself every few years with change of producer, lead actors, aesthetics, and mood, yet still remaining a seemingly self-perpetuating cultural phenomenon, suggests that with *Doctor Who* the BBC hit upon the 'perfect science fiction premise'.[16] The format of the show has changed. During the original television run (1963–89), most stories were multi-episode serials. For New Who, most episodes have been stand-alone stories within season-long story arcs. Different producers have brought different emphases: Philip Hinchcliffe (1975–7) presided over a period of Gothic horror; his replacement, Graham Williams (1977–80) focused on absurdist humour;[17] John Nathan-Turner (1981–89) narrowed the show's appeal through self-referential stories pandering to hard-core fans.[18] New Who's Davies brought much more sophisticated characterisation and personal storylines,[19] while his replacement show-runner Stephen Moffat brought grander science fictional and horror themes.[20]

The clearest marker of change is the Doctor's ability to regenerate when fatally hurt. A fabulous intra-text device that initially allowed the show to continue without the ailing William Hartnell,[21] regeneration has allowed twelve different actors to play the Doctor at the time of writing, each bringing a different persona, often in contrast to their immediate predecessor. Starting with Hartnell (1963–6) as an aged, cantankerous 'grandfather' whose aloofness tended to self-importance, the Second Doctor (Patrick Troughton 1966–9) played the Doctor as a 'cosmic hobo' who ran from danger. Running from danger was not the Third Doctor's way. Jon Pertwee

[13] See <https://en.wikipedia.org/wiki/List_of_Doctor_Who_serials>, last accessed 19 October 2017.

[14] Tulloch and Alvardo, *Doctor Who*, p. 3.

[15] Chapman, *Inside the TARDIS*, p. 54.

[16] Beeler, '*Stargate SG-1* and the Quest for the Perfect Science Fiction Premise', p. 267.

[17] Chapman, *Inside the TARDIS*, pp. 98, 118.

[18] Hills, *Triumph of a Time Lord*, p. 60.

[19] Hills, 'The Dispersible Television Text', p. 28.

[20] Charles, 'The Crack of Doom'.

[21] Chapman, *Inside the TARDIS*, p. 50.

(1970–4) gave an establishment veneer to the Doctor, mostly Earth bound: his Doctor was a 'dandy' in vintage cars working James Bond-like for the alien fighting United Nations Intelligence Taskforce (UNIT). Tom Baker's (1974–81) physically imposing Fourth Doctor reinterpreted Pertwee's aristocratic persona as an Edwardian bohemian-cum-postgraduate drop-out, complete with thick uncontrolled curls and iconic knitted scarf. The Fifth Doctor, portrayed by a young and vulnerable Peter Davidson (1982–4) in an Edwardian cricket jacket, struggled to come out of both Baker's shadow and the shadow of Davidson's other gig as Tristan Farnon in *All Creatures Great and Small* (1978–81, 1990).[22] The aggressive and more prone to violence Sixth Doctor, Colin Baker (1984–7), returned some of the aloof egoism that could be seen in the First Doctor, but with even worse fashion sense. The Seventh Doctor, Sylvester McCoy (1987–9), emerged as a dark clown and considerably more Machiavellian than previous incarnations. The Eighth Doctor, Paul McGann, whose televised tenure lasted only the 1996 telemovie and a 2013 web episode was most notable for breaking a decade-old taboo by kissing his companion, something he had in common with the much angrier, impatient, fatalistic Ninth Doctor (Christopher Eccleston, 2005), suffering survivor's guilt from the Time War. The Tenth Doctor, played by David Tennant (2005–10) married mod-retro-cool[23] with establishment respectability. In this, he was more akin to the Third Doctor (including involvement with UNIT) and was a gentler, almost empathetic character. The Eleventh Doctor, Matt Smith (2010–13) brought a more alien difference and social clumsiness to the Doctor than the affable Tennant. This difference and clumsiness, along with cranky eyebrows and a return to greying hair after the younger Tennant and Smith, characterised the Twelfth Doctor, Peter Capaldi (2013–17). From 2018, along with incoming show-runner Chris Chibnall, the Doctor – after decades of male leads – will be played for the first time by a woman, Jodie Whittaker – another example of the show's elastic mega-text and capacity to regenerate.[24]

In all this change, the central device – and significantly one of the few visuals not to have changed much over the life of the show – has been the TARDIS.[25] While the interior of the TARDIS, always 'bigger on the inside', changes every few years,[26] its exterior has remained inspired by the Gilbert MacKenzie Trench-designed blue London Metropolitan Police telephone

22 Ibid., p. 142.
23 Bould, 'Science Fiction in the United Kingdom', p. 225.
24 Tranter, 'Law, the Digital and Time', p. 521.
25 Britton and Barker, *Reading between Designs*, p. 167.
26 Ibid., pp. 184–9.

Figure 5.1 TARDIS on location. 'The Caves of Androzani' (1983). Permission to reproduce from BBC Photo Archive Library

boxes that were first commissioned in 1929. The TARDIS's visual continuity, as a blue box with a light on the roof, explained by the Doctor as a failure of the 'chameleon circuit' during the maiden episode (set in then broadcast-present 1963 London),[27] provides the first glimpse of the central theme that binds the 'unfoldingness' of *Doctor Who*: time.

The TARDIS, so called by Susan Foreman (Carole Ann Ford), the First Doctor's 'granddaughter' as an acronym of Time and Relative Dimension in Space, is first and foremost a time machine. The TARDIS frees *Doctor Who* from any specific time;[28] the temporal backdrop of episodes ranges from the

[27] Hussein, 'The Unearthly Child', *Doctor Who*.

[28] Robinson, '"Did I Mention it Also Travels in Time?"'

various ends of the universe[29] to the creation of Earth[30] and to its solar obliteration.[31] The Doctor has witnessed and participated in most major events within Earth's (European) history. He has saved from alien interference a who's who of European historical and literary figures: Robespierre,[32] King John,[33] Queen Victoria,[34] H. G. Wells,[35] Homer,[36] Van Gogh,[37] Dickens,[38] Churchill,[39] and Robin Hood,[40] to name but a few. This 'timelessness' – that the Doctor and TARDIS are beyond time, materialising within spacetime only to vanish again with a grinding whir – allows the openness of the *Doctor Who* text. Its narratives are not necessarily located by a time or place, and writers and producers have borrowed from the science fiction archive nearly the full gamut of imagined worlds, races, histories, and places. Indeed, whole books have been written cataloguing the adaptions of genres, stories, and motifs within *Doctor Who*.[41] There is a Dune-inspired episode of mobile sand mining on a desert planet,[42] and so many retellings of *Frankenstein* that the episodes are almost beyond count.[43]

In this, the Doctor adventures within an empty universe. His is a universe that is without a divine; claims to the godhead tend to be the hallmark of delusional aliens, computers, and the like.[44] It is a universe composed only of matter and time.[45] This glimpses the speculative antecedent for the Doctor's universe in H. G. Wells' *Time Machine* (1895).[46] This Wellsian universe of inhuman time, of the flimsily veneer of civilisation, and the

[29] Harper, 'Utopia', *Doctor Who*.
[30] Euros, 'The Runaway Bride', *Doctor Who*.
[31] Euros, 'The End of the World', *Doctor Who*.
[32] Hirsch, 'The Reign of Terror', *Doctor Who*.
[33] Virgo, 'The King's Demons', *Doctor Who*.
[34] Euros, 'Tooth and Claw', *Doctor Who*.
[35] Roberts, 'Timelash', *Doctor Who*.
[36] Leeston-Smith, 'The Myth Makers', *Doctor Who*.
[37] Campbell, 'Vicent and the Doctor', *Doctor Who*.
[38] Euros, 'The Unquiet Dead', *Doctor Who*.
[39] Gunn, 'Victory of the Daleks', *Doctor Who*.
[40] Murphy, 'Robot of Sherwood', *Doctor Who*.
[41] Harmes, *Doctor Who and the Art of Adaption*.
[42] Briant, 'The Robots of Death', *Doctor Who*.
[43] See, for example, Ferguson, 'The War Machines', *Doctor Who*; Maloney, 'Genesis of the Daleks', *Doctor Who*.
[44] See, for example, Black, 'Four to Doomsday', *Doctor Who*; Wareing, 'The Greatest Show in the Galaxy', *Doctor Who*; Talalay, 'Death in Heaven'; Layton, *The Humanism of Doctor Who*, p. 135.
[45] Tranter, '"Her Brain was Full of Superstitious Nonsense"'.
[46] Wells, *The Time Machine*; Tulloch and Alvardo, *Doctor Who*, pp. 121–6.

ceaseless working over of matter by time, is a core element of the *Doctor Who* mega-text. If there is deity in the Doctor's universe(s), it is not the rather pathetic Black and White Guardians from Season 16 (1978–9), but rather Wells' mentor, T. H. Huxley.[47] *Doctor Who* occurs within a particular space, the evolutionary universe, a universe of matter and time, and where reason, civilisation, and life are coincident, random, and chance.[48] It is little wonder that *Doctor Who* is Richard Dawkins' science fiction of choice, having married a former companion (Romana II, Lalla Ward) and made a guest appearance as himself in a story.[49] This empty, random universe explains the continual haphazardness to the Doctor's adventures. The TARDIS rarely goes where it is supposed to. Repeatedly, the wrong that the Doctor rights is revealed not as intentionally malicious, but rather as an accident or misunderstanding – a crash-landed spaceship[50] or a lost alien[51] – something out of place and time – something not needing a solider to combat, but a physician to heal.

This also explains the comedic splicing of genres that also characterises the series. Poignancy and parody, horror and humour, fantastic and farce sit side by side within *Doctor Who* stories. *Doctor Who* is not Dune, a tragedy where spirit is pitted against limit; rather, as Meeker argues, the defining genre for a universe without authoritative meaning is comedy.[52] The Doctor is more a clown than hero, something rendered a bit too obvious in his wardrobe during the Nathan–Turner period. This can be seen in *Doctor Who* alumni. Douglas Adams, the master of the absurdist/poignant science fiction, began as script writer and then script editor with *Doctor Who* in the late 1970s.[53]

This empty vision of the life, the universe, and everything, where the only certainty is time, discloses a specific account of time. It is chronology.[54] Time is ordered as a succession of events; there is no movement.[55] There is a vista of time, of a chronology of events; this happened, then that.[56] There is not becoming as it has been considered from the location of the technical legal subject – just events in time that the chronologist outside of time maps. Here

47 Suvin, *Metamorphoses of Science Fiction*, p. 223.
48 Rose, 'Filling the Void', p. 129.
49 Harper, 'The Stolen Earth', *Doctor Who*.
50 Morshead, 'The Lodger', *Doctor Who*.
51 Campbell, 'Vicent and the Doctor', *Doctor Who*.
52 Meeker, *The Comedy of Survival*, pp. 15–16.
53 Tulloch and Alvardo, *Doctor Who*, p. 160.
54 Tranter, 'In and Out of Time'.
55 Bourne, *A Future for Presentism*, p. 3.
56 McTaggart, *The Nature of Existence*, p. 10 [306].

the Doctor's species name seems apt. He is a Time Lord, and his relation to time can be seen in sovereign-like terms: he lords time.

This lording of time, from a timeless location, reverberates with law as technology. As discussed in Chapter 2, in modernity law has become chronological.[57] This has been apparent to positivism's critics. John Finnis can be pictured in a TARDIS summoning out-of-time moment. Pen clasped at the University of Malawi, he is staking a case for the certainty of the Thomist world-view to save humanity from modernity:

> The primary legal method of showing that a rule is valid is to show (i) that there was at some past time, $t_{1,}$ an act (of a legislature, court, or other appropriate institution) which according to the rules in force at t_1 amounted to a valid and therefore operative act of rule-creation and (ii) that since t_1 the rule thus created has not determined (ceased to be in force) by virtue either of its own terms or of any act of repeal valid according to the rules of repeal in force at times $t_{2,}$ t_3.[58]

From Finnis's speculative location of flourishing, he can see the sterile physics – emphasised through thermodynamic notation (t_1) – of chronology at play in positive law. That is, he glimpses the inhuman emptiness of what it means to make law, to stand beyond time so as to order it.

It is trite to say that law is only a very minor feature of *Doctor Who*, notwithstanding the central icon of a police box. After all, this surface allusion to a legal institution is just a mirage. The Doctor is not a lawman – indeed, in his relationship with his own species, he tends to be an outlaw who originally stole the TARDIS.[59] He was twice brought to account for breaching the Time Lords' vague and hypocritical postulates of non-interference[60] and he regularly expresses frustration and ridicules rule-bound formalists the universe over. A law in literature analysis of *Doctor Who* would come up remarkably short of material. Time Lord courts are uninspired, big-collared, run-of-the-mill television courts. The 'Shadow Proclamation' turns out to be an incipit 'League of Nations'[61] and the various legalities sprouted by the Seventh Doctor tend to just make the aliens angrier.[62] Even the grandiose

[57] See Chapter 2, pp. 70–5.

[58] Finnis, *Natural Law and Natural Rights*, p. 268.

[59] Maloney, 'The War Games', *Doctor Who*; Clark, 'The Doctor's Wife', *Doctor Who.*

[60] Maloney, 'The War Games', *Doctor Who*; Clough, Jones and Mallett, 'The Trial of a Time Lord', *Doctor Who.*

[61] Harper, 'The Stolen Earth', *Doctor Who.*

[62] Clough, 'Delta and the Bannermen', *Doctor Who.*

'Laws of Time' appear mutable.[63] Indeed, the only direction for such an analysis would be in recognising that *Doctor Who*, through repeated representation of idiotic formalists and incompetent and corrupt legal institutions, is a thoroughly anti-law text. The saving direction for such an analysis would be in seeing in the Doctor a fidelity to a higher law. This would run into an ontological barrier in that the dichotomy between positive law and higher law, of a lesser world of semblances, and a pure realm of being, is not the Doctor's empty universe of just time and matter.

So there are few manifestations of either mundane legality or higher law in *Doctor Who*. However, there is timelessness turned to chronology. The Doctor has a personal history. Intra-text successive regeneration numbers off from Hartnell's First.[64] This linearity is made explicit in multiple ways through the text. The anniversary specials see various Doctors sort of working together, complete with gentle ribbing directed to the older, but seen as younger, junior version.[65] Often images of earlier Doctors are used to locate more recent ones.[66] 'Past' companions return[67] and defeated foes come back, again and again. Some regeneration scenes involve montages of that Doctor's companions and triumphs.[68] Often one adventure flows into another. True to his haphazard universe, the Doctor often has to clean up the unexpected consequences of his previous engagements.[69] However, these allusions to the timelessness of modern law, of a location outside time, through which time can be known and ordered, are not the Doctor's; they are the viewers'.

Doctor Who cannot be thought about without the generations of audiences and fans. *Doctor Who*'s uniqueness as a mainstream, family-orientated science fiction means that it has been appreciated by children from behind the sofa who grew to be parents with their own children behind the sofa.[70]

63 Harper, 'Waters of Mars', *Doctor Who.*

64 Smith, 'The Eleventh Hour', *Doctor Who.*

65 Mayne, 'The Three Doctors', *Doctor Who*; Moffatt, 'The Five Doctors', *Doctor Who*; Hurran, 'The Day of the Doctor', *Doctor Who.*

66 For example, Palmer, 'The Family of Blood', *Doctor Who*; Smith, 'The Eleventh Hour', *Doctor Who.*

67 Hawes, 'School Reunion', *Doctor Who*; Payne, 'The Time of the Doctor', *Doctor Who.*

68 Grimwade, 'The Keeper of Traken', *Doctor Who.*

69 Roberts, 'The Face of Evil', *Doctor Who*; Ahearne, 'Bad Wolf', *Doctor Who.*

70 Children hiding behind the sofa are one of the deep cultural memories of *Doctor Who* in England and Australia, so much so that the Museum of the Moving Image in London titled its 1991 *Doctor Who* exhibition 'Behind the Sofa'. Indeed, small children are often said to have listened to *Doctor Who* from 'behind the sofa'. Hills, 'Listening from behind the Sofa?' On intergenerational viewing of *Doctor Who*, see Perryman, *Adventures with the Wife in Space.*

Predating the later fan culture of *Star Trek* and *The X-Files, Doctor Who* spawned appreciation societies the world over and with that fanzines and fan-lits, nurtured by an ever-opportunistic BBC that, from 1963 onwards, produced licensed books, annuals, and merchandise.[71] Dalekmania and Beatlemania went hand in plunger.[72] The weight of this experience of *Doctor Who* is a tendency to reinforce chronology. The child grown to adult can co-locate life milestones with those that the Doctor was overcoming on Saturday evenings, and fan-culture in its ceaseless turning over of episodes drives the Great Chronology – the contested canonical accounts of the Doctor.[73] But something has happened in this remembering of times that were experienced. Remembering and memory are not timeless. These are not statements of the chronologist standing outside of the time-stream. It is not the clinical 't_1'. These are 'timeful' experiences: a lived present that is then recollected, rethought, and reordered as memory; a dynamic past that is continually reassessed, details remembered, and others dimmed; a past where mnemonic moments renew and refresh – much like the BBC's search engine for the online archive of Classic Who stories, which allows searching by way of 'It's the one with . . .'[74] While the Doctor may be a Time Lord, his viewers are only humans, thrown linearly into a universe that is experienced, a future that is always closed and a past that lives on through memory.

Notwithstanding the established title sequence of travelling the time vortex, a pure expression of chronology, even the Doctor does not experience time as chronology. The Doctor often intersects persons and events in reverse chronological order. The sometimes companion/killer/lover/wife River Song (Alex Kingston) plays on this as she keeps meeting the Doctor 'too soon'.[75] There are occasional mentions of the Time Lord's awareness of the passage

[71] Bignell, 'The Child as Adressee', pp. 51–3.

[72] Chapman, 'Fifty Years in the TARDIS', pp. 47–8.

[73] See, for example, Cornell, Day, and Topping, *The Discontinuity Guide*. On 'periodising' *Doctor Who*, see Booth, 'Periodising Doctor Who'.

[74] See <http://www.bbc.co.uk/doctorwho/classic/episodeguide/oohum/index.shtml>, last accessed 22 February 2017.

[75] Euros, 'Silence in the Library', *Doctor Who*; Euros, 'Forest of the Dead', *Doctor Who*; Adam, 'The Time of Angels', *Doctor Who*; Adam, 'Flesh and Stone', *Doctor Who*; Haynes, 'The Pandorica Opens', *Doctor Who*; Haynes, 'The Big Bang', *Doctor Who*; Haynes, 'The Impossible Astronaut', *Doctor Who*; Haynes, 'Day of the Moon', *Doctor Who*; Hoar, 'A Good Man Goes to War', *Doctor Who*; Senior, 'Let's Kill Hitler', *Doctor Who*; Webb, 'The Wedding of River Song', *Doctor Who*; Metzstein, 'The Name of the Doctor', *Doctor Who*; Hurran, 'The Angels Take Manhattan', *Doctor Who*; Mackinnon, 'The Husbands of River Song', *Doctor Who*.

of time,[76] and there is the Doctor's frustration with experiencing linear time when he has lost the TARDIS.[77] The timelessness of the Doctor means that chronological past and future are fluid. The Doctor repeatedly changes the past. Even supposed fixed points in history – the first human colony of Mars, the supposed immutable Time War – opens to his meddling.[78] He has moved between parallel dimensions of alternative times,[79] but ultimately knowledge of his true fate remains obscured. 'Spoilers!' scolds River Song, and the Doctor withdraws his hand from her diary that writes of his future.[80] From this position, the Doctor's life appears chaotic, blown on the time winds, truly timeless.

However, the Doctor is not out of time. He may be an alien face-changer with two hearts and possess a TARDIS, but he seems not to wander too far from the broadcast-present United Kingdom. Ultimately, the Doctor is English – as is confessed to a confused American in the telemovie.[81] In this, *Doctor Who* can be read as a cultural time capsule documenting fifty years of social and broadcasting change in the United Kingdom, from various images of 'independent women' ranging from sixties swinger Polly (Anneke Wills), to naïve intellectual Zoe Herriot (Wendy Padbury), to career woman Sarah Jane Smith (Elisabeth Sladen), to proto-*Xena: Warrior Princess* fantasy pin-up Leela (Louise Jameson), to the anxieties of the common market during the Pertwee era[82] and a nostalgia for empire,[83] to the aggression of early 1980s Thatcher England,[84] to the complexities of cosmopolitan post-imperial United Kingdom[85] where a community of difference from the Tennant tenure – under-employed Londoners Rose Tyler (Billie Piper) and Donna Nobel (Catherine Tate), black middle-class Martha Jones (Freema Agyeman), and gay and omnisexual Captain Jack Harkness (John Barrowman) – is continually threatened by alien destruction. Guest appearances mark moments in British popular culture, from John Cleese[86] to Bill

76 Boak, 'Rose', *Doctor Who*; Hurran, 'The Angels Take Manhattan', *Doctor Who*.

77 Strong, 'The Impossible Planet', *Doctor Who*; Strong, 'The Satan Pit', *Doctor Who*.

78 Harper, 'Waters of Mars', *Doctor Who*; Hurran, 'The Day of the Doctor', *Doctor Who*.

79 Camfield, 'Inferno', *Doctor Who*.

80 Haynes, 'The Big Bang', *Doctor Who*.

81 Sax, *Doctor Who*; Brown, 'Doctor Who: A Very British Alien'.

82 Chapman, *Inside the TARDIS*, p. 82.

83 Grady and Hemstrom, 'Nostalgia for Empire, 1963–1974'.

84 Chapman, *Inside the TARDIS*, p. 157.

85 Gupta, '*Doctor Who* and Race'.

86 Hayes, 'City of Death', *Doctor Who*.

Nighy[87] to Kylie Minogue.[88] However, putting to one side jokes about the BBC's (lack of) budget as the explanation for the Doctor's Englishness and the TARDIS's jammed chameleon circuit, this suggests that the Doctor's existence is not empty. It is full of time.

This explains the significance of memory in *Doctor Who*. The Doctor repeatedly remembers. Indeed, Capaldi's Twelfth Doctor does not become 'doctorish' until he begins to remember.[89] Not a story goes by without the Doctor looking serious and then pronouncing 'This isn't right' as a precursor to making it right. This memory is not to be confused with a chronologist's recording; the Doctor particularly enjoys correcting historians, museums, and archaeologists.[90] Memory – the experience of time – is triumphed over the cold ordering of time. This recognition was made explicit in the first Matt Smith season (2010), where 'cracks in time' were erasing existence. The Doctor overcomes through memory; the past no longer had a physical existence, having faded to white, yet it was in the scattered recollections of Amy Pond (Karen Gillan) that the universe, and the Doctor himself, could be restored.[91]

What can be seen in *Doctor Who*, to adapt Costas Douzinas's phrase is that 'dual time'[92] of sovereignty from Chapter 2. There is the timelessness of linear time and chronology and timefulness of experiential time and memory. Furthermore, there is a preference for experiential time against the meaninglessness of linear time. In facing two past companions, Sarah Jane and Jo Grant (Kat Manning), in the 'Death of the Doctor' (2010) episode of the *Sarah Jane Adventures*, the Doctor urges them to value their memories:

> Because your memories are more powerful than anything else on this planet. Just think of it, Sarah. Remember it, Jo. But properly. Properly. Give the memory weave everything. Every planet. Every face. Every mad man. Every loss. Every sunset. Every scent. Every terror. Every joy. Every Doctor. Every me.[93]

Even the Doctor – actually, especially the Doctor – is a Being-in-time. His time does not quite tick-tock with the rest of the universe, but his meaning and his missions stem from memory. His is not necessarily a warm memory

[87] Campbell, 'Vicent and the Doctor', *Doctor Who*.

[88] Strong, 'Voyage of the Dammed', *Doctor*.

[89] Wheatley, 'Deep Breath', *Doctor Who*.

[90] Euros, 'Silence in the Library', *Doctor Who*; Adam, 'The Time of Angels', *Doctor Who*.

[91] Haynes, 'The Big Bang', *Doctor Who*.

[92] Douzinas, 'Theses on Law, History and Time', p. 17.

[93] Way, 'Death of the Doctor', *The Sarah Jane Adventures*.

of favoured recollections. The thousands of years of the Doctor's past (the assumption is Earth years and not the years of his ancestral planet, Gallifrey) is sorrowful. There are the perennial foes – Daleks, Cybermen, the Master – who keep returning. There are the sad memories of all the young women and occasionally young men who have travelled with him and then grown out of his blue box. There are the time-loops and pasts-that-never-were that he has experienced.[94] There was the loss and responsibility from the interceding Time War that brings the Ninth Doctor to rage, the Tenth Doctor to a sad silence, and the Eleventh Doctor to change the topic of conversation. What *Doctor Who* does, notwithstanding its unfolding-ness, is project, play, and order the West's traditions of time – those exact times from which law as technology emerges. In *Doctor Who*, as with law as technology, time in its complexity imposes.

The locus of linear time and experiential time is event. The event marks the crossing of these two timescales. The event stands out from the mundane of the everyday; it is remembered, and it is noted on calendars. For Heidegger and much of the Western philosophical tradition,[95] the ultimate event – the event that allows Being, so as to be in-time, but also the event most sacred to the ancient chronologists – is death.

Death and the Doctor

The Doctor brings death. Russell T. Davies in the New Who opener 'Rose' (2005) played on this feature of the Doctor's adventures. Rose, the companion-to-be, showing more twenty-first century nous than earlier companions, researches 'the Doctor' and 'blue box' on the Internet before jumping into the TARDIS. This leads her to Clive (Mark Benton) who, in a parody of *Doctor Who* fandom,[96] runs a conspiracy-theory website about the Doctor. According to Clive, the Doctor is a bringer of death; the only certainty if the Doctor is about is that people are going to die. Indeed, Clive goes on to die in an Auton blast.

Davies makes the point in 'Rose' that for a family show it involves a lot of death.[97] Rarely does a *Doctor Who* story go by without several deaths, and during the Hinchcliffe–Tom Baker period, death came thick and fast in each instalment. Continuing this knowing acknowledgement to death in the 2005

[94] Hughes, 'Closing Time', *Doctor Who*; Webb, 'The Wedding of River Song', *Doctor Who*; King, 'Journey to the Centre of the TARDIS', *Doctor Who*; Talalay, 'Heaven Sent', *Doctor Who*; Tranter, 'Narrative and Paradoxes in *Doctor Who* "Time Loop" Stories'.

[95] Braidotti, *Transpositions*, p. 210.

[96] Hills, *Triumph of a Time Lord*, p. 215.

[97] Gibbs, '"Maybe That's What Happens if You Touch the Doctor"'.

'reboot' season, the episode 'The Doctor Dances' has the Doctor dancing precisely because there was no death.[98] The 2011 mid-season finale continues this; the Doctor is told that, generations after his adventures in the Gamma Forests, 'Doctor' has come to be the title of a great warrior.[99] Unlike other television science fictions, where death is pre-coded on to specific characters, the hapless ensign or the malevolent foe, death in *Doctor Who* – in keeping with its empty universe – is more widely distributed. In *Doctor Who*, anyone can die – not just those who deserve it.

There is a need, then, to catalogue the death in *Doctor Who*. There are two types of death. First, there is death where there is a body. This death, as evidenced by remains, is the most common death in *Doctor Who*. More precisely there is a witnessing of the taking of life. Characters crumple to the floor from a Dalek's gun after a fleeting X-rayed skeletal image, they slump from poison, or writhe in agony with a mutation gone wrong. Fleeing humans fall screaming during the 'scourging of Earth' in the season finales for 2006, 2007, and 2008.[100] Forgettable numbers of UNIT soldiers fall in the line of duty to the Third Doctor's and Brigadier Lethbridge-Stewart's (Nicholas Courtney) repulsion of another threat.[101] There is a message to this broadcasted bodily death. Poignant moments, glimpses of the Doctor's tenderness, can be seen when the 'nice' human, animal, mutant, alien, cyborg – whatever – is terminally injured, having intervened at the last minute to save the Doctor and his companion in the climactic moment from the big bad.[102] This template is also deployed in the stories where the bad turns out to be an innocent, a lost, or confused alien, with the Doctor – and Tennant was particularly good at this – sadly apologising.[103] In the Doctor's universe, the spark of life is taken from the innocent and the good, and their 'meat' remains, inert lumps on a BBC soundstage, quarry, or Cardiff street. However, this bodily death is not the only death.

The truly malevolent foes are rarely allowed a bodily death. Their deaths often see the annihilation of the body in pyrotechnics. In 'The Talons of

[98] Hawes, 'The Doctor Dances', *Doctor Who*.

[99] Hoar, 'A Good Man Goes to War', *Doctor Who*.

[100] Strong, 'Doomsday', *Doctor Who*; Teague, 'Last of the Time Lords', *Doctor Who*; Harper, 'Journey's End', *Doctor Who*.

[101] Combe, '*Doctor Who* and the Silurian', *Doctor Who*; Russell, 'Invasion of the Dinosaurs', *Doctor Who*.

[102] Hurran, 'The God Complex', *Doctor Who*; Strong, 'Voyage of the Damned', *Doctor Who*; Mackinnon, 'The Posion Sky', *Doctor Who*.

[103] Hawes, 'New Earth', *Doctor Who*; MacRae, 'The Age of Steel', *Doctor Who*; Teague, 'Last of the Time Lords', *Doctor Who*; Euros, 'Silence in the Library', *Doctor Who*; Goddard, 'The Next Doctor', *Doctor Who*.

Weng-Chiang' (1977),[104] the fifty-first century fugitive Magnus Greel (Michael Spice) dissolves to ash. This scene of bodily decomposition has been repeated for other foes. The Daleks and their assembled war machines seem particularly good at exploding in unison,[105] something that they share with the Sontarans;[106] and in the 2006 finale, the Cybermen are dispatched to the nothing between dimensions, while in the 2014 finale they explode in the sky.[107] Davros, the creator of the Daleks, is never seen dead in his proto-Dalek chair, the twisted remains of a twisted being; his death is only ever alluded to.[108] So a clear coding seems to be at play. The innocent and good leave bodily remains; the truly bad leave nothing.

However, this is not so simple. Three of the Doctor's companions have died (and stayed dead): Katarina (Adrienne Hill), Ardic (Matthew Waterhouse), and Astrid Peth (Kylie Minogue). In death, they did not leave bodies. Katarina floats off into space to save the TARDIS,[109] Ardic is caught on a detonating space freighter,[110] and a spectral Astrid is freed to float the galaxy as dust.[111] Others, like recent companions Rose, Clara Oswald (Jenna Coleman), and Bill Potts (Pearl Mackie), cheat death and bodily remains: Rose in an alternate universe; Clara through a timey-wimey trick that freezes her life in her last heartbeat;[112] and Bill through conversion into a Mondassian cyberman and then union with a liquid space and time-travelling entity.[113] The moralising assumption that the good or innocent leave bodies over to be mourned and the bad turn to nothing is not the way of *Doctor Who*. The right to a body belongs to the small and mundane; the more powerful in this universe, the more that matter and time is bent to will, the less of a body that remains. Companions, as the secondary literature has made abundantly clear, belong with the Doctor – indeed, complete the Doctor.[114] It is the closeness to the Doctor that means that they are deprived of a bodily death.

[104] Maloney, 'The Talons of Weng-Chiang', *DoctorWho.*

[105] Briant, 'Death to the Daleks', *Doctor Who*; Robinson, 'Resurrection of the Daleks', *Doctor Who*; Ahearne, 'The Parting of the Ways', *Doctor Who*; Harper,'Journey's End', *Doctor Who*; MacDonald, 'The Witch's Familiar', *Doctor Who.*

[106] Mackinnon, 'The Posion Sky', *Doctor Who.*

[107] Strong, 'Doomsday', *Doctor Who*; Talalay, 'Death in Heaven', *Doctor Who.*

[108] Maloney, 'Genesis of the Daleks', *Doctor Who*; Grieve, 'Destiny of the Daleks', *Doctor Who*; Robinson, 'Resurrection of the Daleks', *Doctor Who.*

[109] Camfield, 'The Daleks' Master Plan', *Doctor Who.*

[110] Grimwade, 'Earthshock', *Doctor Who.*

[111] Strong, 'Voyage of the Dammed', *Doctor Who.*

[112] Talalay, 'Hell Bent', *Doctor Who.*

[113] Talalay, 'The Doctor Falls', *Doctor Who.*

[114] Amy-Chinn, 'Rose Tyler'.

For, ultimately, Time Lords are denied a body. The Doctor occupies a body and, often at the point of regeneration, laments the soon-to-be passing of that body,[115] but in a blaze of light and some television sleight-of-hand appears in a new one. His supposed end in the tomb on Trenzalore is as twisting cracks of light.[116] Regeneration sends the message that power transcends the body, that it is outside matter. The Master moves on from bodies, not only regenerating – on three occasions seeming to be able to sustain his essence outside of the flesh[117] but in recent seasons comes back sex-changed (as the Doctor, too, is about to do) and called Missy.[118] The Time Lords find a way to reappear to history, Gallifrey and all.[119] The Daleks, Cybermen, and Sontarans just keep coming back. Utter destruction at the Doctor's hands does not seem to prevent them from menacing again. In this category, the body is transcended. There can be seen an essential further feature that unifies the Doctor, Master/Missy, Time Lords, Daleks, Cybermen, and Soltarans: they all possess time travel and they are all takers of life.

Of course, the Master/Missy, Daleks, Cybermen, and Soltarans take life. This is the essential coding that demarks them as foes and the Time Lords in their smug superiority appear, on several occasions, quite capable of sharing in the extermination.[120] However, the Doctor is not just a witness to death, nor simply a cheater of bodily death, but the biggest killer of all. A story rarely goes by without the Doctor's involvement in death. This goes beyond the occasional epic 'kill or be killed' showdown with a malevolent foe. The Doctor euthanises.[121] The Doctor stands by when, for his purposes, another takes life,[122] or he pathetically makes a mistake, miscalculates, gets over-excited, and someone, something dies. That the Doctor is more like an officer or general ordering death is a particular theme in the 2014 season.[123]

115 Euros, 'The End of Time', *Doctor Who*.

116 Metzstein, 'The Name of the Doctor', *Doctor Who*.

117 Grimwade, 'The Keeper of Traken', *Doctor Who*; Sax, *Doctor Who*; Euros, 'The End of Time', *Doctor Who*.

118 Talalay, 'Dark Water', *Doctor Who*; Talalay, 'Death in Heaven', *Doctor Who*; MacDonald, 'The Magician's Apprentice', *Doctor Who*; MacDonald, 'The Witch's Familiar', *Doctor Who*.

119 Euros, 'The End of Time', *Doctor Who*; Payne, 'The Time of the Doctor', *Doctor Who*; Talalay, 'Hell Bent', *Doctor Who*.

120 Clough, Jones and Mallett,'The Trial of a Time Lord', *Doctor Who*; Euros, 'The End of Time', *Doctor Who*.

121 See, for example, Hurran, 'The God Complex', *Doctor Who*; Campbell, 'Vincent and the Doctor', *Doctor Who*.

122 Martin, 'The Web Planet', *Doctor Who*, where the First Doctor allows his companion Barbara to destroy the Animus.

123 Wilmshurst, 'Mummy on the Orient Express', *Doctor Who*; Talalay, 'Death in Heaven', *Doctor Who*.

Of course, the show makes a critical difference between death by Doctor and death by Dalek, Cyberman, Master, and so forth. The Doctor brings death mostly as a last resort, after appeal to emotion and reason has failed. Often there is a macabre calculus involved – this death to prevent greater death or, more often, an innocent heroically sacrifices themselves to save the Doctor and his companion.[124] Unlike the Master/Missy, where life-taking is flippant, or the xeno-racist Daleks, who hate and destroy all non-Dalek life, killing for the Doctor involves sadness, regret, frustration, and weight of decision. The Fourth Doctor pauses to pontificate about whether he should cause the genocide of the Daleks.[125] The Third Doctor is repeatedly frustrated at the needless death that goes with the Brigadier's 'tally-ho' shoot-first policy.[126] The Tenth Doctor offers the Dalek–human hybrid a new planet and a fresh future.[127] The Doctor always pauses and pleads with the Master/Missy, invariably allowing his foiled 'old friend' to slip away.[128] The Doctor only occasionally dances, but he nearly always regrets.

However, notwithstanding this emotional difference between the Doctor and the other life-takers – a difference often emphasised through narratives that have the Doctor destroying Daleks and Cybermen through emotional infection[129] – in a divine-free universe it matters little to the crumpled meat on the floor whether their killer feels sorry or jubilant. The residual imagery is death of the body and bodiless life-taking.

As with time, this body-death complex of bodily death and bodiless life-taking resonates with the alchemist explorations of Chapter 2. To elaborate the argument, modern law is law because behind every technical pronouncement, behind every bland lawyer going through the routine motions of keeping the legal network ticking over, infused in the very air of dark wood panelled Victorian-era courtrooms and in light-filled, modernist, corporate offices, dripping from the forms, peering out from behind the liquid-crystal display (LCD) screen of the junior lawyer's workstation, is death. Robert Cover's now familiar identification that 'legal interpretation takes place in a field of pain and death',[130] like the cracks in the time from the 2010 season of *Doctor Who*, suggests that the legal network is death saturated. As

124 See, for example, Barry, 'The Tomb of the Cybermen', *Doctor Who*; Euros, 'Midnight', *Doctor Who*.

125 Maloney, 'Genesis of the Daleks', *Doctor Who*.

126 Combe, 'Doctor Who and the Silurian', *Doctor Who*.

127 Strong, 'Evolution of the Daleks', *Doctor Who*.

128 Letts, 'Terror of the Autons', *Doctor Who*; Bernard, 'Frontier in Space', *Doctor Who*.

129 Martinus, 'The Evil of the Daleks', *Doctor Who*; MacRae, 'The Age of Steel', *Doctor Who*.

130 Cover, 'Violence and the Word', p. 1,601.

Schmitt observed, in modern law death had been liberated from the specific monstrous body of the sovereign and become infused in every action that was legal.[131] Of course, only the 'bad man' truly appreciates this.[132] Death, the Western materialist tradition repeatedly emphasises,[133] is the ultimate change to the trajectory of matter in time. To kill is to shut off a form of future. The death-event irreversibly excludes a specific embodiment, with all its potentiality, from participation in the becoming of the universe. This is the extreme manifestation of legal power – Cover was foremost writing about capital punishment – but its less extreme manifestations are glimpsed in the everyday working of law. The legal network changes relations within other networks. It reprograms, severing and rewiring connections; further as was seen in Chapter 4, the law network constructs nodes as locus points for rights, responsibilities and resources. In channelling death and time, law frames, delineates, and gives form to life.

To work the legal network – that is, to be 'lawyer' – is to be the wielder of time and death. To be a lawyer of technical legality is to deal in time. Lawyers write future. A contract, agreement, letter, court decision is nothing else but an attempt to fix time, to peer through the time vortex and assume that certain actions will occur. The formal making of law by the politico-legal networks of the West in response to cloning as mapped in Chapter 1 is a grander manifestation of this power over time that procedurally and routinely emanates from the lawyer-node workstations. Lawyers write the past. Formal dispositions, affidavits, interrogatories, statements in letters of advice and demand, order the past. Mere memory and the material artefacts of mnemonic recognition become transmuted into chronology. In this, lawyers work the machines of 'white mythology' that set 'history' into its timeless space apart from the vagrancies of memory.

Further, lawyers of technical legality deal in death; in working the machines, the becoming of the world changes. This is obvious in the fields of legal practice where the biopolitical heritage of modern law manifests close to the surface. In criminal, family, street level, or military law-work, the ordering of biomass is plain to see. Bodies are located, locked away, regulated, and killed in space and time. Total institutions flourish. But even in the more bodiless dimensions to legal practice, the law-work that appears to be solely at the level of tinkering with the networks such as the rarefied heights of commercial and securities law, the Global Financial Crisis (GFC), has been the latest material reminder that the clever work by 'wiz-kids' has material

[131] See Chapter 2, p. 66.

[132] Holmes, 'The Path of Law', p. 477.

[133] Cohen, 'Levinas: Thinking Least about Death'.

consequences on the becoming of the world and the potential and relations of the technical legal subjects within it.[134]

To be a lawyer-node in this moment in the West is to change becoming – to meddle in the primordial elements of the universe, and in so doing give finitude and structure to lesser beings' little lives. It is to be more than a monstrous being; indeed, it is to be a demonic entity whose medium is the primal substance of the universe: death and time. If the technical legal subject that emerged from Chapter 4 can be considered a monster, then the lawyer-node is something more. For the Doctor, monsters are lesser beings:

> *Doctor:* Everyone has nightmares. Even the monsters under the bed have nightmares!
> *Young Reinette:* What do monsters have nightmares about?
> *Doctor:* Me.[135]

In this, the Doctor, Daleks, Cybermen, Sontarans, the Master/Missy, and Time Lords can be seen as something beyond a mere monster. They are all alchemists of time and death, and as such form a community of primal lawyers. Here the 'vast narrative'[136] texts of *Doctor Who* are instructive. The Doctor properly belongs to this demonic community of primal lawyers – whose mastery of time and death means they lord over lesser, temporally limited, and powerless beings; however, his lording is different. The Doctor endures from his fifty-five years of BBC broadcasts because his lordship is, again for want for a better word, 'ethical'. It is this ethics of the Doctor that can be seen as connecting with responsibility for becoming for lawyer-nodes in the technical West: the Doctor provides the paradigm of the technical lawyer.

The Doctor as the Paradigm Technical Lawyer

For the *Doctor Who* secondary literature and fan literature, the Doctor's ethics is a point of conjecture. The ethics of the Doctor is seen as complex and contested. In this, the Doctor's obvious identity as a heteronormative white male of privilege is problematised.

The Doctor changes bodies, but his identity has been fairly consistent. Unlike the Master, he has for the last fifty-five broadcast years been a 'he'. The twelve regenerations have consistently been white, heterosexual males of privilege. The scruffy professor personas of Troughton, McCoy, Smith, and

134 Lipshaw, 'The Epistemology of the Financial Crisis'.
135 Euros, 'The Girl in the Fireplace', *Doctor Who*.
136 Cranny-Francis and Tulloch, 'Vaster than Empire(s)'.

Capaldi, and the everyman of 'every planet has a north'[137] Eccleston, still retain glimpses of the knowing, Byronic, aristocratic airs that are strongly manifest by Hartnell, Pertwee, the Bakers, Davidson, and Tennant. For cultural studies of the past thirty years, this privileged being is in need of change – not necessarily of extermination, but certainly of deconstruction.

The male–female coding in *Doctor Who* is an obvious point of concern, which may be redressed through the casting of Jodie Whittaker as the Thirteenth Doctor. The Doctor can all too easily be seen as the male face of judgement, needing a female voice of care and compassion.[138] This was most clear in the Ninth/Tenth Doctor–Rose partnership, but its echo can be seen in most of the Doctor's relationships with female companions. Sarah Jane would regularly question the Third and Fourth Doctor over his decisions;[139] Clara Oswald did the same to the Twelfth.[140] Further and clearly projected by the female companions in New Who was that the female companion's function was to enlist the episode ally. While the Doctor was prancing around sonic screwdriver-ing and blustering at authority figures, it would be Rose, Martha, Donna, Amy, Clara, or Bill who, through empathy, talk, and care, would make friends with the scared/shy/lost 'small person' (maid/child/alien) who holds the key to the resolution of the episode's narrative. Episode after episode seems to repeatedly show that the Doctor's male 'separation' needs to be balanced by female 'connection'.[141] But this is not universal. The Doctor sometimes has to explain his caring to an enraged female companion who demands bloody justice.

A focus on the male Doctor–female companion(s) relationship leads to the querulous pontificating of sex in the TARDIS. The Doctor clearly has a preference for young, white, English women. Notwithstanding Classic Who's dictate of no sex – Sarah Jane's sultry calls of 'Doc-tor',[142] Leela's (lack of) wardrobe, Tegan Jovanka's (Janet Fielding) leather mini-skirt, Peri Brown's (Nicola Bryant) breasts,[143] real-life couple Tom Baker and Lalla Ward's ad-libbed banter during Season 17 (1979–80) – means that a certain sex discourse was always circulating. Classic Who broadcast heterosexuality from a male perspective.[144] Females possessed sexualised bodies for the

137 Boak, 'Rose', *Doctor Who*.

138 Amy-Chinn, 'Rose Tyler'.

139 Barry, 'Robot', *Doctor Who*; Bromly, 'The Time Warrior', *Doctor Who*.

140 Wilmshurst, 'Mummy on the Orient Express', *Doctor Who*; Bazalgette, 'The Girl Who Died', *Doctor Who*.

141 West, 'Jurisprudence and Gender', p. 2.

142 Chapman, *Inside the TARDIS*, p. 11.

143 Harper, 'The Caves of Androzani', *Doctor Who*; Chapman, *Inside the TARDIS*, p. 143.

144 Tulloch and Alvardo, *Doctor Who*, pp. 208–14; Jowett, 'The Girls Who Waited?', p. 81.

Doctor's and viewers' disembodied gaze.[145] In Classic Who, the TARDIS was a closet, ostensibly keeping sex off the screen yet allowing sexism and the objectification of women. In this context, the relationship between the Fourth and Fifth Doctor and his young male companion, Ardic, resonated as strongly wrong.[146] There were enough intra-text suggestions of what was going on in the TARDIS, and it was not that.

The closeted conservative heterosexuality of Classic Who gets queered, to a certain degree, in New Who. Davies brought sex and sexuality more open into the text. The Ninth and Tenth Doctor are much more comfortable with kissing Rose and expressing romantic attachments. Moffat (as script-writer) and Davies (as producer) also introduced the reoccurring character of Captain Jack, whose adventures with the Doctor and his continuation as the primary character in *Torchwood* earned him the distinction of the first leading queer science fiction television character.[147] However, while Jack clearly desires the Doctor,[148] their screened kiss had a platonic quality.[149] The New Who Doctors – 'Casanova'[150] Tennant and the River Song snogging, Clara's 'boyfriend' Smith, and the settling down for a while with River Capaldi – clearly remain heterosexual – but in a more comfortable, embodied way than the earlier Doctors. Tennant's Tenth Doctor knowingly flirts with females of many species, and Smith's Eleventh Doctor's 'dreams had come at once' when the 'sexy old girl' that is the TARDIS was transmuted into the body of a young human woman.[151] In New Who, the Doctor does have a sexualised body – sex connects him in time and materiality to others – yet this sexuality remains a male heterosexuality of separation. Like Butler's construct males, he seems to resist bonding and settling. The Ninth Doctor's aversion to 'families'[152] and the transient nature of the Doctor's TARDIS families seems to suggest that, like Akin, the Doctor needs his space and his time.

This enacts the tensions already identified within the *Doctor Who* mega-text: of timelessness and timefullness and of the body and bodiless-ness. These complexities can also be seen within the secondary literature's assessment of what can be called the Doctor's contradictory 'politico-ethics'. The

145 Chapman, *Inside the TARDIS*, pp. 6–7.

146 Tulloch and Alvardo, *Doctor Who*, pp. 230–3.

147 Barron, 'Out in Space', p. 217.

148 Davis, 'The Eternal Vigil', p. 85; Duncanson, 'Bodies, Cinema, Sovereignty', pp. 219–20.

149 Ahearne, 'The Parting of the Ways', *Doctor Who*.

150 Prior to *Doctor Who*, Tennant played Casanova in a 2005 television adaption by Davies, Hills, *Triumph of a Time Lord*, p. 161.

151 Clark, 'The Doctor's Wife', *Doctor Who*.

152 Boak, 'Aliens of London', *Doctor Who*.

Doctor clearly stands for certain principles over others.[153] Repeatedly, he takes up the cause of individuals against oppressive collectives, with most of the other primal lawyers portrayed as anti-individual, hierarchical despots.[154] Aside from some well-documented examples to the contrary,[155] the Doctor's preferred method of engagement involves reasoning and non-violence. It could be seen that the Doctor respects what could be called benign cultural diversity. Provided a society manifests the values of peaceful coexistence, non-violence, and talk, it will earn his protection. In this, the Doctor appears to be the paradigm cosmopolitan humanist.[156] This manifests within his strange/estranged attraction to humans. Repeatedly, the Doctor has suggested that humans' modest living, their loving, and their simple deaths when their time is due are what attracts him to them. This tendency was placed in the forefront in the New Who double episodes 'Human Nature/Family of Blood' (2007), where a humanised Doctor falls in love with school nurse Joan Redfern (Jessica Hynes) and the reluctance of the Doctor to leave the possible middle-class life of work, children, and scarlet dressing gown-comfortable old age.[157] These values of domestic life, of peace, and reproduction, are in the storehouse of memory – not the Doctor's, but John Smith's memory-to-come. This is an ethics of the everyday and its temporality is the timefullness of memory.

However, the Doctor is not a humanist of live and let live. John Fiske's 1983 structuralist reading of 'The Creature from the Pit' (1979)[158] argues that behind the Doctor's humanist veneer lies the violence and oppression of the capitalist system where conflict is managed.[159] In 'Family of Blood', the Doctor chooses to be the Doctor and not the human school teacher. The humanism of the Doctor's doing-in-the-universe partly obscures that he is the loci of terrible decision-making. This dimension to the Doctor was made very explicit in the final seasons of Classic Who, in episodes like 'The Cures of Fenric' (1989)[160] and 'Silver Nemesis' (1988),[161] where the clownish superficiality of McCoy's Seventh Doctor evolved into an alien, manipulative

[153] Cull, '"Bigger on the Inside . . ."', p. 100; Gregg, 'England Looks to the Future', p. 652; Dixit, 'Relating to Difference'.

[154] Bould, 'Science Fiction in the United Kingdom', p. 217.

[155] Tulloch and Jenkins, *Science Fiction Audiences*, p. 160.

[156] Orthia, '"Sociopathetic Abscess"', p. 216; Amy-Chinn, 'Rose Tyler'; Layton, *The Humanism of Doctor Who*.

[157] Palmer, 'The Family of Blood', *Doctor Who*.

[158] Barry, 'The Creature from the Pit', *Doctor Who*.

[159] Fiske, '*Doctor Who*', p. 96.

[160] Mallett, 'The Curse of Fenric', *Doctor Who*.

[161] Clough, 'Silver Nemesis', *Doctor Who*.

personality. The Doctor in action and inaction, through deciding to stay or to leave in his blue box, through helping or refusing to aid, dictates the fates of the mere time- and space-bound creatures. The Doctor, sovereign-like, orders time and death so that the 'little people'[162] can live or not. The Doctor's humanism is transposed by the alien will to power of his 'Gallifrey-ism'.

So, the Doctor manifests a complex ethics. He, after all, has two hearts: one heart is the liberal humanist heart of memory and letting live in-time; the other is the will to power of chronology, timelessness, and terrible decisions. A similar binary also circulates with regard to body and identity. While others' bodies are present, in their materiality, in the text – the dead and the sexualised (or, in Jack's case, the un-dead and ultra-sexualised) – the Doctor's vanishes only to reappear again. It is these tensions of humanist/will to power and of connection/separation that allow the Doctor to materialise in a hitherto uncharted universe: legal ethics.

Legal ethics, from its modern birth in the Watergate scandal[163] to more contemporary anxieties over the War on Terror,[164] has struggled with technical lawyering. The primary dispute within legal ethics is how much of a lawyer's conduct must be duty bound and machine-like. The 'zealous' advocacy of the 'standard conception' sees lawyer-nodes as machine components in the network. A lawyer remains ethical if they abide by the 'laws of lawyering' (the professional conduct rules) and the formal dictates of the law network (that is, refrain from illegal activities), and if they pursue their client's lawful instructions.[165] In this view, the lawyer is a tool used by a client for the client's ends; a 'good lawyer' has little autonomy. Provided that a client's wishes are lawful (both according to the wider law and the professional conduct requirements), the lawyer does as instructed. The lawyer role is essentially one of programmed agency (doing what the instructions and the rules tell to do) and technical adviser, suggesting to the client the best technical ways to navigate and operate the law network to achieve the desired ends. This can be seen as technical lawyering: the lawyer is a technician of the legal networks, whose judgement and responsibility are limited to threshold questions of legality or mundane issues of strategy.

The stark technicity of the standard conception and the well-known scenarios of technical lawyering, leading to moral and political controversy, has inspired legal ethicists to generate more noble visions of contemporary lawyer-

162 Harper, 'Waters of Mars', *Doctor Who*.
163 Wasserstrom, 'Lawyers as Professionals', pp. 1, 3.
164 Luban, 'Tales of Terror'.
165 Pepper, 'Counselling at the Limits of the Law'.

ing. Through invocation of 'virtue',[166] 'common morality',[167] or 'judgement',[168] many attempts have been made to draw a more human picture of lawyering that could be seen as more responsible to the social than the controversy-inducing standard conception.[169] These alternative theorisations are another manifestation of the Frankenstein myth, where the monstrous technicity of technical lawyering needs disciplining to be properly human. As the narrative that has been pursued through this book reveals, these human injunctions are essentially doomed. The technicity of lawyering that the standard conception embraces cannot be defined away. The function of the lawyer-node in the network as technician cannot be ignored. Lawyers are rarely in a traditional human setting of sitting behind a desk, paper file in front, secretary waiting patiently in the front office, with time to think, weigh, and decide. Lawyer-nodes are busy, frantic cyborgs,[170] plugged into the law network of bodiless power over life, and behind the frantic mundanity of their information processing there is the ultimate dealing with time and death. To be a technician within the triumph of technology is inescapable. Instead of a romance to a past form of human-scale practice of social leadership, there is need to connect the lawyer-node with responsibility for becoming.

Julian Webb calls for 'a legal ethics, built upon principles of authenticity, responsibility and choice',[171] which represents a theoretical clearing of the way towards this connecting of the lawyer-node with responsibility for becoming. His Heideggerian and Levinasian rethinking of legal ethics generates calls for 'democratic premise' and 'moral agency' in the 'concrete and contextual'.[172] This represents a challenging break to the technicality of 'duty' or humanness of 'virtue' of legal ethics' established narratives. He offers a transgressive reading of Atticus Finch as a myth-ideal for lawyering in the face of Levinas's Other.[173] However, Finch carries baggage: Webb's transgressive reading is just that – transgressive. It goes against the generations of comment and endorsement of Finch as the epitome of the human-scale social leadership of legal ethics' alternative narratives to the standard conception.[174]

It is here that the Doctor can be seen, not just as a primal lawyer – a

[166] Shaffer, 'Moral Theology in Legal Ethics'.

[167] Luban, *Lawyers and Justice.*

[168] Kronman, *The Lost Lawyer.*

[169] Tranter, Bartlett, Corbin, Mortensen, and Robertson, 'Introduction', p. 2.

[170] Thornton, 'The Flexible Cyborg'.

[171] Webb, 'Being a Lawyer/Being a Human Being', p. 144.

[172] Ibid., pp. 146–9.

[173] Ibid., pp. 147–8.

[174] On the contested assessment of Atticus Finch in legal ethics, see Baron, 'The Emperor's New Clothes', pp. 88–9.

demon meddling with time and death – but as a paradigm for technical lawyering. The Doctor's difference from the other primal lawyers can be a myth-ideal for technical lawyering. In doing so, a similar constellation of concepts that were identified in Chapter 4 for the ethics of the technical legal subject reappears, but with different emphases. The Doctor shows how lawyer-nodes can be responsible for becoming through his technical safeguarding of life.

The Doctor is a consummate technologist. A consistent image through the episodes and stories is the Doctor meddling with machines. From the Third Doctor's improvised instruments of dial, cords, and buttons to the Tenth Doctor's cheeky grin as he closes the maintenance cabinet and the machinery whirls to life, the Doctor confidently believes he can fix, modify, or reprogram any technology from any civilisation, from any time. His persistent 'weapon', after all, is a screwdriver. The Doctor is not anti-technological; rather, his being is technological. There is clearly a symbiotic relationship between the Doctor and the machine-like TARDIS. Most of the regeneration scenes occur inside the TARDIS, and the Doctor would not be a Time Lord – with the timeless technicity of the will to power that the species name suggests – without his temperamental 'Type 40 Time Capsule'. Like the Daleks and Cybermen, the Doctor is clearly presented as a cybernetic being.[175]

For Anne Cranny-Francis and Tulloch, this hybridity of the Doctor makes sense of the Doctor's complicated ethics. For them, the Doctor is technical and emotional, and, as such, 'the series explores the nature of embodied human subjectivity as a mixed and muddled sensory, emotional and intellectual complex, not a simple liner Cartesian'.[176] Whereas the Daleks and Cybermen fail through a prioritising of rationality and chronology, over emotions and memory, for the Doctor 'ethical judgment . . . is not based on intellectual or rationalist judgements but on a fully embodied, emotional, sensory and intellectual engagement with the context of judgement'.[177] For them, the Doctor is the master of technique and technologies rather than being mastered by technicity.

But the 'fully embodied, emotion, sensory and intellectual engagement with the context of judgment' that Cranny-Francis and Tulloch identify requires substantiation. What, then, is the Doctor's context of judgement?

The Doctor does not like robots – except robot dogs. Robots remain matter, a false imitation of life. Robots cause violence and hurt that the Doctor overcomes. But what they are never raised to are entities that the Doctor regrets. He does not do his sad-serious face over the charred chassis

175 Fiske, '*Doctor Who*', pp. 10–11.

176 Cranny-Francis and Tulloch, 'Vaster than Empire(s)', p. 354.

177 Ibid.

of a departed robot. The loss of a K9 spurs construction of a new one.[178] The touchstone in this dislike is life. Here, as with *Battlestar Galactica* and *Xenogenesis*, *Doctor Who* consistently presents a vitalistic *zoe*, of a becoming, that needs to be safeguarded. In a universe of matter and time, the Doctor can be seen, again and again, as respecting the becoming of life. His weak cosmopolitan ethics is grounded on openness to this revelling; however, unlike cosmopolitans – such as *Star Trek*'s Captain Jean-Luc Picard – the Doctor's openness to revelling is not a passive live-and-let-live approach. There is a hands-off mentality to the various statements of Star Fleet's Prime Directive.[179] However, the Doctor is not hands off. His safeguarding of becoming is very hands and sonic screwdriver on.

If there is a common opening to *Doctor Who* stories, it can be seen with the Doctor learning about the new context into which he has materialised. There is frantic activity: yo-yos are played with, objects are licked, strangers are accosted, or offered confectionery, and with this engagement, memory is invoked. Behind these techniques of knowing – experimental evidence-gathering and remembering – is the Doctor's confidence that he can master any circumstance, any planet, any time. Sometimes he gets it wrong, but that rarely shakes the confidence. Indeed, it is not confidence, nor is it duty – the Doctor can be seen often running away from duty claims.[180] It is intrinsic to who he is as an alchemist of death and time. This drive to know, to determine the networks of the present so as to diagnose the health of becoming, is repeatedly presented in *Doctor Who* as intrinsic to his being the Doctor. 'This is what I do,' says the Eleventh Doctor to Amy Pond as he whizzes off in the TARDIS to chase Daleks.[181] And, just as future follows present, safeguarding becoming follows in his being. Having learnt the networks of the present, the Doctor does not leave that becoming unmolested in its reaching for the future.

As noted, it is memory – specifically the Doctor's memory – of how things should be, or remembering in complex temporal fashion, how things could be that involves his assessment of the health of becoming. Engaged yet separate, the Doctor takes on to himself responsibility for the circumstance that he has just popped into. Techniques and memory combine to create doing-in-the-world.

While the primary foes see in their powers of time and death a dictate to master, the Doctor often holds off – his actions can be seen as defensive: a

178 Spenton-Foster, 'The Ribos Operation', *Doctor Who*.

179 Joseph and Carton, 'The Law of the Federation'.

180 Harper, 'The Stolen Earth', *Doctor Who*.

181 Gunn, 'Victory of the Daleks', *Doctor Who*.

holding back, a fixing from intrusion. This is seen in the regular repulsion of an alien invasion of broadcast-present Earth narratives. The Doctor chooses to protect the diversity of the status quo against the destruction and uniformity that the invader brings. This does not mean that the Doctor is entirely a conservative figure. Where the 'invasion' brings promises of greater diversity and a quickening of becoming, the Doctor goes from defender to advocate. The Silurian stories – hominid-like reptiles from Earth's past that are awaken from their underground hibernation – end with an angry/despondent Doctor pleading for peace and cooperation between humans and Silurians with the promise of a better future for both species.[182] This cosmopolitan compromise is further evident in the recent Zygon story-arc that has the Doctor facilitating peaceful Zygon cohabitation of Earth.[183] In continuity with this for each repulsion of invasion story, there are narratives where the Doctor is agent for change. The Doctor is not just a defender, but clearly a trickster. The Doctor as trickster has been noted;[184] even intra-text, the anti-Doctor army attempts to build up courage in chanting he is not a trickster, only to have the Doctor appear, trickster-like, in their midst.[185] The Doctor, sonic screwdriver, and TARDIS reflect cultural antecedents of the wizard, wand, and magic cabinet; indeed, 'Gandalf' taunts the Master to the captured and artificially aged Tenth Doctor.[186] The arrival of the TARDIS in a space and a time often spells the end for a nefarious overlord and the freeing of a servile population. The Doctor is both defender and revolutionary – depending on the possible diversity of becoming – of whatever actions will allow freedom, evolution, and peaceful coexistence: in short, whatever facilitates an intensification of affect. The touchstone is life. Safeguarding becoming involves not just a defending of the status quo, but working for change. It involves not a passive watching and learning, but engaging and doing. There is knowledge of the networks of the present; there is through memory assessment of the potentiality for becoming; and then there is the application of techniques grounded in time and death to enhance the possibilities for life.

It is exactly here, with the technical safeguarding of becoming, that the Doctor can be seen as a myth-ideal for the lawyer-nodes of technical legality. But he needs proper understanding. Like the cosmopolitan appreciation of

[182] Combe, '*Doctor Who* and the Silurian', *Doctor Who*; Roberts, 'Warriors of the Deep', *Doctor Who*; Way, 'Hungry Earth', *Doctor Who*; Way 'Cold Blood', *Doctor Who*.

[183] Nettheim, 'The Zygon Invasion', *Doctor Who*; Nettheim, 'The Zygon Inversion', *Doctor Who*.

[184] Rafer, 'Mythic Identity in *Doctor Who*', p. 124.

[185] Hoar, 'A Good Man Goes to War', *Doctor Who*.

[186] Teague, 'Last of the Time Lords', *Doctor Who*.

the Doctor, his ethical lordship of becoming could be seen as another version of the virtue narrative from legal ethics. It could be argued that the Doctor shows how to keep humanity alive inside the law-machine. In doing so, both the technicity of modern lawyering and the Doctor get strangely mangled. The modern lawyer-node and the Doctor are not 'human'. The Doctor is a myth-ideal because of his technical safeguarding of becoming. He works the networks, rendered obvious by computers, machines, the TARDIS. The lawyer-node works the law network. In doing so, the prevailing mode is technical lawyering as identified by the standard conception. There is the franticness of technical decisions – made within six-minute intervals – processed on workstations, logged on a central file management server or the court's mainframe, evidenced in emails, structured by precedents, forms, rules, and instructions. Just as the Doctor's 'victory' – especially during Davies' tenure – often came down to a literal *deus ex machina* of a technological intervention stemming, often indirectly, from the Doctor's technical doing,[187] the lawyer-node remains bound by the law network. Like the Doctor, the lawyer-node is properly a cyborg.

Yet the lawyer-node's participation in the law network is not automated. Lawyers have yet to be replaced by algorithms and AI.[188] The law network provides a total context for decision, but the potential for choice remains.[189] This cannot be seen as freedom of action. Rather, there are instances when lawyer-nodes are presented with choice-moments where it is technically possible, through evidence and memory, to glimpse the impact of alternative actions on becoming. It could be as mundane as a gentler phrasing of a letter, a day's delay in commencing a process, the asking of a further question of a client or witness,[190] or grander, Doctor-like actions, of decisions to act *pro bono publico* or of refusing to act. To be a lawyer means to already be complicit in the power over life that is the law network, just as the Doctor is always complicit and responsible for the becoming of the universe. At this point there is an ultimate choice – one that the Doctor is televised making and remaking again and again. It is easy to just give in to the alchemical power of the law network, to join with the Daleks in their exercise of the powers of time and death in extermination. However, the Doctor's sad memories and his enduring sense of responsibility anchor his resistance to this pull. It is at

187 Hills, *Triumph of a Time Lord*, p. 39.

188 Susskind, *Tomorrow's Lawyers*; Susskind and Susskind, *The Future of the Professions*.

189 Robertson and Tranter, 'Grounding Legal Ethics Learning in Social Scientific Studies of Lawyers at Work'.

190 Tranter, '"Come a Day There Won't be Room for Naughty Men Like Us to Slip about at All"'.

the moment of choice – often small, sometimes grand – that the primal power of the law network over time and death can be channelled by a lawyer-node towards an intensity of affect. The lawyer-node can choose to make a positive continuation of life. The lawyer can, for a moment, become a Doctor.

So, the Doctor can be seen as the paradigm of a technical lawyer. He provides a myth-ideal for lawyer-nodes that it is possible to remain within the total technicity of the law network, but still have the potential to safeguard becoming. But in doing so, the Doctor diagnoses the scary and dangerous real of technical lawyering. To be a lawyer within the modern legal system is a calling to be an alien, a somewhat sad clown-trickster that is not human. It is a calling to be a lord of time and death. It raises the fear of being consumed by the sheer technicity of the law network, to be subsumed – like the Daleks and Cybermen – by its rationality and its primal power. But the Doctor also suggests that seizing the choice-moment where affect can be nurtured can allow a safeguarding of becoming. In this, responsibility for becoming for lawyer-nodes is possible within the law-machine. Even technical lawyers can ensure the potentiality, and beauty, of becoming.

But even so, the alienness will remain. The symptom of disconnection that has been identified in studies of the mental health of lawyers can be seen more properly.[191] It marks the fault line within the complex subject that considers itself human, yet is a lawyer-node during business hours and increasingly beyond.[192] The Doctor's sad loneliness does not provide a resolution to this tension. He does not reconcile his humanist and Gallifreian tendencies. What he does not do is choose to be human. He endures as a paradigm technical lawyer because time and death are always making becoming, and he is forever located in the eye of this storm.

In conclusion, for as long as the technical law of modernity reigns, with its primal substance of time and death, the alien-ness of technical lawyering will endure. To be at the embodied location of the lawyer-node will involve sadness and a holding oneself apart, a feeling out of the body, of a distance of relationships. The Doctor as myth-ideal is a continual urge for technical lawyers not to become a Dalek – locked away as they are in their bumpy armour, waiving a disembodied eye-stork, plunger, and ray-gun at a universe that they hate – but to accept that being a lawyer-node in the law network does involve a demonic working of time and death with the possibility of safeguarding becoming.

To go back in time, the common law once saw lawyering as a melancholy

[191] Sharp, 'The Problem of Mental Ill-Health in the Profession'; Levit and Linder, *The Happy Lawyer*, pp. 3–8.

[192] Thornton, 'Squeezing the Life Out of Lawyers'.

task. The shorthand was that lawyering occurs under the sign of Saturn.[193] For technical lawyering this celestial image should be restored, with one amendment: skating on the rings there should be a blue box.

[193] Goodrich, *Law in the Courts of Love*, p. 80.

6

Mad Max and Mapping the Monsters in the Networks

In the last chapter, the Doctor emerged as a myth-ideal for the lawyer-node of the West. The Doctor embodies what is at stake for the being that, through its immersion with the law network, engages with the primal materials of time and death with the potential to be responsible for becoming. The Doctor's alien safeguarding of becoming – his responsibility made manifest through memory, technical doing, and holding off – demarks the possibilities for technical lawyering within the triumph of technology.

Lawyer-nodes are but one intersection within the networks of the present. The networks produce other node locations, presenting other complex, hybrid, changing beings, other points of difference. Even the law network integrates with other networks to generate other beings – beings that conventionally bear the titles 'judges', 'plaintiff', 'inmates', 'clerk', 'law students', and 'law professors'. It is the last cyborg that is the focus of this chapter. With the triumph of technology, what is the point, the end for legal scholarship? As witnessed in Chapter 3, Heidegger's account of technology's occupation of the Western intellectual horizon in modernity led to his assessment of the end of thinking and the end of genuine scholarship.[1] Like his wider story on the totality of technology, this fall also generates a romantic desire for an imagined past of true intellectual endeavour, and a devaluing of the technicity of modern research life. Indeed, with great scorn, Heidegger condemns 'research man who does not have a library at home'.[2]

Heidegger's quaint criticisms need updating. It is not so much that research woman of the legal academies does not have a home library; it is that she is interfacing with clouds of libraries and repositories through her smart device while in a committee meeting, on public transport, late at night once the children are in bed. Through caresses on a touch-sensitive screen, contemporary scholars of the West are able to access, connect, and process

[1] Heidegger, 'Science and Reflection', pp. 181–2.

[2] Heidegger, 'The Age of World Picture', p. 125.

data in fast and different ways, independent of the old institutions of the paper archive. The fundamental question concerns the end to which this technical capacity should be deployed. How can scholars – particularly legal scholars – be responsible for becoming?

Legal scholars are loci for several networks: the law network with its primal working of time and death, and the research network that manifests in the contemporary university. One is a doing-in-the-world, a participation in the law network's shaping of becoming. The other is a knowing, data-gathering, processing, and producing network. But it is not innocent: its production involves the violence of institutional validation – or silencing or transposing – of voices, stories, and knowledges. A turn to the academy does not exempt the scholar-node from the violence of the law network. The very activity of research involves a setting upon the world to order it, to render becoming into a form amenable to other networks.[3] For the law-scholar node, this participation in violence is compounded by the continuing nexus with the law network. Since Duncan Kennedy, to teach at law school is to prepare future lawyer-nodes for the hierarchical competitive environment of technical lawyering in which the exercise of the powers of time and death are routine, mundane, and hidden.[4] Further, the very object of the law scholar-nodes' investigations means their outputs – the articles, books, grants, reports, advisories, submissions, media statements – feed, restructure, inform, challenge, and facilitate the law network's structuring of becoming. Like the Doctor and lawyer-nodes, law professors are not just embodied little monsters given life and death by the networks of the West, but demonic entities shaping, in multiple ways, those very networks.

This chapter argues that for the law scholar, responsibility for becoming demands aspiring to know the becoming of the world. What is urged is a cartographic project of mapping the monsters within the networks of the present. Instead of imposing preconceived categories, as does the Frankenstein myth, there is a necessity for an openness to the complexity and connections of the present as it strives towards the future. To be responsible for becoming from the scholar's location is to be open to the revealing of the world. This is a call for creativity and methodological hybridity. It involves the striving for truth in the different, in the quirky and in the not official, although there is observation and mapping of the surface eddies and the deep currents of the technological world.[5] As with the lawyer-nodes who remain ever complicit

[3] Heidegger, 'Science and Reflection', p. 172.

[4] Kennedy, *Legal Education and the Reproduction of Hierarchy*; Goodrich, 'Duncan Kennedy as I Imagine Him'.

[5] Braidotti, *Transpositions*, pp. 30–2.

with the law network, this does not mean that law scholar-nodes are removed from the becoming of the world, nor are their mappings of becoming exempt from informing the doings of the politico-legal networks of the West. Rather, in mapping the networks beyond the expected data produced by the Frankenstein myth, the law scholar-node has the opportunity to reorientate, rewire, and reprogram the politico-legal networks, and in so doing enhance the spaces and moments of affect. In knowing how the monsters live within the networks, life in its diversity, complexity, and change becomes prioritised.

The vehicle for this argument is a performative study of a very familiar manifestation of technological Being-in-the-world in the West: the monster that is the human-automobile hybrid.[6] It is shown that George Miller's classic Australian post-apocalyptic science fiction film *Mad Max 2: The Road Warrior* (1981) allows a sophisticated frame through which this monster is known, ordered, and managed within multiple intersecting networks. As such, this chapter presents a way by which legal scholars can be responsible for becoming through knowing the networks of the present.

This argument is in three stages. In the first stage, the film is dissected as a cartographic frame for revealing the network intersections at the human–automobile nexus. Three intersection points are isolated: identity, myth, and biopower. In the second stage, these points are refracted through Australian culture. The human-automobile is shown to be critical for the knowing and ordering of entities, essential to collective myths of possession and prosperity, significant in the distinguishing of 'place' from 'space' and a technical precondition for biopolitical projects like the removal of Indigenous children. What is produced is a very different account of technical legality from that of the Frankenstein myth. The technical legal subject is shown to be embodied not just in human flesh, with all the vagrancies and complexities discussed in Chapter 4, but also embodied by steel, rubber, and chrome. In the third stage, it will be shown how a focus on the human-automobile provides a richer map of the networks of the present than the Frankenstein myth. As such, law scholar-nodes can be responsible for becoming by opening up the networks to affect.

Identity, Myth, and Biopower in *Mad Max 2*

The plot of *Mad Max 2* can be summarised briefly, and without much recourse to the first film or the later ones. Firmly within the post-apocalypse science fiction genre, *Mad Max 2* is set in a future Australia marked by social and technological decline. Max, played with career-establishing charisma by

[6] Urry, 'The "System" of Automobility'.

Mel Gibson, roams a physical, social, and moral desert, his companion the 'Interceptor', 'one of the last V8s', a heavily modified, black, supercharged two-door Australian-made 1970s muscle car. Having abandoned the remnants of civilisation in *Mad Max* by accelerating into the badlands,[7] the second film begins several years later with Max stumbling upon a permanent community. The film suggests that Max has spent the intervening years as a nomad, scavenging fuel, food, and parts from wrecks and debris. In contrast, the community appears to have remade society inside a fortified compound by producing oil.[8]

The narrative quickly establishes itself as a Western:[9] Max the troubled cowboy hero; the Gyro-Captain (Bruce Spence), the goofy side-kick; the inhabitants of the community, the settlers and honest town-folk of the Wild West; the leader of the community, Papagallo (Mike Preston), the town mayor; the 'Interceptor', the wonder horse with which all good cowboys are blessed; and Humungus's gang, the murderous outlaws.[10] Papagallo's community is under siege. Surrounding it are Humungus (Kjell Nilsson) and his horde, demanding the stockpile of fuel and murdering anybody who leaves the sanctuary. Once Max gains entrance into the compound, the narrative turns to escape. After several attempts, including a failure culminating in the destruction of the 'Interceptor', Max drives the community's oil tanker to breach the siege. The tanker draws Humungus's 'dogs of war'[11] away from the compound, allowing the community to leave safely. Ironically, when the tanker is eventually destroyed during the climactic and definitional car-chase finale, Max and viewers discover that it was a diversion, filled with sand.

An emphasis in the *Mad Max* secondary literature has been that the film conveys in punk, post-industrial guise the social contract.[12] In this account, Papagallo's community has been regarded as a nascent state threatened by the forces of violence and anarchy represented by Humungus. It can be seen as a similar speculative projection of Hobbes that was also in *Xenogenesis* with the Human–Oankali construct communities threatened by the huma-only resisters. Within this reading, Max plays the role of an unwitting messiah.[13]

[7] Miller, *Mad Max*.

[8] Falconer, '"We Don't Need to Know the Way Home"', p. 38.

[9] Gibson, *South of West*, p. 160; Williams, 'Beyond *Mad Max III*', p. 309; Martin, *The Mad Max Movies*, p. 39.

[10] Stratton, 'What Made *Mad Max* Popular', pp. 47–8 and Falconer, 'We Don't Need to Know the Way Home', pp. 259–60.

[11] Miller, *Mad Max 2: The Road Warrior* (Humungus).

[12] See Stratton, 'What Made *Mad Max* Popular'; Sharrett, 'Myth, Male Fantasy and Simulacra'; Taylor, 'A Culture of Temporary Culture'.

[13] Sharrett, 'Myth, Male Fantasy and Simulacra', p. 90.

He is the consideration for the social contract; his sacrificial drive of the tanker distracts Humungus, allowing the community to seek a more fertile home. Miller's Max is clearly a hero, and in the journey to the other realm (the badlands) and the confrontation with the terrible father (Humungus), there can be identified certain monomyth correspondences. Indeed, Max is not much of a trickster – like Baltar or the Doctor sponsoring new forms of becoming; rather, he is a Campbell-esque hero whose adventures sustain the status quo.[14] The oil-dependent community that he saves, like the resisters in *Xenogenesis*, are a remnant seeking a return to the pre-apocalyptic old ways.[15] However, there are limits to this account.

As recounted in Chapter 2, Hobbes' pre-social contract human-animals do not need a hero-leader to secure the contract, nor are they contracting in a fall, attempting to preserve civilisation against entropic forces.[16] It is in this latter context of a fall that the film is set – in the unwinding of civilisation, for Hobbes, the time of Behemoth[17] – that is significant. *Mad Max 2* as social contract ignores the features of future and technology that dominate the film. The film is futuristic and post-apocalyptic;[18] however, the apocalypse in *Mad Max 2* is not nuclear.[19] As the prologue relates 'you have to go back to a time when the world was powered by the black fuel and the desert sprouted great cities of pipe and steel . . . the thundering machine spluttered and stopped'.[20] This suggests a prolonged energy crisis leading to economic and ecological social collapse. The paradox of this is the enduring importance of the car for Max's world. Again, the link is made in the prologue:

> On the roads it was a white line nightmare. Only those mobile enough to scavenge, brutal enough to pillage, would survive. The gangs took over the highways, ready to wage war for a tank of juice.[21]

14 Miller, 'The Apocalypse and the Pig'; Martin, *The Mad Max Movies*, p. 55; Broderick, 'Heroic Apocalypse'.

15 Morris, 'White Panic', p. 246.

16 See Chapter 2, pp. 62–3.

17 Hobbes, *Behemoth*.

18 Williams, 'Beyond *Mad Max III*'.

19 Although there is evidence of a nuclear and/or catastrophic military destruction in the final scenes, we see a destroyed Sydney in the third film. See Morris's rough chronology of successive declines and apocalypses in the series, Morris, 'White Panic', p. 242. In the recent 2015 fourth film, the suggestion is more of a climate change collapse. See Branston, 'Apocalyptic Imaginings', p. 807.

20 Miller, *Mad Max 2: The Road Warrior* (opening narration).

21 Ibid.

The wastelands of *Mad Max 2* have their origins in the failure of the internal combustion engine to ground a sustainable civilisation. However, the car retains vitality. The political economy is not marked by a return to simpler forms of energy, but the car in its industrial complexity remains the focus.[22] The importance of the car is further registered on the biography of individual characters. Papagallo was an oil executive. Max was not only a highway cop, but his 'madness' arose from the murder of his wife and child by a motorcycle gang in the first film, where 'in the roar of an engine, he lost everything and became a shell of a man'.[23]

These difficulties with reading the film as social contract are compounded by its situation in a fall. Simply put, it does not represent the state of nature. The desert showdown between Papagallo's community and Humungus's horde is the clash of two rival 'protective associations', to deploy Robert Nozick's phrase.[24] The community and the horde cannot be taken as representing order and disorder. Humungus's gang is distinctly ordered. Just like Papagallo's community, it is strongly hierarchical, if not military (there is evidence that Humungus was an army officer).[25] The gang possesses rituals and relations – admittedly, violent rituals of torture and 'perverse' relationships characterised by homoeroticism and sadomasochism.[26] To regard the film as retelling, as Australian film critic Jon Stratton does, 'the mythology of the conservative fantasy'[27] of the social contract is insufficient.

Instead, a more comprehensive reading of the film tells much more about the relations, connections, and functions of a specific embodied node of the West, the human-automobile. In particular, the film presents itself as a sustained mediation on how various networks process human-automobiles as 'individuals' that can be known, ordered, and managed. In this, the film is not about the old narratives that sustain the West's politico-legal networks, nor is it necessarily an anxiety tale of the end of the West in economic or ecological collapse. It is about how the human-automobile functions within the networks of the present – how embodied nodes are known, ordered, and managed. Within the film, this knowing, ordering, and managing is revealed at three loci points: car as identity, car as myth, and the car as biopower.

Primarily, the car operates to frame the identities of the characters in *Mad Max 2*. It is through this car identity that the characters are known

22 Gibson, *South of West*, p. 163.
23 Miller, *Mad Max 2: The Road Warrior* (opening narration).
24 Nozick, *Anarchy, State, and Utopia*, pp. 12–15.
25 Sharrett, 'Myth, Male Fantasy and Simulacra', p. 87.
26 Falconer, 'We Don't Need to Know the Way Home', p. 262.
27 Stratton, 'What Made *Mad Max* Popular'.

and ordered. Knowledge of the characters – their tendencies, rank, and allegiances – is visually linked to their vehicles. Max provides the archetype of this relationship. Max drives the 'Interceptor', a highly modified police pursuit vehicle. It is a 'piece of history',[28] yet it has been modified for its current role as a high-speed marauder with booby-trapped fuel tanks and 'bug-catcher' supercharger. Max, the ex-policeman, is similarly a piece of history. Just like the car, he is modified. The loss of family and meaning in the wastelands has made him 'mad', an unprincipled pragmatist who in the opening scenes ignores the plight of the roadside wounded. It is significant that it is only after the destruction of the 'Interceptor', when his identity as a road warrior is challenged, that Max's rehabilitation begins,[29] 'and it was here, in this blighted place, that he learned to live again'.[30] This metonymical relationship is reflected in the other characters. The members and machines of Humungus's horde, the rival road warriors, are stylistically similar to Max and the 'Interceptor': black leather and scavenged mementos, but with actual, identifiable cars (like the 'Interceptor' Australian manufactured muscle cars from the 1970s) hiding under the iron rams, wielded armour, and weapons. Humungus is different. His muscle-pumped body and mask demark him not as a remnant, but as a being of the fall.[31] This is reflected in his machine, an ugly six-wheeled monstrosity.[32] It is not a piece of mass-production history that has been appropriated and modified, but a 'one-off', a machine born into the new world of violent scavenging.

In contrast to the leather and material appropriation of the road warriors, Papagallo's community is different. Dressed in flowing robes of light colours and simple cuts, they were nicknamed 'Gucci Arabs' by the production unit.[33] This urbanity is reflected in their vehicles, the most significant being a yellow school bus – an ultimate imagery of safety and domestic peace. Papagallo's role as the rival leader to Humungus is also coded in his vehicle. Like Humungus, Papagallo drives a vehicle that is original, that does not have a link to a mass-production past. However, unlike Humungus's six-wheel beast, Papagallo's machine evidences a degree of beauty. Its silver-bullet body is reminiscent of the Grand Prix cars of the 1930s, speeding modernity into the future.[34] It is through their vehicles that each character's tendencies and

[28] Miller, *Mad Max 2: The Road Warrior*.

[29] Rayner, *Contemporary Australian Cinema*.

[30] Miller, *Mad Max 2: The Road Warrior* (opening narration).

[31] Falconer, 'Selling Australian Space', p. 38.

[32] Stratton, 'What Made *Mad Max* Popular', p. 55.

[33] Sharrett, 'Myth, Male Fantasy and Simulacra', p. 88.

[34] Stratton, 'What Made *Mad Max* Popular', p. 56.

aspirations are known and also through their vehicles that they are ordered. The vehicles code whether they belong inside or outside the compound, and also their status within each community. However, the cars' function extends beyond the knowing and ordering of characters through their identities. The cars also underpin how the characters are ordered and managed through community grounding myths.

In *Mad Max 2*, characters are ordered and managed through specific car-based myths. The central myth within the film is the myth of future prosperity told by members of Papagallo's community. They dream of a better future. They desire to go north; their siren is a bikini model on a postcard for the Sunshine Coast, in sub-tropical Queensland.[35] This northern nirvana is described to Max as 'paradise', where there is nothing better to do than 'breeeeed'.[36] This collective dream of water and breeding orders the community through providing a collective goal and explains the community's submission to Papagallo. The myth justifies the existence of the compound and their oil refining. It also explains Papagallo's more Machiavellian decisions, such as his sacrifice of individuals to Humungus, and his hiding the full details of the escape plan from Max. He needs to manage individuals, to make the hard choices now, in order to provide for a better future.

This myth is based on the car. The car must not only transport the community from the compound to the northern paradise, but symbolically links the dark present of entrapment and danger to the promised future of peace and prosperity. The car plays the role of a sacred vessel consecrating the community through linking it to the promised land: a communion of human, machine, and myth.[37] Given this mythical function of the car, it is fitting that the community's messiah is a road warrior. The car as myth provides for the ordering of individuals as a community and their management. This mythical role suggests a further role of the car in governance, as a direct instrument of biopower in the management of individuals.

The final function of the car in *Mad Max 2* is as a tool of biopower in the management of individuals. Here the car, as a technological object for transportation, is directly utilised in the management of individuals. This occurs in the ordering and management of space and in the direct control over bodies.

The basis for the car's mythical role is its ability to control distance and to render it comprehensible. The car allows an individual to order space, to divide it into familiar places, useable resources, and dangerous spaces. The individuals in Papagallo's community need not identify their desert

[35] Ibid., p. 46.

[36] Miller, *Mad Max 2: The Road Warrior.*

[37] Barthes, *Mythologies*, p. 88.

compound as home; the surrounding land is seen merely as an obstacle, full of danger and hostility that must be traversed. The car allows the inhabitants of the community to order the space surrounding them in such a way as to deny any attachment to the local environment. Instead, it allows individuals to dream of better places elsewhere. Further, these orderings allow the possibility that individuals can be managed to strive for that better place.

However, the car manages individuals more directly than through this ordering of space. It directly manages bodies. The car can take, it can bring, it can contain, and it can kill. Humungus's blockade depends on his road warriors chasing and killing any escapees, leaving their bodies violated and broken beside their violated and broken machines. The primary conflict of the film, between Papagallo and Humungus for the refined oil, is a battle for the bodies of their followers. In the world of *Mad Max 2*, oil creates a future – not just for the individuals in each camp, but for each community. However, the most obvious example of the car managing an individual is the crucifixion scene. Two escaped colonists are returned to the walls of compound screaming and pleading for Papagallo to compromise with Humungus. The cause of their agony is obvious. Not only has the car captured them and returned them to their origin, but their bodies have become part of it. This scene explicitly renders the sovereignty of metal over flesh, bare life's subservience to the machine.

This scene also bloodily summarises how the car facilitates the knowing, ordering, and management of individuals in the film. In it, the road warriors' identity as violent marauders is affirmed through the use of their vehicles for torture. The cars' mythical role is implied in its use as a sacrificial altar. In chasing, catching, and returning the escapee, the car's ordering of space is celebrated, and in mutilating and killing there is no doubt of the car's direct power over life. What emerges from this analysis of the film is that it is a cipher through which the functionality of the human-automobile within the networks of the West can be unthreaded. It is thus in need of a context. For *Mad Max 2*, the most immediate context is Australia.

Mad Max 2 is widely celebrated as the quintessential Australian road film.[38] It does not disguise its Australianness. Gibson does not adopt a North American accent, as he later was to in Hollywood. Indeed, all accents are Australian. The stripped and smashed vehicles are iconic Australian-made cars, Max's Australian Blue Heeler cattle dog, dead kangaroos, the huge, clear sky and red outback from around Broken Hill in New South Wales – even

[38] Sharrett, 'Myth, Male Fantasy and Simulacra', pp. 80–91; Kitson, 'The Great Aussie Car Smash at the End of the World'.

Figure 6.1 Tortured Colonists. *Mad Max 2: The Road Warrior* (1981). Licensed by Warner Bros, Entertainment Inc.

without the remains of Sydney from *Mad Max: Beyond Thunderdome* (1985)[39] – locate *Mad Max 2* as Australian.[40] While the film's framework suggests a way to unthread and comprehend the human-automobile in the West – its functionalities in identity, myth, and biopower – it is to Australia as a context for this unthreading, that this chapter turns.

The Australian Human-automobile

Like other Western nations, Australia manifests a car culture. It is a truism that the car is everywhere; it is a fundamental technical substratum that makes contemporary Australian life possible.[41] What *Mad Max 2* allows, in its focus on identity, myth, and biopower, is a frame to bring forward – to map – this truism. The starting place is the identity function of the car in the knowing and ordering of individuals, and how that knowing and ordering facilitates management.

Like Max in *Mad Max 2*, the 'hoon' is the archetype for the car in

[39] Miller and Oglivie, *Mad Max: Beyond Thunderdome.*

[40] Hodge, 'Aboriginal Myths and Australian Culture', pp. 277–89; Morris, 'White Panic'.

[41] Clarsen, 'Mobility in Australia', p. 123; Davison, *Car Wars*; Redshaw, *In the Company of Cars.*

Australian identity. The dimensions of the hoon are well established. They are young males, predominately from an Anglo-Australian heritage from what used to be seen as 'working-class' suburbs surrounding the large cities, living out the modernist masculine project of risk, speed, and technical proficiency through the modification of older family sedans and public displays of dangerous driving.[42] Cars are fundamental to hoon culture. The cultural hierarchy of better cars, the tribal affiliations to Ford or General Motors Holden, the associated cultural icons of the Gold Coast Grand Prix, the Bathurst 1000 motor race, and the annual – and often riotous – Summernats Street Machine Convention in Canberra mean that cars, the driving of cars, being a passenger in cars, repairing and modifying cars, and saving for a certain car or accessory form a bedrock on which life-meaning and self-identity are based.[43] In Linley Walker's interviews with young men from western Sydney, one of her respondents indicated:

> Yes, a Ford man since I was knee high to a hubcap . . . I'll stick to Fords. Hopefully my kids will be with Fords. There's nothing better, nothing better than a Ford. I've wanted a Ford V8 since I was four years old.[44]

This centrality of the car to identity is not limited to the white, male hoons of Sydney's western suburbs. The car is also fundamental to identity across many cultural demographics. Similar car-based cultures of modification and speed are evident in other communities from non-European backgrounds. While the forms are similar, for young men of Middle Eastern or Asian heritage, the desirable vehicles shift from the Australian-made V8s to the iconic Japanese 'drifter' vehicles of Subaru Impreza WRXs and Nissan Skylines.

This identity function of the car is not restricted to young males. Glenda Jones has documented the pursuit of 'lapping' the main street of regional centres as a female activity.[45] She notes that young women are often the drivers of cars and, through her interviews with young women from rural Tasmania, perceives that for her respondents, the car represents a safe place where genuine socialisation can occur away from alcohol and pubs. It is not surprising that the respondents rated the car their most coveted object.[46] Greg Nobel and Rebecca Baldwin share Jones' conclusion that car identity is gender inclusive. Through a scattered semiotic survey of cars, drivers, and bumper stickers in Sydney, they found that 'the car has become a symbol of

[42] Walker, 'Under the Bonnet', pp. 23–43; Fuller, 'The Hoon: Controlling the Streets?'

[43] Walker, 'Under the Bonnet'.

[44] Ibid., p. 30.

[45] Jones, 'Rural Girls and Cars', pp. 1–6.

[46] Ibid., p. 5.

female breaking out'.[47] They reflect on the level of sexual assertiveness, crude humour, and aggression in the bumper stickers of cars driven by women. Through slogans such as 'Eat My Pussy', continual self-reference as a bitch ('Bad Bitch', 'I am Bitch') and 'One Sly Chick',[48] young women in particular are seen as appropriating a sexist repertoire for their own forms of self-affirmation. It is the car as billboard, as the stand-in for the self, that performs the role.[49] The recent phenomenon of middle-aged women driving SUVs with white icons of a heterosexual nuclear 'My Family' on the rear window reflects a continuation of this car identification.[50]

This car-based identity is not limited to young Australians, and middle-aged and middle-class mothers. Richard Lefrancöis documents that for the aged, the car operates as a symbol of the active social self and a meaningful life. He suggests that the 'strong positive attitudes towards driving . . . may be viewed as a means of self-actualisation, that is to maintain autonomy and freedom'.[51] For the aged, the revoking of a driver's licence becomes a sign of the decline to death, the end of independence, and becoming a social burden. The car is also important for the identities of Indigenous people.[52] The Australian Broadcast Corporation's *Bush Mechanics* (2001)[53] series portrayed the importance of the car for the identity of Indigenous men. The series not only showed the car as an essential instrument in the maintenance of cultural and community life, but revealed that the ability to be a 'bush mechanic' – to keep vehicles going when missing wheels, engine parts, or most of the body – is highly prized and a significant source of community status.[54] While the series humorously tells many stories about contemporary Indigenous life in Central Australia and the material disadvantages facing Indigenous Australia,[55] its popularity rests on its cavalier celebration of car culture – a celebration that resonates with the wider Australian culture.[56]

These examples show that for many Australians their identity is closely

[47] Noble and Baldwin, 'Sly Chicks and Troublemakers', p. 83.

[48] Ibid., pp. 84–5.

[49] Endersby and Towle, 'Tailgate Partisanship', p. 317.

[50] Doyle and Tranter, 'F#ck Your Family!'; Doyle and Tranter, 'Automobility and "My Family" Stickers'.

[51] Lefrancöis, 'Mobility Patterns and Attitudes Toward Driving', p. 26.

[52] Anthony and Blagg, 'STOP in the Name of Who's Law?', p. 48; Young, 'The Life and Death of Cars'; Young, 'Coloring Cars'; Stotz, 'The Colonizing Vehicle'; Peterson, 'An Expanding Aboriginal Domain', p. 205.

[53] Batty, 'Motorcar Ngutju (Good Motorcar)', *Bush Mechanics*.

[54] Probyn-Rapsey, 'Bitumen Films in Postcolonial Australia', p. 101.

[55] Anthony and Tranter, 'Car Crime in the Popular Imagination', p. 7.

[56] Clarsen, 'Still Moving'.

tied to the car. As in *Mad Max 2*, the car facilitates knowledge about the individuals in the car. While most Australians could not tell a 2005 BA Ford Falcon from a 1999 VT Holden Commodore, or a winged and lowered Subaru Impreza WRX from a similarly worked Nissan Skyline, these cars trigger a shared body of knowledge about the occupants – from employment status, education level, and postcode of residential address to ethnic origin, criminal tendency, attitudes towards women and refugees, and consumer preferences.[57] Whether these assumptions are true or false in the immediate instance is immaterial; this car-based knowledge allows Australians to order other individuals, to put them in their allotted place. This knowledge and ordering through the car can be repeated – the late model German SUVs with 'My Family' stickers jostling for space outside a private school; the Toyota four-wheel drives lined up outside the country pub; the shaved middle-aged male in a new white hybrid Toyota Camry; the sign-written ute. Each car allows the driver to be known and ordered: middle-class mothers, farmers or miners, government workers in fleet vehicles and tradespeople.

The significance of the car for Australian identities allows the human-automobile to communicate status, orientation, and age though physical appearance. This symbolic economy of makes, models, and accessories is not limited to private assessments. These knowings are taken up by other networks. Like other law-enforcement agencies post 9/11, the Australian authorities have formalised 'profiling' of the population.[58] At an immediate level, certain cars – particularly models favoured by young men of various cultural backgrounds – attract high levels of surveillance and police attention.[59] This attention is also directed towards drivers who are not in the type of car that general knowledge expects them to be driving. Government welfare officers often enquire and comment on the type and condition of the car as evidence of an individual's suitability for welfare; a new car, or a prestigious make and model, can become findings of fact against the grant of assistance.[60] Further, this management goes beyond the politico-legal networks. At more diffuse levels, the car manages individuals through constituting lifestyles and consumer preferences. The car regularly features in advertising for products and services that have only a tenuous connection to the car. Here, the knowledge of individuals provided by the car allows certain cars to represent the

[57] Walker, 'Hydraulic Sexuality and Hegemonic Masculinity, pp. 181–7; Fozdar, Spittles, and Hartley, 'Australia Day, Flags on Cars and Australian Nationalism'.

[58] Pugliese, 'Preincident Indices of Criminality'.

[59] Walker, Butland, and Connell, 'Boys on the Road', pp. 163–4.

[60] Tranter, 'The Car as Avatar in Social Security Decisions'; Tranter and Kelly, 'Private Motor Vehicle Ownership in Australian Social Security Law'.

target demographic: SUVs and family products, large four-wheel drives for retiree investment funds, the European sedan for the materials of executive life. The car is packaged with product as part of a desirable lifestyle.[61]

The relation between the car and Australian identities allows individuals to be known and ordered. This knowing and ordering occurs at the level of individual human-automobiles, but also politico-legal and consumptive networks. This dimension of the car as identity flows into the second function, the car as myth.

The second function of the car identified in *Mad Max 2* is its ordering and managing of individuals through collective myths of future prosperity. The car maintains a sense of Australian community through an elaborate myth of future prosperity and possession. This can be examined at two sites. The first is the importance of the car in the emergence of 'modern Australia'. The second is the private dream of travelling around Australia in retirement.

While the Australian nation was formed in 1901 by the federation of the six British colonies, the 1920s – the decade over which there was mass adoption of the car – was also when a truly national sense of identity began to emerge. For John William Knott and Georgine Clarsen, there is more to this relationship than coincidence. Knott examines how the car featured in Australian literature from this period, and argues that the car represented the emergence of modern Australia. The car's promise to overcome the hostile, alien Australian bush made it seem like the victory weapon in the colonial battle.[62] With the bush controlled, the colonial period would give way to a better future, a prosperous modern future of social advancement founded on technological solutions.[63] A specific example of the mythical function of the car can be seen in Clarsen's analysis of Marion Bell's 1926 'round-Australia' journey. The high public profile given to the circumnavigation completed by Bell and her daughter made real the car as myth, for in carrying two women[64] around the continent, the car seemed to make good its promise of facilitating a modern Australia based on a technological 'cultural possession' that would lead to a prosperous future.[65] The car as myth established a nation ordered

[61] See Clarsen on the advertising that corresponded with the mid-1950s 'Redex Around-Australia Trials'. Clarsen, 'Automobiles and Australian Modernisation', pp. 358–9.

[62] Knott, 'The "Conquering Car"', p. 26.

[63] Ibid.

[64] Marion Bell's journey was presented as all that more remarkable in that she was a woman supposedly unskilled in the manly tasks of car maintenance and exploration. Bell was an accomplished driver, mechanic, and capitalist. See Clarsen, 'Tracing the Outline of Nation', p. 363.

[65] Ibid. pp. 365–6. For another circumnavigation journey from the 1920s, see Ellis, *The Long Lead*.

and managed to achieve a shared future.[66] The national project was a project of road building.[67] The car became a cipher to order individuals as either backward-looking colonials with romantic notions of the colonial era and the horse, or true citizens of modern Australia.[68] Further, the promise of the myth opened up new vistas for the management of individuals, and provided for a community that saw a shared future in the ordering and managing of themselves, and others, in the achievement of a modern future.[69] Through the managing of larger tracts of land, better communications, faster delivery of services, better responses to natural disasters, and more sophisticated responses to social problems, the car became the emblem for that promised and promising future.[70]

The car can be seen to play a parallel mythical role in the private life of many Australians in the popular aspiration to be a 'grey nomad'.[71] Grey nomads are older Australians 'taking to the road' or 'travelling north' in retirement and semi-retirement in a four-wheel-drive, towing a caravan. This represents a life goal for many Australians.[72] They plan to become grey nomads once work has settled down, after retirement, or when the kids are off their hands.[73] This desirability reflects a story of future prosperity, an ability to afford an expensive car and caravan, and the financial freedom to go travelling for extended periods. In addition, seeing the 'real Australia' strongly reflects Clarsen's view that 'cultural possession' is grounded in travelling around the continent. It plays out the link between seeing the 'real Australia' and a self-identity as a 'real Australian' as a human-automobile who has seen diverse parts of the continent and has authority to speak as an Australian.[74] David Williamson's play *Travelling North* (1980) captures the justification for retirement nomadism in an opening exchange between Frank and his companion Francis: 'We'll travel all over the North. You've had a hard struggle bringing up those daughters of yours and it's time you started to enjoy life.'[75]

This mythic role of the car in Australian governance lies in bringing together individuals as a community aspiring to possession and future pros-

[66] Clarsen, 'Automobiles and Australian Modernisation', p. 353.
[67] Barr, 'A Jurisprudential Tale of a Road, an Office, and a Triangle'.
[68] Knott, 'The "Conquering Car"'.
[69] Clarsen, 'Automobiles and Australian Modernisation', p. 360.
[70] Ibid.
[71] Wu and Pearce, 'The Rally Experience'.
[72] Onyx and Leonard, 'The Grey Nomad Phenomenon'.
[73] Onyx and Leonard, 'Australian Grey Nomads and American Snowbirds', p. 64.
[74] McGrath, 'Travels to a Distant Past', pp. 114–15.
[75] Williamson, *Travelling North*, p. 8.

perity. It not only orders Australians, but also provides for those shared goals to be managed towards. It is public in the sense of a key element in the dreaming of modern Australia and private in the sense of an individual's ordering and managing their life. This mythical dimension of the car can be seen as a complex elaboration of the myth of Papagallo's community in *Mad Max 2*. However, as in the film, this mythical role of the car is based on its technological function: its biopolitical potential.

As anticipated in the examination of the car as identity and the car as myth, the car's role is grounded on its function as transportation. As a transport technology, the car allows individuals to order space in specific ways.[76] For most urban Australians, the car is structurally preordained as the mundane tool of everyday life.[77] The very layout of Australian cities, with suburbs linked to feeder streets, linked to arterial roads, linked to freeways, means that from shopping, to leisure, to work and schools, space becomes reduced to familiar nodes connected via anonymous roads.[78] The car splits reality into two spaces.[79] The first is the familiar living room of the vehicle's interior, a space made place through the accretion of objects and the debris of the driver's life. The second is the space beyond the front bumper – the empty, public space of the road – through which the car must be navigated to arrive at the next familiar place.[80] In this context, the car operates as a transit cocoon, zapping the occupants across space and time to the next life-port.[81] This linking of car, space, and time continues in rural areas, where the common measure of distance is hours of driving. In turn, this demarcation of space and place facilitates the ordering of individuals. The car allows a dual life where interfacing with the public can be reduced to observations through laminated windscreens.[82] Even the grey nomads maintain an Australianism based on 'seeing' the country, and evidence that seeing with souvenir bumper stickers. This disengaged, visual polis is a society composed of human-automobiles. Individuals in the public – especially bare humans without their car prosthetic – are transformed into others occupying a non-place, needing to be watched and avoided.[83]

76 Urry, 'The "System" of Automobility', p. 28.

77 Dowling, Güllner, and O'Dwyer, 'A Gender Perspective on Urban Car Use', pp. 101–10; Dowling, 'Cultures of Mothering and Car Use in Suburban Sydney'.

78 Giblett, 'Magician's Bower'.

79 Herrick, 'King Car: On the Road to Auto-Utopia', pp. 44–6.

80 Costello, 'Learning to Drive', p. 26.

81 Merriman, 'Automobility and the Geographies of the Car'.

82 Morris, 'White Panic', p. 247.

83 Probyn-Rapsey discusses the car subjectivity of urban Australian policing of marginalised suburbs – of the 'retreat to the car' by officers. Probyn-Rapsey, 'Bitumen Films in

Allowing an ordering of space that distances the public reveals the biopolitical function of the car. This can be identified at several levels. Mundanely, the car's essential role in daily life means that, for most Australians, significant portions of the day are spent behind the wheel, where they are known, ordered, and managed within the urban grid. They circulate within a controlled network of cameras, sensors, concrete barriers, painted lines, and parking signs.[84] Additionally, the need for car ownership in order to make the distance comprehensible in terms of place and space means individuals are trapped in a certain frenzy of economic activity so as to afford the car lifestyle. The traces of these orderings can have physical evidence. Accidents happen and many Australians have the scars and mementoes inscribed on their bodies.[85] Dotted along the roadsides are ad hoc shires and memorials to not-to-be-forgotten road warriors, who perished in their vehicle at that place.[86] The crucifixion scene in *Mad Max 2* is explicit recognition that for Australians to be a human-automobile means a sacrifice of not just time, but health, flesh, and blood.[87] Beyond these bodily unions, the biopolitical dimension of the car has other manifestations.

The various welfare programs, informed by the policy of assimilation over the twentieth century whereby Indigenous children were removed from their families and placed in institutions, or in white foster homes, was made technically possible by the car.[88] These programs were a direct attempt by modern Australia to solve outstanding colonial difficulties. The continual existence and perceived ongoing social problems of Indigenous people challenged modern Australia, both in its assertion of cultural possession of the continent and in the future promise of prosperity.[89] The car's promise of technological solutions to social problems made the taking of children, in small,

Postcolonial Australia', p. 107; Manderson and van Rijswijk, 'Introduction to Littoral Readings', pp. 169–70. This protecting from threatening others is particular in the design and marketing of sport utility vehicles (SUVs); McLean, 'SUV Advertising'.

84 On the active surveillance of road users, see Guzik, 'Taking Hold of the Wheel'. On the semiotics of road signs, see Wagner, 'The Rules of the Road'.

85 In 2015, the car claimed 1,101 fatalities or 5.1 fatalities per 100,000 people. In 2013, there were 35,059 hospitalisations from road trauma. Bureau of Infrastructure, *Road Trauma Australia: 2015 Statistical Summary*, pp. 16, 32.

86 Clark, 'Challenging Motoring Functionalism'.

87 Simpson, 'Antipodean Automobility and Crash', p. 3; Lupton, 'Monsters in Metal Cocoons'.

88 See the various laws that facilitated removal of indigenous children discussed by Henriss-Anderssen, 'The "Stolen Generation" in Queensland'; Jones, 'The State and the Stolen Generation'.

89 Haebich, *Broken Circles*, p. 312; Rowse, *White Flour/White Power*, p. 108.

quiet, and discrete ways, possible and desirable. However, the car played a greater role than just an indicator for the policy potential of assimilation. From the 1920s through to the 1970s and beyond, the car was the essential tool in the taking of children away from their families. In survivor accounts from this Stolen Generation, the government agents and their car emerge as cybernetic entities. The act of taking, the vehicle, and the agent of the state merge:

> Mum was at the door, and there was this car on the road outside. There was this white woman standing there . . . One minute we was coming home to the house, and the next instant we was in the car and gone.[90]

In survivor accounts, the car comes to represent the arrival of white authority and the end of family: 'I still can't remember some of the time when I was taken away and placed in Sister Kate's Home . . . However, I do remember a big, black shiny car pulling up with a lady and a man in it.'[91] In many accounts, the car itself is given the role as the active agent in the removal of family. For 'William', one of his earliest memories was his mother's funeral: 'I can remember this utility with a coffin on top with flowers . . . I saw it get driven away knowing there was something inside that coffin that belonged to me.'[92] The car also reappears in the lonely stories of interaction and rejection by white foster parents:

> [T]hey [the foster parents] led me away . . . down a paved street where lots of different coloured cars were parked in a row. I even saw a Ute . . . This was green in colour . . . I kept looking around for my brothers . . . as I didn't want to go anywhere without them. I was told to sit in the back seat of a yellowish, cream-coloured car.[93]

For the family remaining behind, the car came to symbolise the trauma of loss. In Elaine Lomas's poem, an old woman is returned to the day of the taking: 'She screamed and she wailed as she followed the car, but dust in her eyes she couldn't get far.'[94]

The technical capacity of the human-automobile to traverse space and time, to create space and place, to nurture myths of occupation and progress,

[90] Edwards and Read, *The Lost Children*, p. 4.

[91] Mia, 'Life in Sister Katie's Home', p. 129.

[92] Bird, *The Stolen Children*, p. 85; see also Human Rights and Equal Opportunity Commission, *Bringing Them Home*, p. 83.

[93] Bird, *The Stolen Children*, p. 105; Edwards and Read, *The Lost Children*, pp. 78–9.

[94] Lomas, 'When Will They Bring My Tommy Back?'; see also Human Rights and Equal Opportunity Commission, *Bringing Them Home*, p. 129.

produced the Stolen Generation.[95] This shame of modern Australia,[96] only apologised for by Prime Minister Kevin Rudd on behalf of the Australian Government in 2008,[97] shows violently the biopolitical essence, the capacity to change life in fundamental ways of the human-automobile.

In summary, the frame from *Mad Max 2* of identity, myth, and biopolitical functions allows an unthreading of how the human-automobile facilitates knowledge, ordering, and managing in Australia. A complex map is produced, with human-automobiles as the nexus points of multiple networks: at certain moments, a subject location of meaning and identity, and at others an object location as a unit for management, and, then again, an instrument of biopower. What has been achieved, beyond any context-specific findings for the study of Australian culture, legality, and politics, is a way of mapping the networks of the present that takes at its central point a specific, common, embodied moment of technological Being-in-the-world: the human-automobile.

This is not to say that the substantive map of the Australian human-automobile can be imposed, uncritically, on to other Western societies. Clarsen has warns of universalising national automobilities to be a world-wide phenomenon.[98] The complex working of networks over time – of geographies, heritages, wealth, politico-legal traditions, social values, and expectations – renders the manifestations and trajectories of the human-automobile different across even the units that comprise the technological West. American automobility has had, and retains in its becoming, a different accent to European or Australian automobility.[99] But this shows the necessity for the highly specific, embedded, situated, cartographies of highly specific, embedded, situated technological Beings-in-the-world.

Nevertheless, generic features of the human-automobile can be noted. The human-automobile in its constructedness, its circulating and differing functions depending on network, is not the human of the Frankenstein myth. It can do too much, and it is too complicit in the networks of the West to be reduced to this naturalised object state. The human-automobile does not have rights; it has permissions, conventions, policing, parking spaces,[100]

[95] I would like to thank Rebecca Johinke for her comments on the earlier part of this chapter. Johinke, 'Not Quite *Mad Max*'.

[96] Gaita, *A Common Humanity*, p. 87.

[97] *Commonwealth Parliamentary Debates*, House of Representatives, 13 February 2008, pp. 167–73 (Kevin Rudd, Prime Minister); Moses, 'Official Apologies, Reconciliation, and Settler Colonialism'.

[98] Clarsen, 'Automobility'.

[99] Ibid., pp. 27–41.

[100] Marusek, 'Between Disability and Terror'.

scrapyards, and dusty tracks. It is an embodied node of subjectivity, a unit to be managed and a biopolitical instrument. It does not need law to save it from technology. It is because of certain industrial technologies brought together by Karl Benz and Henry Ford, and then refined for 130 years, and it is also because of various technical laws also refined for 130 years. Technical laws facilitating the instruments of licensing and registration,[101] policing,[102] risk allocation,[103] road construction and maintenance,[104] urban planning,[105] consumer and safety standards[106] give form and life to the human-automobile, just as much as the steel, plastic, and glass of the mechanistic components, and the age, gender, sexual orientation, ethnic origins, relationships, memory, and technical skills of the fleshy bits. Like Frankenstein's monster from the many filmic retellings in the Frankenstein archive, 'it lives!', but it lives as a complex of technology, law, and what used to be known as human. Through adopting a frame of analysis that dispenses with the closed Frankenstein categories of 'human', 'technology', and 'law', what has been shown is that detailed, complex maps of the lives of the monsters within the networks of the present can be drawn.

Cartographies of Technical Legality

To be responsible for becoming from the location of the law scholar-node is an invitation to map the monsters and the networks of the Western present. Technical legality describes the world as it is lived. In other words, all activity from the law scholar-node occurs within the ambit of law and technology. Even when the specific technological moments – cloning and Dolly the Sheep, for example – and their science fictional anxieties are not in the foreground, the technicity of law and technological Being-in-the-world

[101] On the origins of these forms of 'car laws', see Tranter, '"The History of the Haste-Wagons"'; Flink, *The Car Culture*; Knott, 'Speed, Modernity and the Motor Car'. On the everydayness of the Australian road rules, see Dent, 'Relationships between Laws, Norms and Practices'.

[102] On the origins of 'policing cars', see Emsley, '"Mother, What *Did* Policemen Do?"'; For contemporary Australian policing of car law, see Mossop, 'Turbo-charging Anti-hoon Legislation'.

[103] On the Australian schemes for compulsory third-party motor vehicle schemes see Brady, Burns, Leiman, and Tranter, 'Automated Vehicles and Australian Personal Injury Compensation Schemes'.

[104] See the High Court of Australia case of *Roads and Traffic Authority v Royal* (2008) 245 ALR 653 as the lead authority in Australia for the liability of road builders.

[105] On the legal and planning networks that perpetuate the ecology of the human-automobile in Australia, see Butler, 'Slicing through Space'.

[106] Lochlann Jain, *Injury*.

remains. The West comprises the becoming of monsters and networks.

In this, law and technology are what law scholar-nodes research and write. Law and technology is not just a subspecies of legal scholarship, published in the many journals of law and technology (JOLTs).[107] In the alternative, to think and write on law in the contemporary West is to study technical legality. The technicity of law and the totality of technological Being-in-the-world are the essential data that the law scholar-node processes. This is where the Frankenstein myth is dangerous. By framing thinking about law and technology according to a narrative of monstrous technology, vulnerable humanity, and saving law, a simplified, static representation of the becoming of the West is sketched. Complexity, constructed-ness, change, multiplicity of meanings and powers are ignored. Law fails to see its own technicity and the entwining of the law network with other networks to give form to contemporary Western life.

This is a problem for any legal scholarship, but is particularly so for law scholar-nodes whose focus is explicitly on law and technology. It can be seen in the poverty of how the car is considered in legal thought. It is a threat against human bodies that needs lawful control,[108] especially with its becoming towards automation.[109] Absent is the fundamental recognition that there has been a century of becoming of the human-automobile in the West, and as such the car is not just a character in legal narratives on accident liability, or criminal negligence; the functionalities of the human-automobile are deeply located and expected by the politico-legal networks.[110] The West is orientated on the needs and capacities of the human-automobile; as such, piecemeal changes to the law would not dramatically change the circulation of this monster. Even as the science fictional future of automated and electric-powered vehicles becomes more manifest, what are still not challenged are the basic functionalities of identity, myth, and biopower of the human-automobile.

What has been revealed by unthreading Australia through the frame suggested by *Mad Max 2* of identity, myth, and biopower is not that this is the total cartography of Western life, or even of the human-automobile. There are many other technologies – digital, pharmaceutical, electrical, and mechanical

[107] Tranter, 'The Law and Technology Enterprise', pp. 33, 77–83.

[108] Fridman, 'The Doctrine of the "Family Car:"'; Spencer, 'Motor-Cars and the Rule in *Rylands v Fletcher*'.

[109] Surden and Williams, 'Technological Opacity, Predictability, and Self-Driving Cars'; Levy, 'No Need to Reinvent the Wheel'; Zohn, 'When Robots Attack'; Glancy, 'Autonomous and Automated and Connected Cars'.

[110] Tranter, 'Disrupting Technology Disrupting Law'.

– that form the cyborgs of the West. There are also other functions of the car that are not brought as clearly forward by *Mad Max 2* – the perverse, erotic, and sexualised of J. G. Ballard's *Crash* (1973)[111] are immediately suggested. However, what has been achieved through *Mad Max 2* and the Australian human-automobile is a partial cartography of technical legality.

In placing the emphasis on the living and becoming of a specific form of technological Being-in-the-world, the networks that sustain, utilise, change, and manage this node are highlighted. The law network's multiple impacts on both an embodied node and its interaction with other networks thus become clearer. Unlike the Frankenstein myth, which imposes categories and obliterates connections and relationships, this mapping of the monsters and networks of the present is open to the complexity of affect. The human-automobile lives in surprising ways. *Bush Mechanics* shows the place of the car for contemporary, remote Indigenous communities, while the Stolen Generation was produced through the biopolitical activities of human-automobile. Police profiling utilises the same symbolic economy of makes and models (of the mechanical and flesh components of the human-automobile) as Australian road warriors do in their daily navigations. Oozing through the nodes and networks is *zoe*. There are unlikely alliances, complicities, and surprises, while at the same time there is also the expected technical working of the machine. The engine usually roars to life, except at the most inconvenient moments when it doesn't. In drafting cartographies that reveal this complexity of affect, the law scholar-node can be responsible for becoming. Instead of generating the expected instrumental input for the politico-legal network – data assessing rules, identifying gaps, noting inefficiencies, registering rights – more complex cartographies can interrupt, reorientate, and rewire the networks of the West.

There are two paths for these vectors of change. The first is the privileged location of the law scholar-node in generating information about the operations of the politico-legal network. As has been seen in Chapter 1, law scholarship is a significant site for the self-reckoning of the legal machine. Agenda-setting, identifying gaps, and working through the technicalities of the law–technology interface does get taken up by law-making sub-routines. The legal scholarship in response to Dolly was processed by advisers, commissions, think-tanks, and departments, into issues papers, reports, recommendations, and, eventually, laws.[112] In going beyond the *Frankenstein* categories to see the interconnections and complexities, the quirky, different, surprises

[111] Ballard, *Crash*; Thomas, 'The Rules of Autogeddon'.

[112] Tranter, 'Biotechnology, Media and Law-making'.

of affect can be noticed. The law-machine will still make law; the primal powers of death and time will still change becoming. This is what the totality of technology means for the law network: the inevitable technicity of law making and remaking the world. However, in feeding more diverse cartographies that see the fluxes of nodes and networks, there are the possibilities that law's making of the world will not carry into the future such destruction of affect as the stolen generation policies, or community shattering road-building or ecological change. The traversing of the planet by the human-automobile is a material fact, the complex product of network histories. The persistence of some of these networks renders it enduring, yet as with any form of technological Being-in-the-world, it is changing, becoming.[113] The law network has contributed and entrenched the human-automobile, yet also can positively direct its manifestation into the future. Safety laws, drink-driving laws, emissions reduction standards, and comprehensive liability laws have all come into being through law scholar-nodes conceiving the human-automobile differently, recording and mapping its impact on affect, and providing privileged data that the politico-legal networks transformed into law. The law scholar-node's function in the networks means it can directly be responsible for becoming through the forms of data about the world that it produces. While functioning not quite as the agent of change of the sovereign Atreides, the Doctor or the lawyer-node – the embodied wielders of the powers of death and time – the law scholar-nodes' privileged proximity can allow their maps to change the world.

This primary way for law scholar-nodes to be responsible for becoming can be seen as supplemented by a secondary path. Their maps and cartographies not only feed the law network, but can be seen as technical manuals for other embodied nodes in their responsibility for becoming. Through knowing the networks of the West better, the law scholar-node can gift the technical legal subject and the lawyer-node – two embodied nodes considered in this book – with more truth about their location, their enduring nature, and their possibilities. In the contemporary West, empowerment depends not on manifestos or natural rights – past, human, strategies for empowerment – but in the epoch of technicity, empowerment is through information, describing, mapping, forensically unthreading the nodes, nexuses, and networks of the present. To link back to *Battlestar Galactica* and Chapter 3, tricksters need plans in their responsibility for becoming. The law scholar-node has a further privileged location in providing the material through which other nodes can plan to fulfil their potential.

[113] Rees, 'Accelerate, Reverse, or Find the Off Ramp?'

In summary, the law scholar-node can be responsible for becoming, but Frankenstein needs to be put aside. Instead of fixed categories of 'technology', 'humanity', and 'law' there is a necessity to map the nodes and networks of the present. In the context of *Mad Max*, Paul Williams has reminded us of the link between the mapping of the unknown 'soft spaces' and the imperial project, especially the colonialist Australian narratives of empty interiors of future possibility.[114] The call for the law scholar-node to map the present is complicit with these tendencies. In the 'Age of the World Picture', as Heidegger laments, the drive to observe, describe, and render the world useful is inescapable.[115] Law scholar-nodes located in this historical moment are not able to go beyond Enframing. Further, their connectedness with the politico-legal networks also means that their productions are not innocent. What is measured and what is written feed into networks of death and time to change life. In her discussion of the 'ethics' of the scholar within the contemporary epoch, Braidotti suggests:

> Post-humanistic acceptance of hybridization and the intermingling of the biological with the cultural, the physical with the technological is neither nihilistic nor decadent . . . It aims at finding accurate cartographies of the changes that are occurring in post-industrial cultures. It is a way of mapping metamorphoses.[116]

The suggestion put forward by this chapter is of alternative cartographic techniques – not an impossible call for a non-technical, pure, and removed mediation. Instead, by going beyond Frankenstein, the complexities of contemporary life become noted. Through 'mapping metamorphoses', the possibilities for change, and responsibility for becoming, are revealed.

This argument was pursued through a performative exercise mapping the human-automobile in the West – or, more precisely, embodied human-automobiles within a specific Western space, namely Australia. Through taking *Mad Max 2* as a lens, it was shown how the human-automobile grounds identity, myth, and biopower. These nexus-points were then transposed on to Australia, showing how the human-automobile is a location for various networks that know, order, and manage Australia.

The concluding image is of life and hope. In *Mad Max 2*, the final scenes are of the community escaping in their rag-tag fleet of vehicles. But unlike *Battlestar Galactica*, the lead vehicle is not military, but rather a vulnerable civilian school bus. However, like *Battlestar Galactica*, where the finale

114 Williams, 'Beyond *Mad Max III*', p. 312.

115 Heidegger, 'The Age of World Picture'.

116 Braidotti, *Transpositions*, p. 170.

reveals that Hera's hybrid descendants had inherited Earth, the voice-over – now revealed to be the grown and old Feral Child (Emil Minty) – narrates how Max's refugees survive and go on to form the Great Northern Tribe. Technology is affirmed, along with myths of progress and technological futures; the precious fuel reserves hidden in the convoy come to allow this becoming. Even after the apocalypse, technological life endures.

Max also endures, although the community does not see the Road Warrior again.[117] He returns in *Mad Max: Beyond Thunderdome* to free other 'lost children' from the desert and from the violent exchanges of 'Bartertown', allowing them to achieve 'Tomorrow-morrow land'.[118] In the long-awaited fourth film, *Mad Max: Fury Road* (2015),[119] chases and battles result in Max (Tom Hardy) and Imperator Furiosa (Charlize Theron) not escaping to the 'Green Paradise' but instead returning as liberators to Joe's Citadel. However, it is Furiosa who seems to take up the vacuum left by Joe; Max is screened as wandering off.[120] At the end of each film, Max remains in the wastelands, traversing, looking, healing, scavenging, mapping.[121] *Mad Max 2* has been used in the chapter as a cipher through which the multiplicities of the human-automobile of the contemporary West can be mapped as a performative example of how law scholar-nodes can be responsible for becoming through developing cartographies of the nodes, nexuses, and networks of the present. In this detailing of complexity, the moments of affect – possibilities for new connections, relations, surprises – are revealed. In this, the productions of law scholar-nodes feed into the process of law change and can be seen as technical manuals for the monsters of the West to achieve the creation, changing, doing, and responsibility that is the potential of technological Being-in-the-world.

Max, with his 1980s punk-meets-new-romantic leathers, can be recoded as myth-ideal for the law scholar-node. While a hero, there is a trickster element to Max. After all, 'We don't need another hero,' Tina Turner belts out in the signature song of the third film.[122] Dispensing with judgements about the progressive or conservative features of the future societies that the saved people of the films become,[123] what Max does do – like Baltar and the

117 Miller, *Mad Max 2: The Road Warrior.*

118 Miller and Oglivie, *Mad Max: Beyond Thunderdome.*

119 Miller, *Mad Max: Fury Road.*

120 Boulware, '"Who Killed the World"'; de Coning, 'Recouping Masculinity'.

121 Williams, 'Beyond *Mad Max III*', p. 310.

122 Turner, 'We Don't Need Another Hero', *Mad Max: Beyond Thunderdome, Original Motion Picture Soundtrack.*

123 Morris, 'White Panic', p. 251.

Doctor – is allow life. His survival in the desert – a survival based on his tenacious skills – allows others to become as well.[124] This is what law scholar-nodes of the contemporary West are called to be when they are challenged to be responsible for becoming: to be privileged road warriors who know the networks and, through the cartographies they create, allow life.

[124] Morris, 'Fate and the Family Sedan', p. 131.

7

Deserts and Technical Legality

The last chapter ended with Max still out there. The Road Warrior endured, even with the ends of civilisation and its fitful restarts, to nurture life. The victory celebrations of the liberated in *Mad Max: Fury Road*, however, seemed partial, for what would happen once the water ran out? With Max nodding and leaving, there remains the possibility for further narration in *Mad Max 5* of the violence, crashes, and becomings of Max's life in the dry expanses of the desert.

Deserts have been a feature of this book's journey of living in technical legality: the deserts of Arrakis, the empty space of *Battlestar Galactica*, the materiality of matter in time of the Doctor's universe and the iconic Australian outback of *Mad Max 2*. Even the hyper-life of the renovated South American rainforests of *Xenogenesis* was a desert, a place of danger and death for Butler's Oankali-saved urbanised humans. These textual and screened deserts were representative of another desert. The triumph of technology in the modern West is often associated with desert imagery. There are concerns with emptiness, uniformity, alien hostility to humanity, a dry space of non-life. This book, taking an alternative perspective, goes *to* the desert. Its charting of hope is predicated on the harsh reality that the desert of the totality of technology needs to be seen as home for us: the monsters that have inherited the West.

Deserts, as seen in Dune and *Mad Max*, are not empty, uniform, and hostile to humanity, dry spaces of non-life. Herbert's imaging of Dune, notwithstanding criticisms that can be made of the depth of his ecological engagement, was based on his seeing in the desert networks of becoming: interconnections between biotic, abiotic, and cultural systems. There is life in deserts, and deserts live. The sands of Arrakis ebb and flow over the millennia of the Dune cycle, yet they endure. Deserts can be home, but to be place and not space requires technical intervention. From Herbert's Freman, to the spaceship-borne technological society of *Battlestar Galactica*, to the re-settlers of the Butler's rehabilitated Earth, to the Doctor's universe traversing blue box, to the survivors of *Mad Max*, life continues, changes, becomes in the desert, through machines, skills, and techniques. Unsurprisingly, to live well within the totality of technology requires an acknowledgement and appreciation of the technical. Nature and culture, and the other old binaries of previous forms of 'human' existence, must be seen as changed. To be at home within the totality of technology, the embodied, hybrid node-in-the-networks that used to be known as human need to acknowledge and embrace – indeed, celebrate – its monstrous technological Being-in-the-world. The now is a moment within a fluxing universe striving towards the becoming of its future. This is an opportunity – a technically mediated opportunity – to be an active participant in the changing of the world – to be responsible for becoming.

All this means that law is changed. The present is the present of technical legality. Law is fundamentally a technology that is changing the world. This means that thinking 'law and technology' – the pragmatic technicalities of how law is to respond, regulate, and react to technological change – holds within it the epoch-defining technicity of law. Its future focus disclosed in its science fictional orientation, its alchemical origins in death and time, its clear agenda to make the world reveal the poverty – indeed, the implosion – of the existing organising narrative of the Frankenstein myth. 'Humanity', or what now is understood as the 'human', is not so pure; technology is not an external monster; and law does not save. In the totality of technology, the desert imagery returns. It does seem that the differences and features of 'humanity', 'technology', and 'law' have been eroded to uniform grains of sand. Instead, a techno-being uses technicity to mediate technology.

However, this sameness is a mirage – much like the blue police box disguises the technological wonder that is the TARDIS. In Heidegger's victory of Enframing, there is – via Haraway and Braidotti – not a fall, but a revealing of life in its material and generative sense. *Zoe* endures; it always has endured. Leviathan's powers of death and time have transformed into the biopolitical machine's law as technology, but living, hoping, and loving remain. The survivors of the Cylon holocaust, Butler's post-nuclear winter, alien-modified humans, the endless 'little people' who continue to become under the Doctor's stewardship and the remnants in *Mad Max* fighting and hoping for better in the Australian outback continue to live. The networks of the present – politico-legal, cultural, consumptive/economic, biotic, informatics – continually change, remaking node-points and the opportunities for life at embodied locations. But this does not mean the passiveness of Agamben's bare life or the liberal myths of rights and freedoms from. It means that responsibility for becoming is technically possible for technological Being-in-the-world, but the scope, opportunities, powers, and possibilities of an embodied node are not the same as for others. The monsters of the West do not occupy identical nexus points within the mega-machine. Instead of the flat sameness of the desert metaphor, the present is a complex set of eddies, currents, histories, and diversity. Unlike the 'human', such as Butler's resister males with their rights, gender and clarity between nature and culture, the contemporary monsters of the West are far less unitary, more connected, located, known, and processed.

This is why this book was a journey of living in technical legality, and why it considered the responsibility for becoming from several specific nodes in the networks. The technical legal subject's ability to choose and nurture life through positive relations, the lawyer-node's possibility to safeguard becoming while necessarily remaining apart, and the law scholar-node's potential to map and rework the networks, each disclose the opportunity for technical doing-in-the-world that could be seen as enhancing affect. This is the message of hope that opened this book. The monsters of the West can live, lawyer, and research within the technical legality of the technological world in life-affirming, positive ways.

The journey of living in technical legality began with law and technology and science fiction. Through examining how the politico-legal networks of the West transmuted Dolly to law, three characteristics of technical legality were revealed. The first was the functioning of science fiction as a storehouse of images of technological futures that structured how certain technologies were conceived. The second was the further science fictionality that structured how these technological futures were to be prepared for in the present. The mega-narrative of vulnerable humanity, amoral technology, and saving law was forged and maintained by the Frankenstein myth. The third was that this making of law in the present to ensure the future disclosed a technicity to law. Law was a tool, an instrument, a technology, through which future was made in the present.

This monstrosity that is law as technology was then considered through Dune and *Battlestar Galactica*. This journey began with the illusion of control, and went to sovereignty, and then saw the stripping away of sovereignty to reveal its essence in the primal alchemy of death and time. The journey then moved on to the exception, the subject, and to the triumph of technology as Enframing. At this point, there was an unexpected ending. *Battlestar Galactica* did not 'end' with the demise of Being, but with technological Being-in-the-world, and with a glimpse of the possibility for responsibility for becoming within the totality of technology. This possibility 'inside the belly of the monster'[1] was then explored in three locations: in the technical

[1] Haraway, quoted in Penley and Ross, 'Cyborgs at Large', p. 12.

legal subject through a detailed reading of Butler's *Xenogenesis*, in the lawyer-node through *Doctor Who*, and in the law scholar-node through *Mad Max 2*.

There is beauty in the desert: the colours of twilight, the red dune framed by a blue in blue sky. And there is life. Even on Herbert's imagined desert planet, Muad'Dib hops, the hawk hunts, Freman live and make culture, and the sandworms rule supreme. This beauty and life are there to be seen, mapped, and appreciated. However, tracks through sand soon fade. Enduring change is the way of the desert.

Technical legality means that the law network, with its technical ability to change bodies in time, is sophisticated, fluxing, and one of many networks that interface in the becoming of the world. It has beauty and colour, and makes a complex space for living through the biopolitical processing of life. The end of this book on technical legality with *Mad Max* and law scholar-nodes is meaningful. In their privileged location as primary revealers of the world, as makers of maps of becoming, law scholar-nodes have a fabulous destiny. They are the tricksters of the tricksters. They occupy a place in the network to be observers of technical legality and witness the beauty of affect along with the ugliness of its violent and destructive other. They note the workings of the machines, and in so doing provide the recordings – the observations, the creative thinking, and the witnessing – for technological Being-in-the-world to create better. But the maps soon fade. Enduring change is the way of deserts and of technically mediated existence. Thus, law scholar-nodes are called to continually produce cartographies of technical legality, so that the West's ever-becoming technological future is better than its ever-becoming technological past.

Bibliography

Secondary Sources

Agamben, Giorgio, *Homo Sacer: Sovereign Power and Bare Life*, trans. Daniel Heller-Roazen (Stanford: Stanford University Press, 1998).

Agamben, Giorgio, *The Open: Man and Animal*, trans. Kevin Attell (Stanford: Stanford University Press, 2004).

Agamben, Giorgio, *State of Exception*, trans. Kevin Attell (Chicago: University of Chicago Press, 2005).

Agamben, Giorgio, *Statis: Civil War as a Political Paradigm*, trans. Nicholas Heron (Edinburgh: Edinburgh University Press, 2015).

Aldiss, Brian, *Trillion Year Spree: The History of Science Fiction* (London: Paladin, 1988).

Alessandria Hurd, Denise, 'The Monster Inside: 19th Century Racial Constructs in 24th Century Mythos of *Star Trek*', *Journal of Popular Culture* 31:1 (1997), pp. 23–35.

Allison, Dorothy 'The Future of Female: Octavia Butler's Mother Lode', in Henry Louis Gates (ed.), *Reading Black, Reading Feminist* (New York: Meridian, 1990), pp. 471–8.

Amy-Chinn, Dee, 'Rose Tyler: The Ethics of Care and the Limit of Agency', *Science Fiction Film and Television* 1:2 (2008), pp. 231–47.

Annas, George J., 'Human Cloning: A Choice or an Echo?', *University of Dayton Law Review* 23:2 (1998), pp. 247–76.

Annas, George J. and Sherman Elias, '*In Vitro* Fertilization and Embryo Transfer: Medicolegal Aspects of a New Technique to Create a Family', *Family Law Quarterly* 17:2 (1983), pp. 199–223.

Annas, George J. and John A. Robertson, 'Human Cloning – Should the United States Legislate Against It?', *ABA Journal* 83:5 (1997), pp. 80–1.

Anthony, Thalia and Harry Blagg, 'STOP in the Name of Who's Law? Driving and the Regulation of Contested Space in Central Australia', *Social and Legal Studies* 22:1 (2013), pp. 43–66.

Anthony, Thalia and Kieran Tranter, 'Car Crime in the Popular Imagination', in Nicole Rafter (ed.), *Oxford Research Encyclopaedia: Criminology and Criminal Justice* (New York: Oxford University Press, 2016).

Asimov, Isaac, *The Rest of the Robots* (London: Panther, 1969 [1967]).

Asimov, Isaac, *In Memory Yet Green* (New York: Doubleday, 1979).

Asimov, Isaac, 'Introduction: The First Century of Science Fiction', in Isaac Asimov,

Martin H. Greenberg and Charles G. Waugh (eds)), *Isaac Asimov Presents: The Best Science Fiction of the Nineteenth Century* (New York: Knightsbridge, 1991 [1981]), pp. 9–12.
Asimov, Isaac, *I, Robot* (New York: Bantam, 2008 [1950]).
Atwood, Margaret, *Oryx and Crake* (London: Bloomsbury, 2003).
Austin, John, *The Province of Jurisprudence Determined* (Amherst: Prometheus Books, 2000 [1832]).
Australian Government, *Legislation Review: Prohibition of Human Cloning Act 2002 and Research Involving Human Embryos Act 2002* (Canberra: Australian Government, 2005).
Australian Health Ethics Committee, *Scientific, Ethical and Regulatory Considerations Relevant to Cloning of Human Beings* (Canberra: National Health and Medical Research Council, 1998).
Back, Kurt W, '*Frankenstein* and Brave New World: Two Cautionary Myths on the Boundaries of Science', *History of European Ideas* 20:1–3 (1995), pp. 327–32.
Baldick, Chris, *In Frankenstein's Shadow: Myth, Monstrosity and Nineteenth Century Writing* (Oxford: Clarendon Press, 1987).
Balkin, Jack M. and Beth Simone Noveck, 'Introduction', in Jack M. Balkin and Beth Simone Noveck (eds), *The State of Play: Law, Games and Virtual Worlds* (New York: New York University Press, 2006), pp. 3–12.
Ballard, J. G., *Crash* (London: Vintage, 1973).
Bararova, Natalyn N. and Yoon Hyung Choi, 'Self-Disclosure in Social Media: Extending the Functional Approach to Disclosure Motivations and Characteristics on Social Network Sites', *Journal of Communication* 64:4 (2014), pp. 569–784.
Baron, Paula, 'The Emperor's New Clothes: From Atticus Finch to Denny Crane', in Reid Mortensen, Francesca Bartlett, and Kieran Tranter (eds), *Alternative Perspectives on Lawyers and Legal Ethics: Reimagining the Profession* (London: Routledge, 2011), pp. 85–107.
Barr, Olivia, 'A Jurisprudential Tale of a Road, an Office, and a Triangle', *Law and Literature* 27:2 (2015), pp. 199–216.
Barron, Lee, 'Out in Space: Masculinity, Sexuality and the Science Fiction Heroics of Captain Jack', in Andrew Ireland (ed.), *Illuminating Torchwood: Essays on Narrative, Character and Sexuality in the BBC Series* (Jefferson: McFarland, 2010), pp. 213–25.
Barthes, Roland, *Mythologies*, trans. Annette Lavers (London: Paladin, 1973).
Barton-Kriese, Paul, 'Exploring Divergent Realities: Using Science Fiction to Teach Introductory Political Science', *Extrapolation* 34:3 (1993), pp. 209–15.
Basson, David, *Battlestar Galactica: The Official Companion* (London: Titan Books, 2005).
Bear, Greg, *Blood Music* (Westminster, MD: Arbor House, 1985).
Beebe, Barton, 'Fair Use and Legal Futurism', *Law and Literature* 25:1 (2013), pp. 10–19.
Beeler, Stan, '*Stargate SG-1* and the Quest for the Perfect Science Fiction Premise', in J. P. Telotte (ed.), *The Essential Science Fiction Reader* (Lexington: University Press of Kentucky, 2008), pp. 267–82.
Belk, Nolan, 'The Certainty of the Flesh: Octavia Butler's Use of the Erotic in the *Xenogenesis* Trilogy', *Utopian Studies* 19:3 (2008), pp. 369–89.

Bell, Dean, 'Human Cloning and International Human Rights Law', *Sydney Law Review* 21:2 (1999), pp. 202–30.

Bell, Derrick, 'Racial Realism', *Connecticut Law Review* 24:2 (1992), pp. 363–79.

Bell-Metereau, Rebecca, 'The How-To Manual, the Prequel, and the Sequel in Post-9/11 Cinema', in Wheeler Winston Dixon (ed.), *Film and Television after 9/11* (Carbondale: Southern Illinois University Press, 2004), pp. 142–61.

Ben-Naftali, Orna and Zvi Triger, 'The Human Conditioning: International Law and Science-Fiction', *Law, Culture and the Humanities* (2013), DOI 10.1177/17438721134992152013.

Bendersky, Joseph W., *Carl Schmitt: Theorist for the Reich* (Princetown: Princetown University Press 1983).

Benjamin, Walter, 'The Work of Art in the Age of Mechanical Reproduction', in Hannah Arendt (ed.), *Illuminations: Essay and Reflections* (New York: Harcourt, Brace and World, 1968), pp. 217–51.

Benjamin, Walter, 'Critique of Violence', in Peter Demetz (ed.), *Reflections: Essays, Aphorisms, Autobiographical Writings* (New York: Schocken Books, 1978), pp. 277–300.

Bennett Moses, Lyria, 'Recurring Dilemmas: The Law's Race to Keep Up with Technological Change', *Journal of Law, Technology and Policy* 7:2 (2007), pp. 239–85.

Bentham, Jeremy, *Of Laws in General* (London: Athlone Press, 1970).

Bentham, Jeremy, 'Anarchical Fallacies', in Jeremy Waldron (ed.), *Nonsense upon Stilts: Bentham, Burke and Marx on the Rights of Man* (London: Methuen, 1987), pp. 46–69.

Berlin, Isaiah, *Against the Current: Essays in the History of Ideas* (New York: Viking Press, 1980).

The Bible Society in Australia, *Good News Bible: Today's English Version* (Canberra: The Bible Society in Australia 1976).

Bignell, Jonathan, 'The Child as Addressee, Viewer and Consumer in Mid-1960s *Doctor Who*', in David Butler (ed.), *Time and Relative Dissertations in Space: Critical Perspectives on* Doctor Who (Manchester: Manchester University Press, 2007), pp. 43–55.

Bird, Carmel, *The Stolen Children: Their Stories* (Sydney: Random House, 1998).

Blackford, Russell, 'Who's Afraid of the Brave New World?', *Quadrant* 47:5 (2003), pp. 9–15.

Blits, Jan H., 'Hobbesian Fear', *Political Theory* 17:3 (1989), pp. 417–31.

Bobbio, Norberto, *Thomas Hobbes and the Natural Law Tradition*, trans. Daniela Gobetti (Chicago: University of Chicago Press, 1993).

Böckenförde, Ernst-Wolfgang, 'The Concept of the Political: A Key to Understanding Carl Schmitt's Constitutional Theory', in David Dyzenhaus (ed.), *Law as Politics: Carl Schmitt's Critique of Liberalism* (Durham, NC: Duke University Press, 1998), pp. 37–55.

Booker, M. Keith, *Science Fiction Television* (Westport: Praeger, 2004).

Booth, Paul, 'Periodising *Doctor Who*', *Science Fiction Film and Television* 7:2 (2014), pp. 195–215.

Borgmann, Albert, *Holding on to Reality: The Nature of Information at the Turn of the Millennium* (Chicago: University of Chicago Press, 1999).

Botting, Fred, *Making Monstrous: Frankenstein, Criticism and Theory* (Manchester: Manchester University Press, 1991).

Bould, Mark, 'Science Fiction in the United Kingdom', in J. P. Telotte (ed.), *The Essential Science Fiction Reader* (Lexington: University Press of Kentucky, 2008), pp. 209–30.

Boulware, Taylor, '"Who Killed the World?": Building a Feminist Utopia from the Ashes of Toxic Masculinity in *Mad Max: Fury Road*', *Mise-en-scène, the Journal of Film & Visual Narration* 1:1 (2016), pp. 1–17, <https://journals.sfu.ca/msq/msq/index.php/msq/article/view/11> (last accessed 7 November 2017).

Bourdieu, Pierre, *The Political Ontology of Martin Heidegger*, trans. Peter Collier (Oxford: Blackwell, 1991).

Bourne, Craig, *A Future for Presentism* (Oxford: Clarendon Press, 2006).

Boyd White, James, 'Law as Rhetoric, Rhetoric as Law: The Arts of Cultural and Communal Life', *University of Chicago Law Review* 52:3 (1985), pp. 684–702.

Brady, Mark, Kylie Burns, Tania Leiman, and Kieran Tranter, 'Automated Vehicles and Australian Personal Injury Compensation Schemes', *Torts Law Journal* 24:1 (2017), 32–63.

Braidotti, Rosi, *Nomadic Subjects: Embodiment and Sexual Difference in Contemporary Feminist Theory* (New York: Columbia University Press, 1994).

Braidotti, Rosi, *Transpositions: On Nomadic Ethics* (Cambridge: Polity Press, 2006).

Branston, Gill, 'Apocalyptic Imaginings', *Environmental Communication* 10:6 (2016), pp. 807–10.

Britton, Piers D. and Simon J. Barker, *Reading between Designs: Visual Imagery and the Generation of Meaning in* The Avengers, The Prisoner, *and* Doctor Who (Austin: University of Texas Press, 2003).

Brock, Caitlin, 'Where We're Going, We Don't Need Drivers: The Legal Issues and Liability Implications of Automated Vehicle Technology', *UMKC Law Review* 83:3 (2015), pp. 769–88.

Broderick, Damien, *Reading by Starlight: Postmodern Science Fiction* (London: Routledge, 1995).

Broderick, Mick, 'Heroic Apocalypse: *Mad Max*, Mythology and the Millennium', in Christopher Sharrett (ed.), *Crisis Cinema: The Apocalyptic Idea in Postmodern Narrative Film* (Washington, DC: Maisonneuve Press, 1993), pp. 251–72.

Brown, J. P. C., 'Doctor Who: A Very British Alien', in R. C. Neighbors and Sandy Rankin (eds), *The Galaxy is Rated G: Essays on Children's Science Fiction Film and Television* (Jefferson: McFarland, 2011), pp. 161–82.

Browning, John G., 'A Long Time Ago, in a Courtroom Far, Far Away, There's No Denying That the Force is All around Us – Even Judges Refer to George Lucas's Pop Culture Science Fiction Saga', *Texas Bar Journal* 77:2 (2014), pp. 158–62.

Brownsword, Roger, 'Stem Cells, Supermen and the Report of the Select Committee', *Modern Law Review* 65:4 (2002), pp. 569–87.

Brownsword, Roger, *Rights, Regulation and the Technological Revolution* (Oxford: Oxford University Press, 2008).

Brownsword, Roger, 'So What Does the World Need Now? Reflections on Regulating Technologies', in Roger Brownsword and Karen Yeung (eds), *Regulating Technologies: Legal Futures, Regulatory Frames and Technological Fixes* (Oxford: Hart, 2008), pp. 23–48.

Bureau of Infrastructure, Transport and Regional Economics, *Road Trauma*

Australia: 2015 Statistical Summary (Canberra: Department of Infrastructure and Regional Development, 2016).
Burke, Debra D., 'Cybersmut and the First Amendment: A Call for a New Obscenity Standard', *Harvard Journal of Law and Technology* 9:1 (1996), pp. 87–145.
Butler, Chris, 'Slicing through Space: Mobility, Rhythm and the Abstraction of Modernist Transport Planning', *Griffith Law Review* 17:2 (2008), pp. 470–88.
Butler, Judith, *Gender Trouble: Feminism and the Subversion of Identity* (New York: Routledge, 1990).
Butler, Octavia E., *Dawn* (New York: Warner Books, 1987).
Butler, Octavia E., *Adulthood Rites* (New York: Warner Books, 1988).
Butler, Octavia E., *Imago* (New York: Warner Books, 1989).
California Advisory Committee on Human Cloning, *Cloning Californiams? Report of the California Advisory Committee on Human Cloning* (Los Angeles, CA: California Department of Health Services, 2002).
Calo, Ryan, 'Robots as Legal Metaphors', *Harvard Journal of Law and Technology* 30:1 (2017), pp. 209–37.
Cameron, Nigel M. de S. and Anna Henderson, 'Brave New World at the General Assesmbly: The United Nations Declaration on Human Cloning', *Minnesota Journal of Law, Science and Technology* 9 (2008), pp. 145–238.
Campbell, Joseph, *The Masks of God: Primitive Mythology* (New York: Penguin, 1959).
Campbell, Joseph, *The Hero with a Thousand Faces* (Princeton: Princeton University Press, 1968).
Canavan, Gerry, 'The Octavia E. Butler Papers', *Eaton Journal of Archival Research in Science Fiction* 3:1 (2015), pp. 42–53.
Carmen, Ira H., *Cloning and the Constitution: An Inquiry into Governmental Policymaking and Genetic Experimentation* (Madison: University of Wisconsin Press, 1985).
Carroll, Noel, *The Philosophy of Horror* (New York: Routledge, 1990).
Carter, Lief H. and Jessica McCann, 'Measuring Humanity: Rights in the 24th Century', in Peter Robson and Jessica Silbey (eds), *Law and Justice on the Small Screen* (Oxford: Hart, 2012), pp. 15–32.
Casey, Jim, '"All this has Happened Before": Repetition, Reimagination, and Eternal Return', in Tiffany Potter and C. W. Marshall (eds), *Cylons in America: Critical Studies in* Battlestar Galactica (New York: Continuum, 2008), pp. 237–50.
Caudill, David S., 'Scientific Narratives in Law: An Introduction', *Law and Literature* 14:2 (2002), pp. 253–74.
Chapman, James, *Inside the TARDIS: The Worlds of* Doctor Who *A Cultural History* (London: I. B. Tauris, 2006).
Chapman, James, 'Fifty Years in the TARDIS: The Historical Moments of *Doctor Who*', *Critical Studies in Television* 9:1 (2014), pp. 43–61.
Charles, Alec, 'War without End? The Family, and the Post-9/11 World in Russell T. Davies's *Doctor Who*', *Science Fiction Studies* 35:3 (2008), pp. 450–65.
Charles, Alec, 'The Crack of Doom: The Uncanny Echoes of Steven Moffat's *Doctor Who*', *Science Fiction Film and Television* 4:1 (2011), pp. 1–24.
Chester, Ronald, 'Cloning for Human Reproduction: One American Perspective', *Sydney Law Review* 23:3 (2001), pp. 319–46.

Chin, Bettina M., 'Regulating Your Second Life: Defamation in Virtual Worlds', *Brooklyn Law Review* 72:4 (2007), pp. 1,303–49.

Clapshaw, Deborah, 'Legal Aspects of Artificial Human Reproduction: Can Law Afford to Play Ostrich?', *Auckland University Law Review* 4 (1980–3), pp. 254–72.

Clark, Jennifer, 'Challenging Motoring Functionalism', *Journal of Transport History* 29:1 (2008), pp. 23–43.

Clarke, Arthur C., *Imperial Earth* (London: Gollancz, 1976).

Clarsen, Georgine, 'Tracing the Outline of Nation: Circling Australia by Car', *Continuum: Journal Media and Cultural Studies* 13:3 (1999), pp. 359–89.

Clarsen, Georgine, 'Still Moving: Bush Mechanics in the Central Desert', *Australian Humanities Review* 25 (2002), pp. 1–12.

Clarsen, Georgine, 'Mobility in Australia: Unsettling the Settled', in Gijs Mom, Gordon Pirie, and Laurent Tissot (eds), *Mobility in History: The State of the Art in the History of Transport, Traffic and Mobility* (Neuchatel: Editions Alphil – Presses Universitaires Suisses, 2009), pp. 123–8.

Clarsen, Georgine, 'Automobiles and Australian Modernisation: The Redex around Australia Trials of the 1950s', *Australian Historical Studies* 41:3 (2010), pp. 352–68.

Clarsen, Georgine, 'Automobility "South of the West": Towards a Global Conversation', in Gijs Mom, Peter Norton, Georgine Clarsen, and Gordon Pirie (eds), *Mobility in History: Themes in Transport* (Neuchatel: Editions Alphil – Presses Universitaires Suisses, 2011), pp. 25–41.

Clute, John and Peter Nicholls, *Encyclopedia of Science Fiction* (New York: St Martin's Press, 1993).

Cockfield, Arthur J., 'Designing Tax Policy for the Digital Biosphere: How the Internet is Changing Tax Laws', *Connecticut Law Review* 34:2 (2002), pp. 333–402.

Cockfield, Arthur J., 'Towards a Law and Technology Theory', *Manitoba Law Journal* 30:3 (2005), pp. 382–415.

Cohen, Daniel Mark, 'Cloning and the Constitution, Cloning and the Constitution, Cloning and the Constitution, Cloning and . . .', *Nova Law Review* 26:2 (2002), pp. 511–44.

Cohen, Richard A., 'Levinas: Thinking Least about Death – Contra Heidegger', *International Journal for Philosophy of Religion*, 60:1 (2006), pp. 21–39.

Conly, Sarah, 'Is Starbuck a Woman?', in Jason T. Eberl (ed.), *Battlestar Galactica and Philosophy: Knowledge Here Begins Out There* (Malden: Blackwell, 2008), pp. 230–41.

Corcos, Christine A., 'I Am Not a Number I am a Free Man! Physical and Psychological Imprisonment in Science Fiction', *Legal Studies Forum* 25:3–4 (2001), pp. 472–83.

Corcos, Christine A., 'Visits to a Small Planet: Rights Talk in Some Science Fiction Film and Television Series from the 1950s to the 1990s', *Stetson Law. Review* 39:1 (2009), pp. 183–246.

Corcos, Christine A., 'More Human than Human: How Some SF Presents AI's Claims to the Right to Life and Self-Determination', *Oxford Journal of Socio-Economic Studies* (2017), <https://ssrn.com/abstract=2908362> (last accessed 7 November 2017).

Corcos, Christine A., Isabel Corcos, and Brian Stockhoff, 'Double-Take: A Second Look at Cloning, Science Fiction and Law', *Louisiana Law Review* 59:4 (1999), pp. 1,041–99.

Cornell, Drucilla, 'Time, Deconstruction, and the Challenge to Legal Positivism: The Call for Judicial Responsibility', *Yale Journal of Law and Humanities* 2 (1990), pp. 267–97.

Cornell, Drucilla, 'The Relevance of Time to the Relationship between the Philosophy of the Limit and Systems Theory', *Cardozo Law Review* 13:5 (1992), pp. 1,579–604.

Cornell, Paul, Martin Day, and Keith Topping, *The Discontinuity Guide: The Definitive Guide to the Worlds and Times of Doctor Who* (Austin: MonkeyBrain Books, 1995).

Costello, Moya, 'Learning to Drive: Reading the Signs', *Meanjin* 58:3 (1999), pp. 22–32.

Cotton, Tenney, 'Mandatory Life Sentence for Murder: Is it Time for Discretion?', *Journal of Criminal Law* 72:4 (2008), pp. 288–97.

Cover, Robert M., 'Violence and the Word', *Yale Law Journal* 95:8 (1986), pp. 1,601–30.

Cranny-Francis, Anne, 'The "Science" of Science Fiction: A Sociocultural Analysis', in J. R. Martin and Robert Veel (eds), *Reading Science: Critical and Functional Perspectives on Discourses of Science* (London: Routledge, 1998), pp. 63–82.

Cranny-Francis, Anne and John Tulloch, 'Vaster than Empire(s), and More Slow: The Politics and Economics of Embodiment in *Doctor Who*', in Pat Harrigan and Noah Wardrip-Fruin (eds), *Third Person: Authoring and Exploring Vast Narratives* (Cambridge, MA: MIT Press, 2009), pp. 343–55.

Crichton, Michael, *Jurassic Park* (New York: Alfred A. Knopf, 1990).

Csicsery-Ronay, Istvan, *The Seven Beauties of Science Fiction* (Middletown: Wesleyan University Press, 2008).

Cull, Nicholas J., '"Bigger on the Inside . . .": *Doctor Who* as British Cultural History', in Graham Roberts and Philip M. Taylor (eds), *The Historian, Television and Television History* (Luton: University of Luton Press, 2001), pp. 95–111.

Curtis, Claire P., 'Theorizing Fear: Octavia Butler and the Realist Utopia', *Utopian Studies* 19:3 (2008), pp. 411–31.

Curtis, Claire P, 'Utopian Possibilities: Disability, Norms, and Eugenics in Octavia Butler's *Xenogenesis*', *Journal of Literary and Cultural Disability Studies* 9:1 (2015), pp. 19–33.

Dan, Joseph, 'Samael, Lilith, and the Concept of Evil in Early Kabbalah', *AJS Review* 5:1 (1980), pp. 17–40.

David, Matthew and Jamieson Kirkhope, 'Cloning/Stem Cells and the Meaning of Life', *Current Sociology* 53:2 (2005), pp. 367–81.

Davies, Stevan L., 'The Lion-Headed Yaldabaoth', *Journal of Religious History* 11:4 (1980), pp. 495–500.

Davis, G. Todd, 'The Eternal Vigil: Captain Jack as Byronic Hero', in Andrew Ireland (ed.), *Illuminating Torchwood: Essays on Narrative, Character and Sexuality in the BBC Series* (Jefferson: McFarland, 2010), pp. 79–89.

Davison, Graeme, *Car Wars: How the Car Won our Hearts and Conquered Our Cities* (Sydney: Allen & Unwin, 2004).

de Coning, Alexis, 'Recouping Masculinity: Men's Rights Activists' Responses to *Mad Max: Fury Road*', *Feminist Media Studies* 16:1 (2016), pp. 174–6.

Deis, Christopher, 'Erasing Difference: The Cylons as Racial Other', in Tiffany Potter and C. W. Marshall (eds), *Cylons in America: Critical Studies in* Battlestar Galactica (New York: Continuum, 2008), pp. 156–68.

Dellamonica, A. M., 'Stripping the Bones: Raising a new *Battlestar* from the Ashes of the Old', in Richard Hatch (ed.), *So Say We All: An Unauthorized Collection of Thoughts and Opinions on* Battlestar Galactica (Dallas: BenBella Books, 2006), pp. 161–70.

Dembling, Paul G., 'National Coordination for Space Exploration: The *National Aeronautics and Space Act* of 1958', *JAG Journal* (February 1959), pp. 16–19.

Dent, Chris, 'Relationships between Laws, Norms and Practices: The Case of Road Behaviour', *Griffith Law Review* 21:3 (2012), pp. 708–27.

Department of Health Chief Medical Officer's Office Expert Group Reviewing the Potential of Developments in Stem Cell Research and Cell Nuclear Replacement to Benefit Human Health, *Stem Cell Research: Medical Progress with Responsibility* (London: Department of Health, 2000).

Derrida, Jacques, *Margins of Philosophy*, trans. Alan Bass (Chicago: University of Chicago Press, 1982).

Derrida, Jacques, 'Force of Law: The "Mystical Foundations of Authority"', in Drucilla Cornell, Michel Rogerfield, and David Grey Carlson (eds), *Deconstruction and the Possibility of Justice* (New York: Routledge, 1992), pp. 3–67.

Dicey, A. V., *Introduction to the Study of the Law of the Constitution* (London: Macmillan, 1959 [1889]).

DiTommaso, Lorenzo, 'History and Historical Effect in Frank Herbert's Dune', *Science Fiction Studies* 19:3 (1992), pp. 311–25.

Dixit, Priya, 'Relating to Difference: Aliens and Alienness in *Doctor Who* and International Relations', *International Studies Perspectives* 13:3 (2012), pp. 289–306.

Dougherty, Candidus and F. Gregory Lastowka, 'Virtual Trademarks', *Santa Clara Computer and High Technology Law Journal* 24:4 (2008), pp. 749–828.

Douzinas, Costas, *The End of Human Rights* (Oxford: Hart, 2000).

Douzinas, Costas, 'Theses on Law, History and Time', *Melbourne Journal of International Law* 7:1 (2006), pp. 13–27.

Douzinas, Costas, *Human Rights and Empire: The Political Philosophy of Cosmopolitanism* (London: Routledge-Cavendish, 2007).

Douzinas, Costas and Adam Gearey, *Critical Jurisprudence: The Political Philosophy of Justice* (Oxford: Hart, 2005).

Dowling, Robyn, 'Cultures of Mothering and Car Use in Suburban Sydney: A Preliminary Investigation', *Geoforum* 31 (2000), pp. 345–53.

Dowling, Robyn, Anna Güllner and Bronwyn O'Dwyer, 'A Gender Perspective on Urban Car Use: A Qualitative Case Study', *Urban Policy Research* 17:2 (1999), pp. 101–10.

Downie, Jocelyn, Jennifer Llewellyn, and Françoise Baylis, 'A Constitutional Defence of the Federal Ban on Human Cloning for Research Purposes', *Queen's Law Journal* 31:1 (2005), pp. 353–85.

Doyle, Kylie and Kieran Tranter, 'Automobility and "My Family" Stickers', *Continuum: Journal of Media and Cultural Studies* 29:1 (2015), pp. 70–83.

Doyle, Kylie and Kieran Tranter, 'F#ck Your Family! The Visual Jurisprudence of Automobility', *International Journal for the Semiotics of Law* 30:1 (2017), pp. 1–22.

Drahos, Peter, 'Law, Science and Reproductive Technology', *Bulletin of the Australian Society of Legal Philosophy* 9 (1985), pp. 270–85.

Drexler, K. Eric and Jason Wejnert, 'Nanotechnology and Policy', *Jurimetrics* 45:1 (2004), pp. 1–22.

Duncanson, Kirsty, 'Tracing the Law through *The Matrix*', *Griffith Law Review* 10:2 (2001), pp. 160–71.

Duncanson, Kirsty, 'Bodies, Cinema, Sovereignty: Using Visual Culture Methodologies to Think about Other Ways that Law Might Work', in Cassandra Sharp and Marett Leiboff (eds), *Cultural Legal Studies: Law's Popular Cultures and the Metamorphosis of Law* (Abingdon: Routledge, 2015), pp. 207–28.

Dworkin, Ronald, *Taking Rights Seriously* (Cambridge, MA: Harvard University Press, 1977).

Dyzenhaus, David, '"Now the Machine Runs Itself": Carl Schmitt on Hobbes and Kelsen', *Cardozo Law Review* 16:1 (1994), pp. 1–19.

Eberl, Jason T. (ed.), *Battlestar Galactica and Philosophy: Knowledge Here Begins Out There* (Malden: Blackwell, 2008).

Edwards, Coral and Peter Read, *The Lost Children: Thirteen Australian Taken from Their Families Tell of the Struggle to Find Their Natural Parents* (Sydney: Doubleday, 1989).

Edwards, Gavin, 'Intergalactic Terror: *Battlestar Galactica* Tackles Terrorism like No Other Show', *Rolling Stone*, 27 January 2006, <http://web.archive.org/web/20090208135051/http://www.rollingstone.com/news/story/9183391/intergalactic_terror>, (last accessed 22 December 2017).

Effross, Walter, 'High-Tech Heroes, Virtual Villains, and Jacked-In Justice: Visions of Law and Lawyers in Cyberpunk Science Fiction', *Buffalo Law Review* 45:3 (1997), pp. 931–74.

Egenfeldt-Nielsen, Simon, Jonas Heide Smith and Susana Pajares Tosca, *Understanding Video Games: The Essential Introduction* (New York: Routledge, 2008).

Eibert, Mark D., 'Human Cloning: Myths, Medical Benefits and Constitutional Rights', *Hastings Law Journal* 53:5 (2002), pp. 1,097–116.

Elgin, Don D., *The Comedy of the Fantastic: Ecological Perspectives on the Fantasy Novel* (Westport: Greenwood Press, 1985).

Ellis, M. H., *The Long Lead: Across Australia by Motor Car* (London: T. Fisher Unwin, 1927).

Ellis, R. J., 'Frank Herbert's Dune and the Discourse of Apocalyptic Ecologism in the United States', in Rhys Garnett and R. J. Ellis (eds), *Science Fiction Roots and Branches: Contemporary Critical Approaches* (London: Macmillan, 1990), pp. 104–24.

Ellul, Jacques, *The Technological Society*, trans. John Wilkinson (New York: Knopf, 1964).

Emsley, Clive, '"Mother, What *Did* Policemen Do When There Weren't Any Motors?" The Law, the Police and the Regulation of Motor Traffic in England, 1900–1939', *Historical Journal* 36:2 (1993), pp. 357–81.

Endersby, James W. and Michael J. Towle, 'Tailgate Partisanship: Political and

Social Expression through Bumper Stickers', *Social Science Journal* 33:3 (1996), pp. 307–19.

Erman, Eva and Niklas Möller, 'What's Wrong with Politics in the Duniverse?', in Jeffery Nicholas (ed.), *Dune and Philosophy: Weirding Way of the Mentat* (Chicago: Open Court Publishing, 2011), pp. 61–74.

Esposito, Roberto, *Bios: Biopolitics and Philosophy*, trans. Timothy Campbell (Minneapolis: University of Minnesota Press, 2008).

Falconer, Delia, '"We Don't Need to Know the Way Home": Selling Australian Space in the *Mad Max* Trilogy', *Southern Review* 27 (1994), pp. 28–44.

Falconer, Delia, '"We Don't Need To Know the Way Home": The Disappearance of the Road in the *Mad Max* Trilogy', in Steven Cohan and Ina Rae Hark (eds), *The Road Movie Book* (London: Routledge, 1997), pp. 249–70.

Farneti, Roberto, 'The "Mythical Foundation" of the State: Leviathan in Emblematic Context', *Pacific Philosophical Quarterly* 82:3–4 (2001), pp. 362–82.

Feenberg, Andrew, *Questioning Technology* (London: Routledge, 1999).

Feenberg, Andrew, *Heidegger and Marcuse: The Catastrophe and Redemption of History* (New York: Routledge, 2005).

Fey, Marco, Annika E. Poppe, and Carsten Rauch, 'The Nuclear Taboo, *Battlestar Galactica*, and the Real World: Illustrations from a Science-Fiction Universe', *Security Dialogue* 47:4 (2016), pp. 348–65.

Fiedler, Frederick A. and Glenn H. Reynolds, 'Legal Problems of Nanotechnology: An Overview', *Southern California Interdisciplinary Law Journal* 3:2 (1994), pp. 593–630.

Finnis, John, *Natural Law and Natural Rights* (Oxford: Clarendon Press, 1980).

Firestone, Shulamith, *The Dialectic of Sex* (New York: William Morrow, 1970).

Fiske, John, '*Doctor Who*: Ideology and the Reading of a Popular Narrative Text', *Australian Journal of Screen Theory* 14–15 (1983), pp. 69–100.

Fitting, Pal, 'Eating Your Way to the Top: Social Darwinism in SF', in Gary Westfahl, George Slusser, and Eric S. Rabkin (eds), *Food of the Gods: Eating and the Eaten in Fantasy and Science Fiction* (Athens, GA: University of Georgia Press, 1996), pp. 172–87.

Fitzpatrick, Peter, *The Mythology of Modern Law* (London: Routledge, 1992).

Fitzpatrick, Peter, *Modernism and the Grounds of Law* (Cambridge: Cambridge University Press, 2001).

Fjellman, Stephen M., 'Prescience and Power: *God Emperor of Dune* and the Intellectuals', *Science Fiction Studies* 13:1 (1986), pp. 50–63.

Flink, James J., *The Car Culture* (Cambridge, MA: MIT Press, 1976).

Ford, James E., '*Battlestar Galactica* and Mormon Theology', *Journal of Popular Culture* 17:2 (1983), pp. 83–7.

Forry, Steven Earl, *Hideous Progenies: Dramatizations of Frankenstein from Mary Shelley to the Present* (Philadelphia: University of Pennsylvania Press, 1990).

Foucault, Michel, *The History of Sexuality Volume 1*, trans. Robert Hurley (New York: Vintage Books, 1978).

Foucault, Michel, 'Governmentality', in Paul Rabinow and Nikolas Rose (eds), *The Essential Foucault* (New York: The New Press, 2003), pp. 229–46.

Fox, Warwick, *Towards a Transpersonal Ecology: Developing New Foundations for Environmentalism* (Boston: Shambhala, 1990).

Fozdar, Farida, Brian Spittles, and Lisa K. Hartley, 'Australia Day, Flags on Cars and Australian Nationalism', *Journal of Sociology* 51:2 (2015), pp. 317–36.

Frank, David John, 'Science, Nature, and the Globalization of the Environment, 1870–1990', *Social Forces* 76:2 (1997), pp. 409–37.

French, Rebecca R., 'Time in Law', *University of Colorado Law Review* 72:3 (2001), pp. 663–748.

Fridman, G. H. L., 'The Doctrine of the "Family Car": A Study in Contrasts', *Texas Technology Law Review* 8 (1976), p. 323.

Friedman, Lawrence, 'Law, Lawyers and Popular Culture', *Yale Law Journal* 98:8 (1989), pp. 1,579–606.

Fukuyama, Francis, *Our Posthuman Future: Consequences of the Biotechnological Revolution* (New York: Farrah, Straus and Giroux, 2002).

Fuller, Glen, 'The Hoon: Controlling the Streets?', in Scott Poynting and George Morgan (eds), *Outrageous! Moral Panics in Australia* (Hobart: ACYS, 2007), pp. 125–36.

Fuller, Lon L., *The Morality of Law* (New Haven: Yale University Press, 1969).

Gaita, Raimond, *A Common Humanity: Thinking about Love and Truth and Justice* (Melbourne: Text Publishing, 1999).

Gauthier, David, *The Logic of Leviathan: The Moral and Political Theory of Thomas Hobbes* (Oxford: Clarendon Press, 1969).

Gaylin, Willard, 'The Frankenstein Factor', *New England Journal of Medicine* 297:12 (1976), pp. 665–7.

George, Susan, 'Fraking Machines: Desire, Gender and the (Post)Human Condition in *Battlestar Galactica*', in J. P. Telotte (ed.), *The Essential Science Fiction Reader* (Lexington: University Press of Kentucky, 2008), pp. 159–91.

Gibbs, Alan, '"Maybe That's What Happens if You Touch the Doctor, Even for a Second": Trauma in *Doctor Who*', *Journal of Popular Culture* 46:5 (2013), pp. 950–72.

Giblett, Rod, 'Magician's Bower: The Car as Communication Technology', *Australian Journal of Communication* 27:2 (2000), pp. 15–24.

Gibson, Ross, *South of West: Postcolonialism and the Narrative Construction of Australia* (Bloomington: Indiana University Press, 1992).

Gibson, William, *Neuromancer* (London: Gollancz, 1984).

Giddens, Thomas, 'Natural Law and Vengeance: Jurisprudence on the Streets of Gotham', *International Journal for the Semiotics of Law* 28:4 (2015), pp. 765–85.

Giddens, Thomas, '*Anderson v Dredd* [2137] Mega-City LR 1', *International Journal for the Semiotics of Law* 30:3 (2017), pp. 389–405.

Glancy, Dorothy J., 'Autonomous and Automated and Connected Cars – Oh My: First Generation Autonomous Cars in the Legal Ecosystem', *Minnesota Journal of Law, Science and Technology* 16:2 (2015), pp. 619–92.

Glut, Donald F., *The Frankenstein Archive: Essays on the Monster, the Myth, the Movies and More* (Jefferson: McFarland, 2002).

Goldsmith, M. M. 'The Hobbes Industry', *Political Studies* 39:1 (1991), pp. 135–47.

Goodrich, Peter, *Languages of Law: From Logics of Memory to Nomadic Masks* (London: Weidenfeld and Nicholson, 1990).

Goodrich, Peter, *Law in the Courts of Love: Literature and Other Minor Jurisprudences* (London: Routledge, 1996).

Goodrich, Peter, 'Duncan Kennedy as I Imagine Him: The Man, the Work, his Scholarship, and the Polity', *Cardozo Law Review* 22:3–4 (2001), pp. 971–90.

Goodrich, Peter and David Grey Carlson, *Law and the Postmodern Mind: Essays on the Physchoanalysists and Jurisprudence* (Ann Arbor: University of Michigan Press, 1998).

Gough, Noel, 'Speculative Fictions for Understanding Global Change Environments: Two Thought Experiments', *Managing Global Transitions* 1:1 (2003), pp. 5–27.

Grady, Maura and Cassie Hemstrom, 'Nostalgia for Empire, 1963–1974', in Gillian Leitch (ed.), *Doctor Who in Time and Space* (Jefferson: McFarland, 2013), pp. 125–41.

Greene, Adam, 'The Regulation of Human Cloning', *George Washington International Law Review* 33:2 (2001), pp. 341–62.

Greene, Eric, 'The Mirror Frakked', in Richard Hatch (ed.), *So Say We All: An Unauthorized Collection of Thoughts and Opinions on* Battlestar Galactica (Dallas: BenBella Books, 2006), pp. 5–22.

Gregg, Peter R., 'England Looks to the Future: The Cultural Forum Model and *Doctor Who*', *Journal of Popular Culture* 37:4 (2004), pp. 648–61.

Gumpert, Matthew, 'Hybridity's End', in Tiffany Potter and C. W. Marshall (eds), *Cylons in America: Critical Studies in* Battlestar Galactica (New York: Continuum, 2008), pp. 143–55.

Gupta, Amit, '*Doctor Who* and Race: Reflections on the Change of Britain's Status in the International System', *The Round Table* 102:1 (2013), pp. 41–50.

Guzik, Keith, 'Taking Hold of the Wheel: Automobility, Social Order, and the Law in Mexico's Public Registry of Vehicles (REPUVE)', *Law and Society Review* 47:3 (2013), pp. 523–54.

Haebich, Anna, *Broken Circles: Fragmenting Indigenous Families 1800–2000* (Fremantle: Fremantle Arts Centre Press, 2000).

Haley, Andrew G., 'Space Law and Metala: A Synoptic View', paper presented at Rendiconti del VII Congresso Internazionale Astronautico, Rome, 1956.

Hamilton, Sheryl N., 'Traces of the Future: Biotechnology, Science Fiction, and the Media', *Science Fiction Studies* 30:2 (2003), pp. 267–82.

Hampton, Jean, *Hobbes and the Social Contract Tradition* (Cambridge: Cambridge University Press, 1986).

Hand, Jack, 'The Traditionalism of Women's Roles in Frank Herbert's *Dune*', *Extrapolation* 26:1 (1985), pp. 24–8.

Haraway, Donna, 'A Manifesto for Cyborgs: Science, Technology and Socialist Feminism in the 1980s', *Socialist Review* 80 (1985), pp. 65–107.

Haraway, Donna, *Primate Visions: Gender, Race, and Nature in the World of Modern Science* (New York: Routledge, 1989).

Haraway, Donna, 'The Biopolitics of Postmodern Bodies: Consitutions of Self in Immune System Discourse', in D. Haraway, *Simians, Cyborgs, and Women: The Reinvention of Nature* (New York: Routledge, 1991), pp. 203–30.

Haraway, Donna, *Modest_Witness@Second_Millennium.FemaleMan©_Meets_OncoMouse™: Feminism and Technoscience* (New York: Routledge, 1997).

Harmes, Marcus K, Doctor Who *and the Art of Adaption: Fifty Years of Storytelling* (Lanham: Rowman and Littlefield, 2014).

Hart, H. L. A., *The Concept of Law* (Oxford: Clarendon Press, 1961).

Hartouni, Valerie, '*Brave New World*: In the Discourses of Reproductive and Genetic

Technologies', in Jane Bennett and William Chaloupka (eds), *In the Nature of Things: Language, Politics and the Environment* (Minneapolis: University of Minnesota Press, 1993), pp. 85–110.

Hatch, Richard (ed.), *So Say We All: An Unauthorized Collection of Thoughts and Opinions on* Battlestar Galactica (Dallas: BenBella Books, 2006).

Hawi, Nazir S. and Maya Samaha, 'The Relations among Social Media Addiction, Self-Esteem, and Life Satisfaction in University Students', *Social Science Computer Review* (2016), DOI 08944393166603402016.

Hayles, N. Katherine, *How We Become Posthuman: Virtual Bodies in Cybernetics, Literature and Informatics* (Chicago: University of Chicago Press, 1999).

Heidegger, Martin, 'Science and Reflection', *The Question Concerning Technology and Other Essays* (New York: Harper and Row, 1977), pp. 155–82.

Heidegger, Martin, 'The Age of World Picture', *The Question Concerning Technology and Other Essays* (New York: Harper and Row, 1977), pp. 115–54.

Heidegger, Martin, 'The Question Concerning Technology', *The Question Concerning Technology and Other Essays* (New York: Harper and Row, 1977), pp. 3–35.

Heidegger, Martin, 'The Origins of the Work of Art', in David Farrell Krell (ed.), *Martin Heidegger: Basic Writings* (London: Routledge, 1993), pp. 139–212.

Heidegger, Martin, *Being and Time*, trans. Joan Stambaugh (New York: State University of New York Press, 1996 [1927]).

Heinlein, Robert A., *Stranger in a Strange Land* (London: New English Library, 1978 [1961]).

Hellstrand, Ingvil, 'The Shape of Things to Come? Politics of Reproduction in the Contemporary Science Fiction Series "Battlestar Galactica"', *NORA—Nordic Journal of Feminist and Gender Research* 19:1 (2011), pp. 6–24.

Henriss-Anderssen, Diana, 'The "Stolen Generation" in Queensland: A Critical Perspective', *Griffith Law Review* 11:2 (2002), pp. 286–308.

Herbert, Frank, *Whipping Star* (New York: G. P. Putnam's Sons, 1970).

Herbert, Frank, *Children of Dune* (London: New English Library, 1976).

Herbert, Frank, 'The ConSentiency and How it Got That Way', *Galaxy Science Fiction*, May 1977, pp. 5–8.

Herbert, Frank, *The Dosadi Experiment* (New York: G. P. Putnam's Sons, 1977).

Herbert, Frank, *Dune* (London: New English Library, 1978 [1965]).

Herbert, Frank, 'Dune Genesis', *Omni*, 2 July 1980, pp. 72–4.

Herbert, Frank, *Dune Messiah* (London: New English Library, 1974 [1969]).

Herbert, Frank, *God Emperor of Dune* (London: New English Library, 1981).

Herbert, Frank, *Heretics of Dune* (London: New English Library, 1984).

Herbert, Frank, *Chapter House Dune* (London: New English Library, 1985).

Herbert, Frank, 'The Tactful Saboteur', in *Eye* (New York: Berkley Books, 1985), pp. 159–90.

Herbert, Frank, Brian Herbert, and Kevin J. Anderson, *The Road to Dune* (London: Hodder and Stoughton, 2005).

Herrick, Andrew, 'King Car: On the Road to Auto-Utopia', *Arena Magazine* 38 (1998), pp. 44–6.

Herz, J. C., *Joystick Nation: How Videogames Ate Our Quarters, Won Our Hearts, and Rewired Our Minds* (New York: Little, Brown and Company, 1996).

Hill, Stephen, *The Tragedy of Technology: Human Liberation Versus Domination in the Late Twentieth Century* (London: Pluto Press, 1988).

Hills, Matt, 'Televisuality without Television? The Big Finish Audios and Discourses of "Tele-centric" *Doctor Who*', in David Butler (ed.), *Time and Relative Dissertations in Space: Critical Perspectives on* Doctor Who (Manchester: Manchester University Press, 2007), pp. 280–95.

Hills, Matt, 'The Dispersible Television Text: Theorising Moments of the New *Doctor Who*', *Science Fiction Film and Television* 1:1 (2008), pp. 25–44.

Hills, Matt, *Triumph of a Time Lord: Regenerating* Doctor Who *in the Twenty-First Century* (London: I. B. Tauris, 2010).

Hills, Matt, 'Listening from behind the Sofa? The (Un)earthly Roles of Sound in BBC Wales' *Doctor Who*', *New Review of Film and Television Studies* 9:1 (2011), pp. 28–41.

Hobbes, Thomas, *De Cive* (Oxford: Oxford University Press, 1983 [1651]).

Hobbes, Thomas, *Behemoth or the Long Parliament* (Chicago: University of Chicago Press, 1990 [1681]).

Hobbes, Thomas, *A Dialogue between a Philosopher and a Student, of the Common Laws of England* (Oxford: Oxford University Press, 2005 [1861]).

Hobbes, Thomas, *Leviathan* (New York: Pearson Longman, 2008 [1651]).

Hodge, Bob, 'Aboriginal Myths and Australian Culture', *Southern Review* 19:3 (1986), pp. 277–89.

Hoeren, Thomas and Anselm Rodenhausen, 'Constitutional Rights and New Technologies in Germany', in Ronald E Leenes, Bert-Jaap Koops, and Paul De Hert (eds), *Constitutional Rights and New Technologies: A Comparative Study* (The Hague: T. M. C. Asser Press, 2008), pp. 137–58.

Hogan, Bernie, 'The Presentation of Self in the Age of Social Media: Distinguishing Performances and Exhibitions Online', *Bulletin of Science, Technology and Society* 30:6 (2010), pp. 377–86.

Holden, Rebecca J., 'The High Costs of Cyborg Survival: Octavia Butler's *Xenogenesis* Trilogy', *Foundation* 72 (1998), pp. 49–57.

Holmes, Oliver Wendell, 'The Path of Law', *Harvard Law Review* 10:8 (1897), pp. 458–78.

Holmes, Stephen, *Passions and Constraint: On the Theory of Liberal Democracy* (Chicago: University of Chicago Press, 1995).

Horning, Richard Allan, 'The Enforceability of Contracts Negotiated in Cyberspace', *International Journal of Law and Information Technology* 5:2 (1997), pp. 109–57.

House of Lords Select Committee on Stem Cell Research, *Stem Cell Research* (London: House of Lords, 2002).

House of Representatives, *Human Cloning: Scientific, Ethical and Regulatory Aspects of Human Cloning and Stem Cell Research* (Canberra: Parliament of the Commonwealth of Australia, 2001).

Howie, Luke, 'They Were Created by Man . . . and They Have a Plan: Subjective and Objective Violence in *Battlestar Galactica* and the War on Terror', *International Journal of Žižek Studies* 5:2 (2016), <http://zizekstudies.org/index.php/IJZS/article/view/265> (last accessed 7 November 2017).

Howse, Robert, 'From Legitimacy to Dictatorship – and Back Again: Leo Strauss's Critique of the Anti-Liberalism of Carl Schmitt', in David Dyzenhaus (ed.), *Law as Politics: Carl Schmitt's Critique of Liberalism* (Durham, NC: Duke University Press, 1998), pp. 56–91.

Huet, Marie-Hélène, *Monstrous Imagination* (Cambridge, MA: Harvard University Press, 1993).

Huh, Jimmy, 'Race in Progress, No Passing Zone: *Battlestar Galactica,* Colorlindness, and the Maintenance of Racial Order', in Sarah E. Turner and Sarah Nilsen (eds), *The Colorblind Screen: Television in Post-Racial America* (New York: New York University Press, 2014), pp. 320–44.

Human Fertilisation and Embryology Authority and Human Genetics Advisory Commission, *Cloning Issues in Reproduction, Sience and Medicine* (London: Human Fertilisation and Embryology Authority and Human Genetics Advisory Commission, 1998).

Human Rights and Equal Opportunity Commission, *Bringing Them Home: National Inquiry into the Separation of Aboriginal and Torres Strait Islander Children from Their Families* (Sydney: Human Rights and Equal Opportunity Commission, 1997).

Humphreys, Sarah A. L., 'Lawmaking and Science: A Practical Look at In Vitro Fertilization and Embryo Transfer', *Detroit College of Law Review* 3 (1979), pp. 429–56.

Hunter, Dan, 'Cyberspace as Place and the Tragedy of the Digital Anticommons', *California Law Review* 91:2 (2003), pp. 439–520.

Huntington, Samuel P., *The Clash of Civilizations and the Remaking of World Order* (New York: Simon and Schuster, 1996).

Hurst, Paul, 'Carl Schmitt's Decisionism', in Chantal Mouffe (ed.), *The Challenge of Carl Schmitt* (London: Verso, 1999), pp. 7–19.

Hutchings, Peter J, 'From Offworld Colonies to Migration Zones: *Blade Runner* and the Fractured Subject of Jurisprudence', *Law, Culture and the Humanities* 3:3 (2007), pp. 381–97.

Huxley, Aldous, *Brave New World* (London: Grafton Books, 1977 [1932]).

Huxley, Thomas H., *Evolution and Ethics* (Princeton, NJ: Princeton University Press, 1989 [1893]).

Ihde, Don, *Bodies in Technology* (Minneapolis: University of Minneapolis Press, 2002).

Ip, John, 'Two Narratives of Torture', *Northwestern Journal of International Human Rights* 7:1 (2009), pp. 35–77.

Isasi, Rosario M. and Bartha M. Knoppers, 'Mind the Gap: Policy Approaches to Embryonic Stem Cell and Cloning Research in 50 Countries', *European Journal of Health Law* 13:1 (2006), pp. 9–26.

Jay, Martin, 'Must Justice be Blind? The Challenge of Images to the Law', in Costas Douzinas and Lynda Nead (eds), *Law and the Image: The Authority of Art and the Aesthetics of Law* (Chicago: University of Chicago Press, 1999), pp. 19–35.

Jenks, C. Wilfred, 'International Law and Activities in Space', *International and Comparative Law Quarterly* 5:1 (1956), pp. 99–114.

Jesser, Nancy, 'Blood, Genes and Gender in Octavia Butler's *Kindred* and *Dawn*', *Extrapolation* 43:1 (2002), pp. 36–61.

Jessup, Philip C. and Howard J. Taubenfeld, *Controls for Outer Space and the Antarctic Analogy* (New York: Columbia University Press, 1959).

Johinke, Rebecca, 'Not Quite *Mad Max*: Brian Trenchard-Smith's *Dead End Drive-In*', *Studies in Australian Cinema* 3:3 (2009), pp. 309–20.

Johns, Adam, 'Octavia Butler and the Art of Pseudoscience', *English Language Notes* 47:2 (2009), pp. 95–107.

Johnston-Lewis, Erika, 'Torture, Terrorism and Other Aspects of Human Nature', in Tiffany Potter and C. W. Marshall (eds), *Cylons in America: Critical Studies in* Battlestar Galactica (New York: Continuum, 2008), pp. 27–40.

Jones, Amanda, 'The State and the Stolen Generation: Recognising a Fiduciary Duty', *Monash University Law Review* 28:1 (2002), pp. 59–84.

Jones, Glenda W., 'Rural Girls and Cars: The Phenomena of "Blockies"', *Rural Society* 2:3 (1991), pp. 1–6.

Joseph, Paul R., 'A Course Whose Time Has Come: Using Science Fiction Materials to Teach Law', *Alternative Law Journal* 22:3 (1997), pp. 111–13.

Joseph, Paul R., 'Science Fiction', in Robert M. Jarvis and Paul R. Joseph (eds), *Prime Time Law: Fictional Television as Legal Narrative* (Durham, NC: Carolina Academic Press, 1998), pp. 155–66.

Joseph, Paul R. and Sharon Carton, 'The Law of the Federation: Images of Law, Lawyers and the Legal System in "Star Trek: The Next Generation"', *University of Toledo Law Review* 24:1 (1992), pp. 43–97.

Joseph, Paul R. and Sharon Carton, 'Perry Mason in Space: A Call for More Inventive Lawyers in Television Science Fiction Series', in Milton T. Wolff and Daryl F. Mallett (eds), *Imaginative Futures: Proceedings of the 1993 Science Fiction Research Association Conference* (San Bernardino: Science Fiction Research Association Press, 1995), pp. 307–16.

Jowett, Lorna, 'The Girls Who Waited? Female Companions and Gender in *Doctor Who*', *Critical Studies in Television* 9:1 (2014), pp. 77–94.

Jung, Leo, 'Fallen Angels in Jewish, Christian and Mohammedan Literature: A Study of Comparative Folk-Lore', *The Jewish Quarterly Review* 16:1 (1925), pp. 45–88.

Kalyvas, Andreas, 'Carl Schmitt and the Three Moments of Democracy', *Cardozo Law Review* 21:5–6 (2000), pp. 1,525–65.

Kamir, Orit, *Every Breath You Take: Stalking Narratives and the Law* (Ann Arbor: University of Michigan Press, 2001).

Kapica, Steven, '"I Don't Feel Like a Copy": Posthuman Legal Personhood and *Caprica*', *Griffith Law Review* 23:4 (2014), pp. 612–33.

Kapica, Steven, '"What a Glorious Moment in Jurisprudence": Rhetoric, Law, and *Battlestar Galactica*', *Law, Culture and the Humanities* 12:3 (2016), pp. 543–65.

Kateb, George, 'Hobbes and the Irrationality of Politics', *Political Theory* 17:3 (1989), pp. 355–91.

Katsh, M. Ethan, 'Rights, Camera, Action: Cyberspatial Settings and the First Amendment', *Yale Law Journal* 104:7 (1995), pp. 1,681–718.

Kaveny, M. Cathleen, 'Cloning and Positive Liberty', *Notre Dame Journal of Law, Ethics and Public Policy* 13:1 (1999), pp. 15–36.

Keating, Kenneth B., 'Reaching for the Stars: Space Law and the New Fourth Dimension', *American Bar Association Journal* 45:1 (1959), pp. 54–92.

Kelsen, Hans, *Introduction to the Problems of Legal Theory*, trans Bonnie Litschewski Paulson and Stanley L. Paulson (Oxford: Clarendon Press, 1992).

Kennedy, Duncan, *Legal Education and the Reproduction of Hierarchy: A Polemic against the System* (Cambridge, MA: Harvard University Press, 1983).

Kennedy, Ellen, '*Hostis* Not *Inimicus: Toward a Theory of the Public in the Work of Carl Schmitt*', in David Dyzenhaus (ed.), *Law as Politics: Carl Schmitt's Critique of Liberalism* (Durham, NC: Duke University Press, 1998), pp. 92–108.

Kennedy, Ellen, *Constitutional Failure: Carl Schmitt in Weimer* (Durham, NC: Duke University Press, 2004).

Kerr, Ian and Katie Szilagyi, 'Evitable Conflicts, Inevitable Technologies? The Science and Fiction of Robotic Warfare and IHL', *Law, Culture and the Humanities* 2016, DOI 17438721135094432014.

Kiersey, Nicholas J. and Iver B. Neumann (eds), Battlestar Galactica *and International Relations* (Abingdon: Routledge, 2013).

King, Laura and John Hutnyk, 'The Eighteenth Brumaire of Gaius Baltar: Colonialism Reimagined in *Battlestar Galactica*', in Arlo Kempf (ed.), *Breaching the Colonial Contract: Anti-Colonialism in the United States and Canada* (Dordrecht: Springer, 2009), pp. 237–50.

Kirby, Michael, *The Law and Modern Technology* (Melbourne: Deakin University Press, 1982).

Kirby, Michael, 'IVF – the Scope and Limitation of the Law', paper presented at Conference on Bioethics and the Law of Human Conception by In Vitro Fertilisation, London, 1983.

Kittler, Friedrich A., *Gramophone, Film, Typewriter*, trans Geoffrey Winthrop-Young and Michael Wutz (Stanford: Stanford University Press, 1999).

Kitson, Michael, 'The Great Aussie Car Smash at the End of the World', *Australian Screen Education* 31 (2003), pp. 64–9.

Klugman, Craig M. and Thomas H. Murray, 'Cloning, Historical Ethics, and the NBAC', in James M. Humber and Robert F. Almeder (eds), *Human Cloning* (Totowa: Humana Press, 1998), pp. 1–51.

Knězková, Klára, 'Frank Herbert's Heroines: Female Characters in *Dune* and its Film Adaptations', Master of Arts thesis, Masaryk University, 2007.

Knott, John William, 'Speed, Modernity and the Motor Car: The Making of the 1909 *Motor Traffic Act* in New South Wales', *Australian Historical Studies* 26:113 (1994), pp. 221–4.

Knott, John William, 'The "Conquering Car": Technology, Symbolism and the Motorisation of Australia before World War II', *Australian Historical Studies* 31:114 (2000), pp. 1–26.

Kolata, Gina, *Clone: The Road to Dolly and the Path Ahead* (New York: William Morrow, 1998).

Konas, Gary, 'Traveling "Further" with Tom Wolfe's Heroes', *Journal of Popular Culture* 28:3 (1994), pp. 177–92.

Korobkin, Russell, 'Stem Cell Research and the Cloning Wars', *Stanford Law and Policy Review* 18:1 (2007), pp. 116–90.

Kronman, Anthony T., *The Lost Lawyer: Failing Ideals of the Legal Profession* (Cambridge, MA: Belknap Press, 1993).

Kukkonen, Taneli, 'God against the Gods: Faith and the Exodus of the Twelve Colonies', in Jason T. Eberl (ed.), *Battlestar Galactica and Philosophy: Knowledge Here Begins Out There* (Malden: Blackwell, 2008), pp. 169–81.

Kungl, Carla, 'Long Live Stardoe', in Tiffany Potter and C. W. Marshall (eds), *Cylons in America: Critical Studies in* Battlestar Galactica (New York: Continuum, 2008), pp. 198–209.

Lane, Margaret I., Susan Cross Bolton, and Rose M. Alexander, '*In Vitro* Fertilization: Hope for Childless Couples Breeds Legal Exposure for Physicians', *University of Richmond Law Review* 17:2 (1983), pp. 311–46.

Lastowka, F. Gregory and Dan Hunter, 'The Laws of the Virtual Worlds', *California Law Review* 92:1 (2004), pp. 1–73.

Latour, Bruno, *We Have Never Been Modern*, trans. Catherine Porter (Cambridge, MA: Harvard University Press, 1993).

Lavi, Shai, 'Cloning International Law: The Science and Science Fiction of Human Cloning and Stem-Cell Patenting', *Law, Culture and the Humanities* 2014, DOI 10.1177/17438721145221552014.

Lawton, Anne, 'The *Frankenstein* Controversy: The Constitutionality of a Federal Ban on Cloning', *Kentucky Law Journal* 87:2 (1999), pp. 277–356.

Layton, David, *The Humanism of Doctor Who: A Critical Study in Science Fiction and Philosophy* (Jefferson: McFarland, 2012).

Le Guin, Ursula, *The Left Hand of Darkness* (London: Granada, 1973 [1969]).

Leaver, Tama, '"Humanity's Children": Constructing and Confronting the Cylons', in Tiffany Potter and C. W. Marshall (eds), *Cylons in America: Critical Studies in* Battlestar Galactica (New York: Continuum, 2008), pp. 131–42.

Lederberg, Josha S, 'Experimental Genetics and Human Evolution', *The American Naturalist* 100:915 (1966), pp. 519–31.

Lee, Roy Skwang, 'The Legal Implications of McGill's High Altitude Research Project', *McGill Law Journal* 10:2 (1964), pp. 158–71.

Leeming, David and Jake Page, *God: Myths of the Male Divine* (New York: Oxford University Press, 1996).

Lefrancöis, Richard, 'Mobility Patterns and Attitudes toward Driving a Car among the Elderly Living in Small Towns and Rural Areas', *Rural Studies* 8:1 (1998), pp. 17–28.

Leslie-McCarthy, Sage, 'Asimov's Posthuman Pharisees: The Letter of the Law Verses the Spirit of the Law in Isaac Asimov's Robot Novels', *Law, Culture and the Humanities* 3:3 (2007), pp. 398–415.

Lessig, Lawrence, *Code and Other Laws of Cyberspace* (New York: Basic Books, 1999).

Lessig, Lawrence, *Code 2.0* (New York: Basic Books, 2006).

Levack, Daniel J. H., *Dune Master: A Frank Herbert Bibliography* (Westport: Meckler, 1988).

Levin, Ira, *The Boys from Brazil* (Melbourne: Hinkler, 1994 [1976]).

Levine, George, 'The Ambiguous Heritage of *Frankenstein*', *The Endurance of Frankenstein: Essays on Mary Shelley's Novel* (Berkeley, CA: University of California Press, 1979), pp. 3–30.

Levit, Nancy and Douglas O. Linder, *The Happy Lawyer: Making a Good Life in the Law* (New York: Oxford University Press, 2010).

Levy, Jeremy, 'No Need to Reinvent the Wheel: Why Existing Liability Law Does Not Need to be Preemptively Altered to Cope with the Debut of the Driverless Car', *Journal of Business, Entrepreneurship and the Law* 9:2 (2016), pp. 355–88.

Lin, Albert C., 'Size Matters: Regulating Nanotechnology', *Harvard Environmental Law Review* 31:2 (2007), pp. 349–408.

Lipshaw, Jeffrey M., 'The Epistemology of the Financial Crisis: Complexity, Causation, Law, and Judgment', *Southern California Interdisciplinary Law Journal* 19:2 (2010), pp. 299–352.

Lloyd, Chris, 'Judge, Jury, Executioner: Judge Dredd, Jacques Derrida, Drones', in Thomas Giddens (ed.), *Graphic Justice: Intersections of Comics and Law* (Abingdon: Routledge, 2015), pp. 201–18.

Lochlann Jain, Sarah S., *Injury: The Politics of Product Design and Safety Law in the United States* (Princeton: Princeton University Press, 2006).

Locke, John, 'The Second Treatise: An Essay Concerning the True Original, Extent, and End of Civil Government', in Ian Shapiro (ed.), *Two Treatises of Government and A Letter Concerning Toleration* (New Haven: Yale University Press, 2003 [1689]), pp. 100–209.

Lodish, Harvey, Arnold Berk, S. Lawrence Zipursky, Paul Matsudaira, David Baltimore and James E. Darnell, *Molecular Cell Biology* (New York: W. H. Freeman, 2000).

Lomas, Elaine, 'When Will They Bring My Tommy Back?', *Aboriginal and Islander Health Worker Journal* 24:4 (2000), p. 6.

Lorio, Kathryn Venturatos, '*In Vitro* Fertilization and Embryo Transfer: Fertile Areas for Litigation', *Southwestern Law Journal* 35:5 (1982), pp. 973–1,012.

Loxdale, Hugh D. and Gugs Lushai, 'Maintenance of Aphid Clonal Lineages: Images of Immortality?', *Infection, Genetics and Evolution* 3:4 (2003), pp. 259–69.

Luban, David, *Lawyers and Justice: An Ethical Case Study* (Princeton: Princeton University Press, 1988).

Luban, David, 'Tales of Terror: Lessons for Lawyers from the "War on Terror"', in Kieran Tranter, Francesca Bartlett, Lillian Corbin, Reid Mortensen, and Michael Robertson (eds), *Reaffirming Legal Ethics* (Abingdon: Routledge, 2010), pp. 56–72.

Luk, Elizabeth M., 'The United Kingdom and Germany: Differing Views on Therapeutic Cloning and How the Belgian Resolution Brings Them Together', *Michigan State University Journal of Medicine and Law* 10:2 (2006), pp. 523–56.

Lupton, Deborah, 'Monsters in Metal Cocoons: "Road Rage" and Cyborg Bodies', *Body and Society* 5:1 (1999), pp. 57–72.

Machiavelli, Niccolò, *The Prince and the Discourses*, trans Luigi Ricci and E. R. P. Vincent (New York: The Modern Library, 1950 [1532]).

MacNeil, William P., 'The Monstrous Body of the Law: *Wollstonecraft vs Shelley*', *The Australian Feminist Journal* 12 (1999), pp. 21–40.

MacNeil, William P., *Lex Populi: The Jurisprudence of Popular Culture* (Stanford: Stanford University Press, 2007).

Malinowski, Bronislaw, 'Magic, Science and Religion', *Magic, Science and Religion and Other Essays* (New York: Doubleday, 1954), pp. 17–92.

Malley, Shawn, '"Does All This Have to Happen Again?" Excavating Heritage in *Battlestar Galactica*', *Science Fiction Film and Television* 7:1 (2014), pp. 1–30.

Manderson, Desmond, *Kangaroo Courts and the Rule of Law: The Legacy of Modernism* (Abingdon: Routledge, 2012).

Manderson, Desmond and Honni van Rijswijk, 'Introduction to Littoral Readings: Representations of Land and Sea in Law, Literature, and Geography', *Law and Literature* 15:2 (2015), pp. 167–77.

Marcuse, Herbert, *One Dimensional Man: Studies in the Ideology of Advanced Industrial Society* (Boston: Beacon Press, 1964).

Marshall, C. W. and Tiffany Potter, '"I See the Patterns": *Battlestar Galactica* and the Things Yhat Matter', in Tiffany Potter and C. W. Marshall (eds), *Cylons in America: Critical Studies in* Battlestar Galactica (New York: Continuum, 2008), pp. 1–10.

Martin, Adrian, *The Mad Max Movies: Mad Max, Mad Max 2 / The Road Warrior, Mad Max beyond Thunderdome* (Sydney: Currency Press, 2003).

Martinich, Aloysius P., *The Two Gods of Leviathan: Thomas Hobbes on Religion and Politics* (Cambridge: Cambridge University Press, 1992).

Marusek, Sarah, 'Between Disability and Terror: Handicapped Parking Space and Homeland Security at Fenway Park', *International Journal for the Semiotics of Law* 20:3 (2007), pp. 251–61.

Marusek, Sarah, 'License Plates: Personalized Jurisdiction and Performativity of Rights', *Law, Culture and the Humanities* 12.3 (2016), pp. 566–81.

McCaffery, Larry, 'The Desert of the Real: The Cyberpunk Controversy', *Mississippi Review* 16:1–2 (1988), pp. 7–15.

McCormick, John P., *Carl Schmitt's Critique of Liberalism: Against Politics as Technology* (Cambridge: Cambridge University Press, 1997).

McDougal, Myers S. and Leon Lipson, 'Perspectives for a Law of Outer Space', *American Journal of International Law* 52:3 (1958), pp. 407–31.

McGrath, Anna, 'Travels to a Distant Past: The Mythology of the Outback', *Australian Cultural History* 10 (1991), pp. 113–24.

McKee, Alan, 'Is *Doctor Who* Australian?', *Media International Australia* 132:1 (2009), pp. 54–66.

McLean, Fiona, 'SUV Advertising: Constructing Identities and Practices', in Jim Conley and Arlene Tigar McLaren (eds), *Car Troubles: Critical Studies of Automobility and Auto-mobility* (Farnham: Ashgate, 2009), pp. 59–76.

McLean, Susan, 'A Question of Balance: Death and Immortality in Frank Herbert's Dune Series', in Carl B. Yoke and Donald M. Hassler (eds), *Death and the Serpent: Immortality in Science Fiction and Fantasy* (Westport: Greenwood Press, 1985), pp. 145–52.

McNamee, Eugene, 'An Egg Shaped Bowl: Law, Innovation and Technology', *Australian Feminist Law Journal* 37:1 (2012), pp. 83–98.

McTaggart, John Ellis, *The Nature of Existence* (Cambridge: Cambridge University Press, 1927).

Meeker, Joseph W., *The Comedy of Survival: Literary Ecology and a Play Ethic* (Tucson: University of Arizona Press, 1997).

Mehaffy, Marilyn and AnaLouise Keating, '"Radio Imagination": Octavia Butler on the Poetics of Narrative Embodiment', *MELUS* 26:1 (2001), pp. 45–76.

Menter, Martin, 'Formulation of Space Law', *USAF JAG Bulletin* 5:5 (1963), pp. 3–9.

Merriman, Peter, 'Automobility and the Geographies of the Car', *Geography Compass* 3:2 (2009), pp. 586–99.

Meyer, Edward, *Machiavelli and the Elizabethan Drama* (Weimar: Verlang von Emil Felber, 1897).

Mia, Tjalaminu, 'Life in Sister Kate's Home: An Oral History', *Studies in Western Australian History* 22 (2001), pp. 125–34.

Miah, Andy, 'Genetics, Cyberspace and Bioethics: Why Not a Public Engagement with Ethics?', *Public Understandings of Science* 14:4 (2005), pp. 409–21.

Miller, George, 'The Apocalypse and the Pig, Or the Hazards of Storytelling', in

Raffaele Caputo and Geoff Burton (eds), *Second Take: Australian Film-Makers Talk* (Sydney: Allen & Unwin, 1999), pp. 30–42.
Miller, Jim, 'Post-Apocalyptic Hoping: Octavia Butler's Dystopian/Utopian Vision', *Science Fiction Studies* 25:2 (1998), pp. 336–60.
Milner, Andrew, *Literature, Culture, Society* (Sydney: Allen & Unwin, 1996).
Minowitz, Peter, 'Prince Versus Prophet: Machiavellianism in Frank Herbert's Dune Epic', in Donald M. Hassler and Clyde Wilcox (eds), *Political Science Fiction* (Columbia: University of South Carolina Press, 1997), pp. 124–47.
More, Thomas, *Utopia*, trans. Paul Turner (Harmondsworth: Penguin, 1965 [1516]).
Morris, David, 'Octavia Butler's (R)evolutionary Movement for the Twenty-First Century', *Utopian Studies* 26:2 (2015), pp. 270–88.
Morris, Meaghan, 'Fate and the Family Sedan', *East–West Film Journal* 4:1 (1989), pp. 113–34.
Morris, Meaghan, 'White Panic or Mad Max and the Sublime', in K. Chen (ed.), *Trajectories: Inter-Asian Cultural Studies* (London: Routledge, 1998), pp. 239–62.
Morton, Timothy, 'Imperial Measures: *Dune*, Ecology and Romantic Consumerism', *Romanticism on the Net* 21 (2001), DOI: 10.7202/005966.
Moses, A. Dirk, 'Official Apologies, Reconciliation, and Settler Colonialism: Australian Indigenous Alterity and Political Agency', *Citizenship Studies* 15:2 (2011), pp. 145–59.
Mossop, Tracy, 'Turbo-Charging Anti-hoon Legislation', *Proctor*, March 2003, pp. 22–3.
Mouffe, Chantal, *The Return of the Political* (London: Verso, 1992).
Muir, John Kenneth, *An Analytical Guide to Television's* Battlestar Galactica (Jefferson: McFarland, 1999).
Mulcahy, Kevin, '*The Prince* on Arrakis: Frank Herbert's Dialogue with Machiavelli', *Extrapolation* 37:1 (1996), pp. 22–36.
Mulkay, Michael, *The Embryo Research Debate: Science and the Politics of Reproduction* (Cambridge: Cambridge University Press, 1997).
Müller, Jan-Werner, *A Dangerous Mind: Carl Schmitt in Post-War European Thought* (New Haven: Yale University Press, 2003).
Mulligan, Rikk, 'The Cain Mutiny: Reflection the Faces of Military Leadership in a Time of Fear', in Tiffany Potter and C. W. Marshall (eds), *Cylons in America: Critical Studies in* Battlestar Galactica (New York: Continuum, 2008), pp. 52–64.
Murphy, Thérèse 'Technology, Tools and Toxic Expectations: Post-Publication Notes on New Technologies and Human Rights', *Law, Innovation and Technology* 1:2 (2009), pp. 181–202.
Murphy, Thérèse, 'The Texture of Reproductive Choice: Law, Enthnography, and Reproductive Technologies', in Thérèse Murphy (ed.), *New Technologies and Human Rights* (Oxford: Oxford University Press, 2009), pp. 195–220.
Murphy, W. T., *The Oldest Social Science? Configurations of Law and Modernity* (Oxford: Clarendon Press, 1997).
Mussawir, Edward, *Jurisdiction in Deleuze: The Expression and Representation of Law* (Abingdon: Routledge, 2011).
National Bioethics Advisory Committee, *Cloning Human Beings: Report and*

Recommendations of the National Bioethics Advisory Committee (Rockville: National Bioethics Advisory Committee, 1997).

Nelson, Anna Lorien and John S. Nelson, 'Institutions in Feminist and Republican Science Fiction', *Legal Studies Forum* 22:4 (1999), pp. 641–53.

Nemes, Irene, 'Therapeutic Cloning in Australia: One Small Stem from Man, One Giant Leap for Mankind', *Journal of Law and Medicine* 16 (2008), pp. 139–60.

Nesteruk, Jeffery, 'A New Narrative for Corporate Law', *Legal Studies Forum* 23:3 (1999), pp. 281–92.

Nicol, Dianne, Donald Chalmers and Brendan Gogarty, 'Regulating Biomedical Advances: Embryonic Stem Cell Research', *Macquarie Law Journal* 2 (2002), pp. 31–59.

Nishime, Leilani, 'Post-9/11 Global Migration in *Battlestar Galactica*', in Shilpa Dave, LeiLani Nishime, and Tasha Oren (eds), *Global Asian American Popular Cultures* (New York: New York University Press, 2016), pp. 197–213.

Noble, Greg and Rebecca Baldwin, 'Sly Chicks and Troublemakers: Car Stickers, Nonsense and the Allure of Strangeness', *Social Semiotics* 11:1 (2001), pp. 75–89.

Nonet, Philippe, 'What is Positive Law?', *Yale Law Journal* 100:3 (1990), pp. 667–99.

Nonet, Philippe, 'Time and Law', *Theoretical Inquires in Law* 8:1 (2007), pp. 311–32.

Norris, Andrew, 'Heideggerian Law beyond Law? Technique, *Recht*, and *Phusis*', *Law, Culture and the Humanities* 2:3 (2006), pp. 341–8.

Nozick, Robert, *Anarchy, State, and Utopia* (New York: Basic Books, 1974).

Olorenshaw, Robert, 'Narrating the Monster: From Mary Shelley to Bram Stoker', in Stephen Bann (ed.), *Frankenstein, Creation and Monstrosity* (London: Reaktion Books, 1994), pp. 159–76.

Olson, Greta, 'The Turn to Passion: Has Law and Literature become Law and Affect?', *Law and Literature* 28:3 (2016), pp. 335–53.

Ong, Walter, *Orality and Literacy: The Technologizing of the Word* (London: Methuen, 1982).

Onyx, Jenny and Rosemary Leonard, 'Australian Grey Nomads and American Snowbirds: Similarities and Differences', *Journal of Tourism Studies* 16:1 (2005), pp. 61–8.

Onyx, Jenny and Rosemary Leonard, 'The Grey Nomad Phenomenon: Changing the Script of Aging', *International Journal of Aging and Human Development* 64:4 (2007), pp. 381–98.

O'Reilly, Timothy, *Frank Herbert* (New York: Frederick Ungar, 1981).

Orthia, Lindy A., '"Sociopathetic Abscess" or "Yawning Chasm"? The Absent Postcolonial Transition in *Doctor Who*', *The Journal of Commonwealth Literature* 45:2 (2010), pp. 207–25.

Orwell, George, *Nineteen Eighty-Four* (London: Penguin, 2009 [1949]).

Osherow, Michelle, 'The Dawn of a New Lilith: Revisionary Mythmaking in Women's Science Fiction', *NWSA Journal* 12:1 (2000), pp. 68–83.

Ott, Brian L., '(Re)Framing Fear: Equipment for Living in a Post-9/11 World', in Tiffany Potter and C. W. Marshall (eds), *Cylons in America: Critical Studies in* Battlestar Galactica (New York: Continuum, 2008), pp. 12–26.

Palumbo, Donald E., *Chaos Theory, Asimov's Foundations and Robots, and Herbert's Dune* (Westport: Greenwood Press, 2002).

Papanikolaou, Eftychia, 'Of Duduks and Dylan: Negotiating Music and the Aural

Space', in Tiffany Potter and C. W. Marshall (eds), *Cylons in America: Critical Studies in* Battlestar Galactica (New York: Continuum, 2008), pp. 224–37.

Parkerson, Ronny, 'Semantics, General Semantics, and Ecology in Frank Herbert's *Dune*', *ETC: A Review of General Semantics* 67:4 (2010), pp. 403–11.

Parrinder, Patrick, 'The Alien Encounter: Or, Ms Brown and Mrs Le Guin', *Science -Fiction Studies* 6:1 (1979), pp. 46–59.

Pasquino, Pasquale, 'Hobbes, Religion and Rational Choice: Hobbes's Two Leviathans and the Fool', *Pacific Philosophical Quarterly* 82:3–4 (2001), pp. 406–19.

Payne, Catherine D., 'Stem Cell Research and Cloning for Human Reproduction: An Analysis of the Laws, the Direction in Which They May be Heading in Light of Recent Developments, and Potential Constitutional Issues', *Mercer Law Review* 61:3 (2010), pp. 943–76.

Pearson, Ashely and Kieran Tranter, 'Code, Nintendo's *Super Mario* and Digital Legality', *International Journal for the Semiotics of Law* 28:4 (2015), pp. 825–42.

Pegues, Juliana Hu, 'Miss Cylon: Empire and Adoption in *Battlestar Galactica*', *MELUS* 33:4 (2008), pp. 189–209.

Peltz, Richard J., 'On a Wagon Train to Afghanistan: Limitations on *Star Trek*'s Prime Directive', *University of Arkansas at Little Rock Law Review* 25:3 (2003), pp. 635–64.

Penley, Constance and Andrew Ross, 'Cyborgs at Large: Interview with Donna Haraway', *Social Text* 25–6 (1990), pp. 8–23.

Pépin, Eugène, 'Space Penetration', *Proceedings of the American Society of International Law* 52 (1958), pp. 229–35.

Pepper, David, *The Roots of Modern Environmentalism* (London: Croom Helm, 1984).

Pepper, Stephen, 'Counselling at the Limits of the Law: An Exercise in the Jurisprudence and Ethics of Lawyering', *Yale Law Journal* 104:7 (1995), pp. 1,545–610.

Peppers, Cathy, 'Dialogic Origins and Alien Identities in Butler's *Xenogenesis*', *Science Fiction Studies* 22:1 (1995), pp. 47–62.

Perryman, Neil, '*Doctor Who* and the Convergence of Media: A Case Study in "Transmedia Storytelling"', *Convergence: The International Journal of Research into Media Technologies* 14:1 (2008), pp. 21–39.

Perryman, Neil, *Adventures with the Wife in Space: Living with Doctor Who* (London: Faber and Faber, 2013).

Peters, Timothy D, 'Allusions to Theology: *I, Robot*, Universalism and the Limits of Law', *Media and Arts Law Review* 13 (2008), pp. 77–92.

Peters, Timothy D., '"The Force" as Law: Mythology, Ideology and Order in George Lucas's *Star Wars*', *Australian Feminist Law Journal* 36:1 (2012), pp. 125–43.

Peterson, Nicolas, 'An Expanding Aboriginal Domain: Mobility and the Initiation Journey', *Oceania* 70:3 (2000), pp. 205–18.

Philippopoulos-Mihalopoulos, Andreas, *Spatial Justice: Body, Lawscape, Atmosphere* (Abingdon: Routledge, 2015).

Piccone, Paul and Garu Ulmen, 'Uses and Abuses of Carl Schmitt', *Telos* 128 (2002), pp. 3–32.

Pierce, John J., *Foundations of Science Fiction: A Study in Imagination and Evolution* (Westport: Greenwood Press, 1987).

Pizzulli, Francis C., 'Asexual Reproduction and Genetic Engineering: A Constitutional Assessment of the Technology of Cloning', *Southern California Law Review* 47:2 (1974), pp. 476–584.

Pohl, Fredrick and C. M. Kornbluth, *Gladiator-at-Law* (London: Pan, 1964 [1955]).

Poniewozik, James, 'Best of 2005: Television', *Time Magazine*, 16 December 2005, <http://www.time.com/time/arts/article/0,8599,1141640,00.html> (last accessed 8 November 2017).

Poole, Steven, *Trigger Happy: The Inner Life of Video Games* (London: Fourth Estate, 2000).

Pop, Virgiliu, 'The Men who Sold the Moon: Science Fiction or Legal Nonsense', *Space Policy* 17:3 (2001), pp. 195–203.

Porte, Antia C., 'Government Regulation of *In Vitro* Fertilization, Recombinant DNA and Cloning Biotechnologies: Where Powers End and Rights Begin', *Nova Law Journal* 3 (1979), pp. 65–104.

Porter, Lynnette, *The* Doctor Who *Franchise: American Influence, Fan Culture and the Spinoffs* (Jefferson: McFarland, 2012).

Postema, Gerald, *Bentham and the Common Law Tradition* (Oxford: Clarendon Press, 1986).

Postigo, Hector, 'From *Pong* to *Planet Quake*: Post-Industrial Transitions from Leisure to Work', *Information, Communication and Society* 6:4 (2003), pp. 593–607.

Potter, Tiffany and C. W. Marshall (eds), *Cylons in America: Critical Studies in* Battlestar Galactica (New York: Continuum, 2008).

Probyn-Rapsey, Fiona, 'Bitumen Films in Postcolonial Australia', *Journal of Australian Studies* 88 (2006), pp. 97–109.

Pryor Ackerman, Erin M., 'Becoming and Belonging: The Productivity of Pleasures and Desires in Octavia Butler's *Xenogenesis* Trilogy', *Extrapolation* 49:1 (2008), pp. 24–43.

Pugliese, Joseph, 'Preincident Indices of Criminality: Facecrime and *Project Hostile Intent*', *Griffith Law Review* 18:2 (2009), pp. 314–30.

Quintero, Maria S., 'Cloning Californians – Report of the California Advisory Committee on Human Cloning and Recent Cloning-Related Legislation', *Santa Clara Computer and High Technology Law Journal* 18:3 (2002), pp. 417–32.

Raab, Felix, *The English Face of Machiavelli* (London: Routledge and Kegan Paul, 1964).

Rafer, David, 'Mythic Identity in *Doctor Who*', in David Butler (ed.), *Time and Relative Dissertations in Space: Critical Perspectives on* Doctor Who (Manchester: Manchester University Press, 2007), pp. 123–37.

Raffel, Burton, 'Genre to the Rear, Race and Gender to the Fore: The Novels of Octavia E. Butler', *Literary Review* 38:3 (1995), pp. 454–61.

Ramsey, Paul, *Fabricated Man: The Ethics of Genetic Control* (New Haven: Yale University Press, 1970).

Raney, Tracey and Michelle Meagher, 'Gender in the Aftermath: Starbuck and the Future of Woman in *Battlestar Galactica*', in *Race, Gender, and Sexuality in Post-Apocalyptic TV and Film* (Basingstoke: Palgrave Macmillan, 2015), pp. 45–57.

Rayner, Jonathan, *Contemporary Australian Cinema: An Introduction* (Manchester: Manchester University Press, 2000).

Redshaw, Sarah, *In the Company of Cars: Driving as a Social and Cultural Practice* (Aldershot: Ashgate, 2008).

Rees, Katherine, 'Accelerate, Reverse, or Find the Off Ramp? Future Automobility in the Fragmented American Imagination', *Mobilities* 11:1 (2016), pp. 152–70.

Reichman, Amnon, 'The Production of Law (and Cinema): Preliminary Comments on an Emerging Discourse', *Southern California Interdisciplinary Law Journal* 17:3 (2008), pp. 457–506.

Reynolds, Glenn Harlan, 'Nanotechnology and Regulatory Policy: Three Futures', *Harvard Journal of Law and Technology* 17:1 (2003), pp. 179–209.

Riggs, Don, 'Future and "Progress" in *Foundation* and *Dune*', in Donald E. Palumbo (ed.), *Spectrum of the Fantastic: Selected Essays from the Sixth International Conference on the Fantastic in the Arts* (Westport: Greenwood Press, 1985), pp. 113–17.

Riley, Meghan K., '"Your Body Has Made a Different Choice": Cognition, Coercion, and the Ethics of Consent in Octavia E. Butler's *Lilith's Brood* and *Fledgling*', *Journal of Cognition and Neuroethics* 3:3 (2015), pp. 113–37.

Roberts, Adam, *Science Fiction* (London: Routledge, 2000).

Roberts, Adam, *The History of Science Fiction* (Basingstoke: Palgrave Macmillan, 2005).

Roberts, Adam, 'Adama and Fascism', in Richard Hatch (ed.), *So Say We All: An Unauthorized Collection of Thoughts and Opinions on* Battlestar Galactica (Dallas: BenBella Books, 2006), pp. 213–22.

Robertson, John A., 'Liberty, Identity, and Human Cloning', *Texas Law Review* 76:6 (1998), pp. 1,371–456.

Robertson, Michael and Kieran Tranter, 'Grounding Legal Ethics Learning in Social Scientific Studies of Lawyers at Work', *Legal Ethics* 9:2 (2007), pp. 211–28.

Robin, Corey, *Fear: The History of a Political Idea* (Oxford: Oxford University Press, 2004).

Robinson, Michael G., '"Did I Mention it also Travels in Time?"', in Sherry Ginn and Gillian Leitch (eds), *The Past from the Present, The Future from the Past: Television Explores Time Travel* (London: Rowman and Littlefield, 2015), pp. 233–43.

Rogers, Juliet, 'Free Flesh: *The Matrix*, the War on Iraq and the Torture of Democracy', *Law, Culture and the Humanities* 3:3 (2007), pp. 416–34.

Rorvik, David M., *In His Image* (Philadelphia: J. B. Lippincott, 1978).

Rose, Christopher, 'How to Teach Biology Using the Movie Science of Cloning People, Resurrecting the Dead, and Combining Flies and Humans', *Public Understandings of Science* 12:3 (2003), pp. 289–96.

Rose, Margaret, 'Cyborg Selves in *Battlestar Galactica* and *Star Trek: The Next Generation*: Genre, Hybridity, Identity', *Journal of Popular Culture* 48:6 (2015), pp. 1,193–210.

Rose, Mark, 'Filling the Void: Verne, Wells and Lem', *Science Fiction Studies* 8:2 (1981), pp. 121–42.

Rowse, Tim, *White Flour/White Power: From Rations to Citizenship in Central Australia* (Melbourne: Cambridge University Press, 1998).

Russ, Joanna, *To Write Like a Woman: Essays in Feminism and Science Fiction* (Bloomington: Indiana University Press, 1995).

Ryan, Michael and Douglas Kellner, 'Technophobia', in Annette Kuhn (ed.), *Alien Zone: Cultural Theory and Contemporary Science Fiction Cinema* (London: Verso, 1990), pp. 58–65.

Salvaggio, Ruth, 'Octavia Butler and the Black Science Fiction Heroine', *Black America Literature Forum* 18:2 (1984), pp. 78–81.

Sanderson, Jay, 'Pigoons, Rakunks and Crakers: Margaret Atwood's Oryx and Crake and Genetically Engineered Animals in a (Latourian) Hybrid World', *Law and Humanities* 7:2 (2013), pp. 218–39.

Sarat, Austin, Lawrence Douglas, and Martha Merrill Umphrey, 'On Film and Law: Broadening the Focus', in Austin Sarat, Lawrence Douglas, and Martha Merrill Umphrey (eds), *Law on the Screen* (Stanford: Stanford University Press, 2005), pp. 1–26.

Saunders, David, *Anti-Lawyers: Religion and the Critics of Law and State* (London: Routledge, 1997).

Scharf, Michael P. and Lawrence D. Roberts, 'The Interstellar Relations of the Federation: International Law and "Star Trek: The Next Generation"', *University of Toledo Law Review* 25:3 (1994), pp. 577–615.

Schauer, Fredrick, *Thinking Like a Lawyer: An Introduction to Legal Reasoning* (Cambridge, MA: Harvard University Press, 2009).

Scheckel, Peggy, 'The Prospect of Cloning Human Beings: Has Knowledge Leapt Ahead of Wisdom?', *DePaul Journal of Health Care Law* 2:3 (1999), pp. 605–38.

Schedle, Per, *Androids, Humanoids, and Other Science Fiction Monsters* (New York: New York University Press, 1993).

Schmitt, Carl, *The Crisis of Parliamentary Democracy*, trans. Ellen Kennedy (Cambridge, MA: MIT Press, 1988 [1923]).

Schmitt, Carl, *The Idea of Representation*, trans. E. M. Codd (Washington, DC: Plutarch Press, 1988 [1923]).

Schmitt, Carl, 'The Age of Neutralizations and Depoliticizations', *Telos* 96 (summer 1993), pp. 130–42.

Schmitt, Carl, *The Leviathan in State Theory of Thomas Hobbes: Meaning and Failure of a Political Symbol*, trans George Schwab and Erna Hilfstein (Westport: Greenwood Press, 1996 [1928]).

Schmitt, Carl, *The Concept of the Political*, trans. George Schwab (Chicago: University of Chicago Press, 1996 [1932]).

Schmitt-v Mühlenfels, Astrid, 'The Theme of Ecology in Frank Herbert's Dune Novels', in *The Role of Geography in a Post-Industrial Society: Proceedings of an International Conference*, 8–12 September 1986 (Vechta 1986).

Scholes, Robert and Eric S. Rabkin, *Science Fiction: History, Science, Vision* (London: Oxford University Press, 1977).

Schwab, George, *The Challenge of the Exception* (New York: Greenwood Press, 1989).

Scigaj, Leonard M., '*Prana* and the Presbyterian Fixation: Ecology and Technology in Frank Herbert's *Dune* Tetralogy', *Extrapolation* 24:4 (1983), pp. 340–55.

Scott, Jonathan, 'Octavia Butler and the Base for American Socialism', *Socialism and Democracy* 20:3 (2006), pp. 105–26.

Sevanthinathan, Pratheep, 'Heavy Regulation of Human Cloning as an Alternative to a Complete Ban', *Quinnipiac Health Law Journal* 10:2 (2007), pp. 219–50.

Shaffer, Thomas, 'Moral Theology in Legal Ethics', *Capital University Law Review* 12:2 (1982), pp. 179–95.

Sharp, Cassandra, '"Riddle Me This . . .?" Would the World Need Superheroes if the Law could Deliver "Justice"?', *Law Text Culture* 16 (2012), pp. 353–78.

Sharp, Michelle, 'The Problem of Mental Ill-Health in the Profession and a Suggested

Solution', in Reid Mortensen, Francesca Bartlett, and Kieran Tranter (eds), *Alternative Perspectives on Lawyers and Legal Ethics: Reimagining the Profession* (Abingdon: Routledge, 2011), pp. 269–88.

Sharp, Patrick B, 'Darwin's Soldiers: Gender, Evolution and Warfare in *Them!* and *Forbidden Planet*', *Science Fiction Film and Television* 1:2 (2008), pp. 215–30.

Sharp, Patrick B., 'Starbuck as "American Amazon": Captivity Narrative and the Colonial Imagination in *Battlestar Galactica*', *Science Fiction Film and Television* 3:1 (2010), pp. 57–78.

Sharrett, Christopher, 'Myth, Male Fantasy and Simulacra in *Mad Max and The Road Warrior*: The Hero as Pastiche', *Journal of Popular Film and Television* 13:2 (1985), pp. 80–91.

Sheldon, David P., 'Claiming Ownership, but Getting Owned: Contractual Limitations on Asserting Property Interests in Virtual Goods', *UCLA Law Review* 54:3 (2007), pp. 751–88.

Shelley, Mary, *Frankenstein: Or, the Modern Prometheus* (New York: Signet, 1965 [1818]).

Short, Sue, '"The Measure of a Man": Asimov's Bicentennial Man, *Star Trek*'s Data and Being Human', *Extrapolation* 44:2 (2003), pp. 209–23.

Siegel, Mark, *Hugo Gernsback, Father of Modern Science Fiction with Essays on Frank Herbert and Bram Stoker* (San Bernardino: Borgo Press, 1988).

Silliman, Barbra Ann, 'Conserving the Balance: Frank Herbert's Dune as Propaganda', PhD thesis, University of Rhode Island, 1996.

Silverman, Eric J., 'Adama's True Lie: Earth and the Problem of Knowledge', in Jason T. Eberl (ed.), Battlestar Galactica *and Philosophy: Knowledge Here Begins Out There* (Malden: Blackwell, 2008), pp. 192–202.

Simeone Jr, Joseph J., 'Space – a Legal Vacuum', *Military Law Review* (April 1962), pp. 43–58.

Simpson, Catherine, 'Antipodean Automobility and Crash: Treachery, Trespass and Transformation of the Open Road', *Australian Humanities Review* 39–49 (2006), <http://australianhumanitiesreview.org/2006/09/01/antipodean-automobility-and-crash-treachery-trespass-and-transformation-of-the-open-road> (last accessed 7 November 2017).

Sisk, David W., *Transformations of Language in Modern Dystopias* (Westport: Greenwood Press, 1997).

Skene, Loane, Ian Kerridge, Barry Marshall, Pamela McCombe, and Peter Schofield, 'The Lockhart Committee: Developing Policy through Commitment to Moral Values, Community and Democratic Processes', *Journal of Law and Medicine* 16 (2008), pp. 132–8.

Skyes, Robbie and Kieran Tranter, '"You Gotta Roll/Rule with It": Oasis and the Concept of Law', *Griffith Law Review* 26:4 (2016), pp. 571–91.

Sleep, Lyndal and Kieran Tranter, 'The Visiocracy of the Social Security Mobile App in Australia', *International Journal for the Semiotics of Law* 30:3 (2017), pp. 494–514.

Smirnoff, Michael, 'The Legal Status of Celestial Bodies', *Journal Air Law and Commerce* 28:4 (1962), pp. 385–404.

Smith, George P. II, 'Intimations of Immortality: Clones, Cyrons and the Law', *University of New South Wales Law Journal* 6:1 (1983), pp. 119–32.

Sobchack, Vivian, 'Science Fiction Film and the Technological Imagination', in

Marita Sturken, Douglas Thomas, and Sandra J. Ball-Rokeach (eds), *Technological Visions: The Hopes and Fears that Shape New Technologies* (Philadelphia: Temple University Press, 2004), pp. 145–58.

Sontag, Susan, 'The Imagination of Disaster', in Sean Redmond (ed.), *Liquid Metal: The Science Fiction Film Reader* (London: Wallflower Press, 2004), pp. 40–7.

Sorell, Tom, 'The Burdensome Freedom of Sovereigns', in Tom Sorell and Luc Foisneau (eds), *Leviathan After 350 Years* (Oxford: Clarendon Press, 2004), pp. 183–96.

Spencer, J. R., 'Motor-Cars and the Rule in *Rylands v Fletcher*: A Chapter of Accidents in the History of Law and Motoring', *Cambridge Law Journal* 42:1 (1983), pp. 65–84.

Spinrad, Norman, *Science Fiction in the Real World* (Carbondale: Southern Illinois University Press, 1990).

Steeves, Sharon M., 'Artificial Human Reproduction: Legal Problems Presented by the Test Tube Baby', *Emory Law Journal* 28:4 (1979), pp. 1,045–79.

Stephenson, Neal, *Snow Crash* (New York: Bantam, 1992).

Stewart, Chip, 'Do Androids Dream of Electric Free Speech? Visions of the Future of Copyright, Privacy and the First Amendment in Science Fiction', *Communication Law and Policy* 19:4 (2014), pp. 433–63.

Stiegler, Bernard, *Technics and Time, 1: The Fault of Epimetheus*, trans. Richard Beardsworth (Stanford: Stanford University Press, 1998).

Stillman, Peter G., 'Dystopian Critiques, Utopian Possibilities, and Human Purposes in Octavia Butler's *Parables*', *Utopian Studies* 14:1 (2003), pp. 15–35.

Stone, Dan, 'Biopower and Modern Genocide', in A. Dirk Moses (ed.), *Empire, Colony, Genocide: Conquest, Occupation, and the Subaltern Resistance in World History* (New York: Berghahn Books, 2008), pp. 162–79.

Stotz, Gertrude, 'The Colonizing Vehicle', in Daniel Miller (ed.), *Car Cultures* (Oxford: Berg, 2001), pp. 223–44.

Stratton, Jon, 'What Made *Mad Max* Popular: The Mythology of a Conservative Fantasy', *Art and Text* 9 (1983), pp. 37–56.

Stratton, Susan, 'The Messiah and the Greens: The Shape of Environmental Action in *Dune* and *Pacific Edge*', *Extrapolation* 42:4 (2001), pp. 303–16.

Strauss, Leo, *The Political Philosophy of Hobbes: Its Basis and Its Genesis* (Chicago: University of Chicago Press, 1952).

Sullivan, John L., 'Transporting Television in Space and Time: The Export of *Doctor Who* to the United States in the 1970s and 1980s', *Journal of British Cinema and Television* 12:3 (2015), pp. 342–63.

Sunstein, Cass R., *The World According to Star Wars* (New York: Dey Street Books, 2016).

Surden, Harry and Mary-Anne Williams, 'Technological Opacity, Predictability, and Self-Driving Cars', *Cardozo Law Review* 38:1 (2016), pp. 121–82.

Susskind, Richard, *Tomorrow's Lawyers: An Introduction to Your Future* (Oxford: Oxford University Press, 2013).

Susskind, Richard and Daniel Susskind, *The Future of the Professions: How Technology will Transform the Work of Human Experts* (Oxford: Oxford University Press, 2015).

Suvin, Darko, *Metamorphoses of Science Fiction; On the Poetics and History of a Literary Genre* (New Haven: Yale University Press, 1979).

Tabachnick, David E., 'Techne, Technology and Tragedy', *Techné* 7:3 (2004), pp. 91–112.

Tabachnick, David E., 'The Politics and Philosophy of Anti-Science', *Techné* 9:1 (2005), pp. 27–43.

Taylor, Paul, 'A Culture of Temporary Culture', *Art and Text* 16 (1984), pp. 94–107.

Teller, Ludwig, 'Peace and National Security in the New Space Age: *The National Aeronautics and Space Act* of 1958', *New York Law Forum* 4 (1958), pp. 276–304.

Tennyson, Alfred, *Tennyson: Poems and Plays* (London: Oxford University Press, 1965).

Thomas, Mark, 'The Rules of Autogeddon: Sex, Death and Law in JG Ballard's *Crash*', *Griffith Law Review* 20:2 (2011), pp. 333–61.

Thornton, Margaret, 'Squeezing the Life Out of Lawyers: Legal Practice in the Market Embrace', *Griffith Law Review* 25:4 (2016), pp. 471–91.

Thornton, Margaret, 'The Flexible Cyborg: Work–Life Balance in Legal Practice', *Sydney Law Review* 28:1 (2016), pp. 1–22.

Tiptree, James Jr, 'Houston, Houston, Do You Read?', in Vonda N. McIntyre and Susan J. Anderson (eds), *Aurora: Beyond Equality* (Robbinsdale: Fawcett, 1976), pp. 36–99.

Tontii, Jarkko, *Right and Prejudice: Prolegomena to a Hermeneutical Philosophy of Law* (Aldershot: Ashgate, 2004).

Touponce, William, *Frank Herbert* (Boston: Twayne, 1988).

Tranter, Kieran, 'Terror in the Texts: Technology – Law – Future', *Law and Critique* 13:1 (2002), pp. 75–99.

Tranter, Kieran, '*Mad Max*: The Car and Australian Governance', *National Identities* 5:1 (2003), pp. 67–81.

Tranter, Kieran, '"The History of the Haste-Wagons": The *Motor Car Act 1909* (Vic), Emergent Technology and the Call for Law', *Melbourne University Law Review* 29:3 (2005), pp. 843–79.

Tranter, Kieran, 'Nomology, Ontology and Phenomenology of Law and Technology', *Minnesota Journal of Law, Science and Technology* 8:2 (2007), pp. 449–74.

Tranter, Kieran, 'Biotechnology, Media and Law-making: Lessons from the Cloning and Stem Cell Controversy in Australia 1997–2002', *Law, Innovation and Technology* 2:1 (2010), pp. 51–93.

Tranter, Kieran, 'The Law and Technology Enterprise: Uncovering the Template to Legal Scholarship on Technology', *Law, Innovation and Technology* 3:1 (2011), pp. 31–83.

Tranter, Kieran, 'The Speculative Jurisdiction: The Science Fictionality of Law and Technology', *Griffith Law Review* 20:4 (2011), pp. 817–50.

Tranter, Kieran, '"Come a Day There Won't be Room for Naughty Men Like Us to Slip about at All": the Multi-Medium Outlaws of *Serenity* and the Possibilities of Post-Literate Justice', *Law Text Culture* 16 (2012), pp. 277–304.

Tranter, Kieran, '"Her Brain was Full of Superstitious Nonsense": Modernism and the Failure of the Divine in *Doctor Who*', in Andrew Crome and James McGrath (eds), *Time and Relative Dimensions in Faith:* Doctor Who *and Religion* (London: Darton, Longman and Todd, 2013), pp. 131–44.

Tranter, Kieran, 'In and Out of Time: Memory and Chronology of *Doctor Who*', in Gillian Leitch (ed.), Doctor Who *In Time and Space* (Jefferson: McFarland, 2013), pp. 82–96.

Tranter, Kieran, 'The Car as Avatar in Social Security Decisions', *International Journal for the Semiotics of Law* 27:4 (2014), pp. 713–34.

Tranter, Kieran, 'Narrative and Paradoxes in *Doctor Who* "Time Loop" Stories', in Sherry Ginn and Gillian Leitch (eds), *The Past from the Present, The Future from the Past: Television Explores Time Travel* (London: Rowman and Littlefield, 2015), pp. 223–32.

Tranter, Kieran, 'Disrupting Technology Disrupting Law', *Law, Culture and the Humanities* 2017, DOI: 10.1177/1743872117704925.

Tranter, Kieran, 'I, Archive: Envisioning and Programing Digital Legality from SyFy's *Caprica*', in Tim Peters and Karen Crawley (eds), *Envisioning Legality: Law, Culture and Representation* (Abingdon: Routledge, 2018), pp. 21–45.

Tranter, Kieran, 'Law, the Digital and Time: The Legal Emblems of *Doctor Who*', *International Journal for the Semiotics of Law* 30:3 (2017), pp. 515–32.

Tranter, Kieran and Judith Kelly, 'Private Motor Vehicle Ownership in Australian Social Security Law', *Journal of Social Security Law* 22:1 (2014), pp. 32–49.

Tranter, Kieran and Bronwyn Statham, 'Echo and Mirror: Clone Hysteria, Genetic Determinism and *Star Trek Nemesis*', *Law, Culture and the Humanities* 3:3 (2007), pp. 361–80.

Tranter, Kieran, Francesca Bartlett, Lillian Corbin, Reid Mortensen, and Michael Robertson, 'Introduction', in Kieran Tranter, Francesca Bartlett, Lillian Corbin, Reid Mortensen, and Michael Robertson (eds), *Reaffirming Legal Ethics* (Abingdon: Routledge, 2010), pp. 1–11.

Travis, Mitchell, 'Making Space: Law and Science Fiction', *Law and Literature* 23:2 (2011), pp. 241–61.

Travis, Mitchell and Kieran Tranter, 'Interrogating Absence: The Lawyer in Science Fiction', *International Journal of the Legal Profession* 21:1 (2014), pp. 23–37.

Tribe, Laurence H., *Channeling Technology through Law* (Chicago: Bracton Press, 1973).

Tribe, Laurence H., 'Technology Assessment and the Fourth Discontinuity: The Limits of Instrumental Rationality', *Southern California Law Review* 46:3 (1973), pp. 616–60.

Tribe, Laurence H., 'Ways Not to Think about Plastic Trees: New Foundations for Environmental Law', *Yale Law Journal* 83:7 (1974), pp. 1,315–48.

Tucker, Jeffrey A, '"The Human Contradiction": Identity and/as Essence in Octavia E. Butler's *Xenogenesis* Trilogy', *Yearbook of English Studies* 37:2 (2007), pp. 164–81.

Tulloch, John and Manuel Alvardo, Doctor Who: *The Unfolding Text* (London: Macmillan, 1983).

Tulloch, John and Henry Jenkins, *Science Fiction Audiences: Watching* Doctor Who *and* Star Trek (London: Routledge, 1995).

Turney, Jon, *Frankenstein's Footsteps: Science, Genetics and Popular Culture* (New Haven: Yale University Press, 1998).

Tyree, J. M., 'Warm-Blooded: True Blood and Let the Right One In', *Film Quarterly* 63:2 (2009), pp. 31–7.

Urry, John, 'The "System" of Automobility', *Theory, Culture and Society* 21:4–5 (2004), pp. 25–39.

Verbeek, Peter-Paul, 'Devices of Engagement: On Borgmann's Philosophy of Information and Technology', *Techné* 6:1 (2002), pp. 69–92.

Verne, Jules, *From Earth to the Moon* (New York: Barnes and Noble, 2005 [1865]).
Vint, Sherryl, *Bodies of Tomorrow: Technology. Subjectivity, Science Fiction* (Toronto: University of Toronto Press, 2007).
Wadington, Walter, 'Artificial Conception: The Challenge for Family Law', *Virginia Journal of International Law* 69:3 (1983), pp. 465–513.
Wagner, Anne, 'The Rules of the Road, A Universal Visual Semiotics', *International Journal for the Semiotics of Law* 19:3 (2006), pp. 311–24.
Wajcman, Judy, *TechnoFeminism* (Cambridge: Polity Press, 2004).
Walker, Alison Tara, 'Destabilizing Order, Challenging History: Octavia Butler, Deleuze and Guattari, and Affective Beginnings', *Extrapolation* 46:1 (2005), pp. 103–19.
Walker, Linley, 'Under the Bonnet: Car Culture, Technological Dominance and Young Men of the Working Class', *Journal of Interdisciplinary Gender Studies* 3:2 (1998), pp. 23–43.
Walker, Linley, 'Hydraulic Sexuality and Hegemonic Masculinity: Young Working-Class Men and Car Culture', in Rob White (ed.), *Australian Youth Subcultures: On the Margins and in the Mainstream* (Hobart: Australian Youth Clearing House, 1999), pp. 178–87.
Walker, Linley, 'Car Culture, Technological Dominance and Young Men of the Working Class', in Stephen Tomsen and Mike Donaldson (eds), *Male Trouble: Looking at Australian Masculinities* (Melbourne: Pluto Press, 2003), pp. 40–68.
Walker, Linley, Dianne Butland, and Robert W. Connell, 'Boys on the Road: Masculinities, Car Culture, and Road Safety Education', *Journal of Men's Studies* 8:2 (2000), pp. 153–69.
Warfield, Angela, 'Reassessing the Utopia Novel: Octavia Butler, Jacques Derrida, and the Impossible Future of Utopia', *Obsidian III* 6:2/1 (2006), pp. 62–70.
Wasserstrom, Richard, 'Lawyers as Professionals: Some Moral Issues', *Human Rights* 5 (1975), pp. 1–24.
Wasson, Sara, 'Love in the Time of Cloning: Science Fictions of Transgressive Kinship', *Extrapolation* 45:2 (2004), pp. 130–44.
Webb, Julian, 'Being a Lawyer/Being a Human Being', *Legal Ethics* 5:1–2 (2005), pp. 130–51.
Weber, Max, *The Protestant Ethic and the Spirit of Capitalism*, trans. Talcott Parsons (London: Routledge, 1992 [1905]).
Weber, Max, *Economy and Society: An Outline of Interpretive Sociology* (Berkeley: University of California Press, 1968 [1925]).
Weber, Samuel, 'Taking Exception to Decision: Walter Benjamin and Carl Schmitt', *Diacritcs* 22:3–4 (1992), pp. 5–18.
Weisberg, Robert, 'The Law–Literature Enterprise', *Yale Journal of Law and Humanities* 1:1 (1988), pp. 1–67.
Weldon, Fay, *The Cloning of Joanna May* (London: Collins, 1989).
Wells, H. G., *The War of the Worlds* (London: Pan, 1975 [1897]).
Wells, H. G., *The Time Machine* (London: J. M. Dent, 1995 [1895]).
West, Robin, 'Jurisprudence and Gender', *University of Chicago Law Review* 55:1 (1988), pp. 1–72.
Westfahl, Gary, 'Space Opera', in Edward James and Farah Mendlesohn (eds), *The Cambridge Companion to Science Fiction* (Cambridge: Cambridge University Press, 2003), pp. 197–209.

White, Eric, 'The Erotics of Becoming: *Xenogenesis* and *The Thing*', *Science Fiction Studies* 20:3 (1993), pp. 394–408.

Williams, Paul, 'Beyond *Mad Max III*: Race, Empire, and Heroism on Post-Apocalyptic Terrain', *Science Fiction Studies* 32:2 (2005), pp. 301–15.

Williamson, David, *Travelling North* (Sydney: Currency Press, 1980).

Wimmler, Jutta, *Religious Science Fiction in* Battlestar Galactica *and* Caprica*: Women as Mediators of the Sacred and Profane* (Jefferson: McFarland, 2015).

Wingfield, Thomas C., 'Lillich on Intersteller Law: U. S. Naval Regulations, *Star Trek*, and the Use of Force in Space', *South Dakota Law Review* 46 (2001), pp. 72–101.

Winner, Langdon, *Autonomous Technology: Technics-out-of-Control as a Theme in Political Thought* (Cambridge, MA: MIT Press, 1977).

Wolcher, Louis E., *Law's Task: The Tragic Circle of Law, Justice and Human Suffering* (Aldershot: Ashgate, 2008).

Wolfe, Patrick, 'Nation and MiscegeNation: Discursive Continuity in the Post-Mabo Era', *Social Analysis* 34:1 (1994), pp. 93–152.

Wolfe, Tom, *The Right Stuff* (New York: Bantam, 1980).

Wood, Robin, *Hollywood from Vietnam to Reagan* (New York: Columbia University Press, 1986).

Wu, Mao-Ying and Philip L. Pearce, 'The Rally Experience: Exploring Motivation Patterns of Australian Grey Nomads', *Journal of Destination Marketing and Management* (2016), DOI: 10.1016/j.jdmm.2016.06.008i2016.

Wurfel, Seymour W., 'Space Law – Is There Any?', *North Carolina Law Review* 37:4 (1959), pp. 269–89.

Young, Alison, *The Scene of Violence: Cinema, Crime, Affect* (Abingdon: Routledge, 2009).

Young, Diana, 'The Life and Death of Cars: Private Vehicles on the Pitjanjatjara Lands, South Australia', in Daniel Miller (ed.), *Car Cultures* (Oxford: Berg, 2001), pp. 35–58.

Young, Diana, 'Coloring Cars: Customizing Motor Vehicles in the East of the Australian Western Desert', in Alison J. Clarke (ed.), *Design Anthropology: Object Culture in the 21st Century* (Vienna: Springer, 2011), pp. 117–27.

Youngerman Miller, Miriam, 'Women of *Dune*: Frank Herbert as a Social Reactionary?', in Jane B. Weedman (ed.), *Women Worldwalkers: New Directions of Science Fiction and Fantasy* (Lubbock: Texas Tech Press, 1985), pp. 181–92.

Zaki, Hoda M., 'Utopia, Dystopia and Ideology in the Science Fiction of Octavia Butler', *Science Fiction Studies* 17:2 (1990), pp. 239–51.

Zaner, Richard M., 'Surprise! You're Just Like Me!: Reflections on Cloning, Eugenics and Other Utopias', in James M. Humber and Robert F. Almeder (eds), *Human Cloning* (Totowa: Humana Press, 1998), pp. 103–52.

Zeender, Marie-Noelle, 'The "Moi-peau" of Leto II in Herbert's Atreides Saga', *Science Fiction Studies* 22:2 (1995), pp. 226–33.

Žižek, Slavoj, *On Belief* (London: Routledge, 2001).

Zohn, Jeffrey R., 'When Robots Attack: How Should the Law Handle Self-Driving Cars That Cause Damage', *University of Illinois Journal of Law, Technology and Policy* 2 (2015), pp. 461–86.

Media

Television

Doctor Who

Ahearne, Joe, 'Bad Wolf', *Doctor Who*, BBC (first screened United Kingdom, 11 June 2005), Television.

Ahearne, Joe, 'The Parting of the Ways', *Doctor Who*, BBC (first screened United Kingdom, 18 June 2005), Television.

Barry, Christopher, 'Robot', *Doctor Who*, BBC (first screened United Kingdom, 28 December 1974–18 January 1975), Television.

Barry, Christopher, 'The Creature from the Pit', *Doctor Who*, BBC (first screened United Kingdom, 27 October–17 November 1979), Television.

Barry, Morris, 'The Tomb of the Cybermen', *Doctor Who*, BBC (first screened United Kingdom, 2–23 September 1967), Television.

Bazalgette, Ed, 'The Girl Who Died', *Doctor Who*, BBC (first screened United Kingdom, 17 October 2015), Television.

Bernard, Paul, 'Frontier in Space', *Doctor Who*, BBC (first screened United Kingdom, 24 Feburary–31 March 1973), Television.

Black, John, 'Four to Doomsday', *Doctor Who*, BBC (first screened United Kingdom, 18–26 January 1982), Television.

Boak, Keith, 'Aliens of London', *Doctor Who*, BBC (first screened United Kingdom, 16 April 2005), Television.

Boak, Keith, 'Rose', *Doctor Who*, BBC (first screened United Kingdom, 26 March 2005), Television.

Briant, Michael E., 'Death to the Daleks', *Doctor Who*, BBC (first screened United Kingdom, 23 Feburary–16 March 1974), Television.

Briant, Michael E., 'The Robots of Death', *Doctor Who*, BBC (first screened United Kingdom, 29 January–19 Feburary 1977), Television.

Bromly, Alan, 'The Time Warrior', *Doctor Who*, BBC (first screened United Kingdom, 15 December 1973–5 January 1974), Television.

Camfield, Douglas, 'The Daleks' Master Plan', *Doctor Who*, BBC (first screened United Kingdom, 13 November 1965–29 January 1966), Television.

Camfield, Douglas, 'Inferno', *Doctor Who*, BBC (first screened United Kingdom, 9 May–6 June 1970), Television.

Campbell, Jonny, 'Vicent and the Doctor', *Doctor Who*, BBC (first screened United Kingdom, 5 June 2010), Television.

Clark, Richard, 'The Doctor's Wife', *Doctor Who*, BBC (first screened United Kingdom, 14 May 2011), Television.

Clough, Chris, 'Delta and the Bannermen', *Doctor Who*, BBC (first screened United Kingdom, 2–16 November 1987), Television.

Clough, Chris, 'Silver Nemesis' *Doctor Who*, BBC (first screened United Kingdom, 23 November–7 December 1988), Television.

Clough, Chris, Ron Jones, and Nicholas Mallett, 'The Trial of a Time Lord', *Doctor Who*, BBC (first screened United Kingdom, 6 September–6 December 1986), Television.

Combe, Timothy, 'Doctor Who and the Silurian', *Doctor Who*, BBC (first screened United Kingdom, 31 January–14 March 1970), Television.

Euros, Lyn, 'The End of the World', *Doctor Who*, BBC (first screened United Kingdom, 2 April 2005), Television.
Euros, Lyn, 'The Girl in the Fireplace', *Doctor Who*, BBC (first screened United Kingdom, 6 May 2006), Television.
Euros, Lyn, 'The Runaway Bride', *Doctor Who*, BBC (first screened United Kingdom, 25 December 2006), Television.
Euros, Lyn, 'The Unquiet Dead', *Doctor Who*, BBC (first screened United Kingdom, 9 April 2006), Television.
Euros, Lyn, 'Tooth and Claw', *Doctor Who*, BBC (first screened United Kingdom, 22 April 2006), Television.
Euros, Lyn, 'Forest of the Dead', *Doctor Who*, BBC (first screened United Kingdom, 7 June 2008), Television.
Euros, Lyn, 'Midnight', *Doctor Who*, BBC (first screened United Kingdom, 14 June 2008), Television.
Euros, Lyn, 'The End of Time', *Doctor Who*, BBC (first screened United Kingdom, 25 December 2009–1 January 2010), Television.
Euros, Lyn, 'Silence in the Library', *Doctor Who*, BBC (first screened United Kingdom, 31 May 2008), Television.
Ferguson, Michael, 'The War Machines', *Doctor Who*, BBC (first screened United Kingdom, 25 June–16 July 1966), Television.
Goddard, Andy, 'The Next Doctor', *Doctor Who*, BBC (first screened United Kingdom, 25 December 2008), Television.
Grieve, Ken, 'Destiny of the Daleks', *Doctor Who*, BBC (first screened United Kingdom, 1–22 September 1979), Television.
Grimwade, Peter, 'The Keeper of Traken', *Doctor Who*, BBC (first screened United Kingdom, 31 January–31 Feburary 1981), Television.
Grimwade, Peter, 'Earthshock', *Doctor Who*, BBC (first screened United Kingdom, 8–16 March 1982), Television.
Gunn, Andrew, 'Victory of the Daleks', *Doctor Who*, BBC (first screened United Kingdom, 7 April 2010), Television.
Harper, Graeme, 'The Caves of Androzani', *Doctor Who*, BBC (first screened United Kingdom, 8–16 March 1984), Television.
Harper, Graeme, 'Utopia', *Doctor Who*, BBC (first screened United Kingdom, 16 June 2007), Television.
Harper, Graeme, 'Journey's End', *Doctor Who*, BBC (first screened United Kingdom, 5 July 2008), Television.
Harper, Graeme, 'The Stolen Earth', *Doctor Who*, BBC (first screened United Kingdom, 28 June 2008), Television.
Harper, Graeme, 'Waters of Mars', *Doctor Who*, BBC (first screened United Kingdom, 15 November 2009), Television.
Hawes, James, 'The Doctor Dances', *Doctor Who*, BBC (first screened United Kingdom, 28 May 2005), Television.
Hawes, James, 'New Earth', *Doctor Who*, BBC (first screened United Kingdom, 15 April 2006), Television.
Hawes, James, 'School Reunion', *Doctor Who*, BBC (first screened United Kingdom, 29 April 2006), Television.
Hayes, Michael, 'City of Death', *Doctor Who*, BBC (first screened United Kingdom, 29 September–20 October 1979), Television.

Haynes, Toby, 'The Big Bang', *Doctor Who*, BBC (first screened United Kingdom, 26 June 2010), Television.
Haynes, Toby, 'The Pandorica Opens', *Doctor Who*, BBC (first screened United Kingdom, 19 June 2010), Television.
Haynes, Toby, 'Day of the Moon', *Doctor Who*, BBC (first screened United Kingdom, 30 April 2011), Television.
Haynes, Toby, 'The Impossible Astronaut', *Doctor Who*, BBC (first screened United Kingdom, 23 April 2011), Television.
Hirsch, Henric, 'The Reign of Terror', *Doctor Who*, BBC (first screened United Kingdom, 8 August–12 September 1964), Television.
Hoar, Peter, 'A Good Man Goes to War', *Doctor Who*, BBC (first screened United Kingdom, 4 June 2011), Television.
Hughes, Steve, 'Closing Time', *Doctor Who*, BBC (first screened United Kingdom, 24 September 2011), Television.
Hurran, Nick, 'The God Complex', *Doctor Who*, BBC (first screened United Kingdom, 17 September 2011), Television.
Hurran, Nick, 'The Angels Take Manhattan', *Doctor Who*, BBC (first screened United Kingdom, 29 September 2012), Television.
Hurran, Nick, 'The Day of the Doctor', *Doctor Who*, BBC (first screened United Kingdom, 23 November 2013), Television.
Hussein, Waris, 'The Unearthly Child', *Doctor Who*, BBC (first screened United Kingdom, 23 November–14 December 1963), Television.
King, Mat, 'Journey to the Centre of the TARDIS', *Doctor Who*, BBC (first screened United Kingdom, 27 April 2013), Television.
Leeston-Smith, Michael, 'The Myth Makers', *Doctor Who*, BBC (first screened United Kingdom, 16 October–6 November 1965), Television.
Letts, Barry, 'Terror of the Autons', *Doctor Who*, BBC (first screened United Kingdom, 2–23 January 1971), Television.
MacDonald, Hettie, 'The Magician's Apprentice', *Doctor Who*, BBC (first screened United Kingdom, 19 September 2015), Television.
MacDonald, Hettie, 'The Witch's Familiar', *Doctor Who*, BBC (first screened United Kingdom, 26 September 2015), Television.
Mackinnon, Douglas, 'The Poison Sky', *Doctor Who*, BBC (first screened United Kingdom, 3 May 2008), Television.
Mackinnon, Douglas, 'The Husbands of River Song', *Doctor Who*, BBC (first screened United Kingdom, 25 December 2015), Television.
MacRae, Tom, 'The Age of Steel', *Doctor Who*, BBC (first screened United Kingdom, 20 May 2006), Television.
Mallett, Nicholas, 'The Curse of Fenric', *Doctor Who*, BBC (first screened United Kingdom, 25 October–15 November 1989), Television.
Maloney, David, 'The War Games', *Doctor Who*, BBC (first screened United Kingdom, 19 April–21 June 1969), Television.
Maloney, David, 'Genesis of the Daleks', *Doctor Who*, BBC (first screened United Kingdom, 8 March–12 April 1975), Television.
Maloney, David, 'The Talons of Weng-Chiang', *Doctor Who*, BBC (first screened United Kingdom, 26 Feburary–2 April 1977), Television.
Martin, Richard, 'The Web Planet', *Doctor Who*, BBC (first screened United Kingdom, 13 Feburary–20 March 1965), Television.

Martinus, Derek, 'The Evil of the Daleks', *Doctor Who*, BBC (first screened United Kingdom, 2 May–1 July 1967), Television.
Mayne, Lennie, 'The Three Doctors', *Doctor Who*, BBC (first screened United Kingdom, 30 December 1972–20 January 1973), Television.
Metzstein, Saul, 'The Name of the Doctor', *Doctor Who*, BBC (first screened United Kingdom, 18 May 2013), Television.
Moffatt, Peter, 'The Five Doctors', *Doctor Who*, BBC (first screened United Kingdom, 25 November 1983), Television.
Morshead, Catherine, 'The Lodger', *Doctor Who*, BBC (first screened United Kingdom, 12 June 2010), Television.
Murphy, Paul, 'Robot of Sherwood', *Doctor Who*, BBC (first screened United Kingdom, 6 September 2014), Television.
Nettheim, Daniel, 'The Zygon Invasion', *Doctor Who*, BBC (first screened United Kingdom, 31 October 2015), Television.
Nettheim, Daniel, 'The Zygon Inversion', *Doctor Who*, BBC (first screened United Kingdom, 7 November 2015), Television.
Palmer, Charles, 'The Family of Blood', *Doctor Who*, BBC (first screened United Kingdom, 2 June 2007), Television.
Payne, Jamie, 'The Time of the Doctor', *Doctor Who*, BBC (first screened United Kingdom, 25 December 2013), Television.
Roberts, Pennant, 'The Face of Evil', *Doctor Who*, BBC (first screened United Kingdom, 1–22 January 1977), Television.
Roberts, Pennant, 'Warriors of the Deep', *Doctor Who*, BBC (first screened United Kingdom, 5–14 January 1984), Television.
Roberts, Pennant, 'Timelash', *Doctor Who*, BBC (first screened United Kingdom, 9–16 March 1985), Television.
Robinson, Matthew, 'Resurrection of the Daleks', *Doctor Who*, BBC (first screened United Kingdom, 8–16 March 1984), Television.
Russell, Paddy, 'Invasion of the Dinosaur', *Doctor Who*, BBC (first screened United Kingdom, 12 January–16 Feburary 1974), Television.
Sax, Geoffrey, *Doctor Who*, Universal/BBC (first screened United Kingdom, 27 May 1996), Telemovie.
Senior, Richard, 'Let's Kill Hitler', *Doctor Who*, BBC (first screened United Kingdom, 27 August 2011), Television.
Smith, Adam, 'Flesh and Stone', *Doctor Who*, BBC (first screened United Kingdom, 1 May 2010), Television.
Smith, Adam, 'The Eleventh Hour', *Doctor Who*, BBC (first screened United Kingdom, 3 April 2010), Television.
Smith, Adam, 'The Time of Angels', *Doctor Who*, BBC (first screened United Kingdom, 24 April 2010), Television.
Spenton-Foster, George, 'The Ribos Operation', *Doctor Who*, BBC (first screened United Kingdom, 2–23 September 1978), Television.
Strong, James, 'Doomsday', *Doctor Who*, BBC (first screened United Kingdom, 8 July 2006), Television.
Strong, James, 'The Impossible Planet', *Doctor Who*, BBC (first screened United Kingdom, 3 June 2006), Television.
Strong, James, 'The Satan Pit', *Doctor Who*, BBC (first screened United Kingdom, 10 June 2006), Television.

Strong, James, 'Evolution of the Daleks', *Doctor Who*, BBC (first screened United Kingdom, 28 April 2007), Television.
Strong, James, 'Voyage of the Dammed', *Doctor Who*, BBC (first screened United Kingdom, 25 December 2007), Television.
Talalay, Rachel, 'Dark Water', *Doctor Who*, BBC (first screened United Kingdom, 1 November 2014), Television.
Talalay, Rachel, 'Death in Heaven', *Doctor Who*, BBC (first screened United Kingdom, 8 November 2014), Television.
Talalay, Rachel, 'Heaven Sent', *Doctor Who*, BBC (first screened United Kingdom, 28 November 2015), Television.
Talalay, Rachel, 'Hell Bent', *Doctor Who*, BBC (first screened United Kingdom, 5 December 2015), Television.
Talalay, Rachel, 'The Doctor Falls', *Doctor Who,* BBC (first screened United Kingdom, 1 July 2017), Television.
Teague, Colin, 'Last of the Time Lords', *Doctor Who*, BBC (first screened United Kingdom, 30 June 2007), Television.
Virgo, Tony, 'The King's Demons', *Doctor Who*, BBC (first screened United Kingdom, 15–16 March 1983), Television.
Wareing, Alan, 'The Greatest Show in the Galaxy', *Doctor Who*, BBC (first screened United Kingdom, 14 December 1988–4 January 1989), Television.
Way, Ashley, 'Hungry Earth', *Doctor Who*, BBC (first screened United Kingdom, 22 May 2010), Television.
Way, Ashley, 'Cold Blood', *Doctor Who*, BBC (first screened United Kingdom, 29 May 2010), Television.
Webb, Jeremy, 'The Wedding of River Song', *Doctor Who*, BBC (first screened United Kingdom, 1 October 2011), Television.
Wheatley, Ben, 'Deep Breath', *Doctor Who*, BBC (first screened United Kingdom, 23 August 2014), Television.
Wilmshurst, Paul, 'Mummy on the Orient Express', *Doctor Who*, BBC (first screened United Kingdom, 11 October 2014), Television.

Battlestar Galactica
Alcalá, Félix Enríquez, 'Exodus Part I', *Battlestar Galactica*, Sci Fi Channel/NBC Universal (first screened United States, 16 October 2006), Television.
Alcalá, Félix Enríquez, 'Exodus Part II', *Battlestar Galactica*, Sci Fi Channel/NBC Universal (first screened United States, 23 October 2006), Television.
Alcalá, Félix Enríquez, 'Razor', *Battlestar Galactica*, Sci Fi Channel/Universal Studios Home Entertainment (first screened United States, 24 November 2007), Television.
Bellisario, Donald, 'The Hand of God', *Battlestar Galactica*, American Broadcasting Corporation/Universal Studios (first screened United States, 29 April 1979), Television.
Colla, Richard A., 'Saga of a Star World', *Battlestar Galactica*, American Broadcasting Corporation/Universal Studios (first screened United States, 17 September 1978), Television.
Edwards, Paul, 'The Hub', *Battlestar Galactica*, Sci Fi Channel/NBC Universal (first screened United States, 6 June 2008), Television.
Hardy, Rod, 'Act of Contrition', *Battlestar Galactica*, Sci Fi Channel/NBC

Universal (first screened United States of America, 28 January 2005), Television.

Hardy, Rod, 'Litmus', *Battlestar Galactica*, Sci Fi Channel/NBC Universal (first screened United States, 11 February 2005), Television.

Hardy, Rod, 'The Farm', *Battlestar Galactica*, Sci Fi Channel/NBC Universal (first screened United States, 12 August 2005), Television.

Hardy, Rod, 'Epiphanies', *Battlestar Galactica*, Sci Fi Channel/NBC Universal (first screened United States, 20 January 2006), Television.

Hardy, Rod, 'A Day in the Life', *Battlestar Galactica*, Sci Fi Channel/NBC Universal (first screened United States, 18 February 2007), Television.

Hardy, Rod, 'Sine Qua Non', *Battlestar Galactica*, Sci Fi Channel/NBC Universal (first screened United States, 27 May 2008), Television.

Hayers, Sidney, 'Galactica Discovers Earth Part I', *Galactica 1980*, American Broadcasting Corporation/Universal Studios (first screened United States, 27 January 1980), Television.

Head, James, 'Black Market', *Battlestar Galactica*, Sci Fi Channel/NBC Universal (first screened United States, 27 January 2006), Television.

Hemingway, Anthony, 'Six of One', *Battlestar Galactica*, Sci Fi Channel/NBC Universal (first screened United States, 11 April 2008), Television.

Horder-Payton, Gwyneth, 'No Exit', *Battlestar Galactica*, Sci Fi Channel/NBC Universal (first screened United States, 13 February 2009), Television.

Kroeker, Allan, 'Resistance', *Battlestar Galactica*, Sci Fi Channel/NBC Universal (first screened United States of America, 5 August 2005), Television.

Mimica-Gezzan, Sergio, 'You Can't Go Home Again', *Battlestar Galactica*, Sci Fi Channel/NBC Universal (first screened United States, 4 February 2005), Television.

Mimica-Gezzan, Sergio, 'The Captain's Hand', *Battlestar Galactica*, Sci Fi Channel/NBC Universal (first screened United States, 17 February 2006), Television.

Mimica-Gezzan, Sergio, 'Precipice', *Battlestar Galactica*, Sci Fi Channel/NBC Universal (first screened United States, 6 October 2006), Television.

Moore, Ronald D., 'Disquiet Follows My Soul', *Battlestar Galactica*, Sci Fi Channel/NBC Universal (first screened United States, 23 January 2009), Television.

Nankin, Michael, 'Maelstrom', *Battlestar Galactica*, Sci Fi Channel/NBC Universal (first screened United States, 4 March 2007), Television.

Nankin, Michael, 'The Ties that Bind', *Battlestar Galactica*, Sci Fi Channel/NBC Universal (first screened United States, 18 April 2008), Television.

Nankin, Michael, 'Sometimes a Great Notion', *Battlestar Galactica*, Sci Fi Channel/NBC Universal (first screened United States, 16 January 2009), Television.

Nankin, Michael, 'Someone to Watch Over Me', *Battlestar Galactica*, Sci Fi Channel/NBC Universal (first screened United States, 27 February 2009), Television.

Olmos, Edward James, 'Islanded in a Stream of Stars', *Battlestar Galactica*, Sci Fi Channel/NBC Universal (first screened United States, 6 March 2009), Television.

Olmos, Edward James, 'The Plan', *Battlestar Galactica*, Sci Fi Channel/NBC Universal (first screened United States, 10 January 2010), Television.

Pate, Jonas, 'Colonial Day', *Battlestar Galactica*, Sci Fi Channel/NBC Universal (first screened United States, 18 March 2005), Television.

Rose, Wayne, 'Dirty Hands', *Battlestar Galactica*, Sci Fi Channel/NBC Universal (first screened United States, 25 February 2007), Television.

Rose, Wayne, 'Guess What's Coming to Dinner?' *Battlestar Galactica*, Sci Fi Channel/NBC Universal (first screened United States, 16 May 2008), Television.
Rose, Wayne, 'Blood on the Scales', *Battlestar Galactica*, Sci Fi Channel/NBC Universal (first screened United States, 6 February 2009), Television.
Rymer, Michael, 'Battlestar Galactica Mini-series', *Battlestar Galactica*, Sci Fi Channel/NBC Universal (first screened United States, 8–9 December 2003), Television.
Rymer, Michael, '33', *Battlestar Galactica*, Sci Fi Channel/NBC Universal (first screened United States, 14 January 2005), Television.
Rymer, Michael, 'Kobol's Last Gleaming Part II', *Battlestar Galactica*, Sci Fi Channel/NBC Universal (first screened United States, 1 April 2005), Television.
Rymer, Michael, 'Scattered', *Battlestar Galactica*, Sci Fi Channel/NBC Universal (first screened United States, 15 July 2005), Television.
Rymer, Michael, 'Pegasus', *Battlestar Galactica*, Sci Fi Channel/NBC Universal (first screened United States, 23 September 2005), Television.
Rymer, Michael, 'Resurrection Ship Part I', *Battlestar Galactica*, Sci Fi Channel/NBC Universal (first screened United States, 6 January 2006), Television.
Rymer, Michael, 'Resurrection Ship Part II', *Battlestar Galactica*, Sci Fi Channel/NBC Universal (first screened United States, 13 January 2006), Television.
Rymer, Michael, 'Lay Down Your Burdens Part II', *Battlestar Galactica*, Sci Fi Channel/NBC Universal (first screened United States, 10 March 2006), Television.
Rymer, Michael, 'Collaborators', *Battlestar Galactica*, Sci Fi Channel/NBC Universal (first screened United States, 27 October 2006), Television.
Rymer, Michael, 'The Eye of Jupiter', *Battlestar Galactica*, Sci Fi Channel/NBC Universal (first screened United States, 15 December 2006), Television.
Rymer, Michael, 'Rapture', *Battlestar Galactica*, Sci Fi Channel/NBC Universal (first screened United States, 21 January 2007), Television.
Rymer, Michael, 'The Woman King', *Battlestar Galactica*, Sci Fi Channel/NBC Universal (first screened United States, 11 February 2007), Television.
Rymer, Michael, 'Crossroads Part II', *Battlestar Galactica*, Sci Fi Channel/NBC Universal (first screened United States, 25 March 2007), Television.
Rymer, Michael, 'He that Believeth in Me', *Battlestar Galactica*, Sci Fi Channel/NBC Universal (first screened United States, 4 April 2008), Television.
Rymer, Michael, 'The Road Less Traveled', *Battlestar Galactica*, Sci Fi Channel/NBC Universal (first screened United States, 2 May 2008), Television.
Rymer, Michael, 'Revelations', *Battlestar Galactica*, Sci Fi Channel/NBC Universal (first screened United States, 13 June 2008), Television.
Rymer, Michael, 'Daybreak Part II', *Battlestar Galactica*, Sci Fi Channel/NBC Universal (first screened United States, 20 March 2009), Television.
Satlof, Ron, 'The Return of Starbuck', *Galactica 1980*, American Broadcasting Corporation/Universal Studios (first screened United States, 4 May 1980), Television.
Turner, Brad, 'Flesh and Bone', *Battlestar Galactica*, Sci Fi Channel/NBC Universal (first screened United States, 25 February 2005), Television.
Woolnough, Jeff, 'The Hand of God', *Battlestar Galactica*, Sci Fi Channel/NBC Universal (first screened United States, 11 March 2005), Television.

Woolnough, Jeff, 'Home Part II', *Battlestar Galactica*, Sci Fi Channel/NBC Universal (first screened United States, 26 August 2005), Television.

Woolnough, Jeff, 'Downloaded', *Battlestar Galactica*, Sci Fi Channel/NBC Universal (first screened United States, 24 February 2006), Television.

Young, Robert, 'The Son also Rises', *Battlestar Galactica*, Sci Fi Channel/NBC Universal (first screened United States, 11 March 2007), Television.

Young, Robert, 'Deadlock', *Battlestar Galactica*, Sci Fi Channel/NBC Universal (first screened United States, 20 February 2009), Television.

Other

Batty, David, 'Motorcar Ngutju (Good Motorcar)', *Bush Mechanics*, Australian Broadcasting Corporation (first screened Australia, 2 October 2001), Television.

Harrison, John, *Dune*, Science-Fiction Channel (first screened United States, 3 December 2000), Television.

Reiner, Jeffrey, 'Pilot', *Caprica*, SyFy (first screened United States, 22 January 2010), Television.

Scheerer, Robert, 'Measure of Man', *Star Trek: The Next Generation*, Paramount Television (first screened United States, 12 March 1989), Television.

Senensky, Ralph, 'Bread and Circuses', *Star Trek*, Paramount Television (first screened United States, 15 March 1968), Television.

Yaitanes, Greg, *Children of Dune*, Science-Fiction Channel (first screened United States, 16 March 2003), Television.

Way, Ashley, 'Death of the Doctor', *The Sarah Jane Adventures*, BBC (first screened United Kingdom, 26 October 2010), Television.

Film

Allen, Woody, *The Sleeper*, United Artists (first screened United States, 17 December 1973), Film.

Baird, Stuart, *Star Trek Nemesis*, Paramount Pictures (first screened United States, 13 December 2002), Film.

Bay, Michael, *The Island*, DreamWorks (first screened United States, 22 July 2005), Film.

Emmerich, Roland, *Independence Day*, 20th Century Fox (first screened United States, 2 July 1996), Film.

Lucas, George, *Star Wars: Attack of the Clones*, 20th Century Fox (first screened United States, 16 May 2002), Film.

Lynch, David, *Dune*, Universal Pictures (first screened United States, 14 December 1984), Film.

Marquand, Richard, *Star Wars: The Return of the Jedi*, 20th Century Fox (first screened United States, 25 May 1983), Film.

Miller, George, *Mad Max*, Roadshow Film Distributors (first screened Australia, 12 April 1979), Film.

Miller, George, *Mad Max 2: The Road Warrior*, Warner Bros (first screened Australia, 24 December 1981), Film.

Miller, George, *Mad Max: Fury Road*, Warner Bros Pictures (first screened Australia, 14 May 2015), Film.

Miller, George and George Oglivie, *Mad Max: Beyond Thunderdome*, Warner Bros (first screened Australia, 10 July 1985), Film.

Ramis, Harold, *Multiplicity*, Columbia Pictures (first screened United States, 17 July 1996), Film.
Schaffner, Franklin J., *The Boys from Brazil*, 20th Century Fox (first screened United States, 5 October 1978), Film.
Scott, Ridley, *Blade Runner*, Warner Bros (first screened United States, 16 December 1982), Film.
Spielberg, Steven, *Jurassic Park*, Universal Studios (first screened United States, 11 June 1993), Film.
Spottiswoode, Roger, *The 6th Day*, Columbia Pictures (first screened United States, 17 November 2000), Film.
Wachowski, Andy and Larry Wachowski, *The Matrix*, Warner Bros (first screened United States, 31 March 1999), Film.

Other Media

Dylan, Bob, 'All Along the Watchtower', *John Wesley Harding* (Columbia), 1967, Album.
Turner, Tina, 'We Don't Need Another Hero', *Mad Max beyond Thunderdome Original Motion Picture Soundtrack* (Capitol), 1985, Album.
Westwood Studio, *Dune II: The Building of a Dynasty*, Virgin Interactive, 1992, Computer game.

Primary Legal Sources

International and European Statements and Agreements

Additional Protocol to the Convention for the Protection of Human Rights and Dignity of the Human Being with regard to the Application of Biology and Medicine, on the Prohibition of Cloning Human Beings, 12 January 1998, Europ. T.S. No. 168, <http://conventions.coe.int/Treaty/en/Treaties/html/168.htm>, last accessed 9 February 2017.
United Nations Declaration on Human Cloning, G. A. Res. 59/280, U.N. Doc A/RES/59/260 (23 March 2005).
Universal Declaration on the Human Genome and Human Rights, UNESCO, 29th General Conference, 11 November 1997.

National Legislation, Regulations, and Bills

Australia
Prohibition of Human Cloning Act 2002 (Cth).
Prohibition of Human Cloning for Reproduction Act 2002 (Cth).
Research Involving Human Embryos Act 2002 (Cth).
Research Involving Human Embryos Regulation 2003 (Cth).

Canada
Assisted Human Reproduction Act, S. C., c.2.

France
Act No. 2004-900 of 6 August 2004 relative to bio-ethics [*relative à la bioéthique*] *JO* 7 August 2004, art 28.

Germany
Gesetz zum Scvhutz von Embryonen [Embryo Protection Law], v. 13.12.1990 (BGB1. I S. 2746).

New Zealand
Human Assisted Reproductive Technology Act 2004 (NZ) no 92.

South Africa
National Health Act, 2003 (no 61 of 2003).

United Kingdom
Human Reproductive Cloning Act 2001, Chapter 23.
Human Fertilisation and Embryology Act 1990, Chapter 37.
Human Fertilisation and Embryology Act 2008, Chapter 22.

United States
Cal. Health & Safety Code §§ 24185, 24187, 24189 (2001)
Human Cloning Prohibition Act of 2003, H.R. 534, 108th Cong. (2003).
Human Cloning Research Prohibition Act, H.R. 222, 109th Cong. (2005).
Human Cloning Prohibition Act of 2005, H.R. 1357, 109th Cong. (2005).
Human Cloning Prohibition Act of 2007, H.R. 2560, 110th Cong. (2007).
Human Cloning Prohibition Act of 2009, H.R. 110, 111th Cong. (2009).

Cases

Phonographic Performance Company of Australia v Federation of Commercial Television Stations (1998) 195 CLR 158.
Prohibitions del Roy [1607] EWHC KB J23; 77 ER 1342.
Roads and Traffic Authority v Royal (2008) 245 ALR 653.
Twentieth Century-Fox Film Corp v MCA, Inc (1983) 715 F.2d 1327.

Parliamentary Debates

Australia
Commonwealth Parliamentary Debates, House of Representatives, 20 August 2002, 5242 (Simon Crean).
Commonwealth Parliamentary Debates, House of Representatives, 20 August 2002, 5255 (Nicola Roxon).
Commonwealth Parliamentary Debates, House of Representatives, 20 August 2002, 5884 (Daryl Melham).
Commonwealth Parliamentary Debates, House of Representatives, 21 August 2002, 6068 (Alexander Downer, Minister for Foreign Affairs).
Commonwealth Parliamentary Debates, House of Representatives, 28 August 2002, 6055 (Petro Georgiou).
Commonwealth Parliamentary Debates, House of Representatives, 28 August 2002, 6066 (Barry Wakelin).
Commonwealth Parliamentary Debates, House of Representatives, 28 August 2002, 6087 (Bruce Scott).
Commonwealth Parliamentary Debates, Senate, 6 November 2006, 5 (Natasha Stott Despoja).

Commonwealth Parliamentary Debates, Senate, 12 November 2002, 6105 (Nick Sherry).
Commonwealth Parliamentary Debates, House of Representatives, 30 November 2006, 13–16 (Julia Gillard).
Commonwealth Parliamentary Debates, House of Representatives, 30 November 2006, 25 (Julia Irwin).
Commonwealth Parliamentary Debates, House of Representatives, 30 November 2006, 63 (Dick Adams).
Commonwealth Parliamentary Debates, House of Representatives, 13 February 2008, 167–73 (Kevin Rudd, Prime Minister).

United Kingdom
Hansard (House of Lords) 28 April 1999 Col 317 (Lord Alton of Liverpool).
Hansard (House of Lords) 28 April 1999 Col 329 (Lord Rea).
Hansard (House of Lords) 26 November 2000 Col 20 (Lord Brennan).
Hansard (House of Commons) 19 December 2000 Col 221 (Yvette Cooper, Pontefract and Castleford).

Newspapers and Websites

'List of Doctor Who Serials', <https://en.wikipedia.org/wiki/List_of_Doctor_Who_serials> (last accessed 19 October 2017).
Ahuja, Anjana, 'Could the Cure for all Diseases be Banned?', *The Times* (London), 17 June 2004, 8.
BBC, 'Classic Doctor Who Episode Guide', <http://www.bbc.co.uk/doctorwho/classic/episodeguide/oohum/index.shtml> (last accessed 22 February 2017).
Birkett, Dea, 'Cloning is Good: We Should Slide with Enthusiasm and Boldness Down the Slippery Slope', *The Guardian* (Manchester), 23 January 2001, 20.
Brown, Brian A., 'Cloning: Where's the Outrage?' *The Wall Street Journal* (New York), 19 February 1998, 1.
Colman, Alan, 'Why Cloning Would be Inhuman', *The Times* (London), 15 June 1998, 17.
Coyne, Andrew, 'Think Twice before Fearing the Advent of Cloning', *Toronto Star* (Toronto), 27 February 1997, 29.
Crane, David, 'Don't Rush to Ban Cloning Research', *Toronto Star* (Toronto), 2 December 2002, 2.
Dempsey, John, 'Sci Fi's "Battlestar" Shines Brightly', *Variety* (New York), 11–17 April 2005, 18.
Devine, Frank, 'Crackpot Reasoning Behind Ungodly Cloning Rush', *The Australian*, 13 August 2001, 13.
Editorial, 'To Clone a Sheep', *The Washington Post*, 26 February 1997, 18.
Friend, Tim, 'Hello Dolly! Breakthrough with Sheep Could Herald Human Cloning', *USA Today* (McLean), 24 February 1997, 1.
Hawkes, Nigel, 'Legal Barriers will Prevent Apocalypse Now, if Not Later', *The Times* (London), 26 February 1997, 3.
Jenkins, Henry, 'Confessions of an Aca-Fan', <http://henryjenkins.org> (last accessed 25 February 2017).
Kolata, Gina, 'Gene Genie', *The Australian*, 3 January 1998, 14.
Leech, Graeme, 'The Genetic Gene', *The Australian,* 1 March 1997, 22.

McKie, Robin, 'Scientists Clone Adult Sheep', *The Observer* (London), 23 February 1997, 1.

McNamara, Mary, 'The Hit that Zaps Sc-Fi Cliches', *Multichannel News*, 28 March 2005, 33–4.

Postrel, Virginia, 'Should Human Cloning Be Allowed? Yes, Don't Impede Medical Progress', *The Wall Street Journal*, 5 December 2001, A.20.

Ragg, Mark, 'Right or Wrong? Cloning Ourselves', *The Australian*, 8 June 1998, 10.

Stott Despoja, Natasha, 'To Clone or Not to Clone', *The Australian,* 26 February 1997, 12.

Sutherland, John, 'The Ideas Interview: Julian Savulescu Eugenics Need Not be Nazi, and Drugs in Sport are Good, Oxford's Leading Ethicist tells John Sutherland', *The Guardian* (London), 10 October 2005, 24.

Trafford, Abigail, 'Fear of Cloning and the Ewe To-Do', *The Washington Post,* 11 March 1997, Z.06.

Index

CPSIA information can be obtained
at www.ICGtesting.com
Printed in the USA
BVHW040846010720
582685BV00008B/22